UNCLE BUBBA'S SAVANNAH SEAFOOD

EARL "BUBBA" HIERS
WITH POLLY POWERS STRAMM

SIMON & SCHUSTER

New York London Toronto Sydney

SIMON & SCHUSTER
Rockefeller Center
1230 Avenue of the Americas
New York, NY 10020

SIMON & SCHUSTER and colophon are registered trademarks of Simon & Schuster, Inc.

Food photography © Alan Richardson
Food stylist: Michael Pederson
Prop stylist: Deborah E. Donahue
Photographs: page ii © Christine Hall, page x © Russ Bryant, and unless otherwise noted, all other
photographs are from the author's personal collection and are used with permission.

Frontispiece (p.ii): *From left, top,* Trevor and Jay; Ian, Dawn, Bubba, and Corrie.

Designed by Joel Avirom, Jason Snyder, and Meghan Day Healey

Manufactured in the United States of America

ISBN-13: 978-0-7432-9283-2

Hey, y'all, this is especially for my big sister,
Paula Hiers Deen.

ACKNOWLEDGMENTS

When it comes to thanking people, I feel like one of those good-looking Hollywood actors who wins an Academy Award, runs down to the stage and stands at the microphone not knowing what to say.

When I first told my family, friends, and co-workers that I wanted to write a cookbook they couldn't have been more encouraging. They offered recipes and everything else under the sun. I know I can count on them and I hope they realize that, with the Lord willing, I'll be there for them.

I want to thank everyone who shared recipes with me but I'm afraid I'll leave somebody out and step on a few toes. But I have to try my best to name the folks who were generous enough to help me start and finish this project.

I couldn't have done it all without recipes given to me by my Aunt Trina Bearden and Aunt Glennis Hiers. Others whose recipes I love are Betty Archer, Amy Beaver, Bo Beaver, Kathy and Buddy Bethea, Deane Brown, Robin Dermer, Jill Hiers, Susan Greene, Lisa Jackson, Ineata "Jellyroll" Jones, Kathy Kueker, Sheila Kueker, Joanne Lair, Beth O'Brien, and Virginia Robertson.

Polly Powers Stramm, who has been writing professionally for thirty years, sat down with me and helped me organize my thoughts and put them on paper. Polly and I worked closely with good cook Ashley Strickland, who tested and fine-tuned the recipes that I've collected through the years.

A million thanks to my literary agent, Janis Donnaud, and Simon & Schuster editor Sydny Miner, who shepherded me through the process from the early days on to the end when the book went to print. Thanks also to folks like Sydny's asistant Michelle Rorke, design director Linda Dingler and designer Joel Avirom, art director Jackie Seow and photographer Alan Richardson for the cover and food photography, copyeditors Suzanne Fass and Mara Lurie; as well as publisher David Rosenthal, associate publishers Eileen Boyle and Deborah Darrock, and publicists Tracey Guest and Julia Prosser.

My Aunt Peggy Ort has looked out for me all my life and even more so after Mama and Daddy died. When she heard I was doing this book, she spent hours going through family photos and recipes. She also jotted down helpful kitchen tips from newspaper and magazine articles that she clipped and saved over a lifetime.

Obviously, I wouldn't be where I am today without my big sister, Paula Hiers Deen, who has paved the way for me in every sense of the word. Without Paula's support, sensible advice, and unconditional love, I'd probably be a lost soul. I can also say the same about my nephews, Bobby and Jamie Deen, who are like my brothers.

My children, Jay and Corrie, mean the world to me and always have. I'm particularly thankful that I found a wonderful woman like my wife, Dawn, who has two fine sons, Iaen and Trevor, who make our family complete.

CONTENTS

FOREWORD

by Paula Deen

I'll never forget February 28, 1954, the day Mama and Daddy told me I had a new little brother. Dwight Eisenhower was president, but the best thing to happen that year as far as I was concerned was the birth of my baby brother. I was seven years old and I thought I had a brand-new doll baby to play with. Mama and Daddy named him Earl Hiers Jr., but from the very start he was always Bubba.

When children lose their parents at an early age, they tend to grow even closer, and that's what happened with Bubba and me. By the time I was 23, I was already grown and married and starting my own family, so when Mama and Daddy died, it was just natural that Bubba, who was still a teenager, would come and live with us.

Food was always the glue that held our family together, and that is still true to this day. Through

Little Paula and Baby Bubba

good times and bad, we have managed to find a way to gather at the supper table, and bow our heads and count our blessings.

When I started my first restaurant with Jamie and Bobby, I dreamed that someday my boys and I would find a way to drag Bubba into the business with us.

And anybody who knows Paula Deen knows that when I make up my mind about something, you just better give up and give in!

It took some doing, but finally Bubba sold his successful landscaping company in Albany and moved to Savannah to lend us his much-needed expertise in business matters.

With The Lady & Sons restaurant about to bust out of our original building, Bubba helped us take on the enormous challenge of buying and renovating a building at Whitaker and Congress streets in downtown Savannah. Suddenly, we went from a 90-seat restaurant to a 15,000-square-foot operation that serves 1,500 to 2,000 meals a day, seven days a week.

Bitten by the restaurant bug, Bubba was itching to get started on a place of his own when I came up with the crazy notion of opening a seafood restaurant. By a stroke of good luck, we found a beautiful building with a drop-dead view of Georgia's famous coastal marshes.

And that's how Uncle Bubba's Oyster House was born. My precious baby brother couldn't be prouder of his new restaurant, and I couldn't be prouder of him.

I just know you're going to enjoy trying this new batch of family recipes, all of which have the special Bubba touch.

INTRODUCTION

It's not everybody who's lucky enough to make a living at what they love best. Me? I'm one of the lucky ones, and boy, don't I know it! My whole life has been about cooking, eating, and swapping stories.

Now that I have a restaurant where I get to do those things on a daily basis, I try never to forget just how blessed I am. Most every day I put on my baseball cap and visit with the fine folks who are eating in our restaurant. I stop by each table and eyeball what they've ordered. Could be a plateful of my chargrilled oysters or Georgia sweet shrimp with homemade cocktail sauce. Either one will make you want to clean your plate and beg for more.

I always say, "Hey, y'all, I'm Uncle Bubba. Where y'all from?" People appreciate the personal attention and lots of times say they never realized that there really is an Uncle Bubba. I say, "Yep, that's me, and I'm proud to be a good ole Southern boy."

My family and I have never been what you would call fancy diners. Growing up in southwest Georgia, we never had white tablecloths or silver candlesticks. We just wanted to eat good, laugh a lot, and have a good time. When I opened the doors at Uncle Bubba's Oyster House I tried to carry on what I describe as down-home Southern style. I want people to come just as they are and enjoy what I think is the greatest seafood ever, like my oyster stew, for instance. It's just like the stews I ate when I was a boy growing up, made by my Mama, Corrie Paul Hiers, and my Granny

Paul. (That's what I preferred to call her; Paula called her Grandmomma Paul.) To make oyster stew, we start with sautéed onion, pour in real milk, add some real butter and a few other special ingredients, and then add the best oysters you've ever put in your mouth.

Like I said before, I'm proud of the name Bubba. Yep, people kid me about it all the time but I just laugh because it's a nickname that fits my personality. I was named for my daddy, Earl Wayne Hiers Sr. He was a great guy who never met a stranger. He and Mama didn't want me to be called Little Earl or Junior so they called me Bubba, which in the South is slang for brother. Most of you know that I am Paula Deen's one and only baby brother.

But believe it or not, Bubba isn't my only nickname. My Granny Hiers called me Sonny Boy. Come to think of it, that's what she called everybody. One story about her gets me laughing out loud every time I tell it. When I got out of high

Mama and Daddy at River Bend

school I was dying to have a motorcycle bigger than the Honda 50 I scooted around on in Albany, Georgia. My Aunt Peggy Ort, my Mama's sister, just about had a fit when Mama bought me that first motorcycle. She reminds me of that motorcycle all the time and how she couldn't believe that her sister would buy a motorcycle for a fifteen-year-old boy. Anyway, after high school I bought a Honda 750 and decided to ride it to Florida because I had met a girl who lived around Winter Haven, which was close to where Daddy's relatives lived.

I grew up around good cooks. I can still taste the chicken, with the secret barbecue sauce, that Daddy used to put on the grill. It was truly finger-lickin' good. Food like that was my downfall when it came to my weight. When I went to college I started working out because I wanted to get to know some of the good-lookin' girls on campus. I went to the gym and, before long, I had dropped about thirty pounds. So, lookin' all handsome, I took one of my old belts, strapped it around my suitcase, hooked it to the back of the motorcycle and took off down Interstate 75. My first stop was Winter Haven because I wanted to visit Daddy's baby brother, Uncle Bob, who, by the way, used to be a model in New York. (I guess that's where me and Paula get some of our good looks from.)

Around the corner from Uncle Bob was where Daddy's Mama lived. I pulled into Granny Hiers's driveway and saw her pushing open the screen door. She waved at me and said, "Hey Sonny Boy, come on in."

We sat in her living room laughing and talking for a while and all of the sudden, she leaned up and looked at me through her thick glasses and said with a little giggle, "Tell me your name again, Sonny Boy." It tickled me so much that I almost wet my pants. Then it dawned on me that she hadn't seen me since I'd lost weight. She just died laughing and hurried over to hug and kiss me all over again. She told me she thought I was her next door neighbor's boyfriend because he had a motorcycle, too. Then, of course, she had to offer me something to eat because that's what we do in our family. She could make the best country fried steak, smothered in gravy and onions. It was so tender you could cut it with a fork.

Food stories like that seem to follow me everywhere but they don't always have whatcha call happy endings. When I was a senior in high school or a freshman in college (I forget which), I was living with my sister Paula because we had lost our parents by the time I was sixteen. Paula's seven years older than I am, and she was married and raising two boys, Jamie and Bobby, who have always been like little brothers to me even though I'm their uncle.

One night Paula and I decided to grill steaks. Money was always pretty tight, so this dinner was an extra special treat for us. We laid out the steaks on the counter and went outside to light the charcoal grill. Paula and I walked back in the kitchen and we couldn't believe what we were looking at.

We had a boxer named Deacon (Daddy named him), and we were all ready to put those pretty steaks on the grill before Deacon changed our plans. That dog was staring at us with one of those juicy steaks hanging out of both sides of his jaw. Somehow Paula and I scraped up enough money to replace the steak. Paula sent me back to the grocery store and sent Deacon to his doghouse to think about what he had done.

I guess it's only fittin' that I should be in the restaurant business because that's where I got my start in life. When I was born, we lived about ten miles from Albany, Georgia, at a place called River Bend on the Flint River. My granddaddy and granny on my Mama's side, John L. Paul and Irene Paul, operated a motel, restaurant, swimming pool, lounge, and skating rink at River Bend. My parents had the service station and a little store across the street where they sold souvenirs, Coca-Colas, ice cream, Moon Pies, pecans, and Georgia peaches to the Northern tourists who were driving through Georgia on their way to the Florida panhandle.

From the get-go I was forever in the kitchen getting under Granny Paul's feet or in the way of Sam, her head cook. They always worried about me because I would be right there when they were frying huge pans of chicken or pulling trays of homemade biscuits out of the oven. I always managed to sneak a piece of Granny Paul's cake or pecan pie, but she didn't mind. She knew that there was one thing I didn't want and that was my stomach hurtin' because it was empty.

Back then I thought the Coca-Cola man who drove the big red truck was somethin' special because Coca-Colas were my absolute favorite. That Coca-Cola driver would pull up to the restaurant, slide open the truck's back door, and show me what seemed like millions of green glass Coke bottles. I learned from watchin' Mama and Granny Paul that you can use Coke to make sauces for good ole fried chicken and country hams. Me? I just liked to drink 'em.

I never tired of listening to stories that Aunt Peggy or Granny Paul would tell me about River Bend. One even had to do with that Coca-Cola truck. One day when I was about three years old, I went missing—or at least everybody thought so. I had only climbed on the back of the Coke truck and nobody knew where I was. Mama was panicking, sure enough. She was clutching her apron, and yellin', "Where's Bubba?" over and over again. Finally somebody found me on the back of the truck. Boy, did I get my you-know-what tore up. Never did chase that truck again, though.

There's one more River Bend story that Paula, Aunt Peggy, and Granny Paul used to love to tell everybody. It seems a couple from up North pulled up to the gas pump, and Les, who worked at the station, walked out to fill up their car with gas, check the oil, and clean the windshield, while they snacked on cheese and peanut butter crackers and a Coke. Les had a big old four-door Plymouth that I liked to play in. So while Les was seeing about the car, the man and woman watched me bouncing up and down on the front seat of that old Plymouth.

They went on their way, switched on the radio, and heard that a little boy from up North had been kidnapped. I fit the description of that boy and they got to thinking about it and put two and two together. They stopped at a pay phone, called the sheriff, and told him that they thought they had found the missing boy. The next thing Mama knew the sheriff's car came to a screeching halt in front of the store. The sheriff demanded to know who that little boy was. That got Mama so flustered that she could hardly find my birth certificate to prove that I belonged to her.

After we moved into town, Daddy had a used-car lot and would come home every day at noon for a hot meal. Whether it was breakfast, lunch, or supper, Mama always put good food on the table for us. For lunch she might fry chicken and fix macaroni and cheese and okra. If it was summertime she'd slice some homegrown tomatoes and, no matter what, she was always baking biscuits. After finishin' a breakfast of scrambled eggs, crisp bacon, buttery grits, and biscuits covered with grape jelly, I'd hardly let that screen door slam behind me before I'd be daydreaming about Mama's hot and gooey chocolate chip cookies that she'd have waiting for me when I got out of school.

One summer day when Daddy came home at noontime for lunch he brought a Shetland pony that he took on at the car lot. He gave that pony to me and I named him Tony. I'm telling you, I felt like the biggest bigshot around because I would grab a handful of Mama's cookies and lead Tony around the neighborhood like a dog. Nobody else had a pony, especially one like Tony. I couldn't ride him because he was mean as hell, so I would just walk him around and show him off. One day Tony must've had a hankerin' for cookies because he hauled off and bit me on the shoulder. I ran home crying and the next day Tony was gone. To this day, I wonder if Daddy traded him for a Buick or a Chevy.

Sometimes I'd get in the kitchen and try to do some cooking myself but Mama, in her sweet way, would say, "Bubba, honey, I'll take over. You go outside and

Bubba at bat

play." Thank goodness I never caught the house on fire. I do remember grilling out with friends most every weekend. If I close my eyes I can still see Mama and the other ladies sitting in their lawn chairs and the men standing around the grill bragging about who was the best cook or who caught the biggest fish. They'd cook hamburgers or chicken, or fry some fish that they caught on their latest fishing trip.

I loved baseball more than anything in the world. When I wasn't eating, I played baseball every minute that I could. I dreamed of being another Mickey

Mantle or Roger Maris. One time my buddies and I broke into the concession stand at the ball park. We "borrowed" baseballs and a case of potato chips that we carried to school. Boy, I sure was popular that day. It's a wonder I didn't get put in jail.

I managed to survive my youth and even went to college for a while. But college wasn't for me so I tried my hand at different jobs in Albany. While I was selling cars and living in an apartment complex, I met a registered nurse named Jill. She was a single mom with a six-year-old named Jay, who was the cutest little ole boy I'd ever seen. Jill and I were married and I adopted Jay. Later we had a daughter who we named Corrie, after my mother. Meanwhile, I started a little business in Albany that I named Yard Busters, which grew into a successful landscaping and groundskeeping company. Unfortunately, when Corrie was in high school, Jill and I divorced. My sister, Paula, had moved to Savannah but we couldn't stand being that far apart. She begged me to come to Savannah to be with her and Bobby and Jamie. I finally took the plunge, found a buyer for my house and business, and headed for Savannah. I don't regret a minute of it.

By then The Lady & Sons was rocking and rolling at 311 West Congress Street in the heart of Savannah's Historic District. Paula was doing so well that she wanted to open another restaurant that I would run. One day she came to me and said, "Bubba, we live in this beautiful Southern coastal city. Why don't we open a place where we can do some of the delicious Southern seafood recipes that we grew up eatin'?"

I said, "Let's do it."

We went around and around about the name. We thought about The Lady and Her Brother and The Lady's Brother but then one day I walked in the office and she said, "Bubba, we've come up with a name. Uncle Bubba's Oyster House." We found a fantastic location on a pretty deepwater creek on the way to Tybee Island, which is Savannah's beach.

Now it seems like I've come full circle. I ain't on the Flint River no more, but being on the creek reminds me of the good old days with Mama, Daddy, Paula, and our grandparents. I was truly blessed to meet a wonderful woman named Dawn a few years after I moved to Savannah, and we were married at Paula's house while I was writing this book. She has two fine sons named Trevor and Ian. Now I'm happily the father of four, which is perfect because there's always room for more folks at my table. I guess good food and good times are the threads that have bound me and my family and friends together. So that's why I decided to write this cookbook. I want to share these recipes and family stories with all the folks who've asked for them, and even the less fortunate souls who haven't been lucky enough—yet—to visit Savannah and Uncle Bubba's for a taste of real Southern hospitality.

BEFORE YOU GET STARTED . . .

Don't forget to keep these tips in mind before you start fixing my delicious recipes! They're pretty much common sense, but I wanted to remind you anyway.

All vegetables and fruits should be thoroughly rinsed. Onions and garlic are peeled before use, and if no type of onion is specified, use your favorite. Sugar is granulated white sugar unless otherwise specified. Pans may be greased with more of the same fat used in a recipe, or sprayed with a cooking spray.

And last but not least, recipes followed by an asterisk are from Uncle Bubba's Oyster House. Enjoy!

BUBBA'S JUMPSTART APPETIZERS

UNCLE BUBBA'S CHARGRILLED OYSTERS*

BAKED OYSTERS WITH CRAB

CRAB MARTINI*

SEAFOOD NACHOS*

CALAMARI*

SAUTÉED FROGS LEGS

AUNT TRINA'S FAVORITE SHRIMP BOULETTES

JOSIE'S SHRIMP YUMMIES

PICKLED SHRIMP

FRIED DILL PICKLES*

SHORE IS GOOD SEAFOOD DIP*

BUFFALO CHICKEN DIP

TONI'S CHEESE WAFERS

HOT CHICKEN WINGS*

Jamie, Bubba, and Bobby on a fishing trip

Sautéed frogs legs are one of my all-time favorite appetizers and as good as any piece of Southern fried chicken anywhere, anyhow. Sometimes I even eat a few sets for a meal and, when I do, I usually giggle like crazy when I recall the first time I went frog gigging.

It was the early 1970s when my buddy Stump and I were both about sixteen. He got his unusual nickname because he was about five feet two inches tall and all muscle from lifting weights all the time. Stump was forever crackin' jokes and cuttin' the fool so there was no doubt in my mind that we would have fun when we set out to go gigging. We loaded up our hunting gear, which consisted of a gigantic flashlight with a handle, a long frog gig (like a skinny pitchfork with three short prongs), and paddles for the johnboat, which is a flat aluminum boat that's perfect for shallow water. Because of his muscles and all, Stump had the job of carrying the cooler on his shoulder.

It was one of those hot, muggy south Georgia nights, when the crickets were singing to high heavens and the bullfrogs were croaking, and we could hardly hear ourselves think. I tell you right now, we were definitely on the lookout for snakes and alligators.

All at once, I looked up and saw the cooler floating. Stump had stepped into a hole and had gone in water over his head. We rescued him and everybody had a good laugh at that one. We were still giggling when we pushed the boat off into the swamp. We knew we had reached the perfect spot for gigging when we shined the flashlight on the bank and saw six or eight frogs sitting in the mud staring at us with great big ole red eyes. We gigged a whole bunch, threw them in the cooler, and went home for some good eatin'.

Naturally, I had to include a recipe for sautéed frogs legs. I don't go gigging anymore because I simply buy my frogs legs at our local seafood store. If your town doesn't have a seafood store, most of the larger grocery chains carry them. It won't be as fun as my first experience with frogs legs but the taste will be well worth the time.

In addition to frogs legs, I'm sharing recipes for a bunch of other goodies, including Uncle Bubba's Chargrilled Oysters, straight from my restaurant to your supper table.

UNCLE BUBBA'S CHARGRILLED OYSTERS*

Serves 4 to 6

I ain't pullin' your leg when I say that people come from miles around to eat Uncle Bubba's Chargrilled Oysters. We grill 'em over an open flame but you can cook them right in the oven.

Serve with some French bread to sop up all those buttery juices.

1 cup (2 sticks) butter

½ teaspoon garlic powder

12 to 16 oysters on the half shell

1 cup grated Parmesan cheese

Bubba shucking oysters at the restaurant

(cont. on next page)

Place the butter in a small saucepan on high heat and bring to a boil. Skim off all of the foam that rises to the top and discard. Then stir in the garlic powder.

FOR THE GRILL:

Put the oysters on an open-flame grill and sprinkle Parmesan cheese over them. (Do not cover completely with cheese.) Let cook until cheese starts to brown (2 to 3 minutes). Drizzle garlic butter generously over each oyster. Cook another 1 to 2 minutes and remove from heat. Serve immediately.

OR FOR THE OVEN:

Preheat the broiler and line a broiler pan with foil. Place the oysters on the pan and sprinkle grated Parmesan cheese over them, being careful not to cover the oysters completely. Broil 2 to 3 minutes, until the cheese starts to brown. Remove the pan from the broiler and turn over each oyster. Generously spoon garlic butter over each oyster and return them to the broiler and cook 1 to 2 minutes more. Being careful not to lose any of the butter and oyster liquor, place the oysters on a platter and serve immediately.

BAKED OYSTERS WITH CRAB

Serves 4 to 6

The combination of crab and oysters is a seafood lover's dream. Plus, this recipe is so dadgum simple to fix and serve. Try it, you'll see and you'll thank me for it!

One 8-ounce package cream cheese, softened

1 cup grated Parmesan cheese

1 pound lump crabmeat, picked clean of shells

1 teaspoon salt

1 teaspoon pepper

1 teaspoon garlic powder

1 minced shallot

1 cup cooked chopped bacon

¼ cup chopped fresh basil

12 to 16 oysters on the half shell

Preheat the oven to 350°F.

Combine the cream cheese, Parmesan, crabmeat, salt, pepper, garlic powder, shallot, bacon, and basil. Place the oysters on a baking sheet and spoon the mixture onto the oysters in the half shell, putting a generous rounded mound of topping on each. Bake for 7 to 10 minutes, until the topping is bubbly and browned. Serve immediately.

CRAB MARTINI*

Serves 4 to 6

When this delicious appetizer is ready to serve, add a sprinkle of a seafood seasoning such as Old Bay. I like to garnish it with a lemon wedge and an olive to make it really look like a Martini.

12 to 15 fresh asparagus spears

1 cup mayonnaise

2 tablespoons spicy mustard (I like Dijon)

2 or 3 small tomatoes, diced

Juice and grated zest of 1 lemon

1 pound lump crabmeat, picked clean of shells

1 pound claw crabmeat, picked clean of shells

Lemon pepper and seasoned salt to taste

Lemon wedges

Old Bay Seasoning, for garnish

Pimento stuffed olives, for garnish

Blanch the asparagus by placing the spears in boiling salted water for 1 minute and immediately shocking them in an ice water bath. Drain and dry the asparagus. Trim the very bottom of the spears and discard. Cut off the top 2 inches of the asparagus and set aside for garnish. Finely chop the remaining asparagus.

Combine the chopped asparagus with the mayonnaise, mustard, tomatoes, lemon zest, and lemon juice. Gently fold the crabmeat into the asparagus mixture and season to taste with lemon pepper and seasoned salt.

Place the Old Bay Seasoning into a shallow dish. Run a lemon wedge around the rim of a martini glass and dip the rim into the Old Bay. Repeat with the remaining martini glasses. Divide the crab mixture among the prepared glasses and garnish with a sprinkle of Old Bay, the asparagus tops, lemon wedges, and olives.

SEAFOOD NACHOS*

Serves 4 to 6

At Uncle Bubba's Oyster House we serve this outstanding version of nachos over a plateful of warm corn tortilla chips. People always ask for more chips so they can eat every morsel.

1 large bag corn tortilla chips (16 ounces)

2 cups shredded Cheddar cheese (8 ounces)

2 cups shredded pepper Jack cheese (8 ounces)

1 tablespoon butter

1 clove garlic, minced

8 ounces crabmeat, picked clean of shells

½ pound shrimp, boiled, peeled, deveined, and tails removed, chopped

½ pound scallops, muscle removed, chopped

1 cup heavy cream

16 ounces grated Parmesan cheese

½ teaspoon salt

½ teaspoon ground pepper

½ teaspoon garlic powder

1 cup shredded iceberg lettuce

1 cup Pico de Gallo (page 29)

10 to 12 pickled jalapeño slices

Sour cream

Preheat the oven to 375°F.

In a large baking pan place a layer of the tortilla chips and cover with the shredded Cheddar and pepper Jack cheeses. Bake the chips for 2 to 3 minutes, or until the cheeses are melted. Remove the dish from the oven and set aside.

In a large sauté pan over medium-high heat, melt the butter and sauté the garlic until soft. Add the crabmeat, shrimp, and scallops and sauté for 3 minutes.

Add the cream to the seafood and stir for 2 to 3 minutes, until the sauce has thickened. Add the Parmesan cheese and stir to combine.

Remove the seafood mixture from the heat, stir in the salt, pepper, and garlic powder, and pour on the tortilla chips. Top the nachos with shredded lettuce, Pico de Gallo, jalapeños, and a large dollop of sour cream. Serve immediately.

CALAMARI*

Serves 4 to 6

Sometimes I tease folks and tell them that a dish of calamari is really just a plateful of onion rings because they tend to get all nervous when they think about eating squid.

1 quart buttermilk

2 tablespoons garlic powder

2 pounds squid, tubes only, cleaned and cut into ¼- inch rings

1 gallon peanut oil

4 cups Uncle Bubba's Fry Mix (page 38)

2 tablespoons (¼ stick) butter

1 cup diced tomatoes (fresh or canned and drained)

1 cup drained bottled banana peppers, sliced

1 teaspoon minced garlic

Combine the buttermilk, garlic powder, and calamari in a large bowl, cover, and put in the refrigerator to marinate for at least 1 hour.

Heat the peanut oil in a Dutch oven over medium-high heat to 350°F.

Drain the calamari. In a large separate bowl, toss the calamari with the fry mix to coat thoroughly. Remove excess fry mix from the calamari by lightly tossing in a fine mesh strainer.

Carefully place the battered squid in batches into the hot oil. Fry each batch for 3 to 4 minutes, stirring continuously so that the pieces don't stick together. When the calamari is crispy and golden brown, immediately remove it from the oil using a clean strainer or slotted metal spoon and place on a paper towel to drain. In a large sauté pan melt the butter and add the tomatoes, peppers, and garlic. Once heated through, add the calamari to the pan and toss gently just until well combined.

Serve immediately.

SAUTÉED FROGS LEGS

Serves 4 to 6 as an appetizer, 6 to 10 as a main course

Everytime I whip up a batch of frogs legs I think of my buddy Stump and can't help but laugh even after all these years. These can be served as an appetizer or as an entree.

1 cup peanut oil

8 to 10 sets frogs legs

Uncle Bubba's House Seasoning (page 26)

Uncle Bubba's Fry Mix (page 38)

One 12-ounce can or bottle beer

Bubba as a high school senior

In a large skillet, heat the peanut oil to 350°F. Sprinkle the frogs legs with House Seasoning. Dredge the legs in the fry mix, dip into the beer to coat, and coat again with the fry mix. Working in batches, sauté each for 2 to 3 minutes. Remove from the oil when golden brown and drain on paper towels.

AUNT TRINA'S FAVORITE SHRIMP BOULETTES

Serves 8 to 10

My Aunt Trina Bearden lives in Houma, Louisiana. This is one of her fine recipes. I can assure you that they make a great addition to any party.

1 pound raw shrimp, peeled and deveined, tails removed

1 medium onion, cut in chunks

1 medium all-purpose potato, peeled and cut in chunks

Half bunch fresh parsley, finely chopped

2 or 3 green onions (scallions), chopped

¼ cup finely chopped green bell pepper

1 egg, beaten

3 tablespoons all-purpose flour

Salt and pepper

3 tablespoons vegetable shortening

Using the grinder attachment on a mixer, or in a food processor, grind the shrimp, onion, and potato together. In a bowl, combine the shrimp mixture with the chopped parsley, green onion, and green pepper. Stir in the egg and flour to make a batter. Season to taste with salt and pepper.

Melt the shortening in a large skillet over medium-high heat. When the shortening is hot, drop the batter by tablespoonfuls into the pan and sauté 2 to 3 minutes per side, until browned and crisp. Drain on paper towels, then serve immediately.

JOSIE'S SHRIMP YUMMIES

Serves 4

Yummy is truly the perfect word to describe this recipe, given to me by Joanne Lair. I kid you not—when I first tasted these I thought I was eating dessert. I'm convinced that the cream sherry makes the difference. I could eat an entire plateful and still want more.

1 sleeve Ritz crackers

3 tablespoons melted butter

3 tablespoons cream sherry

Salt and pepper

12 large raw shrimp, peeled and deveined

Lettuce leaves

Preheat the oven to 350°F.

To make the stuffing, crush the crackers thoroughly and place in a small bowl with the melted butter and sherry. Mix thoroughly, and add salt and pepper to taste. The crackers will soak up the sherry and butter to make a thick paste.

Slice each shrimp down the back to create a pocket. Stuff the shrimp with the cracker mixture. Place in a lightly greased baking pan and bake for 10 minutes, or until the shrimp turn pink.

Arrange the lettuce leaves on a serving platter or on individual plates. Place the shrimp on top of the lettuce and serve.

PICKLED SHRIMP

Serves 12 to 16

I never can get enough pickled shrimp. I like to serve them at parties to add a touch of spice to a buffet. People eat them so fast, you'd think they were salted peanuts. Everybody always wants the recipe, so here it is!

4 pounds shrimp, cooked, peeled, and deveined

6 to 8 large white onions, sliced thin

1½ cups vegetable oil

2 cups white vinegar

¼ cup capers, drained

1 to 1½ tablespoons tomato paste

1 teaspoon sugar

⅓ cup prepared horseradish

Salt and red pepper

Place a layer of shrimp and a layer of onion rings in a very large glass container (a mayonnaise jar is good), alternating layers until all are used. In a large bowl, combine the oil, vinegar, capers, tomato paste, sugar, horseradish, and salt and red pepper to taste until well blended. Pour the sauce over the shrimp, put the cover on the jar, and refrigerate for 24 hours before serving. Pickled shrimp can be stored in the refrigerator for one week.

FRIED DILL PICKLES*

Serves 12 to 14

Here in the South, we like everything fried, even our pickles. And as we say at Uncle Bubba's Oyster House, it ain't a seafood house without Fried Dill Pickles.

One 24-ounce jar kosher dill pickle spears

1 teaspoon garlic powder

½ cup Louisiana hot sauce (I like Texas Pete)

½ cup buttermilk

1 gallon peanut oil

2 cups Uncle Bubba's Fry Mix (page 38)

Drain the juice from the pickle jar and refill the jar with the garlic powder, hot sauce, and buttermilk. Marinate the pickles for at least 30 minutes.

In a Dutch oven over medium-high heat, heat the oil to 350°F. Drain the pickles. Put the fry mix in a large mixing bowl, and toss the pickles to coat thoroughly. Shake off the excess mix by tossing lightly in a strainer and deep fry the pickles in batches for 3 to 5 minutes, depending on the size of the spears.

When golden brown, remove the pickles from the oil with a clean strainer or slotted metal spoon and place on paper towels to drain off any excess oil. Serve immediately.

SHORE IS GOOD SEAFOOD DIP*

Serves 10 to 12

This mighty fine dip can be served with tortilla chips, bread rounds, or celery.

1 tablespoon butter, plus extra for the baking dish

1 medium-size green bell pepper, finely chopped

1 medium-size yellow onion, finely chopped

2 celery stalks, finely chopped

One 10.75-ounce can condensed cream of mushroom soup

1 cup mayonnaise

Two 8-ounce packages cream cheese, softened

2 cups grated Parmesan cheese

8 ounces crabmeat, picked clean of shells

½ pound shrimp, boiled, peeled, deveined, and tails removed, chopped

Salt and pepper

1½ cups shredded Cheddar cheese (6 ounces)

Preheat the oven to 375°F. Grease well a 13 by 9-inch baking dish.

Melt the butter in a medium sauté pan. Saute the green pepper, onion, and celery until the vegetables are soft and the onion is translucent. Set aside to cool.

While the vegetables are cooling, in a large bowl, combine the soup, mayonnaise, cream cheese, and Parmesan cheese. Gently mix in the crab and shrimp, and season to taste with salt and pepper. Mix in the sautéed vegetables.

Pour the mixture into the prepared pan and top with the shredded cheddar. Bake the dip for 15 to 20 minutes, until the cheese is melted and the sides are bubbly.

BUFFALO CHICKEN DIP

Serves 8 to 10

Watch out for this one—it's mighty spicy. Be sure to have plenty of ice-cold drinks nearby. This recipe can also be made in a slow cooker if you run short of stovetop space. Combine all the ingredients except the celery and crackers in the slow cooker and cook on low for 2 hours or until the cheese has melted and the mixture is smooth.

Two 10-ounce or four 5-ounce cans chunk chicken, drained

¾ cup Louisiana hot sauce (I like Texas Pete)

Two 8-ounce packages cream cheese, cubed

1 cup bottled ranch-style salad dressing

1½ cups shredded Cheddar cheese (6 ounces)

1 bunch celery, washed, trimmed, and cut into sticks

Crackers

In a Dutch oven or heavy pot over medium heat, combine the chicken and hot sauce. Stir in the cream cheese and salad dressing and heat until the cream cheese melts. Mix in half of the Cheddar cheese. (If using a slow cooker, transfer mixture to the cooker and sprinkle remaining cheese on top. Cover and cook until bubbly.)

Sprinkle the remaining cheese on top, cover, and cook on low heat until bubbly, about 30 minutes. Serve with celery and/or crackers.

TONI'S CHEESE WAFERS

Makes about 24

Toni Nix was part of Mama and Daddy's circle of friends in Albany. They'd get together nearly every weekend to grill out supper and play cards. My Aunt Trina Bearden found this recipe in a box Mama had. It was written on a score pad sheet from a card game.

½ cup (1 stick) butter or margarine, softened

2 cups grated Cheddar cheese (8 ounces)

1 cup self-rising flour (see Tip)

1½ cups cornflakes

¼ teaspoon cayenne pepper

Mama and Daddy

Preheat the oven to 350°F. Grease a cookie sheet. In a medium bowl, mix all the ingredients until well combined.

Roll dough into a log 1½ inches in diameter and slice into ¼-inch-thick wafers. Place the wafers about 1 inch apart on the cookie sheet. Bake for 30 minutes, or until golden and crispy. Cool before serving.

TIP: If you can't find self-rising flour, use 1 cup regular all-purpose flour, and add 1½ teaspoons baking powder and ¼ teaspoon salt.

HOT CHICKEN WINGS*

Serves 4 to 6

These marinated chicken wings are as hot as an August day in south Georgia. But I sure do love anything spicy and they're the best, as long as you have a cool drink within arm's reach.

30 chicken wings, wingtips removed

About 2 cups Uncle Bubba's Chicken Wing Marinade (page 37)

1 gallon peanut oil

Louisiana hot sauce for dipping

Blue Cheese Dressing (page 35) for dipping

Place the wings in a large bowl or plastic bag and pour the marinade over the wings. Marinate for at least 1 hour, refrigerated. The longer they marinate, the hotter the wings.

When ready to serve, heat the oil in a Dutch oven to 350°F. Shake off the excess marinade and fry the wings for 8 to 10 minutes, or until crispy. Serve with Louisiana hot sauce or Blue Cheese Dressing.

SEASONINGS, SAUCES, DRESSINGS, AND SUCH

UNCLE BUBBA'S HOUSE SEASONING*

COCKTAIL SAUCE*

TARTAR SAUCE*

PICO DE GALLO*

UNCLE BUBBA'S MARINARA SAUCE*

UNCLE BUBBA'S SOUTHERN BEURRE BLANC*

HONEY MUSTARD*

BLUE CHEESE DRESSING*

THOUSAND ISLAND DRESSING*

UNCLE BUBBA'S CHICKEN WING MARINADE*

UNCLE BUBBA'S FRY MIX*

Bubba and Paula in the '70s

At Uncle Bubba's Oyster House we take pride in the homemade salad dressings, sauces, marinades, and frying mix we use on our seafood, chicken, and vegetables. We add a little special something to our recipes because we know our patrons are extra special folks.

I'm including nearly a dozen recipes for the dressings and such because people always want to know why our food tastes so gosh darn good. Back when I was growing up, Granny Paul, Mama, and Paula always were experimenting with different ways to turn ordinary recipes into extraordinary surprises. I learned from the best and I hope you enjoy the results!

UNCLE BUBBA'S HOUSE SEASONING*

Makes 1¾ cups

I mix this up in a small bowl and keep it right next to my stove so when I cook, it'll be handy. You can also keep it in a shaker.

1 cup salt

¼ cup garlic powder

¼ cup onion powder

¼ cup pepper

Combine all the ingredients in a small bowl. Store in a covered jar or shaker.

COCKTAIL SAUCE*

Makes 2½ cups

You don't have that zing in cocktail sauce without the horseradish. I eat cocktail sauce with all kinds of seafood and I even like to spread a little on crackers while I'm waiting for my meal.

2 cups ketchup

¼ cup prepared horseradish

2 tablespoons Worcestershire sauce

1 tablespoon hot sauce (I like Texas Pete)

Juice of 1 lemon

½ teaspoon pepper

In a bowl, mix together all of the ingredients. Cover and chill until ready to serve.

You can store this sauce in a sealed container or a squeeze bottle and refrigerate for up to a week.

TARTAR SAUCE*

Makes 2½ cups

This is my take on traditional tartar sauce. It's good on any kind of seafood.

1 cup diced white onion

1 cup dill pickle relish, drained, or 5 to 6 dill pickle spears, chopped

1 cup mayonnaise

1 teaspoon fresh lemon juice

Salt and pepper

In a food processor, puree the onion and relish. In a medium bowl, combine the pureed onion and relish with the mayonnaise and lemon juice. Season with salt and pepper to taste. Serve immediately or refrigerate, covered, until needed.

You can store this sauce in a sealed container or squeeze bottle and refrigerate for up to a week.

PICO DE GALLO*

Makes 6 cups

Without the fruit and honey, this would be just like salsa. That's fine, but I like the lively combination of pineapple, lemon, lime, and honey that gives this sauce a tropical sweet taste. At Uncle Bubba's Oyster House, we pile a heaping helping of this on our Seafood Nachos (page 10).

5 medium-size garden tomatoes, peeled, seeded, and chopped

1 medium-size green bell pepper, diced

1 medium-size red bell pepper, diced

1 large red onion, diced

1 jalapeño, seeded and finely minced

1 cup diced canned pineapple, drained

1 tablespoon Louisiana hot sauce (I like Texas Pete)

1 teaspoon grated lemon zest

1 teaspoon fresh lemon juice

1 teaspoon grated lime zest

1 teaspoon fresh lime juice

1 tablespoon honey

¼ cup chopped fresh cilantro

In a large bowl, mix together all of the ingredients until well combined. Serve immediately or refrigerate, covered, until needed.

You can store Pico de Gallo in a sealed container and refrigerate up to a week.

UNCLE BUBBA'S MARINARA SAUCE*

Makes 4 cups

A dippin' dish of marinara sauce goes with crispy fried calamari. It is great on pasta, which especially pleases Uncle Bubba's youngest guests.

4 tablespoons (½ stick) butter

1 medium-size red onion, diced

¼ medium-size green bell pepper, diced

¼ medium-size red bell pepper, diced

1 celery stalk, diced

½ carrot, diced

½ cup chopped fresh oregano, or ¼ cup dried

½ cup chopped fresh basil, or ¼ cup dried

1 cup dry white wine

½ teaspoon heavy cream

1½ tablespoons chopped garlic

1 tablespoon granulated sugar

1 tablespoon dark, packed brown sugar

1 tablespoon beef base (such as Better Than Bouillon, More Than Gourmet, or Bear Creek) (see Tip)

1 tablespoon chicken base (see Tip)

Two 14-ounce cans diced tomatoes in juice

In a saucepan, melt the butter and sauté the onion, green and red peppers, celery, and carrot until the onions are translucent. Add the oregano, basil, wine, and cream. Cook for 10 minutes to reduce the wine. Add the garlic, sugars, beef and chicken bases, and the tomatoes. Bring to a boil.

Carefully transfer the sauce to a food processor or blender and blend until smooth. Return the sauce to the pot and simmer for 1 hour or until thickened.

You can store this sauce in a sealed container and refrigerate for up to a week.

TIP: If you can't get beef or chicken base, dissolve 1 teaspoon powdered bouillon in 3 teaspoons warm water.

UNCLE BUBBA'S SOUTHERN BEURRE BLANC*

Makes 1 cup

At Uncle Bubba's we love to use our Southern Beurre Blanc sauce on our Crab Cakes (page 107). Beurre Blanc is just a French name for a butter sauce. What makes mine special is the Crab Butter recipe that goes with it. We slice a medallion of crab butter and put it on our piping hot stuffed flounder just before it is taken to the table.

3 tablespoons dry white wine

3 tablespoons diced onion

¼ cup Crab Butter (recipe follows)

½ cup heavy cream

In a small saucepan combine the wine and onions and cook over medium heat for 2 minutes until the wine has evaporated. Add the crab butter and stir until melted. Bring the mixture to a simmer. Add the heavy cream in a slow drizzle, stirring gently until combined. Serve immediately with the seafood of your choice.

CRAB BUTTER

Makes one 8-inch log

4 ounces claw crabmeat, picked clean of shells

1 pound (4 sticks) unsalted butter, softened

2 tablespoons crab or seafood base

2 green onions (scallions), thinly sliced

Fold the crab, butter, crab base, and onions together in a large bowl and mix until smooth. Remove from the bowl and shape into a log. Serve immediately or wrap in plastic and store in the freezer until needed. (When you're ready to use the crab butter, transfer it from the freezer to the refrigerator.)

Bubba with his catch

HONEY MUSTARD*

Makes 3 cups

Yum, yum, yum. I like honey mustard on a good tossed salad, chicken fingers, and sometimes even fried seafood.

2 cups mayonnaise

½ cup honey

¼ cup yellow mustard

1 tablespoon whole-grain mustard

1 teaspoon fresh lemon juice

1 teaspoon fresh orange juice

½ teaspoon prepared horseradish

Pinch of paprika

Salt and pepper

Combine all of the ingredients in a small bowl and mix until well incorporated. Serve immediately or refrigerate, covered, until needed.

You can store Honey Mustard in a sealed container and refrigerate up to a week.

BLUE CHEESE DRESSING*

Makes about 4½ cups

I love to pour blue cheese dressing over a wedge of iceberg lettuce with tomatoes, bacon, and red onions. I also use it as a refreshing dip for Hot Chicken Wings.

2 cups mayonnaise

¾ cup crumbled blue cheese

¼ cup sour cream

2 tablespoons chopped fresh parsley

2½ teaspoons fresh lemon juice

2½ teaspoons red wine vinegar

Kosher salt and pepper

Buttermilk, for thinning

In a medium bowl, whisk together the mayonnaise, blue cheese, sour cream, parsley, lemon juice, vinegar, and salt and pepper to taste until well combined. Add a little buttermilk to reach the consistency desired.

Serve immediately, or store, covered, up to a week in the refrigerator.

THOUSAND ISLAND DRESSING*

Makes about 2½ cups

This is another tasty dressing for tossed salads.

2 tablespoons red wine vinegar

2 tablespoons sugar

1 cup mayonnaise

½ cup ketchup

⅓ cup dill pickle relish, or 2 finely chopped dill pickle spears

2 hard-boiled eggs, finely chopped

1 tablespoon chopped fresh parsley

3 green onions (scallions), green parts, finely chopped

Kosher salt

Pepper

Worcestershire sauce

In a small bowl, whisk together the vinegar and sugar until the sugar is dissolved. Stir in the mayonnaise, ketchup, dill relish, eggs, parsley, and onions, and mix well. Adjust the seasoning with salt, pepper, and Worcestershire. Serve immediately or refrigerate, covered, for up to a week.

UNCLE BUBBA'S CHICKEN WING MARINADE*

Makes about 2¼ cups

Louisiana hot sauce is the key to opening up the flavor in this marinade. This makes enough for 30 party-size wings. (When you are ready, go back to the Hot Chicken Wings* recipe on page 22.)

2 cups Louisiana hot sauce (I like Texas Pete)

2 tablespoons Cajun seasoning (available in the spice aisle in grocery store)

2 tablespoons cayenne pepper

1 tablespoon garlic powder

In a small bowl, whisk together all the ingredients until well-blended. Store covered in a jar.

UNCLE BUBBA'S FRY MIX*

Makes 7 cups

We use this to coat chicken, seafood, calamari, dill pickles, and vegetables. Make up a batch of this anytime and have it ready when you're in the mood to fry.

6 cups self-rising flour (see Tip)

1 cup self-rising white cornmeal (see Tip)

1 teaspoon salt

1 teaspoon pepper

In a large bowl, combine all the ingredients. This recipe makes a ton, so store it in a large resealable plastic bag in the freezer until you need it.

TIP: If you can't find self-rising flour, use 6 cups all-purpose flour plus 3 tablespoons baking powder and 1½ teaspoons salt. If you can't find self-rising cornmeal, use ¾ cup plus 3 tablespoons white cornmeal, 1 tablespoon baking powder, and ½ teaspoon salt.

BREADS, ROLLS, AND MORE

BANANA NUT BREAD

PERFECT CORNBREAD

GRANDMOTHER'S ROLLS

BEER ROLLS

MAMA'S SOUTH GEORGIA ICEBOX ROLLS

RAISED BISCUITS

UNCLE BUBBA'S CORN MUFFINS*

SKILLET CORNBREAD

Little Bubba with a buzz cut

If I didn't know better I'd think my middle name was bread. Excuse the pun, but I was born and bred to eat bread of all kinds. I guess that goes back to my childhood when Granny Paul turned her back and I snitched her hot biscuits out of the oven.

In this section I've included several family recipes—like Mama's South Georgia Icebox Rolls—as well as others that I've collected through the years. Give me a hot roll or a piece of cornbread right out of the iron skillet (yep, you heard me right) and I'm in heaven.

BANANA NUT BREAD

Makes 2 loaves

This is a dee-licious way to use bananas that have stayed on the counter too long and need to be used pronto. I like to eat it right out of the oven for breakfast but it's really good anytime, warm or cool. It also freezes well.

5 large, very ripe bananas

1 cup vegetable oil

3 cups sugar

4 eggs

3⅓ cups all-purpose flour

1½ teaspoons salt

2 teaspoons baking soda

1 cup chopped pecans

Preheat the oven to 325°F. Lightly grease two 9 by 5-inch loaf pans.

In a large bowl, mash the bananas until smooth. Beat in the oil and sugar until well combined. Add the eggs one at a time and beat until combined.

In a medium bowl, stir together the flour, salt, and baking soda. Add this to the banana mixture and stir just until combined. Stir in the pecans.

Pour the batter into the two prepared pans. Bake for 1 hour, or until a toothpick inserted into the middle of the bread comes out clean. Cool for 10 minutes in the pans, then turn out onto a rack to cool completely.

TIP: Only grease the bottom of the loaf pans so a lip won't form around the edge of the bread.

PERFECT CORNBREAD

Serves 8 to 10

Give me a square of perfect cornbread and I'll be indebted to you forever. I love it hot out of the oven and slathered with butter.

1 cup all-purpose flour, sifted

¼ cup sugar

4 teaspoons baking powder

¾ teaspoon salt

1 cup yellow cornmeal

2 eggs

1 cup milk

¼ cup vegetable shortening

Preheat the oven to 425°F.

Generously grease an 8-inch square baking pan or a cast-iron skillet. Sift the flour with the sugar, baking powder, and salt into a large bowl. Stir in the cornmeal and add the eggs, milk, and shortening. Using a mixer, beat just until smooth. Do not overbeat.

Pour into the prepared pan. Bake for 12 to 15 minutes, and serve hot.

GRANDMOTHER'S ROLLS

Makes 24 rolls

Jill Hiers's grandmother, the late Mattie King of Buena Vista, Georgia, was affectionately called "GiGi." This is GiGi's recipe for lip-smackin'-good rolls. If you want to prepare the dough ahead of time, it will keep in the refrigerator, covered, for several days.

½ cup vegetable shortening

One ¼-ounce package active dry yeast

½ cup boiling water

½ cup lukewarm water (100 to 110°F)

3 cups all-purpose flour, sifted

1 egg

¼ cup sugar

1 teaspoon salt

Place the shortening in a large heatproof bowl. Place the yeast in another small bowl. Pour the boiling water over the shortening and the lukewarm water over the yeast. Set both aside.

When the shortening has melted and the mixture has cooled, beat in 2 cups of the flour, the egg, the dissolved yeast, the sugar, and the salt. Add the remaining flour and beat with a spoon until the batter leaves the spoon. Cover the bowl and refrigerate for at least 2 hours or until it has doubled in size.

Grease a baking sheet. Remove the dough from the refrigerator, punch down, and shape the dough into small rolls and place them on the prepared baking sheet two inches apart. Cover lightly and let stand in a warm place until they double in size again. While the rolls are rising, preheat the oven to 400°F. Bake the rolls for 12 to 15 minutes, until golden brown.

BEER ROLLS

Makes 24 rolls

With a name like Bubba I had to include a recipe for beer rolls. I actually have several recipes but I like this one given to me by Deane Brown, who is a server at Uncle Bubba's Oyster House.

4 cups baking mix (I use Bisquick)

4 tablespoons sugar

Two 12-ounce cans or bottles domestic beer, room temperature

Preheat the oven to 350°F. Grease two 12-cup muffin tins.

In a large bowl, mix the baking mix, sugar, and beer until smooth. Pour into the prepared muffin tins and bake for 30 to 35 minutes, until brown.

MAMA'S SOUTH GEORGIA ICEBOX ROLLS

Makes 24 rolls

My Aunt Trina wrote down this recipe for me. Even though she has lived in Houma, Louisiana, for years, she has never forgotten her south Georgia roots.

2 cups milk

⅓ cup sugar

½ cup vegetable shortening

One ¼-ounce package active dry yeast

About 5 cups all-purpose flour

1 teaspoon baking powder

½ teaspoon baking soda

2 teaspoons salt

In a small saucepan, scald the milk. Add the sugar and shortening and stir until dissolved. Set aside until the mixture is 110 to 115°F. Dissolve the yeast in the milk mixture.

Sift 2 cups of the flour in a separate bowl, and beat in the yeast mixture until smooth. Cover and let rise in a warm place for 2 hours.

Stir in baking powder, soda, and salt, and enough additional flour for a soft dough, about 3 cups. Turn the dough out on a floured board and knead until smooth. Place in a covered bowl in the refrigerator until ready to use.

When you are ready to bake, grease a baking sheet. Shape the dough into 24 rolls and place them on the prepared baking sheet 2 inches apart. Cover lightly and let stand in a warm place until they double in size again. While the rolls are rising, preheat the oven to 350°F. Bake for 30 minutes, until golden brown.

RAISED BISCUITS

Makes 2½ dozen

I have a handwritten copy of this recipe from my mama, Corrie Paul Hiers, who learned to cook from her mother, Irene "Granny" Paul. One of my earliest memories is watching them cook side-by-side in the kitchen at River Bend near Albany. For those of you who don't make biscuits too often, I've made the directions more detailed.

One ¼-ounce package active dry yeast

2 cups buttermilk, heated to 110 to 115°F

4 cups all-purpose flour

½ teaspoon baking soda

½ teaspoon baking powder

1 teaspoon salt

2 tablespoons sugar

3 tablespoons vegetable shortening, creamed at room temperature

Melted butter

In a large bowl, combine the yeast and the buttermilk. Add the flour, baking soda, baking powder, salt, and sugar alternately with shortening. Let it rise until it doubles in size, then punch down once.

Shape the dough into biscuits by hand or roll the dough out and cut out biscuits with a round cookie cutter. Place on 1 or 2 baking sheets, about 2 inches apart, and brush with melted butter. Let rise until double in bulk. Preheat the oven to 400°F.

Bake until brown, about 20 to 30 minutes. Serve hot.

UNCLE BUBBA'S CORN MUFFINS*

Makes 12 muffins

At Uncle Bubba's Oyster House we pride ourselves in serving food that's just a little bit different from what you'll get at other places. The cream-style corn added to these muffins makes them extra special.

Uncle Bubba's Oyster House on Whitemarsh Island in Savannah

1 cup self-rising yellow cornmeal (see Tip)

¾ cup self-rising flour (see Tip)

½ teaspoon salt

½ teaspoon cayenne pepper (optional)

½ cup vegetable oil

2 eggs

1 cup sour cream

One 8-ounce can cream-style corn

Preheat the oven to 375°F. Grease a 12-cup muffin tin.

In a large bowl, stir together the cornmeal, flour, salt, and cayenne, if using. In another bowl, beat together the oil, eggs, and sour cream until well blended. Stir in the corn. Add the corn mixture to the flour and stir until just mixed.

Pour the batter into the prepared muffin tin. Bake for 18 to 22 minutes, until golden brown.

TIP: If you can't find self-rising cornmeal, use ¾ cup plus 3 tablespoons regular cornmeal plus 1 tablespoon baking powder. Increase the salt to 1 teaspoon. If you can't find self-rising flour, use ¾ cup all-purpose flour plus 1⅛ teaspoons baking powder.

SKILLET CORNBREAD

Serves 6 to 8

Using an cast-iron skillet to make cornbread reminds me of days gone by and memories that will never be forgotten. Baking the cornbread in the skillet gives it a wonderful crisp crust.

2 tablespoons bacon drippings or butter

2 cups buttermilk

1 egg, beaten

1 teaspoon baking soda

1 teaspoon salt

1 teaspoon baking powder

1½ cups yellow cornmeal

Preheat oven to 450°F.

Heat a 10-inch cast iron skillet with drippings until smoking hot.

In a medium bowl stir together the buttermilk, egg, baking soda, salt, baking powder, and cornmeal just until moistened. Pour the cornmeal batter into the hot pan and spread evenly. Bake in the oven for 15 to 20 minutes or until golden brown.

SALADS, SOUPS, AND SIDES

Nothin' Better!

SAVANNAH SHRIMP SALAD*

CHILLED SHRIMP AND RICE SALAD

VIDALIA ONION AND LUMP BLUE CRAB SALAD

KATHY'S DIG DEEP SALAD

AUNT PEGGY'S GREEK SALAD

ZESTY PASTA SALAD

OYSTER STEW*

CRAB STEW*

GUMBO*

UNCLE BUBBA'S FAVORITE COLE SLAW*

CRUNCHY COLE SLAW

RED BEANS AND RICE

RICE-BROCCOLI CASSEROLE

HOPPIN' JOHN

OKRA AND TOMATOES

BAKED MACARONI AND CHEESE

COLLARD GREENS

CHEESY SQUASH CASSEROLE

BUTTER BEANS

Little Bubba with his Mama

When I was a young un', my Mama would buy fresh produce every week from Mr. Mock's tiny grocery store on Magnolia Street in Albany, Georgia. We'd see practically everybody in town there while we were pushing the cart down those skinny aisles. Mr. Mock would have fresh green beans, vine-ripe tomatoes, corn on the cob, butter beans, and most everything else under the sun. Sometimes when we got home, Mama would send me out on my bicycle back to Mr. Mock's if she realized that she had forgotten something that she wanted to cook for supper.

Usually, though, when we got home from the grocery store, Mama couldn't wait to put me to work. She'd sit me in front of the television set with bowlfuls of beans to snap and shell, and there I'd sit, snapping and shelling. I hated it but I knew if I wanted to eat good, I was gonna have to earn it.

Seeing all those fresh vegetables on the table in front of me made all that work well worthwhile. Naturally, I want to share some of my favorite recipes for vegetable salads, soups, and stews (like oyster and crab), and good ole Southern sides like okra and tomatoes, and collard greens.

SAVANNAH SHRIMP SALAD*

Serves 4 to 6

I like to cool off on a summer's day with a plate of fresh shrimp salad on a bed of lettuce, with a few crackers and a large glass of sweet iced tea. A shrimp salad sandwich makes an easy, quick lunch.

2½ pounds shrimp

1 cup mayonnaise

2 hard-boiled eggs, finely chopped

1 cup chopped celery

3 green onions (scallions), finely chopped

Salt and lemon pepper

Place the shrimp in a large pot and cover with water. Over medium-high heat, bring the pot to a boil and cook the shrimp for 4 minutes. Remove the shrimp and let cool. Peel, devein, remove the tails, and chop the shrimp, and place in a large bowl.

Add the mayonnaise, eggs, celery, green onions, and salt and lemon pepper to taste, and mix well.

CHILLED SHRIMP AND RICE SALAD

Serves 6 to 8

I always appreciate a good salad, especially when it's hot as a firecracker in Savannah. Shrimp and rice are a classic Southern combination. And this recipe is so easy to make. What more could you ask for?

2 pounds shrimp

Old Bay Seasoning

4 cups cooked and cooled white rice

1 cup chopped green bell pepper

1 cup chopped celery stalks and leaves

1½ cups mayonnaise

Pepper

Shell, devein, and remove the tails from the shrimp, then cut them in half lengthwise. Boil the shrimp with a sprinkling of Old Bay Seasoning. Let cool.

In a large bowl, combine the shrimp, rice, green pepper, celery, and mayonnaise. Season to taste with pepper and additional Old Bay Seasoning. Mix well, cover, and chill overnight.

VIDALIA ONION AND LUMP BLUE CRAB SALAD

Serves 4

If you like crabmeat, you'll love this salad. It's also great for anyone on a diet. Serve it on a bed of lettuce or drain it slightly and serve "naked," with some crackers on the side.

½ cup white wine vinegar

¼ cup sugar

Pinch of salt

Pinch of pepper

1 medium Vidalia or other sweet onion, thinly sliced

1 medium cucumber, peeled, seeded, and thinly sliced

1 medium tomato, diced

1 medium yellow tomato, diced

1 pound fresh lump blue crabmeat, picked clean of shells

¼ cup virgin olive oil

4 green onions (scallions), thinly sliced

4 large basil leaves, chopped

In a large bowl, whisk together the vinegar, sugar, salt, and pepper. Add the Vidalia onion and cucumber. Marinate for 1 to 2 hours at room temperature.

Add the tomatoes, crab meat, olive oil, green onions, and basil. Toss gently. Serve on a bed of lettuce or drain slightly and serve "naked."

KATHY'S DIG DEEP SALAD

Serves 12 to 14

My friend Susan Greene sent me this salad recipe that came from her buddy Kathy Bethea. She said Kathy and her husband, Buddy, serve it on their yacht, which they named "It Is Always Friday." This salad is perfect with fish, chicken, or beef.

1 head iceberg lettuce, chopped

2 medium red onions, chopped

1 green bell pepper, chopped

1 red bell pepper, chopped

3 or 4 ribs celery, chopped

One 8-ounce can sliced water chestnuts, drained

One 10-ounce package frozen green peas thawed but not cooked

2 cups mayonnaise (I like Hellmann's or Best Foods)

Grated Romano cheese

3 hard-boiled eggs, sliced

4 strips bacon, cooked, drained, and crumbled

1 or 2 medium garden tomatoes, sliced

In a large glass bowl, layer the lettuce, onions, green and red peppers, celery, water chestnuts, and peas. Spread the mayonnaise on top and sprinkle with cheese. Do not stir. Cover and refrigerate for 24 hours.

About 45 minutes before serving, remove from the refrigerator, and garnish with the sliced eggs, bacon, and tomatoes.

AUNT PEGGY'S GREEK SALAD

Serves 4 to 6

Aunt Peggy has served me this salad plenty of times. We either eat it with soup or a sandwich or stuff it in a pita half and drizzle with the dressing.

1 large head romaine lettuce, torn into bite-size pieces

¼ cup chopped fresh parsley

3 green onions (scallions), white and green tops, sliced

2 medium garden tomatoes, cubed

½ cup crumbled feta cheese (2 ounces)

¼ cup Kalamata olives, pitted and chopped

Greek Dressing (recipe follows)

In a large bowl toss together the lettuce, parsley, onions, and tomatoes. Top with the cheese, olives, and Greek dressing and toss again.

GREEK DRESSING

Makes 1 cup

3 cloves garlic

1 teaspoon salt

1 teaspoon pepper

¼ cup fresh lemon juice

¾ cup olive oil

In a food processor, pulse the garlic, salt, and pepper until chopped. Add the lemon juice and pulse three times. With the food processor running, pour the oil through the food chute in a slow, steady stream and process until smooth and thick.

ZESTY PASTA SALAD

Serves 6 to 8

Amy Beaver of Albany shared this tasty recipe with me. When you're serving seafood or steak, swap the coleslaw or tossed salad for this pasta salad for a change. You can also add shredded chicken or grilled shrimp to make this a main dish.

One 16-ounce package angel hair pasta, cooked, drained, and cooled

One 4-ounce jar sliced pimientos, drained

8 green onions (scallions), chopped

One 2.25-ounce can, or ¼ cup, sliced black olives, drained

¾ cup vegetable oil

3 tablespoons steak seasoning salt
(I use McCormick's Grill Mates Montreal Steak Seasoning)

3 tablespoons mayonnaise

4 tablespoons fresh lemon juice

Pepper

Dash of Tabasco sauce

In a large bowl, combine the pasta, pimientos, onions, and olives. In a small bowl whisk the oil, steak seasoning salt, mayonnaise, lemon juice, pepper to taste, and Tabasco sauce until well blended. Pour over the pasta.

OYSTER STEW*

Serves 4

This recipe from Uncle Bubba's Oyster House is a family favorite and made to order with our freshly shucked oysters. We like to serve it with saltine crackers, oyster crackers, or croutons, and a side of Louisiana hot sauce.

½ cup (1 stick) butter

3 green onions (scallions), green tops, thinly sliced

1 pint shucked oysters, juice reserved

4 cups milk

1 tablespoon salt

1 teaspoon freshly ground pepper

Over medium heat, melt the butter in a heavy medium saucepan. Sauté the green onions until tender. Add the oysters and cook until the edges begin to curl, stirring frequently. Add the milk, oyster juice, salt, and pepper and heat the milk until small bubbles form around the edge of the pot. Do not allow the stew to boil. Serve immediately.

CRAB STEW*

Serves 6 to 8 as a starter, 3 to 4 as an entree

This is one of our most popular dishes at Uncle Bubba's. Some people eat a cup as an appetizer while others order a bowl as their meal. Either way, it's a tasty treat that can't be beat.

½ cup fennel bulb, trimmed and chopped

1 celery stalk, chopped

¼ cup chopped yellow onion

½ cup (1 stick) butter

¾ cup self-rising flour (see Tip)

2 tablespoons crab base (see Tip)

2 quarts heavy cream

2 tablespoons cooking sherry

2 cups half-and-half

1 quart milk

2 pounds crabmeat, picked clean of shells

Salt and pepper

In a food processor, finely chop the fennel, celery, and onion. Melt the butter on medium-high heat in a large heavy saucepan. Add the vegetables and sauté until soft. Stir in the flour until it is all absorbed and no lumps remain. Continue to stir and cook the mixture for 8 to 10 minutes, until it spreads out and becomes bubbly.

Stir in the crab base, heavy cream, sherry, half-and-half, and milk. Bring the mixture to a boil, then reduce the heat to a low simmer. Allow the stew to thicken for no more than 8 to 10 minutes, then remove from heat. Gently stir in the crab meat and season to taste.

TIP: If you can't find self-rising flour, use ¾ cup all-purpose flour plus 1⅛ teaspoons baking powder. If you can't find crab base, you can substitute a seafood bouillon (shrimp or lobster) or seafood base.

GUMBO*

Serves 4 to 6

A bowl or cup of gumbo, served over rice like we do at Uncle Bubba's, is just about as good as you can get. My recipe calls for shrimp stock and shrimp base. If you have trouble finding shrimp stock you can make your own. Just bring 4 cups water, shrimp shells from at least 1½ pounds of shrimp, half an onion, 1 tablespoon whole peppercorns, a bay leaf, and one-quarter bunch of parsley to a boil and simmer, uncovered, for 45 minutes. Strain the stock. It will keep for 3 to 4 days in a tightly covered container in the refrigerator. Shrimp bouillon cubes are available in the Hispanic section of some grocery stores. You can use it like shrimp stock; just follow the directions on the side of the package.

½ cup (1 stick) plus 1 tablespoon butter

¾ cup all-purpose flour

½ cup chopped yellow onion (about ½ small onion)

¼ cup chopped celery (about 1 stalk)

¼ cup chopped green bell pepper (about ¼ pepper)

1 clove garlic, minced

1½ cups sliced cooked smoked sausage

3 cups shrimp stock

2 cups bottled clam juice

1 tablespoon shrimp base

1 tablespoon dried parsley flakes

1 tablespoon Cajun seasoning (available in the spice aisle in the grocery store)

1 teaspoon dried thyme leaves

1 teaspoon dried basil leaves

½ teaspoon finely ground black pepper

½ teaspoon coarsely ground black pepper

2 bay leaves

1 teaspoon gumbo file (optional, depending on how thick you want it)

1 cup sliced okra, fresh or frozen

1 cup chopped canned tomatoes, with juice

1 green onion (scallion), thinly sliced

Cooked white rice (optional)

Make a roux: In a large heavy saucepan, over low heat, melt ½ cup of the butter. Add the flour, and cook on low heat for 30 to 45 minutes or until the roux is dark brown. Brown does not mean burnt; if you burn the roux you have to throw it out and start over again. Remove about 1 tablespoon of the roux and set it aside.

In small sauté pan, over low heat melt the remaining 1 tablespoon of butter, sweat the onion, celery, green pepper, and garlic until the vegetables are soft and the onions are translucent. Add the vegetables to the roux.

In the pan you used to sweat the vegetables, sauté the smoked sausage until tender and add it to the vegetable and roux mixture.

Add the shrimp stock, clam juice, shrimp base, parsley, Cajun seasoning, thyme, basil, peppers, bay leaves, gumbo file, okra, and tomatoes, and stir to mix. Simmer on medium-low heat until thick, about 1 hour. (If you are using frozen okra, add 3 to 4 minutes cooking time.)

Before serving, remove the bay leaves and add the remaining roux. Cook for at least 5 minutes on low heat. Add the green onion and serve immediately, over her white rice if you like.

UNCLE BUBBA'S FAVORITE COLE SLAW*

Serves 6 to 8

At Uncle Bubba's we shred the cabbage and carrots ourselves but, if you're in a hurry, you can pick up a bag of pre-shredded slaw in the produce section at the grocery store.

1 large head green cabbage

1 carrot

¾ cup mayonnaise

¼ cup white vinegar

¼ cup sugar

1 small yellow onion, finely chopped

1 small green bell pepper, finely chopped

1 teaspoon dried parsley flakes

Celery seed

Salt and pepper

Uncle Bubba's House Seasoning (page 26)

Remove and discard the tough outer leaves of the cabbage. Cut in quarters and remove the core. Slice the cabbage as thinly as possible. Place the cabbage in a large bowl.

Rinse the carrot well, peel, and shred, and add to the cabbage. Set aside.

In a separate bowl, mix the mayonnaise, vinegar, sugar, onion, green pepper, parsley flakes, celery seed, salt, pepper, and House Seasoning to taste.

Pour the mixture over the cabbage and carrot mixture and toss with a spoon, or by hand, until evenly coated. Adjust the seasoning as needed. Let the cole slaw sit for at least 30 minutes in the refrigerator.

Toss the cole slaw immediately before serving to reincorporate the dressing.

CRUNCHY COLESLAW

Serves 4 to 6

Sometimes when I'm in the mood for a little crunch in my coleslaw, I fix this version, with crispy ramen noodles, almonds, and sesame seeds. I like to serve this as a side, with fried shrimp or oysters.

Add the ramen noodles just before serving; the noodles will soften as the slaw sits.

½ cup olive oil

2 tablespoons sugar

2 tablespoons white vinegar

One 3-ounce package chicken-flavored ramen noodles

One package shredded coleslaw

One 2.25-ounce package (2 teaspoons) slivered almonds, toasted

2 tablespoons sesame seeds, toasted

In a small bowl, mix the oil, sugar, and vinegar with the seasoning envelope included in the package of ramen noodles. Let stand 30 minutes.

In a large bowl, combine the coleslaw, almonds, and sesame seeds. Pour the dressing over all and stir until well coated. Crush the ramen noodles over the top. Serve immediately.

RED BEANS AND RICE

Serves 6 to 8

My fondness for Cajun dishes just keeps on keeping on. I like to serve this with Fried Chicken (pages 82 and 83) and Skillet Cornbread (page 50).

½ pound dried red kidney beans (1¼ cups)

1 smoked ham hock

1 bay leaf

½ cup chopped celery

½ cup chopped onion

1 tablespoon Louisiana hot sauce (I like Texas Pete)

¼ teaspoon cayenne pepper

2 teaspoons dried thyme

1 tablespoon white vinegar

2 cups sliced smoked sausage, thinly sliced

Salt and pepper

3 cups cooked white rice

In a large heavy saucepan, cover the beans with water and bring to a boil; drain.

Return the beans to the pot and add 4 cups water, the ham hock, bay leaf, celery, onion, hot sauce, cayenne pepper, thyme, and vinegar. Bring to a boil; reduce heat, cover, and simmer 1 hour.

Remove the ham hock and discard and add the smoked sausage. Simmer, covered, for 30 minutes.

(cont. on next page)

Season with salt and pepper and stir in the cooked rice. Cook uncovered 10 more minutes, or until any remaining liquid has evaporated. Remove the bay leaf before serving.

TIP: Don't stir your rice while it's cooking because stirring tends to make it sticky.

RICE-BROCCOLI CASSEROLE

Serves 10 to 12

This is a great combination of rice and broccoli that makes two sides in one.

Cooking spray

¼ cup (½ stick) butter

1 cup chopped celery

½ cup chopped onion

2 cups cooked rice

Two 10-ounce packages frozen broccoli, chopped and cooked until almost done

One 10.75-ounce can condensed cream of mushroom soup

One 10.75-ounce can condensed cream of chicken soup

1 cup processed cheese sauce

Preheat the oven to 350°F. Coat a 13 by 9-inch baking pan with cooking spray.

In a large skillet over medium-high heat, melt the butter and sauté the celery and onion. Stir in the rice, broccoli, mushroom soup, chicken soup, and cheese sauce. Pour the mixture into the prepared baking pan and bake for 30 minutes.

HOPPIN' JOHN

Serves 4 to 6

I like to follow tradition, and down South it's a New Year's Day custom to eat Hoppin' John and collards (page 76) for good luck during the coming year. I've been lucky the last few years and now I know why.

1 pound dried black-eyed peas

2 tablespoons vegetable oil

1 smoked ham hock

1 medium yellow onion, chopped

2 teaspoons salt

1 teaspoon dried parsley flakes

1 teaspoon dried thyme leaves

2 cups long-grain white rice, uncooked

Pepper

Rinse and pick over the black-eyed peas to remove any dust or stones.

In a large heavy saucepan, bring 8 cups of water to a boil along with the oil, ham hock, and onion. Add the peas and simmer, covered, for 2½ hours. Remove the ham hock and discard.

Add salt, parsley, thyme, 2 cups water, and the rice. Cover and simmer for an additional 30 minutes. Add pepper to taste and additional salt, if necessary. Serve this dish with hot sauce on the side.

OKRA AND TOMATOES

Serves 4 to 6

One of my all-time favorite vegetable dishes is okra and tomatoes, which simply can't be beat in my memory book. I remember Mama serving hot, steaming bowls of this all the time when Paula and I were growing up.

1 tablespoon peanut oil

¼ pound bacon, chopped

1 medium-size yellow onion, diced

1 medium-size green bell pepper, diced

½ teaspoon minced garlic

Salt

½ teaspoon seasoned salt

¼ teaspoon garlic powder

4 cups diced tomatoes with their juice, fresh
(about 3 to 4 large tomatoes), or canned

½ cup (1 stick) butter

1 tablespoon chicken base

4 cups sliced fresh or frozen okra

Pepper

(cont. on next page)

Little Bubba flexing

In a large skillet, heat the oil over medium heat. Add the bacon, onion, green pepper, and garlic and sauté until the vegetables are soft and the onions are translucent. Add ¼ teaspoon salt, the seasoned salt, garlic powder, tomatoes, 1 cup water, the butter, chicken base, and okra. Bring to a boil, reduce the heat, and simmer, covered, for 1 hour, stirring occasionally. Season to taste with salt and pepper.

Uncle Bubba's Chargrilled Oysters

OPPOSITE:
Oven Fried Chicken with Skillet Cornbread
and Red Beans and Rice

BELOW:
Vidalia Onion and
Lump Blue Crab Salad

OPPOSITE:
Uncle Bubba's Crab Cakes

ABOVE:
Gumbo with Uncle Bubba's
Corn Muffins and Mama's South Georgia
Icebox Rolls

BELOW:
Uncle Bubba's Key Lime Pie

OPPOSITE:
Uncle Bubba's Crab-Stuffed Flounder

Pickled Shrimp

BAKED MACARONI AND CHEESE

Serves 10 to 12

When I think of comfort food, this version of macaroni and cheese tops my list. A plate of this always makes me feel better.

1 pound elbow macaroni, cooked and drained

4 cups shredded sharp Cheddar cheese (1 pound)

3 eggs, beaten

3 cups milk

1 tablespoon dry mustard

Salt and pepper

Preheat the oven to 350°F. Grease a 13 by 9-inch baking pan.

Place half the prepared macaroni in the prepared pan. Cover with 1½ cups of the cheese. Top with the remaining macaroni, then cover with the remaining cheese.

Whisk together the eggs, milk, mustard, and salt and pepper to taste and pour evenly over the contents of the pan.

Bake for 1 hour, or until the cheese is melted and lightly browned.

COLLARD GREENS

Serves 6

Here's one of the good luck recipes that I eat on New Year's and plenty of other days, too. Be sure to wash the collard greens real good before cooking. There's nothing worse than a mouthful of sandy greens!

1 smoked ham hock

1 tablespoon Louisiana hot sauce (I like Texas Pete)

2 pounds collard greens, trimmed, very well washed, and chopped

White vinegar

Salt and pepper

Bring the ham hock, 8 cups water, and hot sauce to a boil in a stockpot. Boil, covered, for 30 minutes.

Stir in collard greens. Reduce the heat, cover, and simmer 1 hour, or until the greens are tender and no longer bitter.

Remove the ham hock and shred the meat into the greens. Season with the greens with vinegar, salt, and pepper to taste.

CHEESY SQUASH CASSEROLE

Serves 6 to 8

Ashley Strickland, who did a super job of testing the recipes in this book for me, gave me her version of squash casserole, a classic Southern side dish. All I have to say is that it's *umm-mm* good.

1 tablespoon vegetable oil

6 medium yellow summer squash, thinly sliced

1 large Vidalia or other sweet onion, thinly sliced

½ cup sour cream

½ cup grated Parmesan cheese

1 cup shredded sharp Cheddar cheese (4 ounces)

Salt and pepper

1 sleeve Ritz crackers, crushed medium to fine

Preheat the oven to 350°F. Grease a 2-quart casserole.

Heat the oil in a large skillet over medium heat. Add the squash and onion, and sauté until tender and the liquid has evaporated. Transfer to a bowl and stir in the sour cream, cheeses, and salt and pepper to taste. Place in the prepared casserole and sprinkle the cracker crumbs evenly over the top. Bake for 20 minutes, or until the top is golden and bubbly.

BUTTER BEANS

Serves 6 to 8

Mercy me! I can't get enough of butter beans. I eat them with everything, but most especially with beef stew over rice. That's my choice for one of the top ten meals of all time.

3 slices streak o' lean or bacon (see Tip)

4 cups chicken broth

1 pound fresh or frozen butter beans
(use fresh or frozen lima beans if butter beans aren't available)

Salt and pepper

Rinse the streak o' lean in cold water; pat dry. Heat the streak o' lean in a medium saucepan over medium-high heat until the fat renders. Add the chicken broth and butter beans and bring to a boil. Reduce the heat, cover, and simmer 25 minutes or until beans are tender. Season with salt and pepper to taste.

TIP: Streak o' lean is a form of fatback. It's like lard but firmer.

ENTREES

*Just a Fancy Name for Meats
and Seafood*

UNCLE BUBBA'S FRIED CHICKEN*
OVEN-FRIED CHICKEN
LIP-SMACKIN'-GOOD CHICKEN CASSEROLE
OVEN-BAKED BARBECUED CHICKEN
BO'S GRILLED CUBED STEAK ROLLUPS
OLD-TIME BEEF STEW
TENDER BEEF POT ROAST
ITALIAN STEAK
NO-FAIL LASAGNA
BEEF BURGUNDY
SOUR CREAM PORK CHOPS
FRIED QUAIL
DOVE WITH SHERRY GRAVY
UNCLE BUBBA'S FRIED SHRIMP*
BBQ SHRIMP*
LOW COUNTRY BOIL
SHRIMP AND GRITS*
SALMON AND GRITS
UNCLE BUBBA'S CRAB CAKES*
DEVILED CRAB
UNCLE BUBBA'S CRAB STUFFED FLOUNDER*
UNCLE BUBBA'S FRIED OYSTERS*
SCALLOPED OYSTERS
CRAWFISH ÉTOUFFÉE

I'm as lucky as a pig in mud to have lots of good cooks on both sides of my family; so many of our family traditions are built around food and the supper table. One of my all-time favorite memories is the long Thanksgiving weekends we spent at my Uncle Bernie and Aunt Glennis Hiers's home place up in the country in southeast Georgia.

Little Bubba by the boat

I'll never forget all the food that kept coming out of Aunt Glennis's kitchen. It wouldn't have been Thanksgiving without baked turkey and cornbread dressing but she also set a table full of vegetables like collard greens and fresh butter beans.

After the turkey dinner and leftovers (if there were any), we were ready for bream and catfish caught right out of Uncle Bernie's pond. By the time Saturday rolled around we would have cranked up the cooker and had a fish fry with homemade hush puppies, coleslaw, and all the fixin's.

We'd eat like crazy, watch football, and laugh and holler at the stories everybody told. The children would ride ponies and take turns on the go-carts. The best part (other than the food) was being all together with the rest of the family. When Aunt Glennis got to where she couldn't do the cookin', the family came to Savannah to eat and spend time with Paula and me, and our families.

UNCLE BUBBA'S FRIED CHICKEN*

Serves 4

At Uncle Bubba's Oyster House we serve my fried chicken with cole slaw and fries, but at home I like to eat it with fresh vegetables and biscuits.

2 tablespoons seasoned salt (I use Lawry's)

2 tablespoons of Uncle Bubba's House Seasoning (page 26)

1 chicken, cut into 8 pieces (about 3 to 4 pounds)

1 cup of Louisiana hot sauce (I like Texas Pete)

5 eggs

1 gallon peanut oil

4 cups self-rising flour (see Tip)

Combine the seasoned salt and House Seasoning in a small bowl. Massage the mixture into the chicken pieces. Place the chicken in a heavy resealable plastic bag or a baking pan large enough to hold the pieces in one layer. In a medium bowl, whisk together the hot sauce and eggs until well combined. Pour enough of the mixture over the chicken to coat it, but do not drown it. Allow the chicken, covered, to marinate in the refrigerator for at least 1 hour and up to 8 hours. (Discard leftover marinade.)

When ready to fry, heat the oil to 350°F in a Dutch oven. While the oil is heating, place the flour in a large bowl. Shake off the excess marinade from a chicken piece and coat in the flour. Shake off the excess flour and set the chicken aside on a rack. Fry the chicken, turning once, 8 to 10 minutes for white meat and 13 to 15 minutes for dark meat. Allow each piece to drain on paper towels before serving.

TIP: If you can't find self-rising flour, use 3¾ cups all-purpose flour mixed with 2 tablespoons baking powder and 2 teaspoons salt.

OVEN-FRIED CHICKEN

Serves 4 to 6

This is a slightly different take on Southern fried chicken, which I dearly love. Mama and Grandma Paul used to serve fried chicken all the time when Paula and I were growing up. Alongside they'd serve up rice and gravy, fresh okra and tomatoes (page 73), and creamed corn.

MARINADE

1 cup buttermilk

½ cup unflavored yogurt

2 teaspoons spicy brown mustard

2 teaspoons Louisiana hot sauce (I like Texas Pete)

2 teaspoons dried tarragon (1 teaspoon if fresh)

2 teaspoons grated lemon zest (about 1 large lemon)

2 teaspoons paprika

2 teaspoons salt

One 2½-pound chicken, cut into serving pieces, *or* 4 to 6 boneless, skinless chicken breast halves

COATING

1½ cups all-purpose flour

½ cup plain oatmeal

(cont. on next page)

In a small bowl, mix together the buttermilk, yogurt, mustard, hot sauce, tarragon, lemon zest, paprika, and salt. Put the chicken in a heavy resealable plastic bag or a baking pan large enough to hold the pieces in one layer and pour the buttermilk mixture over it. Seal the bag or cover the pan with plastic and marinate in the refrigerator for at least 4 hours and up to 8 hours or overnight.

Preheat the oven to 450°F. Grease a baking pan large enough to hold the chicken pieces in one layer.

Place the flour and oatmeal in a brown paper bag. One piece at a time, place the chicken in the bag and shake until coated. Place the piece skin side down in the prepared baking dish. Continue until all the pieces are covered in the flour mixture. Bake for 40 minutes, turning once, until the chicken is golden brown.

LIP-SMACKIN'-GOOD CHICKEN CASSEROLE

Serves 4 to 6

This is almost like chicken pie but not quite. I'm partial to the addition of the herb-seasoned dressing because I can eat a ton of dressing—and not just at Thanksgiving!

2 medium carrots, peeled and sliced

1 medium yellow onion, sliced

1 teaspoon salt

½ teaspoon pepper

One 3- to 4-pound chicken, quartered, or 2 bone-in chicken breasts

One 10.75-ounce can condensed cream of chicken soup

Two 10.75-ounce cans condensed cream of mushroom soup

One 8-ounce bag herb-seasoned dressing

Fill a stockpot with enough well-salted water to cover the chicken. Add the carrots, onion, and salt and pepper and bring to a boil. Place the chicken in the pot, reduce the heat, and simmer, covered, for 30 minutes. When the chicken is done, remove it and let cool. Strain and reserve the broth and discard the vegetables.

Preheat the oven to 350°F. When the chicken is cool enough to handle, remove and discard the skin and bones. Cut the meat into bite-size pieces.

In a large bowl, combine the chicken with both soups and stir thoroughly. Pour into a 13 by 9-inch baking pan, and cover the mixture evenly with the dry dressing. Pour 1⅔ cups of the reserved broth over the dressing. Bake for 30 minutes, or until bubbly.

OVEN-BAKED BARBECUED CHICKEN

Serves 4 to 6

If you like barbecued chicken but you don't want to fire up the grill and get into all that mess, you might want to try this recipe for a change.

1 medium yellow onion, chopped

2 tablespoons white vinegar

2 tablespoons granulated sugar

3 tablespoons light, packed brown sugar

¼ cup fresh lemon juice

1 cup ketchup

1½ teaspoons prepared whole mustard

½ cup chopped celery

3 tablespoons Worcestershire sauce

1 tablespoon cane syrup (I like Alaga, available from www.whitfieldfoods.com)

Salt and cayenne pepper

One 1½- to 2-pound chicken, cut into serving pieces

In a medium saucepan, combine the onion, vinegar, sugars, lemon juice, ketchup, mustard, ½ cup water, the celery, Worcestershire, syrup, and salt and cayenne pepper to taste. Simmer for 30 minutes.

Preheat the oven to 350°F. Place the chicken in a baking pan large enough to hold the pieces in one layer. Pour the sauce over the chicken and bake for 1 hour, basting occasionally.

BO'S GRILLED CUBED STEAK ROLLUPS

Serves 4 to 6

My nephew Bo Beaver lives in my hometown of Albany, Georgia. He made these for me once and I've been eating them ever since.

¼ cup Dale's Steak Sauce (available from www.dalesseasoning.com),
or your favorite steak sauce

2 teaspoons Cavender's Seasoning (available from www.greekseasoning.com),
or other Greek-style seasoning

1 pound cubed steak, in 4 to 6 pieces

4 to 6 slices sharp Cheddar cheese

1 jalapeño pepper, seeded and sliced into 4 to 6 strips

4 to 6 slices bacon

Preheat a grill to medium-high.

Combine the steak sauce, Greek seasoning, and meat in a large bowl. Marinate for 15 minutes.

Place a slice of cheese and a strip of jalapeño on top of a piece of steak; roll the steak and wrap with a slice of bacon, securing the roll with a toothpick. Repeat with the remaining pieces of meat. Grill, turning occasionally, for 25 to 30 minutes; 15 to 20 minutes, turning occasionally, if you prefer your meat less well-done.

OLD-TIME BEEF STEW

Serves 4 to 6

When I was growing up, Mama would sometimes serve this beef stew over rice, along with fresh butter beans and corn on the cob. We'd call it "half and half."

2 tablespoons vegetable oil

2 pounds stew beef, cut into 1-inch cubes
(boneless chuck, tip, or round roast work well in this dish)

1 teaspoon Worcestershire sauce

1 whole clove garlic

1 medium onion, sliced

1 large bay leaf (or 2 small)

1 tablespoon salt

1 teaspoon sugar

½ teaspoon pepper

½ teaspoon paprika

Pinch of ground allspice or cloves

3 medium-size carrots, peeled and cut into bite-size pieces

3 medium potatoes, peeled and cut into bite-size pieces

3 celery stalks, cut into bite-size pieces

2 tablespoons all-purpose flour

In a Dutch oven over medium-high heat, heat the vegetable oil and brown the beef. Add 2 cups water, the Worcestershire sauce, garlic, onion, bay leaf, salt, sugar, pepper, paprika, and allspice. Bring to a boil. Cover, reduce the heat, and simmer for 1½ hours.

Remove the bay leaf and garlic. Add the carrots, potatoes, and celery. Cover and simmer an additional 35 to 40 minutes over low heat.

Dip out 1 cup of the hot liquid from the beef stew into a small

Mama in her apron

heatproof bowl. In another small bowl, stir ¼ cup water and the flour until smooth. Pour the flour mixture into the hot liquid, stir until well combined, and return to the pot. Stir the stew over low heat until it becomes thick.

TENDER BEEF POT ROAST

Serves 4 to 6

I dearly love a recipe that's easy and tastes so doggone good. I like to serve this with one or two fresh vegetables and homemade biscuits. It makes for a great Sunday dinner, reheats well, and makes delicious sandwiches, if you have any leftovers.

One 3-pound chuck roast

Salt and pepper

2 large carrots, peeled and cut into 3-inch pieces

2 celery stalks, cut into 3-inch pieces

1 medium-size onion, sliced

2 cloves garlic, sliced in half

1 bay leaf

One 10.75-ounce can condensed French onion soup

1 cup dry red wine

1½ cups beef broth

2 tablespoons all-purpose flour

Preheat the oven to 375°F. Sprinkle all sides of the chuck roast with salt and pepper. Place the meat in a roasting pan with tall sides. Combine the carrots, celery, onion, garlic, bay leaf, onion soup, ½ soup can water, the red wine, and beef broth. Pour over the roast and bake, uncovered, for 3 to 4 hours, or until the meat is fork-tender.

Remove the meat from the pan and let it rest. Strain the pan juices into a saucepan, reserving the vegetables, if desired (discard the bay leaf). In a small bowl whisk together the flour and 1 cup water. Stir into the pan juices and bring the mixture to a boil. Continue to whisk until the gravy is thickened. Slice the pot roast and place it on a serving dish. Surround the meat with the vegetables, if you like. Serve the gravy over the pot roast or on the side.

ITALIAN STEAK

Serves 4 to 6

Aunt Trina lives out yonder in Houma, Louisiana, and like all the Hiers family, she likes to cook. This is a quick, easy, and filling dinner. Serve it with a tossed salad and fresh green beans.

1½ cups Italian seasoned bread crumbs

½ teaspoon dried basil (¼ teaspoon if fresh)

½ cup grated Romano cheese

6 or 7 garlic cloves, minced

Salt and pepper

3 eggs

1 pound round steak, pounded ¼-inch thick and cut into 4 to 6 pieces

2 tablespoons olive oil

In a shallow bowl, combine the bread crumbs, basil, Romano cheese, garlic, and salt and pepper to taste. Lightly beat the eggs in a separate shallow bowl. Dip the steaks into the beaten eggs to coat. Dip in the bread crumb mixture on both sides and pat gently so the crumbs stick. Heat the oil in a large skillet over medium heat and fry the steaks 1 to 2 minutes on each side, until brown. Do not crowd the pan. Do not overcook the meat unless you like tough, chewy meat.

TIP: If you need to cook your steak in more than one batch, you may need to add more oil to your pan after each batch has cooked.

NO-FAIL LASAGNA

Serves 6 to 8

This lasagna freezes beautifully uncooked. Just defrost the lasagna before baking. Let it stand for 10 minutes before you cut and serve it; it will hold together better.

2 pounds ground beef

2 cloves garlic, minced

Two 6-ounce cans tomato paste

One 14-ounce can whole tomatoes

1 teaspoon salt

1 teaspoon dried oregano

Dash of pepper

6 to 8 regular lasagna noodles (not no-boil)

One 12-ounce container cottage cheese

1 egg, beaten

8 ounces sliced Swiss cheese

3 cups shredded mozzarella (¾ pound)

Grated Parmesan cheese

Lightly grease a 3-quart casserole.

In a large, deep skillet, brown the beef and garlic. Stir to break up meat. When browned, drain off fat.

Return to heat and add the tomato paste, tomatoes, salt, oregano, and pepper. Stir to combine. Cover and simmer for 20 minutes, stirring occasionally.

(cont. on next page)

Cook the noodles according to directions, drain, and separate them by rinsing them in cold water.

Preheat the oven to 350°F. In a small bowl, mix the cottage cheese and egg until well combined. In the prepared casserole, layer the sauce, noodles, Swiss cheese, mozzarella, and cottage cheese mixture. Repeat the layers, ending with a layer of sauce. Sprinkle the lasagna with the Parmesan. Bake for 20 to 30 minutes, until the lasagna is bubbling and the cheese is melted. Let stand 10 minutes before cutting.

BEEF BURGUNDY

Serves 4

My wife, Dawn, served this to me at a romantic dinner. She not only cooks but she's beautiful, too. What more could a guy ask for?

2 pounds lean beef, cut into 1-inch cubes
(boneless chuck, tip, or round roast work well in this recipe)

One 10.75-ounce can condensed golden mushroom soup (I use Campbell's)

1 cup Burgundy or other dry red wine

One 2-ounce envelope dried onion soup mix (I use Lipton)

1 cup sliced mushrooms, canned and drained or fresh

Preheat the oven to 325°F. In a Dutch oven, combine the beef, soup, wine, soup mix, and mushrooms. Cover and bake for 2 hours.

TIP: I spotted this advice, more or less, in the Sunday newspaper: When getting married and combining households, two cooks say "I love you" by giving up some cherished tools to make room for their partner's.

© Christine Hall

Bubba and Dawn

SOUR CREAM PORK CHOPS

Serves 4

These pork chops will melt in your mouth, they're so tender. You can use boneless or bone-in chops. Serve this over rice.

2 tablespoons vegetable oil

4 pork chops

1 medium-size onion, thinly sliced

One 8-ounce can sliced mushrooms, drained

1 cup beef broth

1 teaspoon prepared yellow mustard

1 tablespoon chopped fresh parsley

1 teaspoon paprika

Salt and pepper

1 cup sour cream

In a large skillet over medium-high heat, heat the oil and brown the pork chops on both sides. Separate the onion slices into rings and layer evenly on top of the pork chops. Scatter the mushroom slices over the onion rings.

In a small bowl, combine the broth, mustard, parsley, paprika, and salt and pepper to taste. Pour the mixture over the pork chops and simmer, covered, for 1½ hours.

Stir in the sour cream and cook for an additional 15 minutes until heated through. Do not let it boil.

FRIED QUAIL

Serves 4 to 6

After a successful day of quail hunting with my buddies in south Georgia, I like to fire up the cast-iron skillet and serve quail with garlic-cheese grits and biscuits. After eating that feast, I guarantee you that we all have to take a nap.

1 cup all-purpose flour

½ teaspoon salt

½ teaspoon pepper

½ teaspoon garlic powder

12 quail, cleaned, plucked, cut in halves and lightly salted
(available frozen from www.dartagnan.com)

4 tablespoons vegetable shortening, vegetable oil, or lard

MILK GRAVY

3 tablespoons pan grease (left from frying quail)

3 tablespoons all-purpose flour

1½ cups milk

Salt and pepper

In a shallow dish combine the flour, salt, pepper, and garlic powder. Dredge each quail half in the seasoned flour. In a cast-iron skillet over medium-high heat, melt enough shortening to measure ½-inch deep. When the fat is smoking hot, place the quail in the fat, skin side down first, and cook for 3 to 4 minutes per side. Don't crowd the skillet. You will need to cook the quail in batches, and set the cooked pieces aside in a covered container.

(cont. on next page)

To prepare the milk gravy, carefully drain off all but 3 tablespoons of grease from the skillet. Whisk the flour into the remaining pan grease until dissolved. Cook over medium-low heat until the gravy is milk chocolate brown. Gently whisk in the milk and cook until thickened. Season with salt and pepper to taste. Serve immediately over the hot quail.

Bubba and a buddy with a mess of birds

DOVE WITH SHERRY GRAVY

Serves 4 to 6

My dear friend Virginia Robertson, who is a fantastic cook, shared this recipe for dove with me. You might not have dove where you live but we do down South, and I can't get enough of them during hunting season.

12 doves, washed, cleaned, and plucked

1 cup all-purpose flour

Salt

Pepper

1 teaspoon garlic powder

2 tablespoons vegetable shortening, vegetable oil, or lard

¼ cup sherry

Split each dove in half. Combine the flour, 1 teaspoon salt, 1 teaspoon pepper, and garlic powder in a shallow dish. Dredge each dove in the flour mixture and shake off excess. Reserve the remaining flour mixture.

In a large cast-iron skillet, heat the shortening to 350°F. Brown the doves on both sides. Place into a Dutch oven.

Add 2 to 3 tablespoons of the remaining flour mixture to the skillet and whisk until well combined. Brown the mixture, taking care that it does not burn. Whisk in 1 cup water and the sherry, making sure the are no lumps. Pour this mixture over the doves. Cover and cook on medium heat 40 to 45 minutes, until doves are tender. Season the gravy with salt and pepper to taste.

UNCLE BUBBA'S FRIED SHRIMP*

Enough for 4 to 6 Po' Bubbas

At Uncle Bubba's Oyster House we're proud as can be to serve sweet, wild Georgia shrimp. Guests also love our version of the po' boy sandwich, which we've nicknamed Fried Shrimp Po' Bubba. We serve it on a toasted hoagie roll with tartar sauce on the side.

2 pounds, uncooked shrimp, peeled (tails left on), deveined, and butterflied

Salt and pepper

3 eggs

½ cup Louisiana hot sauce (I like Texas Pete)

2 cups Uncle Bubba's Fry Mix (page 38)

Peanut oil for deep frying

Lightly sprinkle the shrimp with salt and pepper. In a small bowl mix the eggs, ¼ cup water, and hot sauce. Place the fry mix in a shallow dish. Dip each shrimp in the egg mixture and then in the fry mix.

Heat 3 to 4 inches of peanut oil in a Dutch oven to 350°F. Place the shrimp in the pot and fry until golden brown. Remove with a clean strainer or slotted spoon and drain on paper towels.

TIP: If the fry mix gets lumpy you can sift it to make smooth.

BBQ SHRIMP*

Serves 6 to 8 as an appetizer or 4 as an entree portion

This is a popular item at Uncle Bubba's Oyster House. It can be served as either an appetizer or as an entree. Either way, it's a real elbow licker.

4 tablespoons clarified butter (see page 146)

½ cup light beer

5 teaspoons mesquite barbecue seasoning

1 teaspoon coarsely ground black pepper

1 pound large shell-on shrimp, heads off or on

1 medium-size tomato, diced, for garnish

2 green onions (scallions), diced, for garnish

Lemon wedges, for garnish

In a large skillet over medium-high heat, melt the butter. When the butter is melted, add the beer, barbecue seasoning, and pepper, and bring to a boil. Add the shrimp and cook about 3 minutes or until the shrimp turn pink. Do not overcook the shrimp or they will be rubbery. Remove the shrimp from heat and place in a serving dish with the sauce. Garnish with tomatoes, green onions, and lemon wedges.

LOW COUNTRY BOIL

Serves 4

This makes a wonderful casual supper. It can literally be thrown together when friends are coming over. I don't bother with serving bowls; I just pour it out onto a patio table covered with newspaper.

Crab boil seasoning (I use Old Bay)

12 baby red potatoes

6 ears corn, shucked and silk removed

One 12-ounce can or bottle domestic beer

1 medium-size white onion, quartered

2 packages smoked sausage, cut into 1-inch pieces

1 pound medium to large raw shrimp, in the shell

In a stockpot, pour enough water to cover all the ingredients. Add a sprinkling of crab boil seasoning appropriate for the amount of water used. Bring to a boil. Add the potatoes, corn, beer, and onion. Reduce the heat and simmer for 30 minutes. Add the smoked sausage. Cook 20 minutes more. Add the shrimp and cook about 3 minutes or until the shrimp turn pink. Drain the liquid into the sink and pour the boil onto a big serving platter or bowl. Sprinkle with extra crab boil seasoning.

SHRIMP AND GRITS*

Serve 4 to 6

You can't possibly live in the South all your life and not fix grits with just about everything—even shrimp. I've even converted some Northerners to grits. Can you believe it?

GRITS

4 tablespoons (½ stick) butter

2 teaspoons salt

2 cups quick grits

GRAVY

¼ cup chopped bacon

½ cup diced onion

2 tablespoons each, diced red and green bell peppers

¼ cup diced leek

½ teaspoon minced garlic

36 medium shrimp, peeled, tails removed, and deveined

¾ cup flour

½ cup dry white wine

1 quart heavy cream

½ teaspoon salt

½ teaspoon pepper

½ teaspoon garlic powder

(cont. on next page)

In a medium saucepan on medium-high heat, bring 6 cups water, the butter, and salt to a boil. Slowly whisk in the grits. Continue whisking occasionally for about 5 minutes, until the grits are thick and tender. Remove from the heat and keep warm.

For the gravy, sauté the bacon in a large heavy saucepan over medium-high heat until the fat is rendered. Stir in the onion, peppers, leek, and garlic and cook until soft. Add the shrimp and stir to combine. Sprinkle in the flour, and stir, making sure all of the flour is well incorporated. Add the wine and cream, stirring well until the sauce has thickened. In a small bottle or bowl, mix the salt, pepper, and garlic powder and season the gravy to taste.

Serve the shrimp gravy over grits.

TIP: For creamier grits, add a small amount of heavy cream.

SALMON AND GRITS

Serves 4

Ineata Jones has worked for my sister, Paula, at The Lady & Sons restaurant for years. She's so much like family that we've even given her a nickname—Jellyroll. She came up with this recipe; it may not be the prettiest dish but it's certainly one of the best, and it makes a fabulous Sunday brunch.

GRITS

4 tablespoons (½ stick) butter

2 teaspoons salt

2 cups quick grits

SALMON

4 tablespoons (½ stick) butter

1 medium-size yellow onion, diced

½ medium-size green bell pepper, diced

One 14.75-ounce can salmon, undrained

1 teaspoon Uncle Bubba's House Seasoning (page 26)

In a medium saucepan over medium-high heat bring 6 cups water, the butter, and salt to a boil. Slowly whisk in the grits. Continue whisking occasionally for about 5 minutes, until the grits are thick and tender. Remove from the heat and keep warm.

(cont. on next page)

In a large skillet, over medium-high heat melt the butter and sauté the onion and green pepper until tender. Add the salmon, 1¼ cups water, and the House Seasoning, and simmer for 10 minutes. Serve over hot grits.

TIP: It doesn't matter if the canned salmon's red or pink.

Bubba and Paula at Uncle Bubba's

UNCLE BUBBA'S CRAB CAKES*

Makes sixteen 3-ounce cakes

At Uncle Bubba's we pan-sear our crab cakes and serve them atop spinach and a bed of rice, with a choice of our tasty beurre blanc (page 32), tartar (page 28), or cocktail sauce (page 27).

3 tablespoons butter

6 green onions (scallions), green tops, thinly sliced

1 clove garlic, minced

1 small green pepper, finely chopped

5½ tablespoons mayonnaise

⅓ cup heavy cream

3 tablespoons spicy mustard (I like Dijon)

¼ teaspoon salt

¼ teaspoon pepper

¼ teaspoon garlic powder

Pinch of cayenne pepper

2 eggs

2 teaspoons chopped fresh parsley

Juice of 1 lemon

20 saltine crackers, crumbled medium to fine

1 pound lump crabmeat, picked clean of shells

1 pound claw crabmeat, picked clean of shells

1 tablespoon vegetable oil

(cont. on next page)

In a medium skillet, melt 1 tablespoon of the butter and sauté the onions, garlic, and peppers until soft. Let cool.

In a mixing bowl, combine the sautéed vegetables, mayonnaise, heavy cream, mustard, salt, pepper, garlic powder, cayenne pepper, eggs, parsley, and lemon juice until well incorporated. Gently mix in the saltine crackers and crab meat. Form into 3-ounce patties (about the size of the top of a cupcake). Set aside.

Heat the remaining 2 tablespoons of butter and the oil in a large sauté pan over medium-low heat. Place the crab cakes in the pan and sauté for 3 to 5 minutes per side until golden brown. Remove from the heat and place on paper towels to remove any excess oil.

VARIATION: At Uncle Bubba's we also like to stuff shrimp with our crab cake mix. Butterfly the peeled shrimp by making a slit down the back, but don't cut all the way through. Fill the shrimp with as much crab cake mixture as you like and wrap in a half strip of bacon, secured with a toothpick. Broil for 8 to 10 minutes until the bacon is crispy and the shrimp is pink.

DEVILED CRAB

Serves 4

This is a super simple way to fix deviled crab and it's so yummy. I like to serve it with either Tartar Sauce (page 28) or Cocktail Sauce (page 27) and a heaping helping of Uncle Bubba's Favorite Cole Slaw (page 66).

2 slices toast, very crisp sandwich-size bread

1 pound lump crabmeat, picked clean of shells

1 tablespoon Worcestershire sauce

Juice of one lemon

½ cup (1 stick) butter, softened

1 egg, beaten

Salt and pepper

Cleaned crab shells or foil crab shapes

Preheat the oven to 400°F. Grate the toast into a large bowl and soften with 1 tablespoon water. Add the crabmeat, Worcestershire sauce, lemon juice, butter, egg, salt, and pepper and combine. Stuff in crab shells or aluminum foil crab shapes (or in mounds on a greased baking sheet), and brown for about 15 to 20 minutes.

UNCLE BUBBA'S CRAB-STUFFED FLOUNDER*

This is one of the most popular entrees at Uncle Bubba's Oyster House. I think it's because it combines three of our most delicious recipes—grilled flounder, our special crab cake mix, plus our scrumptious crab butter.

One 8- to 10-ounce filet of flounder

4 ounces Uncle Bubba's Crab Cake mix (page 107)

½ teaspoon each salt and pepper

½ teaspoon paprika

One 1-inch slice of crab butter (page 32)

Fresh parsley (optional)

Preheat the oven to 350°F. Using a fillet knife, carefully open the flounder by cutting along the left and right sides of the seam down the middle of the fish to make pockets. Lay the cut sides back. Prepare the crab cake mix, stuff the flounder, and press the sides down to cover the crab cake mix. Sprinkle with salt, pepper, and paprika. Coat a glass baking dish with cooking spray and bake for 20 minutes. Without removing the dish from the oven, turn the oven to broil and broil for five additional minutes. When the fish is done, remove it from the oven. Slice a medallion of crab butter and place it on top of the grilled fish. Sprinkle fresh parsley on top for added color.

UNCLE BUBBA'S FRIED OYSTERS*

When I go shopping for oysters to fry, I choose good-size, select oysters. Obviously, at Uncle Bubba's Oyster House we sell a whole bunch of oysters all year round. I believe that if you shuck it, they will come.

12 oysters per person

Salt and pepper

Uncle Bubba's Fry Mix (page 38)

Hot sauce (optional)

Peanut oil for deep frying

Drain the oysters, sprinkle lightly with salt and pepper, and dredge each one in the fry mix. Lay out the oysters on a baking sheet and sprinkle with hot sauce if desired. Pour two inches of peanut oil in a skillet and heat to 350°F. Fry the oysters in batches until crisp and golden brown.

SCALLOPED OYSTERS

Serves 4 to 6

Looking for an easy and delicious way to serve oysters without pulling out the oyster knives and shucking a few? This is it. You can buy shucked oysters from your local fresh fish market.

1 cup dried bread crumbs

1½ cups cracker crumbs (I like Ritz)

¾ cup (1½ sticks) butter, melted

1 pint oysters, drained with ½ cup liquor reserved

1 teaspoon salt

Dash of pepper

Dash of nutmeg

2 tablespoons chopped fresh parsley

¼ cup milk

Preheat the oven to 350°F.

Grease a 13 by 9-inch baking dish. In a medium bowl, mix the bread crumbs and cracker crumbs with the butter. Line the bottom of the prepared casserole with half of the crumbs. Arrange a layer of oysters, sprinkle with salt, pepper, nutmeg, and parsley, a layer of crumbs, another layer of oysters with seasonings, and top with the crumb mixture. Pour the milk and oyster liquid over all.

Bake for 1 hour or until mixture is puffed and browned.

CRAWFISH ÉTOUFFÉE

Serves 6 to 8

Paula and I love the aroma and spicy taste of Cajun cooking. When we were deciding on menu items for Uncle Bubba's we knew we had to include this.

Étouffée comes from the French word *étouffer,* meaning to smother. At Uncle Bubba's we smother a big plate of rice with crawfish étoufée.

½ cup (1 stick) butter

¾ cup all-purpose flour

½ cup chopped bacon

1 clove garlic, minced

2 cups diced medium-size yellow onion

1 cup chopped celery

½ cup chopped red bell pepper

½ cup chopped green bell pepper

1 cup domestic beer

4 cups bottled clam juice

Pinch of cayenne pepper

1 tablespoon Cajun seasoning (available in the spice aisle of the grocery store)

½ teaspoon white pepper

¼ cup finely chopped fresh parsley

1 bay leaf

1 cup half-and-half

1 pound crawfish meat, raw or precooked and frozen

(*cont. on next page*)

In a Dutch oven, melt the butter in over medium-high heat. Add the flour and stir until the mixture begins to smell nutty and look thick. Add the bacon and garlic and cook for five minutes. Add the onion, celery, and bell peppers and continue to cook five minutes more. Add the beer, clam juice, cayenne pepper, Cajun seasoning, white pepper, parsley, bay leaf, half-and-half, and crawfish. Mix well and simmer until thick, 45 minutes to 1 hour.

DESSERTS

My Favorite!

AUNT GLENNIS'S RED VELVET CAKE

ALL-TIME FAVORITE CARAMEL CAKE

CHEWY CAKE

AUNT JESSIE'S CHOCOLATE
POUND CAKE

GRANDMOTHER PAUL'S SOUR CREAM
POUND CAKE*

NEVER-FAIL POUND CAKE

BUTTERSCOTCH POUND CAKE

KATHY KUEKER'S CARROT CAKE

LEMON CHEESE CAKE

BETTY PORTER'S FRUITCAKE

GEORGIA PEACH CAKE

FIG PRESERVE CAKE

AUNT PEGGY'S CHEESECAKE

BAKED BLUEBERRY FRENCH TOAST

CHOCOLATE CRÈME BRÛLÉE*

CHOCOLATE ALMOND PIE

UNCLE BUBBA'S KEY LIME PIE*

UNCLE BUBBA'S SOUTHERN
PECAN PIE*

BOURBON CHOCOLATE PECAN PIE

MILLION-DOLLAR DESSERT

VIRGINIA BRUNCH SURPRISE

OATMEAL MACAROONS

STAR'S COOKIES

SIMPLY DELICIOUS CHOCOLATE
COOKIE BARS

NEVER-FAIL PEANUT BRITTLE

A GIFT FROM PAULA:

SWEET POTATO DOUGHNUTS WITH MAPLE ICING

WHITE CHOCOLATE–CRANBERRY CHEESECAKE

QUEEN OF HEARTS DECADENT DESSERT

One look at pudgy me in my school pictures from Magnolia Elementary School in Albany, Georgia, and you can tell that desserts and I get along just fine. I guess I'd say I've had a sweet tooth (or a dozen) all my life. Sometimes it's almost as good to hear the stories about desserts as eating them. (Not really.)

Bubba in the first grade

Since I was an itty bitty thing, my Aunt Peggy has told me about the sweets Granny Paul made when my Mama, Aunt Peggy, and Aunt Trina were girls. Mama's family didn't hardly have two nickels to rub together so Granny Paul made up for material things by baking cakes, cookies, and melt-in-your-mouth jelly rolls for her three daughters. Aunt Peggy said jelly rolls were Granny's specialty. To this day, Aunt Peggy says those jelly rolls were the best she's ever tasted. She says she can still remember how Granny Paul would put a jelly roll on a sheet of waxed paper and tuck it around and 'round with her fingers until it was just right.

My all-time favorite dessert is my Aunt Glennis Hiers's Red Velvet Cake. I'll never forget her standing in her apron in her kitchen at the house near Statesboro, Georgia, and slicing through the sweet white icing to that delicious red cake underneath. Oh boy! It makes my mouth water just thinking about it.

I've also added plenty of other recipes for all kinds of cakes, pies, cookies, and a few other sweet things in between. Enjoy!

AUNT GLENNIS'S RED VELVET CAKE

Serves 10 to 12

I didn't realize this until recently, but my cousin told me that Aunt Glennis Hiers used to sell her Red Velvet Cake. I'm sure people came from miles around to buy this layered delicacy that I've enjoyed for so many years.

CAKE

One 18.25-ounce package yellow cake mix

4 eggs

½ cup condensed milk

½ cup (1 stick) butter, softened

One 3-ounce package regular vanilla pudding mix

2 ounces red food coloring

CREAM CHEESE ICING

Three 8-ounce packages cream cheese, softened

1½ cups (3 sticks) butter, softened

3 cups confectioners' sugar

3 cups pecans, chopped

Preheat the oven to 350°F. Grease 3 round 8-inch cake pans, or three 9-inch pans for thinner layers. In a large bowl, using a mixer, combine the cake mix, eggs, 1 cup water, the condensed milk, butter, pudding mix, and food coloring until well blended. Pour the batter into the prepared pans and bake for 30 to 35 minutes, until a toothpick inserted in the center of the cake comes out clean. Let the layers cool in the pans for 5 to 10 minutes, then turn them onto racks to cool completely before icing.

In a clean large bowl, using a mixer, beat the cream cheese, butter, and sugar until smooth and creamy. Stir in the pecans. Frost the cake between the layers, then on the top and sides.

ALL-TIME FAVORITE CARAMEL CAKE

Talk about melting in your mouth! One slice of this cake and you'll think you've won the lottery. It's definitely a winner.

CAKE

½ cup (1 stick) butter, softened

1 cup vegetable shortening

3 cups sugar

6 eggs

3 cups all-purpose flour

¼ teaspoon salt

¼ teaspoon baking powder

1 cup whole milk

1 teaspoon almond extract

1 teaspoon vanilla extract

CARAMEL ICING

3⅓ cups sugar

¾ cup (1½ sticks) butter

One 5-ounce can evaporated milk

2 tablespoons whole milk

1 teaspoon vanilla extract

Preheat the oven to 325°F. Grease and flour a 10-inch tube pan.

In a large bowl, using a mixer, cream the butter and shortening. Beat in the sugar until the mixture is fluffy. Add the eggs one at a time, beating well after each addition. Sift the flour with the salt and baking powder. Add the flour mixture alternately with the milk, beginning and ending with flour. Stir in the almond and vanilla extracts. Pour the batter into the prepared pan.

Bake for 1½ hours, or until a toothpick inserted in the middle of the cake comes out clean. Cool the cake in the pan 10 minutes, then turn out onto a wire rack to cool completely before icing.

To make the icing, in a heavy medium saucepan over medium heat, combine 3 cups of the sugar, the butter, evaporated milk, and whole milk. Bring to a boil and boil for 3 minutes.

In another medium saucepan, over medium-high heat, combine the remaining ⅓ cup sugar with 1 tablespoon water, or enough water to make the mixture like wet sand. Brush down the sides of the saucepan with a pastry brush dipped in water. Bring the mixture to a boil, stirring with a small whisk to make sure that all the sugar has dissolved. Continue boiling until it is dark mahogany colored.

Carefully add the milk mixture to the caramel; it will splatter. Bring mixture to a boil and boil for 3 minutes. Remove from the heat and stir in the vanilla. Using a mixer, beat the icing until thick and smooth. Ice the top, inside, and outside of the tube cake.

TIPS: If some of the caramel splatters on you, rub the burned spot with ice and peel off the caramel.

If one spot of the liquid caramel seems to be getting brown faster than the rest, gently stir to distribute the heat in the saucepan. Brushing down the sides of the saucepan will prevent the formation of crystals. This is important because caramel icing is tricky to work with. If crystals form, the sugar becomes granular again and the texture will be grainy.

CHEWY CAKE

Serves 10 to 12

Another of my Aunt Glennis's specialties is Chewy Cake. One bite and you'll see how it got the name. It's always yummy in my tummy because it has coconut in it. Did I mention how it's quick and easy?

One 1-pound package or bag light brown sugar

2 cups self-rising flour (see Tip)

½ cup (1 stick) butter or margarine, softened

3 eggs, beaten

1 cup sweetened flaked coconut

1 tablespoon vanilla extract

2 cups chopped pecans

1 cup semisweet chocolate chips

Preheat the oven to 350°F. Lightly grease a 13 by 9-inch baking pan.

In a large bowl, mix together the brown sugar, flour, butter, eggs, coconut, vanilla, pecans, and chocolate chips until well combined. Spread the batter evenly in the prepared pan and bake for 30 to 35 minutes, until a toothpick inserted through the middle comes out clean. Cool the cake completely in the pan before cutting it into squares.

TIP: If you can't find self-rising flour, use 2 cups minus 1 tablespoon all-purpose flour mixed with 1 tablespoon baking powder and ½ teaspoon salt.

AUNT JESSIE'S CHOCOLATE POUND CAKE

Serves 10 to 12

My Aunt Jessie Dixon was Daddy's sister and very much a Southern lady. I never heard her say a harsh word to anyone. She shared this recipe with the members of the First Baptist Church of Eagle Lake, Florida, when they put together a cookbook as a fund-raiser.

1 cup butter (2 sticks), softened

½ cup (1 stick) margarine

3 cups sugar

5 eggs

3 cups cake flour

5 tablespoons unsweetened cocoa powder

½ teaspoon salt

½ teaspoon baking powder

1 cup whole milk

1 teaspoon vanilla extract

ICING

One 1-pound package confectioners' sugar

¼ cup unsweetened cocoa powder

4 tablespoons (½ stick) butter

½ cup evaporated milk

1 teaspoon vanilla extract

(cont. on next page)

Preheat the oven to 325°F. Grease and flour a 10-inch tube pan.

In a large bowl, using a mixer, cream the butter and margarine. Add the sugar gradually and continue beating until light and fluffy. Add the eggs one at a time, beating well after each addition.

Sift together the flour, cocoa, salt, and baking powder. Add to the butter mixture alternately with the milk, beginning and ending with flour. Stir in the vanilla. Pour the batter into the prepared pan. Bake 1¼ hour to 1½ hours, until a toothpick inserted through the middle of the cake comes out clean. Cool in the pan for 10 minutes, then turn the cake out onto a wire rack to cool completely before icing.

In a medium bowl, using a mixer, beat the sugar, cocoa, butter, milk, and vanilla until well blended and completely smooth. Ice the top, inside, and outside of the tube cake.

GRANDMOTHER PAUL'S SOUR CREAM POUND CAKE*

Serves 10 to 12

Granny Paul must have baked a zillion pound cakes during her lifetime. I remember eating slices just out of the oven with whipped cream on top. When strawberries were in season and growing in the fields around Albany, we'd always buy a couple of baskets of those bright red berries to top our cake slices. I can attest to the fact that it's truly a Southern delight. At Uncle Bubba's we serve our sliced pound cake with whipped cream and sliced strawberries cooked in simple syrup. (Simple syrup is equal parts water and sugar, dissolved, by cooking over low to medium heat.)

1 cup (2 sticks) unsalted butter, at room temperature

3 cups sugar

1 cup sour cream

3 cups all-purpose flour

¼ teaspoon baking soda

6 eggs

1 teaspoon vanilla extract

Preheat the oven to 325°F. Grease and flour a 10-inch tube pan or two 9 by 5-inch loaf pans.

In a large bowl, using a mixer, cream together the butter and sugar. Add the sour cream and beat until well blended. Sift the flour and baking soda together. Add the flour mixture and eggs to the creamed mixture in thirds, beating until smooth each time. Stir in the vanilla. Pour the batter into the prepared pan and bake for 1⅓ to 1½ hours, until a toothpick inserted in the middle of the cake comes out clean. Cool in the pan. Serve warm or cool.

NEVER-FAIL POUND CAKE

Serves 10 to 12

The late Nellie L. Hiers was my grandmother, but I always called her Granny Hiers. I remember sitting in her living room in Florida and being served a slice of this cake more than once. Unlike traditional pound cakes, this one requires that you begin cooking it in a cold oven.

½ cup (1 stick) butter, softened

3 cups sugar

5 eggs

3 cups cake flour

1 cup milk

2 teaspoons lemon extract

Daddy and Granny Hiers

Grease and flour a 10-inch tube pan.

In a large bowl, using a mixer, cream the butter and sugar until light and fluffy. Add the eggs one at a time, beating well after each addition. Add the flour and milk alternately, beginning and ending with the flour. Stir in the lemon extract. Spoon the batter into the prepared pan.

Place in oven and bake at 325°F for 1 hour. Increase the temperature to 350°F and bake for 30 minutes more. Do not open the oven door while baking. After 30 minutes, insert a toothpick into the center of the cake to see if it comes out clean. If it doesn't, continue baking at 350°F until the toothpick comes out clean. Cool the cake in the pan for 10 minutes, then turn out onto a wire rack to cool.

BUTTERSCOTCH POUND CAKE

Serves 10 to 12

The flavor of butterscotch always reminds me of the candy that Mama and Daddy sold at the store at River Bend. Those were fun times.

3 cups sugar

1 cup (2 sticks) butter, softened

½ cup vegetable oil

8 ounces cream cheese, softened

3 cups flour

6 eggs

1 bag (11 ounces) butterscotch chips

1 cup chopped pecans

Preheat the oven to 325°F. Grease and flour a 10-inch tube pan.

In a large bowl, using a mixer, cream together the sugar, butter, oil, and cream cheese. Add the flour and eggs alternately, starting and ending with flour. Stir in two thirds of the butterscotch chips and all the pecans. Pour into the prepared pan.

Bake for 1 hour and 15 minutes. Reduce the heat to 300°F and bake for 20 minutes more, or until a toothpick comes out clean when inserted in the middle of the cake. Let the cake rest in the pan for 10 minutes, then turn out onto a wire rack to cool completely. In a small saucepan over medium heat melt the remaining butterscotch chips. Pour over the top of the cooled cake.

KATHY KUEKER'S CARROT CAKE

Serves 15 to 20

Crushed pineapple makes this cake moist. And cream cheese icing has always been one of my favorites.

2 cups plus 2 tablespoons all-purpose flour

2 cups sugar

2 teaspoons baking powder

2 teaspoons baking soda

2 teaspoons ground cinnamon

1 teaspoon salt

1¼ cups vegetable oil

4 eggs

2 teaspoons vanilla extract

2 cups peeled and finely grated carrots

One 8-ounce can crushed pineapple, drained

1 cup chopped pecans

ICING

One 8-ounce package cream cheese, softened

4 tablespoons (½ stick) butter or margarine, softened

5 cups confectioners' sugar

2 tablespoons milk

1 teaspoon vanilla extract

Preheat the oven to 350°F. Grease and flour and 13 by 9-inch baking pan.

In a large bowl, using a mixer, beat the flour, sugar, baking powder, baking soda, cinnamon, salt, and oil for two minutes. Add the eggs and vanilla and beat for 2 minutes. Stir in the carrots, pineapple, and pecans.

Pour into the prepared pan and bake for 45 to 50 minutes, until a toothpick inserted in the center of the cake comes out clean. Cool the cake in the pan. Let the cake cool completely before icing the top of the cake.

For the icing: In a medium bowl, with a mixer, beat the cream cheese and butter until smooth. Gradually beat in the confectioners' sugar and milk as needed to make the icing a spreadable consistency. Stir in the vanilla.

LEMON CHEESE CAKE

When you first glance at the name of this recipe you might think it's cheesecake but it's not. It's really a traditional Southern layer cake and a darn good one at that! The frosting is similar to divinity candy.

CAKE

⅔ cup (about 1⅓ sticks) butter

2 cups sugar

3 cups all-purpose flour

3 teaspoons baking powder

½ teaspoon salt

1 cup milk

1 teaspoon vanilla extract

5 egg whites, beaten to stiff peaks

LEMON CURD FILLING

5 egg yolks

1 cup sugar

½ cup (1 stick) butter, melted

Juice and grated zest of 2 lemons

SEVEN-MINUTE ICING

2 egg whites

1½ cups sugar

1 tablespoon light corn syrup

Dash of salt

1 teaspoon vanilla extract

Preheat the oven to 350°F. Grease three 9-inch round cake pans.

In a large bowl, using a mixer, cream the butter and sugar until light and fluffy. Sift the flour, baking powder, and salt twice. Add the flour mixture and milk alternately to the creamed mixture, beginning and ending with the flour. Stir in the vanilla. With a spatula, gently fold in the beaten egg whites. Pour the batter evenly into the prepared pans.

Bake for 25 to 30 minutes, rotating the cake pans halfway through baking, until a toothpick inserted near the center comes out clean. Cool the cakes in the pans for 10 minutes, then turn out onto wire racks to cool completely before filling and icing.

To make the filling, beat the egg yolks, sugar, melted butter, lemon juice, and zest in a medium bowl until light yellow. Transfer mixture to a heavy medium saucepan. Cook over low heat until thickened, about 7 minutes, whisking constantly. Cool completely before spreading on cake.

For the frosting, place the egg whites, sugar, syrup, ⅓ cup cold water, and salt in the top of a double boiler. Beat with a mixer over boiling water until the mixture stands in peaks; about 7 minutes. Remove from the heat and stir in the vanilla.

To assemble the cake, place one layer on a serving plate or cake stand. Cover with half of the cooled lemon curd filling. Top with another cake layer. Cover that layer with the remaining filling. Top with the remaining layer. Frost the top and sides of the cake with the seven-minute frosting.

TIP: The pans need to be rotated when baking, because there are three in there at once. If they aren't rotated, they'll bake unevenly.

BETTY PORTER'S FRUITCAKE

Serves 10 to 12

My Aunt Peggy Ort of Albany sent me this recipe for fruitcake. It was adapted from a recipe clipped from a Columbus, Mississippi, newspaper in 1965. She says margarine doesn't work as well as butter for this cake and that all ingredients should be at room temperature. Unlike many fruitcakes, this is nonalcoholic, so everyone can enjoy it. It makes for a wonderful holiday treat.

1 pound shelled pecans or other nuts, broken into pieces or coarsely chopped

8 ounces (1 cup) candied pineapple, chopped

8 ounces (1 cup) candied cherries, chopped

1 pound package golden or dark raisins

4 cups sifted all-purpose flour

1½ teaspoons baking powder

½ teaspoon salt

¾ cup (1½ sticks) butter

2½ cups sugar

6 eggs

3 ounces (6 tablespoons) rum extract

Preheat the oven to 325°F. Grease and flour a 10-inch tube pan.

In a medium bowl mix the nuts, pineapple, cherries, and raisins. In a large bowl, mix the flour, baking powder, and salt. In another large bowl, cream the butter and the sugar. Alternately add to the butter mixture 2 of the eggs, 1 ounce of the extract, and one third of the flour mixture. Continue in the same sequence with eggs, flavoring, and flour until all is used and blended together. Stir in the nut and fruit mixture.

Pour into the prepared pan and bake for 1½ to 2 hours, until a toothpick inserted in the middle of the cake comes out clean. Let the cake rest for 15 minutes before removing it from the pan and cooling on a wire rack. Allow to cool thoroughly before cutting.

GEORGIA PEACH CAKE

Serves 12 to 15

This recipe came from my Aunt Trina, who is just a few years older than my sister Paula. She said she and Paula used to fix this in their "young housewife" days. It's nice for brunch, or as a snack with a cup of coffee or tea.

CAKE

One 18.25-ounce package yellow cake mix

One 21-ounce can peach pie filling

3 eggs

½ teaspoon vanilla extract

½ cup chopped pecans

TOPPING

½ cup sugar

½ cup all-purpose flour

4 tablespoons (½ stick) butter or margarine

½ teaspoon vanilla extract

Preheat the oven to 350°F. Grease a 13 by 9-inch baking pan.

In a large bowl, using a mixer at medium speed, combine the cake mix, pie filling, eggs, vanilla, and pecans until well combined. Pour the batter into the prepared pan.

To make the topping, combine the sugar, flour, butter, and vanilla in a small bowl, using a fork or your fingers until it resembles large bread crumbs. Sprinkle the topping over the cake batter and bake for 40 to 45 minutes, until a toothpick inserted in the middle comes out clean. Cool in pan on wire rack. Then cut into squares and serve.

FIG PRESERVE CAKE

Serves 20

Paula and I love this cake recipe; it is so unbelievably moist and delicious. If you prefer a banana cake, just swap the fig preserves for 1½ cups mashed bananas. It's so good you'll think you've died and gone to heaven. Thank you, Sheila Kueker!

2 cups all-purpose flour

1 teaspoon salt

1 teaspoon baking soda

1½ cups sugar

1 cup vegetable oil

3 eggs

1 cup buttermilk

1¾ cup fig preserves

1 cup chopped pecans

1 teaspoon vanilla extract

1 teaspoon liquid butter flavoring (I use Braswell's, available in 1-ounce bottles)

SAUCE

½ cup (1 stick) butter

¾ cup sugar

1 tablespoon light corn syrup

1 tablespoon vanilla extract

½ cup buttermilk

½ teaspoon baking soda

Preheat the oven to 325°F. Grease or spray with cooking spray a 13 by 9-inch baking pan.

Sift the flour, salt, soda and sugar in a large mixing bowl. Add the oil and beat well with a mixer. Add the eggs and beat until well blended. Continue to beat, gradually adding the buttermilk. Add the fig preserves, nuts, vanilla, and butter flavoring and mix well. Pour into the prepared pan.

Bake for 45 minutes. Prepare the sauce while the cake is baking, and pour over the cake immediately after taking it out of the oven.

Melt the butter in a small saucepan. Stir in the sugar, corn syrup, vanilla, buttermilk, and baking soda. Bring to a boil and boil for 3 minutes.

Serve the cake warm or cooled. Store this cake covered and in the refrigerator.

AUNT PEGGY'S CHEESECAKE

Serves 8

Good cooking runs in our family and my Aunt Peggy is no exception. I can't wait to dress up her recipe for cheesecake during peach season. I peel and slice a few really ripe, juicy peaches to put on top of the cheesecake. But I have to admit that having a sliver of cheesecake by itself is nearly as scrumptious.

You'll need to start this the day before you plan to serve it.

CRUST

1½ cups graham cracker crumbs

½ cup (1 stick) butter, melted

1 tablespoon sugar

FILLING

Two 8-ounce packages cream cheese, softened

1 cup sugar

3 eggs

1 teaspoon vanilla

TOPPING

2 cups sour cream

3 tablespoons sugar

½ teaspoon vanilla

Preheat the oven to 350°F.

For the crust, in a medium bowl combine the butter, crumbs, and sugar until well blended. Press into the bottom and one inch up the sides of a 9-inch springform pan, using the back of a large spoon.

In a large bowl, using a mixer, beat the cream cheese, sugar, eggs, and vanilla until creamy. Pour into the prepared crust. Bake for 35 to 45 minutes. Be sure the center is firm before removing the cheesecake from the oven. Place on a rack and allow to cool completely. Release the springform, and place onto a platter.

In a small bowl, blend the sour cream, sugar, and vanilla until smooth. Spread on top of the cake and chill overnight.

Store this cake covered and in the refrigerator.

Aunty Peggy

BAKED BLUEBERRY FRENCH TOAST

Serves 6 to 8

Robin Dermer serves this special recipe at brunch. She uses challah bread instead of white bread, but says any bread is just fine. Whichever bread you get, unsliced bread is easier to remove the crust from than a full loaf.

You'll want to put this together the night before and bake it just before your brunch.

TOAST

12 pieces of sliced white bread, crust removed and cut into 1-inch cubes

Two 8-ounce packages cream cheese, cut into 1-inch cubes

1 cup blueberries, picked over and rinsed

12 large eggs

$\frac{1}{3}$ cup maple syrup

2 cups milk

SAUCE

1 cup sugar

2 tablespoons cornstarch

1 cup blueberries, picked over and rinsed

1 tablespoon unsalted butter

Butter a 13 by 9-inch glass baking dish. Arrange half of the bread cubes in the prepared dish. Scatter the cream cheese cubes over the bread and sprinkle the blueberries over the cream cheese. Arrange the remaining cubes of the bread over the blueberries. In a large bowl, whisk together the eggs, syrup, and milk, and pour evenly over the bread mixture. Cover with foil and chill overnight.

Preheat the oven to 350°F. Bake on the middle rack of the oven for 30 minutes. Remove the foil and bake for an additional 30 minutes or until puffed and golden. Serve the toast with the sauce.

In a small saucepan, stir together the sugar, cornstarch, and 1 cup water, and cook over moderately high heat, stirring occasionally, for 5 minutes or until thickened. Stir in the blueberries and simmer, stirring occasionally, for 10 minutes or until the blueberries burst. Add the butter and stir until melted.

CHOCOLATE CRÈME BRÛLÉE*

Makes 6 to 8

At Uncle Bubba's we like to serve this scrumptious version of crème brûlée with chocolate whipped cream and strawberries, but it's out of this world just about any way you serve it. You can use a baking torch to make the sugar crust but if you don't have one, use the broiler. Place the ramekins in a flameproof baking pan. Place the pan as close to the broiler as possible (put the rack on the highest level). Carefully watch the custards and cook until the sugar has melted and browned, 3 to 5 minutes.

I like to garnish these with fresh mint leaves and a sliced strawberry.

3 cups heavy cream

2½ tablespoons chocolate-flavored liqueur

Sugar

1 ounce (1 square) unsweetened chocolate, finely chopped

1½ teaspoons vanilla extract

1 tablespoon plus 1½ teaspoons unsweetened cocoa powder

8 eggs yolks

Preheat the oven to 300°F.

In a medium bowl, mix the cream, liqueur, ¾ cup sugar, the chocolate, vanilla, and cocoa powder. Pour the mixture into a heavy medium saucepan and heat, stirring occasionally, until bubbles form around the edges. Remove the pan from heat.

In a separate large bowl, beat the egg yolks just to combine. Temper the eggs by adding a little of the hot cream mixture, whisking continuously. Whisk the egg mixture back into the remaining hot cream. Strain the mixture through a fine-mesh strainer into a heatproof pitcher and pour into 6 to 8 flameproof ramekins.

Line a baking pan with a folded clean kitchen towel. Place the ramekins on the towel. Fill the baking dish with water to ¼ inch below the tops of the ramekins. Bake for 30 to 45 minutes, depending on size of your ramekins, until the custard has set and is firm. Remove the baking pan from the oven and let stand until cool.

Remove the ramekins from the water and refrigerate until ready to serve.

Sprinkle an even layer of sugar over the chilled custards. Using a baking torch, melt and evenly brown the sugar covering. Within minutes the tops will harden. Serve immediately.

CHOCOLATE ALMOND PIE

Serves 6 to 8

This is a no-bake pie that will leave you begging for more. It's got two of my favorite ingredients in the whole wide world—Hershey Bars and marshmallows. What a combination!

Four 1.45-ounce bars Hershey's Milk Chocolate with Almonds

½ cup milk

20 large marshmallows

1 teaspoon vanilla extract

1 cup heavy cream

1 storebought 9-inch graham cracker crust

Whipped cream, for garnish (optional)

Crushed cookies, for garnish (optional)

Melt the candy bars, milk, vanilla, and marshmallows in the top of a double boiler over boiling water, stirring until well blended and smooth. Remove from the heat and cool.

Whip the cream to stiff peaks and gently fold it into the cooled chocolate mixture, trying to maintain as much volume as possible. Pour the pie filling into the crust and chill overnight. Top with whipped cream, your favorite crushed cookie, or serve by itself.

TIP: A quick way to cool down the chocolate filling is to place the pot over an ice-water bath and stir until cool.

UNCLE BUBBA'S KEY LIME PIE*

Serves 4 to 6

Most folks probably think of Florida when Key lime pie comes to mind. Well, I'm here to tell you that we dearly love Key lime pie at Uncle Bubba's Oyster House in Savannah and so do our guests. Slice the pie with a hot, wet knife and it won't stick to the knife.

If you can't find fresh Key limes, a good quality bottled juice is fine.

CRUST

1¾ cups graham cracker crumbs

¾ cup sugar

½ cup slivered almonds

¼ cup clarified butter (see Tip)

FILLING

1 teaspoon vanilla extract

One 14-ounce can sweetened condensed milk

¼ cup Key lime juice (I like Nellie and Joe's Key Lime Juice)

Grated zest and juice of 1 Key lime

3 egg yolks

Grease a 9-inch pie pan.

In a small bowl, mix the graham cracker crumbs, sugar, and almonds. Add the clarified butter and mix well. Press evenly into the prepared pan.

(cont. on next page)

Preheat the oven to 325°F.

In a medium bowl, combine the vanilla, condensed milk, Key lime juice, lime zest and juice, and egg yolks, and mix well. Pour into the pie crust. Bake for 20 minutes. Let stand at room temperature for 20 to 30 minutes, and refrigerate until you are ready to serve.

TIP: To clarify butter, gently heat butter until all is melted. Once the butter has melted and separated, use a spoon to remove the white foam from the top. Carefully pour off the golden liquid, leaving behind the milky solids without mixing them back into the butter. Discard the solids. About ¾ of the original amount will be left. The clarified butter is ready to use. Store extra in the refrigerator.

UNCLE BUBBA'S SOUTHERN PECAN PIE*

Serves 6 to 8

This is the pecan pie we serve at Uncle Bubba's Oyster House. I like it with a scoop of vanilla ice cream plopped on top.

4 tablespoons (½ stick) unsalted butter, softened

1 cup packed light brown sugar

1 tablespoon all-purpose flour

Pinch of salt

½ cup cane syrup (I like Alaga, available at www.whitfieldfoods.com)

4 eggs

1 teaspoon vanilla extract

1 cup chopped pecans

One 9-inch deep dish pie crust, unbaked

Preheat the oven to 325°F.

In a large bowl, using a mixer, cream the butter, sugar, flour, and salt until smooth. Add the syrup, eggs, and vanilla, and mix well. Place the chopped pecans into the bottom of the pie crust. Pour the filling into the pie shell, covering the pecans. Bake the pie for 45 to 50 minutes, until firm. Cool on a wire rack to desired temperature.

BOURBON CHOCOLATE PECAN PIE

Serves 6 to 8

This twist on a traditional pecan pie is extremely rich, so if you're a chocoholic you'll love it the way it is. If you'd like, use half the amount of chocolate chips for a lighter tasting pie. Adding some shredded coconut would also be a nice variation. A large scoop of vanilla ice cream or whipped cream is another great way to cut the richness, believe it or not!

½ cup firmly packed dark brown sugar

½ cup granulated sugar

1 tablespoon all-purpose flour

3 eggs

2 tablespoons condensed milk

1 teaspoon vanilla extract

½ cup (1 stick) butter, melted

1 cup chocolate chips

1 tablespoon bourbon or strong coffee

1 cup chopped pecans

½ cup sweetened flaked coconut (optional)

One 9-inch pie crust, unbaked

Preheat the oven to 350°F.

In a large bowl, stir together the sugars, flour, eggs, condensed milk, vanilla, butter, chocolate chips, bourbon, and pecans. Pour into the pie crust. Bake for 40 to 50 minutes, until firm. Cool on a wire rack to desired temperature.

MILLION-DOLLAR DESSERT

Serves 4 to 6 (12 to 15 pieces)

I wish I had a million bucks for every time I've fixed this easy dessert. It's a welcome end to any meal!

½ cup (1 stick) butter or margarine, softened

1 cup self-rising flour (see Tip)

½ cup chopped pecans

One 8-ounce package cream cheese, softened

1 cup confectioners' sugar

One 8-ounce carton frozen whipped topping, thawed (I like Cool Whip)

Two 3-ounce packages instant chocolate pudding

3 cups milk

Preheat the oven to 350°F. Mix together the butter, flour, and ¼ cup of the nuts until the mixture resembles cookie dough. Press into the bottom of an ungreased, large square or rectangular casserole (13 by 9 or 8 by 8—the size of the dish will determine the thickness of your dessert bars). Bake the crust for 10 minutes, or until firm. Cool the crust completely.

Meanwhile, in a large bowl, using a mixer, beat the cream cheese, sugar, and half of the whipped topping until smooth. Spread the cream cheese mixture evenly in the cooled crust.

In a medium bowl, whisk together the pudding and the milk until thick and smooth. Spread the pudding over the cream cheese mixture.

In a small bowl, gently combine the remaining whipped topping and the nuts. Spread evenly over the pudding layer. Refrigerate for at least 6 hours, or preferably overnight.

TIP: If you can't find self-rising flour, use all-purpose flour and add 1½ teaspoons baking powder and ¼ teaspoon salt.

VIRGINIA BRUNCH SURPRISE

Serves 8 to 10

This is so easy and mighty scrumptious. You'll blow your cover as a great cook if you let your guests know how easy it is!

One 18.25-ounce package yellow cake mix

½ cup (1 stick) butter, softened

½ cup plus 2 tablespoons sweetened shredded coconut

3 medium-size red or green apples, cored and sliced, peeled or unpeeled

½ cup sugar

1 teaspoon ground cinnamon

Two 8-ounce cartons or one 16-ounce carton sour cream

2 eggs

Preheat the oven to 350°F. Grease a 13 by 9-inch baking pan.

Mix the cake mix, butter, and coconut together; the mixture will be crunchy. Press into a prepared pan. Be sure to cover the bottom and the sides. Bake for 10 minutes. Remove from the oven.

Arrange the apple slices evenly on top of the cake. In a small bowl, mix the sugar and cinnamon, and sprinkle on top of the apples. In a separate small bowl, beat the sour cream and eggs. Pour evenly on top of the cake. Bake an additional 20 to 25 minutes, until golden and puffy.

OATMEAL MACAROONS

Makes 6 dozen cookies

You have to try these. Think of oatmeal cookies with cinnamon and pecans.

1 cup vegetable shortening

1 cup firmly packed light brown sugar

1 cup granulated sugar

½ teaspoon vanilla extract

2 eggs

1¼ cups all-purpose flour, sifted

1 teaspoon baking soda

½ teaspoon salt

½ teaspoon ground cinnamon

3 cups uncooked old-fashioned (not quick-cooking or instant) oatmeal

½ cup chopped pecans

Preheat the oven to 350°F. Grease a cookie sheet.

In a large bowl, combine the shortening, sugars, vanilla, and eggs. Sift the flour with the baking soda, salt, and cinnamon. Add to the shortening mixture and stir until thoroughly combined. Fold in the oatmeal and pecans. Roll the dough into 1-inch balls and place on the prepared cookie sheet, 1 inch apart. Bake for 12 to 15 minutes, until firm. Remove and cool on a wire rack. Bake in batches, or on multiple pans, or freeze some of the dough and store in an airtight container for later use.

STAR'S COOKIES

Makes 4 dozen

It's important to let these babies cool before you take them up off the cookie sheet. That is, if you can wait to eat a bunch! As for me, I can't hardly wait to sample 'em.

1 cup (2 sticks) butter

1 cup granulated sugar

1 cup firmly packed light brown sugar

2 eggs

1 teaspoon vanilla extract

½ teaspoon salt

2 cups uncooked old-fashioned (not quick-cooking or instant) oatmeal

2 cups all-purpose flour

1 teaspoon baking soda

½ teaspoon baking powder

1 cup chopped pecans

2 cups crispy rice cereal (I like Rice Krispies)

Preheat the oven to 375°F. Grease a cookie sheet.

Cream the butter and the sugars until light and fluffy. Add the eggs, vanilla, salt, oatmeal, flour, baking soda, baking powder, pecans, and cereal and stir until well blended. Drop by teaspoonsfuls onto the prepared cookie sheet 2 to 3 inches apart. Bake for 12 to 15 minutes. Cool on wire racks.

SIMPLY DELICIOUS CHOCOLATE COOKIE BARS

Makes 24 to 36 bars

Susan Greene of Albany shared this with me. When I make this I like to use Oreos but you can substitute any brand of chocolate sandwich cookie. They truly turn out like candy bars, which I love.

2 cups finely crushed creme-filled chocolate sandwich cookies
(about 24 cookies)

4 tablespoons (½ stick) butter, melted

One 12-ounce package semisweet chocolate chips

One 14-ounce can sweetened condensed milk

1 teaspoon vanilla extract

1 cup chopped pecans

Preheat the oven to 350°F. Combine the cookie crumbs and butter, and press firmly into the bottom of a 13 by 9-inch baking pan.

In a medium saucepan, over medium heat, melt 1 cup of the chocolate chips with the condensed milk and the vanilla. Pour evenly over the prepared crust. Top with the nuts and the remaining chocolate chips. Bake 20 minutes or until set. Cool, and chill if desired. Cut into bars and store tightly covered at room temperature.

NEVER-FAIL PEANUT BRITTLE

We used to sing a song about goober peas. Y'all do know those are peanuts, don't you? It went something like this, "Goodness how delicious, eating goober peas." (You'll need a candy thermometer to make this recipe.)

1 tablespoon butter, plus extra for the pan

3 cups sugar

1 cup light corn syrup

3 cups raw peanuts without skins,
or substitute boiled unsalted peanuts without skins

1 teaspoon salt

2 teaspoons baking soda, sifted

Butter a jelly roll pan.

In a large saucepan, boil the sugar, corn syrup, and ½ cup water until a thread spins. (The candy thermometer will read or say "thread" or you can do a cold water test.) Add the peanuts and stir until candy thermometer reaches 280°F and the mixture becomes hard. Remove pot from the heat and add 1 tablespoon butter, the salt, and the baking soda, and stir them into the mixture. Pour and spread over the bottom of the prepared pan. Cool in the pan. Break into pieces and enjoy!

Store in an airtight container.

TIP: The cold water test: Drop a teaspoon of the sugar mixture into a glass of ice water. If it doesn't dissolve and forms a thread, it's ready.

A GIFT FROM PAULA

My sister said she'd never forgive me if I didn't let her surprise me with a gift for my cookbook. So what did she go on and do? She presented me with three delicious dessert recipes from her unbelievably popular magazine, *Cooking with Paula Deen.* She describes these scrumptious recipes as the icing on the cake for a job well done. That's just like Paula. Her generosity and her talents just can't be matched.

SWEET POTATO DOUGHNUTS WITH MAPLE ICING

Makes 2½ dozen

When Paula and I were kids, Mama would plop us down in front of the television in the living room and, in a few minutes, bring us a bag of hot doughnuts straight from the fryer. Never heard of sweet potato doughnuts? Well, now you have and they're delicious.

3½ cups all-purpose flour, plus extra for kneading

1 cup sugar

2 teaspoons baking powder

½ teaspoon baking soda

½ teaspoon ground cinnamon

½ teaspoon salt

2 large eggs, lightly beaten

1 cup sour cream

1 cup mashed cooked sweet potato (about 1 medium)

Vegetable oil, for frying

Maple icing (recipe follows)

1 cup finely chopped pecans

In a medium bowl, combine the flour, sugar, baking powder, soda, cinnamon, and salt. In a large bowl, combine the eggs, sour cream, and sweet potato. Gradually add the flour mixture, stirring to combine. Turn the dough out onto a heavily floured surface; knead lightly 4 or 5 times (dough will be sticky). Roll out the dough to ½-inch thickness. Cut out the dough with a doughnut cutter (or use 2¼-inch round cutter and a ¾-inch cutter). Reroll dough as needed.

In a Dutch oven, heat the vegetable oil over medium heat to 360°F. Cook the doughnuts in batches in the oil for 2 minutes per side, or until lightly browned. Drain on paper towels. Ice top of doughnuts with maple icing and sprinkle with chopped pecans.

MAPLE ICING

Makes 1 cup

2⅔ cup confectioners' sugar

3 to 4 tablespoons milk

¼ teaspoon maple flavoring

In a small bowl, combine the confectioners' sugar and 3 tablespoons milk; stir well. Add additional milk to reach desired consistency. Stir in maple flavoring.

WHITE CHOCOLATE-CRANBERRY CHEESECAKE

Serves 6 to 8

Looking for a different way to serve cranberries at Thanksgiving? This cheesecake is made with cranberries three ways—cranberry sauce, fresh cranberries, and cranberry preserves. What a treat!

One 16-ounce can whole berry cranberry sauce

2 cups graham cracker crumbs

1¼ cups sugar

6 tablespoons (¾ stick) butter, melted

Three 8-ounce packages cream cheese, softened

3 large eggs

One 3.5-ounce bar white chocolate, melted and cooled slightly

2 cups fresh cranberries

¼ cup cranberry preserves, melted (optional)

In a small saucepan over medium-low heat, cook the cranberry sauce, stirring frequently, for 35 minutes, or until reduced to 1 cup. Cover and chill 2 hours.

Preheat the oven to 350°F. In a medium bowl, combine the cracker crumbs, ¼ cup of the sugar, and the butter. Press firmly on bottom and 1 inch up sides of a 9-inch springform pan. Bake 8 minutes. Remove from oven and let cool, leaving oven on.

In a large bowl, beat the cream cheese and remaining 1 cup sugar with a mixer until fluffy. Beat in the eggs one at a time, beating well after each addition. Stir in the chocolate. Spoon half of the batter into the cooled crust. Spread the reduced cranberry sauce over batter. Top with the remaining batter. Bake 45 minutes. Let cool completely on wire rack. Chill 8 hours before serving.

Garnish with fresh cranberries, and brush with melted preserves, if desired. Cheesecake can be made ahead and frozen up to one month.

Little Bubba ready for football

QUEEN OF HEARTS DECADENT DESSERT

I use cookie cutters in the shape of card suits—diamonds, spades, clubs, and hearts. It reminds of my childhood when Mama and Daddy's friends would come over and play cards. That's my preference but you can use any shape cookie cutter. Just cut out the brownies and put the scraps in a plastic bag and freeze to eat later with vanilla ice cream.

Here's a time saver: Bake both batches of brownies at the same time.

White Chocolate Brownies (recipe follows)
Fudgey Chocolate Brownies (page 161)
Strawberry–Cream Cheese Frosting (page 162)

Spread each White Chocolate Brownie with a thin layer of Strawberry–Cream Cheese Frosting. Top with Fudgey Chocolate Brownie cutouts.

WHITE CHOCOLATE BROWNIES

Makes about 30 cutout brownies

1 cup (2 sticks) butter

Six 1-ounce squares white chocolate

1½ cups sugar

4 large eggs

1½ cups all-purpose flour

1 teaspoon vanilla extract

Preheat the oven to 350°F. Line a 13 by 9-inch baking pan with aluminum foil.

In a medium saucepan, melt the butter and chocolate over low heat; set aide to cool slightly. In a large bowl, combine the sugar and eggs; beat with mixer until fluffy. Gradually beat in the flour and vanilla. Stir in the chocolate mixture until smooth. Pour into the prepared pan. Bake for 30 minutes. Let cool completely in the pan. Lift the brownies from the pan using the foil as handles.

FUDGEY CHOCOLATE BROWNIES

Makes about 30 cutout brownies

1 cup (2 sticks) butter

Five 1-ounce squares unsweetened chocolate

1¾ cups sugar

4 large eggs

1½ cups all-purpose flour

½ teaspoon salt

1 teaspoon vanilla extract

Preheat the oven to 350°F. Line a 13 by 9-inch baking pan with aluminum foil.

In a medium saucepan, melt the butter and chocolate over low heat; set aside to cool slightly. In a large bowl, combine the sugar and the eggs; beat with a mixer until fluffy. Gradually beat in the flour, salt, and vanilla. Stir in the melted chocolate mixture until smooth. Pour into the prepared pan. Bake for 28 minutes. Let cool completely in the pan. Lift the brownies from the pan using foil as handles.

STRAWBERRY-CREAM CHEESE FROSTING

Makes about 2 cups

One 3-ounce package cream cheese, softened

¼ cup (½ stick) butter, softened

3 tablespoons strawberry preserves

2½ cups confectioners' sugar

In a medium bowl, beat the cream cheese, butter, and strawberry preserves until combined. Gradually beat in confectioners' sugar.

METRIC EQUIVALENCIES

LIQUID EQUIVALENCIES

Customary	Metric
¼ teaspoon	1.25 milliliters
½ teaspoon	2.5 milliliters
1 teaspoon	5 milliliters
1 tablespoon	15 milliliters
1 fluid ounce	30 milliliters
¼ cup	60 milliliters
⅓ cup	80 milliliters
½ cup	120 milliliters
1 cup	240 milliliters
1 pint (2 cups)	480 milliliters
1 quart (4 cups)	960 milliliters (.96 liter)
1 gallon (4 quarts)	3.84 liters

DRY MEASURE EQUIVALENCIES

Customary	Metric
1 ounce (by weight)	28 grams
¼ pound (4 ounces)	114 grams
1 pound (16 ounces)	454 grams
2.2 pounds	1 kilogram (1,000 grams)

OVEN TEMPERATURE EQUIVALENCIES

Description	°Fahrenheit	°Celsius
Cool	200	90
Very slow	250	120
Slow	300–325	150–160
Moderately slow	325–350	160–180
Moderate	350–375	180–190
Moderately hot	375–400	190–200
Hot	400–450	200–230
Very hot	450–500	230–260

INDEX

THE *NEW* ENCYCLOPEDIA OF SCHOOL LETTERS

THE *NEW* ENCYCLOPEDIA OF SCHOOL LETTERS

*P. Susan Mamchak
and
Steven R. Mamchak*

PRENTICE HALL
Englewood Cliffs, New Jersey 07632

©1990 by

PRENTICE-HALL, Inc.
Englewood Cliffs, NJ

10 9 8 7 6 5 4 3 2 1

Library of Congress Cataloging-in-Publication Data

The new encyclopedia of school letters / by P. Susan Mamchak and Steven R. Mamchak.
   p. cm.
Rev. ed. of: Encyclopedia of school letters. c1979.
ISBN 0-13-612656-1
   1. Schools—Records and correspondence—Forms. 2. Form letters.
I. Mamchak, Steven R. II. Mamchak, P. Susan, 1944– Encyclopedia of school letters.
III. Title.
LB2845.7.M35 1990
651.7′4—dc20   89-48884
                                             CIP

Printed in the United States of America

ISBN 0-13-612656-1

PRENTICE HALL
BUSINESS & PROFESSIONAL DIVISION
A division of Simon & Schuster
Englewood Cliffs, New Jersey 07632

DEDICATION

. . . to Ingrid Pedersen:

a little this;

a little that;

a lot of LOVE . . .

ABOUT THE AUTHORS

P. SUSAN MAMCHAK has been active in education for over 20 years, holding a number of positions from substitute teacher to school disciplinarian. She holds a degree in behavioral science and has lectured extensively on teacher effectiveness and interpersonal relations.

STEVEN R. MAMCHAK is an educator with over 28 years of experience in the New Jersey public school system. He has lectured, has hosted his own radio show, and is the recipient of the New Jersey Governor's Recognition of Excellence in Teaching Award.

The MAMCHAKS are the authors of over 14 books on education and effective communication techniques. Their books include *Complete School Communications Manual* and *School Administrator's Public Speaking Portfolio: With Model Speeches and Anecdotes.*

How This *New* Encyclopedia
Will Better Serve Your Needs

If one thing is certain about American education, it is this—NOTHING stands still. It has been over a decade since *Encyclopedia of School Letters* was published. In that time, not only have we gotten older, a bit grayer, and it is hoped, a little wiser, but we have *all* witnessed education changing rapidly and inexorably. The "Middle School," for example, was an interesting "concept" ten years ago, and it has become one of the fastest-growing "items" today; yesterday, a job description might have been, "Teach!" while today every item is spelled out for legal purposes; ten years ago, AIDS referred to maps and textbooks, rather than the devastating scourge that plagues our nation. NOTHING stands still.

There are some truths, however, that are timeless. In the introduction to the original *Encyclopedia of School Letters* we wrote:

> As an Administrator, you begin your day five minutes before you are ready for it and finish it an hour after you thought it had ended. There are just *so many duties,* not the least of which is that you are faced each day with tasks which call upon your skills in the art of written communication. There are letters and memos to parents, other administrators and faculty members; in-house communications and bulletins; policy statements and public relations work—the list seems endless and the paperwork never ending.

Certainly, *that* is a truth which applies today more than ever!

That is why *The NEW Encyclopedia of School Letters* was written. Administrators *still* realize that time spent locked in an office doing paperwork is time when they are *not* functioning as visible educational leaders. Administrators *still* need to manage their paperwork before that "paper tiger" rises up and devours them. Administrators *still* can use models of forms, memos, bulletins, announcements, and letters of all types to free their time while still providing the most powerful of written communications. Administrators *still* realize that they can profit from the sharing of models of communications which have worked for other educators in similar situations—and we *know* that the sharing of knowledge is what education is all about.

We have taken the claim, "If'n it ain't broke, don't fix it!" to heart. If an item was viable ten years ago and still applies with equal vigor, it stayed in. An item left only if it were dated, no longer applied, or there was something better or stronger with which to replace it. An item was *not* placed in this current volume because it was "new," but because it was *better!*

Even so, almost 70 percent of this book is brand new. The topics remain the same, of course, for they are the topics which are central to education and always have been, and those topics which are new are those which have come to prominence of late, such as AIDS and middle school. Under these time-honored topics, however, are many new and vital forms, memos, letters and the like which you can use in drafting *your* written communications with the knowledge that they are timely, effective, accurate communications that have been used and *are being used* in American education right now—today!

From an "Absentee Breakdown Form" to a "Resolution on Attendance Zones," we believe that you will find the most complete and comprehensive collection of model forms and letters anywhere. From a pointed "Letter on the Abuse of" the school's telephones to a memorandum on the "Use of Protective Gloves" when dealing with ill children, this book is as contemporary as this morning's headlines. From a principal's "Special Letter to Parents" about school photographs to a "Welcome to Parents and Students" at an orientation program, here are communications that handle the day-to-day requirements of a functioning school. From a "Memo on Animals in Class" and their use in science to a "Notice on the Showing of" PG- and R-rated movies in a classroom, here are communications that do not flinch from handling the challenging aspects of today's educational scene. From the "Philosophy of" a middle school to an "Inspirational Message to Students" at the end of the school year, here are bulletins and memos and letters that penetrate to the heart of education and capture the minds of your audience. This is a book that you, as a professional educator, *can use*.

Whether you need to formulate a "Code of Behavior," reprimand a substitute teacher "For Poor Service," compose a "Memo on Student Aides" in the main office, write a "Letter to Parents Concerning" standardized testing, send an individual a "Letter on a Major Infraction" concerning alcohol or drug abuse, or engage in the pleasant task of mailing someone a "Letter on a Job Well Done," this is the place you will find what you need and more.

Take a comprehensive list of topics as contemporary as the evening news on television; provide under each topic the finest forms, memos, bulletins, and letters that are currently being used to advantage in our nation's schools; add to this a table of contents so detailed that it serves as its own index, allowing you to find exactly what you need when you need it; include the fact that within the body of the book, every topic is cross-referenced to others where additional suitable information may be found—and you have a practical resource worthy of your consideration.

In the introduction to the original *Encyclopedia of School Letters* we concluded:

> This is not a book which you will find gathering dust on a bookshelf. Rather, it is a volume which will occupy a featured position on your desk among those items which you use, use day in and day out, use now—and throughout the entire school year.

Well . . . some things never change!

P. Susan Mamchak

Steven R. Mamchak

──── TABLE OF CONTENTS ────

ABSENCE (See Also: ATTENDANCE; CUTTING; DISMISSAL PROCEDURES; SIGN-IN SHEETS; TARDINESS)

. . .Absentee Breakdown Form

Date: _____

GRADE	TOTAL NUMBER OF STUDENTS ABSENT		RUNNING TOTAL
	boys	girls	
K			
1			
2			
3			
4			
5			
6			
7			
8			
9			
10			
11			
12			
Total			

. . .Absentee Form

(A) for a student

FORM FOR STUDENT ABSENCE

Name: _____ Grade: _____

Home Room: _____ Date: _____

This is to state that I was absent from school on (give date(s)): _____

_____

because (state reason): _____

_____

    I hereby state that the above is the true reason for my absence.

                Signature of Student: _____

                Signature of Parent: _____

(B) for a teacher

                        Date: _____

REASON FOR ABSENCE FROM DUTY

Name of Employee: _____

Grade and/or Subject: _____

        I hereby certify that my absence from duty on

_____ was caused by _____

_____

_____

Number of Days Absent: _____

Substitute(s): _____

        Signature of
        School Employee: _____

This form is to be filled out and returned to the principal's office after each absence.

. . .Absentee Report

(A) monthly absentee report

ABSENTEE REPORT

for the month of

_____, 19 _____

School: _____

Date	1	2	3	4	5	6	7	8	9	10	11	12	Running Total
1													
2													
3													
4													
5													
6													
7													
8													
9													
10													
11													
12													
13													
14													
15													
16													
17													
18													
19													
20													
21													
22													
23													
24													
25													
26													
27													
28													
29													
30													
31													
Total													

(B) *yearly absentee report*

REPORT ON ABSENTEES

School: _____

For the School Year: _____

| Month | Number of Absences in Grade | | | | | | | | | | | | | Total | Running Total |
	K	1	2	3	4	5	6	7	8	9	10	11	12		
Sept.															
Oct.															
Nov.															
Dec.															
Jan.															
Feb.															
Mar.															
Apr.															
May															
June															
Yearly Total															

Signature: _____

Title: _____

. . .Letter on Excessive Absence

(A) *to a student*

Dear Adam,

Would you believe that almost half a school year has gone by? It has, and just as we designed it to be, it has been a period of growth, both mental and physical, for our students. Over these few months both the faculty and administration of Rock Township High School have been delighted to take note of this progress and to aid and encourage it.

That is precisely why we are so concerned with you and your attendance over these past few months. Our records indicate that you have been absent 31 days from the start of school until now.

Certainly you must be aware that school policy provides drastic action for excessive absence that is unexcused. This is due to the fact that we wish you to learn and to perform at your maximum capacity, and this cannot be done if you are not physically present to participate.

We sincerely ask you to consider this seriously, and we look forward to seeing you at school on a more regular basis in the future. We have every hope that you will participate voluntarily in your education.

Yours sincerely,

Copies: Central Administration
          Parents of Adam Brady
          Our files

(B) *to a teacher*

Dear Mr. Garling,

Quite frankly, we are very concerned. In the past six-month period, you have been absent from school and your teaching duties a total of 43 days. It is obvious that this has totally drained all of your accumulated sick-leave time as well as any personal time allotted to you via contractual obligations.

Certainly, such excessive absence is an indication that something is amiss. As always, we stand ready to help in whatever way we can. If there is a serious problem, please share it with us and allow us to help you.

Frankly, we are concerned about you, and we are also concerned about your class. Such an amount of absence on the part of the teacher is bound to have an effect upon the learning of the students. It is precisely for these students that we all entered education, so we know that you must be concerned as well.

Please make an appointment with me at your earliest convenience in order that we may discuss this matter more fully.

Please, let us help.

Yours sincerely,

COPIES: Central Administration
          Our files

ACCEPTANCE (See Also: ACHIEVEMENT; DEGREES; IDEAS; NEGOTIATIONS; RESIGNATION; STUDENT TEACHER)

. . .By a Candidate of a Position

Dear Dr. Sorrenti,

I cannot begin to tell you how happy it makes me to return the contract forms you sent me. Needless to say, I am delighted, and I accept with gratitude.

It is far more than gratitude, however, that I hope to offer to you and to the students of Rock Township High School in the days and years to come. You may be assured that I shall give the best that I am personally able to provide in order to justify your faith in me and to see to it that the students of Rock Township receive the quality education they deserve.

It is with great enthusiasm and anticipation that I look forward to assuming my duties as principal of Rock Township High School.

Yours sincerely,

. . .Of a Candidate for a Position

Dear Dr. Benson,

As Superintendent of Schools of Rock Township, I have had occasion to write letters for any number of negative reasons. That is why I am so overjoyed to write to you concerning a positive decision of the Rock Township Board of Education made at the June 19, 19XX meeting; one which, I am certain, will have a positive influence upon the students of Rock Township.

In short—you got the job!

I am enclosing the contract which I would like you to sign and return right away, and I'd like you to call for an appointment within the next week, as I know that we will have much to discuss.

I want you to know that your credentials and references and the erudite way in which you handled the interview convinced us that you are the person to lead us into the next decade at Rock Township High School. We know we have the best person available.

Yours sincerely,

. . .Of an Idea

Dear Kenny,

I sometimes think that I am the most fortunate of people to have ingenious and creative people like you in the school.

The idea you were kind enough to share with me at our last faculty meeting is an outstanding one, reflective of the concern for the welfare of our school and its students which I have come to expect from you. Your idea will, when implemented, solve an overcrowding problem that could have become very serious.

I'd like you to set up an appointment with me so we can move ahead on your idea.

Again, let me thank you for your most valuable contribution.

Sincerely,

. . .Of Responsibility

Dear Dr. Smith,

Harry Truman had a sign on his desk which read, "The Buck Stops Here!" This letter is my attempt to emulate that sentiment.

I fully understand the policies of Rock Township relative to the use of the school building after regular school hours, and I can understand how they were developed to protect our students and regulate the use of our buildings. I understand and appreciate.

However, a situation has developed within our student body where a number of students are anxious to formulate a group for positive interaction with the community, a goal which we certainly all share. When these students approached me with a community matter that required virtually immediate attention, I took the responsibility and opened the school to them at night. I will personally be there to supervise and see to it that all goes well.

Because I felt it was a pressing need, and since you were out of town and could not be reached, I felt I could do no less. I shall be happy to speak to you as soon as possible and explain more fully.

In the meantime, the "Buck" has stopped here, and it is in my pocket whenever you want to see it.

Yours sincerely,

ACCOUNTABILITY (See Also: ACHIEVEMENT; COMPLAINTS; EVALUATION; GRADES; INSTRUCTION; LEARNING DISABILITIES; MAINSTREAMING; MINORITIES; OBSERVATION; PHILOSOPHY; SPECIAL EDUCATION; YEAR-END MATTERS)

. . .Form for

Name: _____   Date: _____

Subject Area: _____

Test Used: _____

Standardized Norm of Test: _____

NAME	SEPTEMBER SCORE	JUNE SCORE	DIFFERENTIAL + or −
Class Median			

Special Problems:

Signature: _____

. . .Letter to Parents Concerning

Dear Parents,

This letter is so important that I hope it doesn't end up being tossed aside unread. That, I'm afraid, is the fate of many communications from school. Therefore, if you are reading this, be thankful that your son or daughter had the responsibility to bring it home.

You see, here we are at the start of yet another school year, and everyone waits in anticipation to see what that year will bring. I know that is true of the faculty, administration, and students, and I am certain that you must feel some of it as well.

While I am certainly no gifted seer into the future, I would like to make a prediction as to what this year will bring. It will bring happiness and success to some and failure and disappointment to others; and this is a prophecy that WILL come true.

You see, we are all accountable to ourselves and to each other for what we do and do not do in our lives. To those students whose accountability includes taking advantage of the education that is being offered daily at Rock Township High School, then they will be the successful ones, and their days here will be happy ones indeed.

If, on the other hand, a student feels no accountability for his or her own education, then it is a difficult time that lies ahead for that person. I would only remind such an individual that here at Rock Township High School, we never fail a student; we merely record the grades the student does or does not give himself or herself.

Let us look forward to a year filled with challenge befitting the champions we all have within us and which we are all capable of becoming.

I look forward to working with you and your child during the coming school year.

Yours sincerely,

. . .Policy Statement on

In a democratic society, each person is ultimately responsible for his or her actions and is accountable for those actions to the body of society. In a like manner, we in education are responsible for the education of all students and must stand accountable for that education.

Common sense, however, dictates that many variables, not the least of which is the degree of motivation of the individual student, influence the outcomes of education.

We feel, therefore, that we must be accountable for doing all within our power to see that every student has every opportunity the school provides for his or her education. That, combined with individual motivation and cooperation from the student and the home, should, we hope, provide the maximum in education for all concerned.

ACHIEVEMENT (See Also: ACCEPTANCE; ACCOUNTABILITY; CONGRATULATIONS; DEGREES; GIFTED STUDENTS; NATIONAL HONOR SOCIETY; THANKS)

. . .Certificates of Achievement (Two Forms)

(A) first form

ROCK TOWNSHIP HIGH SCHOOL

_____

is awarded this
Certificate of Achievement
for

_____

_____

PRESENTED THIS _____ DAY OF _____, 19 _____

_____

_____

(B) *second form*

Date: _____

To Whom It May Concern:
This is to certify that _____
a student at Rock Township High School, has indicated a high degree of

achievement in that _____

_____
In testimony thereof, this certificate is gratefully presented.

Signed: _____

. . .Letter Acknowledging Achievement

Dear Wayne,

On behalf of the entire school, I wish to congratulate you for your outstanding achievement of coming in second in the state gymnastics program. What an outstanding effort on your part, and how proud we are of you!

While many will see only the medal and certificate, we look and see the hours and hours of dedication and hard work that went into the honor you have achieved. You may be as proud of that dedication as you are justly proud of your accomplishment.

We sincerely hope that you will continue to contribute to gymnastics and remain a credit to the discipline as you continue to be a credit to this school and your entire community.

Yours sincerely,

J. Benson, Principal

ADDRESS (See Also: ATTENDANCE; PERMANENT RECORDS; ZONING)

. . .Change of Address Form for a Student

CHANGE OF ADDRESS FORM

Name: _____ Date: _____

School: _____ Grade: _____

Name of Parent or Guardian: _____

Old Address: _____

Assigned Bus Stop, If Any: _____

New Address: _____

Telephone Number: _____ Transportation: Yes _____ No _____

This form is to be filled out and presented to the Guidance Office upon student's change of address within the township.

. . .Change of Address Form for a Teacher

CHANGE OF ADDRESS FORM

Name: _____ Date: _____

School: _____ Grade or Subject: _____

This is to inform you that my address has changed as indicated below:

Old Address: _____

_____ Zip _____

Telephone Number: _____

New Address: _____

_____ Zip _____

Telephone Number: _____

My telephone number is (   ) listed   (   ) unlisted.

. . .Letter on Address Clarification

Dear Parent/Guardian:

We are certain that you realize how important it is for an institution of our size to keep proper records. Indeed, not only is it necessary for us to keep accurate records for our own daily functioning, but the law rightfully requires this of us as well.

Therefore, we are certain that you will help us in clarifying the address of your son/daughter who is a student in our school.

This is the way our records currently show your child's name and address:

NAME: _____

ADDRESS: _____

CITY/TOWN: _____ STATE: _____ ZIP: _____

If the information above is NOT CORRECT, please fill in the correct information on the address form below. If it is correct, simply write "OK" across the blank form below:

NAME: _____

ADDRESS: _____

CITY/TOWN: _____ STATE: _____ ZIP: _____

In either case, please sign this form where indicated below and return it to us via your son/daughter.

Thank you for taking this time to help us with this very important matter. We appreciate your concern.

Yours sincerely,

J. Benson, Principal

PARENT SIGNATURE: _____

DATE: _____

AIDS (ACQUIRED IMMUNE DEFICIENCY SYNDROME)
(See Also: ACCOUNTABILITY; COUNSELING; DRUGS; ILLNESS; MEDICAL; PSYCHOLOGICAL SERVICES)

. . .General Message on

We live in perilous and unusual times. Often situations offer us challenges that sharpen us and allow us to grow. At other times, situations may seem almost impossible yet allow us to see ourselves and others work together for a common cause. In any situation, we have the opportunity to shrink from the task or meet it head on and learn from it and grow with it.

Like it or not, AIDS (Acquired Immune Deficiency Syndrome) is a fact of modern life. This disease, virtually unknown a decade ago, poses a major threat to society and a challenge to each and every one of us.

We in education must stand ready to meet that challenge as we work to fulfill our directive of educating the children of America. This includes children with AIDS, children from homes with AIDS, and children who need to be educated about this potential destroyer of lives.

Without prejudice, without fear, and armed with knowledge coupled with compassion and understanding, we in education will work together for a common cause; we will meet the challenge; and we will grow together in the doing.

We are educators.

We can do no less.

. . .Memo to Faculty

To: Faculty
From: John Benson, Principal
Re: Students with AIDS

I am told that the only way to slay a dragon is to strike at the heart of the beast, so let's get right to it.

Yes, we have a student with AIDS. No, I'm not going to tell you who that student is. I tell you that the teachers who are involved with this student know the identity, and they have voluntarily offered to keep it secret. We are doing this for the child's welfare, *and for no other reason.* A student deserves an education, not an onslaught of pointed fingers and whispered innuendos. The student's identity will remain in confidence.

I know for a fact that you all attended the inservice meeting on AIDS that was given by the county health organization. Therefore, as knowledgeable professionals, you are aware that there is nothing to fear as we go about our duties as educators. We have always done an outstanding job in that respect and you know how proud I am of you in this regard. I know that we shall continue to provide that quality education and that all of our students . . . ALL of our students . . . will benefit from your professionalism, integrity, and concern.

Keep those swords sharp, ladies and gentlemen, and there is not a dragon that can hope to stand against us.

. . .Use of Protective Gloves

To: Faculty and Staff
From: Janet Simpson, RN
Re: Protective Gloves

Enclosed with this note, you will find two latex gloves. Yes, one size fits all, and you can wear them on either hand.

I suggest that you keep these gloves in a convenient location where they may be gotten to quickly. The top drawer of your desk is fine. Then, if a situation arises where you must come into contact with the bodily effluent of a student (blood, saliva, vomit, mucus, etc., sorry, but I must be graphic), it is strongly suggested that you take the one or two seconds required to don the latex gloves *prior* to touching the student.

Many of you have told me that teaching is like living inside a petri dish what with the huge number of disease and bacteria our students carry to us each day. Using the latex gloves minimizes the chance of infection, and that can only be a benefit to all of us. While recent findings indicate that, as far as AIDS is concerned, *only contact with blood* presents a hazard, let us not leave ourselves vulnerable to the many infectious situations with which we come into contact. If we go overboard, let it be on the side of SAFETY!

Please, keep them where you can get at them—and use them.

ANIMALS   (See Also: ACCOUNTABILITY; NURSE; THANKS)

. . .Letter to Parents Concerning

Dear Parents:

When I went to school (a few hundred years ago), I was always bringing in things from home—cookies that my mother made for the class, my stamp collection, the science project my father and I made in the cellar. As far as anyone can tell, this practice is still going on. Kids like to bring things from home to share with their classmates.

While all this may be a fitting and proper part of education, it enters an entirely different realm when the "something" from home is in the shape of a live animal.

In all honesty, we have had students bring in everything from hamsters to golden retrievers. While seemingly harmless, animals can and often do pose a problem in school. Animals bite, animals know nothing about using lavatory facilities, and sometimes animals are sick when they come into contact with our students. Given the natural gregariousness and eagerness of our students and the generally shy demeanor of most animals, the animal doesn't get a holiday, either.

Therefore, I am asking the parents to please notify the school well in advance of bringing an animal to school and be advised that you will be required to supervise the animal brought into school. Should a child bring in an animal to the school without advance warning, we will try to keep the animal as comfortable as possible until you come pick it up.

We want school to be a fun place, but we want it to be safe as well.

Thank you for your understanding and your cooperation.

. . .Memo on Animals in Class

TO: All Staff
FROM: Administration
RE: Live Animals in a Classroom

In the study of science, it may seem proper at times for live animals to be present in the classroom for observation purposes. The presence of live animals in any classroom, however, should only be permitted when a science teacher approves of it and supervises the activity. When that situation occurs, certain precautions should necessarily follow:

1. Live animals must be caged.

2. Live animals are not to be handled by any student at any time. They are for observation only, not for handling.

3. Live animals brought into school are under stress. Therefore, students are to remain clear of cages and must never poke a finger or other object into a cage.

4. Animals are to be transported by the owner. They are to be brought in *only* on the day of the project or observation and are to be removed by the owner as soon as the project or observation has been completed.

While we regret the necessity of reminding everybody in a memo such as this, it is important for you to know that four students have been referred to the school nurse so far this year for animal bites. In those instances, those cute little critters weren't so cute after all.

Thank you!

APPRECIATION (See Also: CITIZENSHIP; SECRETARY; STUDENT COUNCIL; THANKS; VOLUNTEERS; YEARBOOK)

. . .Certificate of

ROCK TOWNSHIP HIGH SCHOOL

This Certificate Is Presented
to

_____

in grateful appreciation for

_____

_____

Presented this _____ day of _____, 19 _____

_____, (title) _____

. . .Letters of

(A) to an administrator

Dear Mrs. Kelty,

I deeply appreciate your recent efforts on behalf of our students by allowing our home economics class to visit with your kindergarten classes. I am certain that the practical experience they gathered in child care will prove a benefit to each student as well as to their future families.

It could not have been done, however, without your cooperation, understanding, and kindness. I am personally grateful for all three, and I deeply appreciate this current kindness as well as all the kindnesses you have so frequently shown us in the past.

I trust you know that if we may ever be of service to you or your school, you need only ask.

Yours sincerely,

J. Benson

(B) *to a parent*

Dear Mr. Griggs,

One of the joys of my job is getting to meet wonderfully concerned parents such as yourself. The recent trip you arranged to the New York Stock Exchange was simply outstanding. Our students are still talking about it.

It is obvious to me and to our faculty that a great, great deal of time, effort, coordination, and just plain hard work went into the day at the Stock Exchange that you so graciously arranged for us. You managed to take a subject that, frankly, most students find somewhat dull and made it into a dynamic, living experience that none will soon forget.

I am totally sincere when I tell you that the faculty and I deeply appreciate what you have done for our students. Your reward could be found etched into the faces of our kids as they discovered a new knowledge about a major factor in our economy.

Again, my deep personal appreciation goes to you, and should you ever decide to leave that investment firm of yours, look me up—there's always a place on our faculty for someone like you!

With best personal regards,

J. Benson

(C) *to a student*

Dear Carol Anne,

We have received in our office a letter from the Floral Park Nursing Home expressing their appreciation for the recent donations of both clothing and time spent with patients that your home economics class provided last week. I am writing to you because your teacher informs me that you were selected by your classmates to be the leader of this project. Mrs. Scott also tells me of your virtually untiring efforts on behalf of this project.

Therefore, it is only proper that you should know how much that nursing home and its patients appreciated the work you put in to the project.

Personally, I want you to know what a fine thing both I and the faculty of this school think your project was and how greatly we appreciate your efforts, and having the pleasure of meeting you in our classes each and every day.

Keep it growing.

Yours sincerely,

J. Benson

(D) *to a teacher*

Dear Bill,

If I asked you why you did it, I know you would quip (as you have in the past) that you just couldn't pass up the opportunity to inflict pain on yourself. We all laugh at your cleverness, but those of us on the inside of education know only too well about the reality of the "pain."

Taking on an extra assignment such as you have for five straight years now *must* be a labor of love, and the love you put into it is evident in the benefits our students reap from your work, most of it behind the scenes and unheralded.

That's why I just want you to know how deeply I personally, as well as the students and faculty of this school, appreciate all you do when nobody sees, all the hours you put in when everyone else has gone home, and the effort that manifests itself in the quality of our students' lives.

We greatly appreciate you, Bill, and we are honored to serve with you.

Yours sincerely,

John Benson

ASSEMBLIES   (See Also: GRADUATION)

. . .Assignment of Assembly Schedule

YEARLY ASSEMBLY SCHEDULE

Each teacher shall be responsible for one (1) assembly during the school year. Please fill in the following form by placing your name next to the time you prefer to give your assembly. Placement is on a first-come, first-serve basis. The number one (1) after a month indicates the first half of the month (from the 1st through the 15th) while a two (2) indicates the second half (from the 16th through the last day). When this form has been completely filled, it will be copied and distributed to the staff as a reminder of due dates.

DATE	TEACHER	DATE	TEACHER
Sept. (2)		Feb. (1)	
Oct. (1)		Feb. (2)	
Oct. (2)		Mar. (1)	
Nov. (1)		Mar. (2)	
Nov. (2)		Apr. (1)	
Dec. (1)		Apr. (2)	
Dec. (2)		May (1)	
Jan. (1)		May (2)	
Jan. (2)		June (1)	

. . .Letter Regarding

(A) *outstanding assembly*

Dear Mrs. Harris,

What a delight it was to watch the assembly program which you and your class presented for the school this morning. It was so evident that some monumental effort and hard work went into it. The result was a performance that both faculty and students deeply enjoyed and benefited from. That's no easy task, and you and your class accomplished it beautifully.

I shall make time to drop in later this week and tell the children personally how much I appreciated their efforts. In the meantime, please tell them how much I enjoyed it. And please know how much I personally appreciate your efforts on behalf of your students and this school.

Yours sincerely,

J. Benson

(B) *poor assembly*

Dear Sir:

Your brochure was a major factor in our selection of your group to present an assembly program for our school. That brochure promises "an hour of fun." The performance barely lasted thirty minutes. The brochure proclaims that "clowns pour from the stage while acrobats perform feats of daring and skill." Sir, *one* clown who later did a handstand hardly constitutes fulfillment of the promise of your literature. In short, we are disappointed, we are underentertained, and we are angry.

While we feel that it would be well within our rights to withhold payment for such an obvious misrepresentation, we are enclosing a check for the "performance." You may be assured, however, that this will be your "final curtain" at our school, and I shall let the administrators of other township schools know my feelings as well.

Sincerely,

J. Benson

. . .Memo to Teachers on

MEMO

To: ALL TEACHERS
From: J. BENSON, PRINCIPAL
Re: ASSEMBLIES

Everyone likes assemblies—the students enjoy them and, from comments I've heard, so does the faculty. Assemblies have a definite place in education as an instrument for the social growth of the student. They are not merely a "time to get out of class."

It is important, therefore, that we impress upon our students the proper behavior during an assembly, and it is equally important that all teachers sit with their classes and supervise behavior during the entire program.

I know that I can count upon your cooperation in this matter, and I look forward to some fine assemblies in the future.

. . .Policy on

We believe that assemblies are an integral part of the education of the children in our schools. We believe that they are a means for teaching social interaction in group situations as well as broadening the educational and cultural backgrounds of all students.

We also believe that all assemblies should provide information and entertainment in line with the community's standards. We also believe that no student or group of students should be made to feel slighted, neglected, or outcast because of the content of any assembly.

All assemblies should be beneficial to all attending.

. . .Procedures for

ASSEMBLY PROCEDURES

The following procedures will apply to all assemblies:

1. All teachers will wait until called to the assembly over the public address system.
2. Teachers in rooms 100, 101, 102, and 103 will enter by Door B and take seats in sections M, N, O, and P.
3. Teachers in rooms 104, 105, 106, and 107 will enter by Door C and take seats in sections I, J, K, and L.
4. Teachers in rooms 200, 201, 202, and 203 will enter by Door A and take seats in sections A, B, C, and D.
5. Teachers in rooms 204, 205, 206, and 207 will enter by Door B and take seats in sections E, F, G, and H.
6. Teachers will sit with and supervise their classes during the assembly.
7. Upon completion of the assembly, teachers will wait until their section is dismissed by word from the stage.
8. Teachers will supervise their classes going to and coming from the assembly.
9. Emergencies in the assembly will be handled by the teacher in whose class it occurs, and the student or students shall be taken out the nearest exit.
10. In the event of teacher absence, the above procedures will be handled by the substitute. Regular teachers will assist in the supervision of those classes whenever possible.

ATTENDANCE (See Also: ABSENCE; ADDRESS; CLASS; FACULTY MEETINGS)

. . .Entry/Change/Withdrawal Form

CIRCLE ONE: REGISTRATION (enter)   CHANGE   WITHDRAW

STUDENT DATA BASE TO BE COMPLETED   DATE: _____
        BY SCHOOL PERSONNEL   Month   Day   Year

STUDENT NAME _____ STUDENT NUMBER _____

SCHOOL _____ GRADE _____

CHECK ONE: _____ Male _____ Female

E CODE _____ (1-White, 2-Black, 3-Hispanic, 4-American Indian,
                          5-Asian/Pacific Islander, 6-other)

ENTER:

  Name of Previous School _____

  Street _____

  City, State, Zip _____

  Check One: Public _____   Private _____

CHANGE/WITHDRAW:

  Transfer in district—new school _____

  Withdraw: transfer to another school   _____ YES _____ No

        in State   YES _____   NO _____

        PUBLIC _____   PRIVATE _____   PAROCHIAL _____

        NAME OF SCHOOL _____

If 9th, 10th, 11th, 12th Grade:
  Did student pass H.S.P.T.   _____ Yes _____ No

HOMEROOM INSTRUCTOR

  NAME _____ NUMBER _____

GUIDANCE COUNSELOR

  NAME _____ NUMBER _____

EVIDENCE OF AGE: BIRTH CERTIFICATE _____

                     BAPTISMAL CERTIFICATE _____

                     SCHOOL RECORDS _____

NOTE: THIS FORM IS TO BE COMPLETED THE DAY A STUDENT ENTERS/
        CHANGES/WITHDRAWS AND FORWARDED TO THE APPROPRIATE
        DEPARTMENTS.

DISTRIBUTION:
  1. Data Procesing Department
  2. Director of Special Services and Guidance (classified students ONLY)
  3. SCHOOL

. . .Letter on Perfect Attendance

Dear Mr. & Mrs. Butler,

This is to inform you that your daughter, Angela, will be receiving an award for "Perfect Attendance" for the current school year during promotion ceremonies to be held next Thursday at the school. Angela is one of only three students who will be presented with this award.

You have every right to be proud of your daughter who has made such a wonderful effort to take advantage of the opportunities that are offered in school. Her eagerness for education cannot help but be satisfying.

Yours sincerely,

John Benson

. . .Memo on Attendance Procedures

MEMO

To: ALL TEACHERS
From: J. BENSON, PRINCIPAL
Re: ATTENDANCE PROCEDURES

To improve the procedures for taking attendance and to eliminate the possibility of class cutting, the following procedures will be implemented:

  (1) All Home Room teachers will take attendance and send the attendance cards of those absent to the main office at the conclusion of Home Room period. Students who report after morning exercises should have their cards sent to the main office in a special envelope marked "Tardy."

  (2) In the main office all attendance will be correlated and an Attendance Bulletin published. The Bulletin shall contain the names of students absent or tardy listed alphabetically, boys and girls, and by grade. The number after a name indicates the number of consecutive days absent, while a "T"

indicates a tardy student and the time listed when the student reported to school. This Bulletin shall be delivered to teachers during Period 3.

(3) Teachers shall take attendance in all classes and record the names of absent students.

(4) At the end of the day, teachers will check their class absences against the Attendance Bulletin. Any student who was absent from class and whose name does not appear on the Attendance Bulletin is to have his or her name placed on a separate sheet which is to be turned in to the office at the end of the school day.

(5) That list shall be checked and returned to the teacher with a disposition of each case, as "absent . . . not on list"; "sent home . . . ill"; "cut class"; etc. It will then be up to the teacher involved to initiate the proper disciplinary procedures where warranted.

. . .Sample Attendance Card

ATTENDANCE CARD

Name: _____

Grade: _____ Home Room: _____ H.R. Teacher: _____

ABSENT—"X" on date   Tardy—Date circled

Sept.	Oct.	Nov.	Dec.	Jan.	Feb.	Mar.	Apr.	May	June	Weekday	Key
—	3	—	—	WV	—	—	3	1	—	Mon.	CD–Columbus
—	4	1	—	3	—	—	4	2	—	Tues.	Day
—	5	2	—	4	1	1	5	3	—	Wed.	
—	6	3	1	5	2	2	6	4	1	Thurs.	ED–Election
—	7	4	2	6	3	3	7	5	2	Fri.	Day
—	CD	7	5	9	6	6	10	8	5	Mon.	IS–In Service
6	IS	ED	6	10	7	7	11	9	6	Tues.	LB–Lincoln's
7	12	IS	7	11	8	8	12	10	7	Wed.	Birthday
8	13	TC	8	12	9	9	13	11	8	Thurs.	MD–Memorial
9	14	TC	9	13	10	10	14	12	9	Fri.	Day
12	17	14	12	16	LB	13	17	15	12	Mon.	SV–Spring
13	18	15	13	17	14	14	18	16	13	Tues.	Vacation
14	19	16	14	18	15	15	19	17	14	Wed.	
15	20	17	15	19	16	16	20	18	15	Thurs.	TC–Teacher's
16	21	18	16	20	17	17	21	19	16	Fri.	Convention
19	24	21	19	23	WB	20	24	22	19	Mon.	TH–Thanksgiving
20	25	22	20	24	21	21	25	23	20	Tues.	Holiday

Sept.	Oct.	Nov.	Dec.	Jan.	Feb.	Mar.	Apr.	May	June	Weekday	Key
21	26	23	21	25	22	22	26	24	21	Wed.	WB–Washington's
22	27	TH	22	26	23	23	27	25	22	Thurs.	Birthday
23	28	TH	23	27	24	SV	28	26	23	Fri.	
26	31	28	WV	30	27	SV	—	MD	—	Mon.	WV–Winter
27	—	29	WV	31	28	SV	—	30	—	Tues.	Vacation
28	—	30	WV	—	—	SV	—	31	—	Wed.	
29	—	—	WV	—	—	SV	—	—	—	Thurs.	
30	—	—	WV	—	—	SV	—	—	—	Fri.	

									Possible Number of Days	
									Number of Days Absent	
									Times Tardy	

AWARDS (See Also: CITIZENSHIP; HONOR ROLL; NATIONAL HONOR SOCIETY; SCHOLARSHIPS; SPORTS)

. . .Announcement to Parents

Dear Mr. and Mrs. Denning,

It gives me great pleasure and a good deal of personal satisfaction to inform you that your daughter, Ann Marie, has been chosen to receive this year's Gordon Medal of Outstanding Citizenship.

Perhaps you are aware that the Gordon Medal is an annual award presented to that senior student at Rock Township High School who has best personified those qualities of citizenship and leadership that are reflective of the highest ideals of American society.

I am happy to report that Ann Marie was the outstanding choice of students and faculty alike. I personally feel that no finer choice could have been made.

The medal will be presented during graduation ceremonies. Meanwhile, may I congratulate you on this singular honor which your daughter so richly deserves.

Sincerely,

J. Benson, Principal

. . .Letter to Award Recipient

Dear Buddy,

I cannot begin to tell you how pleased and delighted I was to learn that you would be receiving the Academic Merit Award at graduation ceremonies next week. Over your four years in this school I have come to know you well through your unselfish work with our student council, and your academic prowess has not escaped my notice, either.

It has been a pleasure dealing with someone who is a credit to himself and his family, and when I hand you that Academic Merit Award next Thursday evening, I will consider it an honor to do so.

I wish you every success and happiness in your future.

With best regards,

J. Benson, Principal

BACK-TO-SCHOOL NIGHT OR ACTIVITY
(See Also: OPEN HOUSE; PUBLIC RELATIONS)

. . .Announcement to Parents

Dear Parents,

Yes, it's that time of the year again. School has begun in earnest, and your children are beginning to settle down to the routine that will take them through the next ten months of their growth.

We would really like you to know our plans for this upcoming time, and we'd like to meet you and have you meet us as well. As we get to know each other, we will certainly come to an understanding of how we, together, can best help your child grow and mature over this coming year.

We are holding our annual "Back-to-School" Night on Thursday, September 24, 19XX, from 7:00 P.M. to 10:00 P.M. at the school, and we would be most happy if you would accept our invitation and come visit with us. The evening will start with a *brief* PTA meeting in the gym at 7:00 P.M., after which parents will follow their child's schedule through an abbreviated school day and meet all of his or her teachers. It should be an enjoyable evening for everyone.

We look forward to seeing you there!

. . .Follow-up Letter to Those Involved

Dear _____,

Do you know what makes a meeting such as last Thursday's "Back-to-School" Night a success? I do. It's the hard work and personal dedication of the people who are involved in it. It's YOU!

Throughout the evening and on the following day I received so many compliments on the general nature of the evening and the quality of the faculty and staff that there would not be room on this paper for the wonderful comments about you. This is highly to your credit.

It is more than evident to me that your professionalism, concern, and dedication to the highest ideals of education were more than evident to all who attended, and were the single contributing factor to the evening's success.

I personally thank you for all that you did to add to this outstanding evening.

Yours sincerely,

J. Benson

. . .Program for

TO ALL PARENTS

Welcome to Rock Township High School's Annual Back-to-School Night! We hope you will enjoy the program that awaits you. Please take this opportunity to get to know your child's teachers, and don't forget to drop by the main office and introduce yourself. We'll be happy to meet you.

J. Benson, Principal

BACK-TO-SCHOOL NIGHT

8:00—General Meeting in Auditorium; Explanation of Program.

8:30—Program Begins. Parents will follow their son's or daughter's schedule. Each "period" will be seven minutes in length. Change of periods will be announced over the public address system:

8:30—8:37—Period 1	9:20—9:27—Period 5
8:40—8:47—Period 2	9:30—9:37—Period 6
8:50—8:57—Homeroom	9:40—9:47—Period 7
9:00—9:07—Period 3	9:50—9:57—Period 8
9:10—9:17—Period 4	10:00—Program Concludes

10:00—Coffee, Cake, and Conversation. There will be an informal get-together in the cafeteria to which you are all cordially invited.

11:00—Good Night! We hope you enjoyed yourself! Come back soon!

. . .Thanks to Parents

Please allow me to take this opportunity to thank you for your kind words regarding our very successful "Back-to-School" Night. It is occasions like this that reinforce my belief that there is truly no limit to what we can do **together** as long as we act honorably.

You give me faith that there will be no problem over this coming school year that the home and school cannot solve together, and I know that your child will be receiving a **quality** education.

Again, thank you for attending; thank you for helping to make the evening a success; thank you for caring!

As I said to the assembled parents last night, "Drop in any time!"

You don't need an invitation!

With best regards,

John Benson, Principal

BEHAVIOR (See Also: DISCIPLINE; REPRIMANDS; SUSPENSION; VANDALISM)

. . .Code of Behavior

There is no doubt in our minds that one of the greatest challenges facing Rock Township's school staff each day is promoting a wholesome and supportive learning atmosphere throughout the school. Promoting effective discipline in Rock Township requires a comprehensive program supported by everyone. We believe that a well-disciplined school not only guarantees a safe and comfortable environment for all, and has a friendly and cooperative atmosphere, but also offers the same set of rules for everyone and provides equal application of all rules.

This year we are asking all staff members to set the following class-room standards for all students:

> I. BE PRESENT AND ON TIME.
>
> II. BRING LEARNING MATERIALS.
>
> III. RESPECT OTHER PEOPLE AND THEIR PROPERTY.
>
> IV. BE PREPARED TO PARTICIPATE.

When teachers discuss class rules with their own students, further delineation of each of these will become necessary.

In terms of disciplining for infraction of these rules, we recommend the following steps be taken:

1. Informal conference (such as after-class discussion)

   The posting of these "Guidelines for Success" in each classroom is "warning" enough.

2. Detention (hold a formal student/teacher conference).

3. Speak with the student's guidance counselor in the hopes that the situation can be resolved before it becomes a problem. Perhaps, you may wish to have the student present when you speak with his or her counselor.

4. Parent phone contact.

5. After these steps, if problem persists, refer student to the appropriate administrator.

The following incidents should result in immediate referral:

1. Smoking in school.

2. Fighting beyond pushing and shoving.

3. Profanity to any teacher or supervisor.

4. Vandalism.

5. Threatening or actual violence directed toward teacher or student.

6. Possessing or being under the influence of a controlled substance.

7. Stealing.

8. Throwing food in cafeteria.

Rules and procedures are a part of life no matter where we work or attend school. When rules are fair and students follow them because they know exactly what is expected of them, their day will be a lot easier (and ours, as well) and Rock Township will be a most orderly place to learn and work.

. . .Letter of Policy to Parents

Dear Parents,

In answer to many parental inquiries, the following is the policy of the Board of Education on Behavior:

The Rock Township Board of Education has the authority to make reasonable and necessary rules governing the behavior of students in school. These rules will apply to all students going to, attending, and returning from school and those on school-approved activities.

Teachers have the responsibility to maintain a suitable environment for learning.

Administrators have the responsibility to maintain and facilitate the educational programs. The principal is authorized by state statute to suspend students for cause. Rules and regulations will be published and reviewed with students at the opening of each school year and will be posted in a prominent location within the school. Copies will be made available to students and parents upon request.

So that infractions of the rules established for student conduct may be treated equitably and consistently, the Board has approved a disciplinary action schedule for the district's secondary schools. School administrators will administer discipline within the guidelines of this schedule and other specific policies relating to student behavior adopted by the Board.

The intent of this schedule is to provide students with a definition of the limits of acceptable behavior and to equip school administrators for their disciplinary responsibilities. The schedule will be interpreted by the principals and their designees in a manner which they deem just, given the circumstances of the individual case. Additionally, administrators will have the authority to enforce other reasonable disciplinary actions which they find warranted by situations not covered in the disciplinary action schedule.

This policy, it is hoped, will answer many questions. If you would like any further clarification, please call me at 234-5678.

Sincerely,

J. Benson, Principal

. . .Letter on Major Violation

To All Students:

Perhaps you are mature enough to accept this: One of the most difficult things any person will ever do is to watch someone he or she cares about suffer and be able to do nothing about it. If you don't know that by now, you will soon enough.

Yesterday afternoon, I stood by in the Emergency Room of Parkview Hospital and watched helplessly as a team of doctors worked feverishly to save the life of one of our students, one of your classmates. As I write this letter to you, he remains in "guarded" condition; the prognosis for his recovery is still uncertain.

Minutes before this scene occurred, this student was standing in the halls of this school preparing to go to class. He could not know that another student who was recklessly violating our behavior code by running in the halls would slam into him, knocking him down a flight of steps, and causing a major concussion and possible fractured skull.

This incident happened because one student was flagrantly disregarding the rules. That student thought only of himself. Now another student lies critically injured because of it.

We do not make rules simply to fill up a sheet of paper! They are for your benefit and protection, and *they will be enforced!*

It was a hard thing to watch one of our students suffer; it will be a hard thing when I deal with the student who caused the suffering and deal with him to the full extent that the law and the Board of Education permit.

I don't want to go through either procedure again!

Understand that the rules are for you; obey them!

. . .Principal's Message on

(A) to students

In any school it is necessary that rules and regulations be established for the safety and well-being of all. Each student is expected to recognize that the school's authority extends from within the building itself to the walls surrounding it, to the playgrounds, and to the buses and bus stops. Some of the more common rules are listed below:

1. Students are to follow the instructions of the teacher in the classroom.

2. Smoking, profanity, and fighting are forbidden.

3. Students are not to engage in an action that is potentially or actually harmful to the safety of other students or adults (running in the halls, throwing an object, pushing or shoving, etc.).

4. Students are not to damage any school property deliberately.

5. Students are not to bring to school the following: radios, water pistols or any other type of "toy" gun, cigarettes or any other form of tobacco, firecrackers, matches, sharp or pointed instruments, or any other dangerous object or substance.

6. Students with projects completed in shop areas may not take them home on school buses.

7. Students are not to leave the classroom without permission, cut classes, or be absent from school without proper reason.

In an effort to see that the rules are enforced in a fair and consistent manner, Rock Township High School has adopted a discipline system. The discipline system explains what is expected of each student and tells the student what will happen if a rule is violated. The purpose of the system is to help each student fully understand what is expected so he or she will not get into trouble.

(B) to teachers

MEMO

To: ALL TEACHERS
From: J. BENSON
Re: BEHAVIOR

Behavior is everyone's concern. We have spent a goodly amount of time and trouble formulating a code of behavior which we all feel is meaningful, reasonable, and enforceable, and which will aid in the smooth functioning of our school. Now, therefore, it is essential that we *all* enforce the code uniformly. It is, in the long run, the consistency of discipline rather than its severity which make it the most effective.

Let us all resolve to consistently and uniformly enforce this excellent code which we have all worked so hard to attain.

BOARD OF EDUCATION (SCHOOL BOARD)
(See Also: FINANCIAL; NEGOTIATIONS; AND ALL STATEMENTS OF POLICY)

. . .Congratulations to a New Member

Dear Mrs. Jordan,

Please accept my congratulations on your recent election to the Rock Township Board of Education. You have before you a task equal to your talents as you work for the ultimate goal of the best possible education for every student in Rock Township.

I wish you success in your endeavors and pledge my cooperation in working toward common educational goals.

If I may be of service, please do not hesitate to call upon me.

Sincerely,

J. Benson, Principal

. . .Letter of Protest to

Members of the Board of Education:

In the past, whenever you have done something that has furthered our common goal of providing the best possible education for the children of Rock Township, I have been among the first to publicly acclaim your actions. Therefore, when something is about to happen which will have a detrimental effect upon our system, I feel it incumbent upon me to openly protest your decision.

Your proposal to delete the Activity Arts programs from our secondary schools due to budget restrictions strikes a blow to the heart of education, which is to educate the total child. While a person may exist without art, he or she cannot live without it, and to eliminate this program as "nonessential" is to take a shortsighted view that can only harm the very students we have sworn to educate and help grow into mature adults.

It is my fervent hope that you will reconsider this proposed action and take it under deep advisement prior to *any* action on your part.

Yours sincerely,

J. Benson

. . .Letter of Support for

Dear Board Members:

Obviously, your job is not an easy one, and, as the saying goes, "You can't please everybody!" That was never so true as recently when you made a unanimous decision to reinstate the Activity Arts programs at the secondary level. While the pressure to assuage budgetary problems by haphazard cutting of programs was certainly clear, I can only admire the courage of the Board in considering the educational merit of the program rather than its fiscal cost. Many students who have yet to take the course will thank you for your farsightedness.

Rest assured that you have my personal thanks as well as my total support in your courageous decision.

Yours sincerely,

J. Benson

. . .Message to the Public

ROCK TOWNSHIP BOARD OF EDUCATION

The control of the Rock Township School District lies with its Board of Education which has been duly constituted and is governed by the state's educational statutes. The Board exercises its powers through the adoption of bylaws and policies for the organization and operation of the school district and is responsible for district operation through its chief executive officer, the Superintendent of Schools.

The Board consists of nine members. Each year three members of the Board are chosen by the community for a full three-year term at an annual election held on the first Tuesday in March. To qualify to represent the community at large, the candidate must be a citizen and resident of the district for at least two years and must be able to read and write. Board vacancies occurring by resignation, expulsion, or death are filled by a majority vote of the Board within two calendar months of the vacancy. Other vacancies or those not filled within the prescribed time are appointed by the County Superintendent of Schools. A Board member does not receive compensation for services.

All citizens have the right to advance notice of and attendance at all public meetings of the Board of Education. Announcements of meetings may be found at the front entrance to the Board of Education

Office, 123 Crescent Road, at each of the 15 schools within the district, and once a year in local newspapers. The following descriptions of the types of meetings conducted by the Board have been prepared to help the community understand the operation of the Board.

Regular Public Meetings

Required by law to be held at least once a month, this is a meeting at which formal and official actions are taken by the Board of Education. The Rock Township Board usually holds such meetings on the first and third Wednesday of each month, the first to handle all items requiring official action and the second to authorize payment of bills. At these meetings there is time set aside for the public to speak and bring their concerns to the attention of the Board. However, if a resident wishes to speak on an agenda item prior to a vote being taken, a written request to do so must be submitted in advance to the Board president and a majority of the Board must agree to hear the request at that time.

Committee of the Whole Meetings (Workshop Meetings)

The purpose of a Committee of the Whole Meeting is to discuss issues and formulate motions to be acted upon at the next regularly scheduled meeting of the Board. No formal action is taken at such a meeting. Although the community may attend meetings of this nature it cannot participate in any of the discussions nor is time set aside for the public to speak. However, if a resident feels that a concern should be considered by the Board, the resident can request permission to speak, in writing, subject to approval by the majority of the Board.

Special Meetings

Special Meetings are those established by state statutes such as public hearings on school budgets, a proposed building referendum, etc. The community may attend and speak at all such special meetings, prior to formal action being taken by the Board.

Emergency Meetings

Emergency meetings may be called without advance notice being given to the community, but discussion and action are restricted to the item causing the emergency. A resolution setting forth the reason for the emergency must first be adopted by the Board.

Public Exclusion at Meetings

The community, as permitted by law, will be excluded from meetings or portions of meetings when items to be discussed might jeopardize the public interest or infringe upon the rights of an individual or individuals. Such an exclusion would include collective bargaining or negotiations sessions, employment termination evaluation and/or discipline of any present or prospective employee, and sessions in which information, if disclosed, would invade the personal privacy of an individual. The Board, however, must take formal action at a public meeting.

Agenda and Minutes

Agenda for all meetings are posted at the front entrance of the Board of Education Office and in the district's 15 schools. Minutes are available during normal working hours and copies of meeting notices and agenda are mailed at the request of a resident at a cost of 50 cents per page. An initial deposit of $10.00 is required from a resident who wishes to be placed on the mailing list.

BUDGET (See Also: ACTIVITIES OR ITEMS THAT REQUIRE A BUDGET, SUCH AS FIELD TRIPS, BUDGET FORM FOR . . .)

. . .Guidelines for Preparation of

To: ALL COORDINATORS, DIRECTORS, AND SPECIALISTS
From: J. BENSON
Re: BUDGET PREPARATION

The following guidelines are to be followed in the preparation of your 19XX–19XX Budget:

1. Distribute all forms as soon as possible.

2. Request your teachers to return all forms no later than Monday, October 20, 19XX.

3. Categorize all requests by budget account categories on summary sheets:

2304.05	Contracted services, repairs
2305.05	Instructional supplies
2306.05	Teachers' in-state travel and expenses
2406.05	Textbooks (all books except workbooks)
2504.05	Library book binding
2505.05	Library books, magazines
2506.05	Library travel, postage
2604.05	AV contracted services, repairs
2606.05	AV materials
2704.05	Guidance contracted test correcting

2705.05	Guidance supplies
2706.05	Guidance travel, expenses, printing
3205.05	Health (clinic) supplies
3206.05	Health (clinic) travel, postage, etc.
3370.05	Field trips
3515.05	Athletic and intramural supplies
7306.05	New equipment
7406.05	Replacement of equipment

4. Fill in a summary sheet for each of the categories in 3 above.

5. Check that all items are in proper categories.

6. Check arithmetic carefully.

7. All totals above last year's amounts must be explained thoroughly in writing. Unrealistic requests will be returned for trimming. All programs, old or new, and large individual items need written explanations. Small, miscellaneous items (under $10 each) may be combined and listed as follows:

   —Miscellaneous laboratory supplies such as test tubes, beakers, clamps, etc. $50.00

   —Other sewing supplies such as pins, needles, thread, tape, and buttons. $45.00

8. Turn in all forms arranged by budget categories, carefully checked and totaled, no later than Monday, October 27, at 8:55 A.M. Attach summary sheet on top. Include all sheets, even if blank.

. . .Letter Concerning

Dear Parents,

As you are aware, the Board of Education is in the process of formulating next year's school budget. The Board members have neither an enviable nor an easy task before them. They are faced with a Herculean challenge of keeping a cap on rising property taxes while assuring the students of Rock Township that they will receive the best possible education.

As a resident of Rock Township, I pay the same taxes you do and I like paying them as much as you do. As principal of Rock Township High School, however, I have a rare opportunity to see, firsthand, what those tax dollars have meant for the children of our community. I assure you that every cent has been well invested in your children's future.

Therefore, if you have any concerns about the upcoming budget, now is the time to make those concerns known. Contact the members of the Board of Education, or let me know, and I will pass on your observations.

Let's make certain we have a budget that we may all vote for with a clear conscience and every hope for a bright future for all our children.

Yours sincerely,

J. Benson

. . .Notice to Teachers

MEMO

To: ALL STAFF MEMBERS INVOLVED WITH
          BUDGET MAKING
From: J. BENSON, PRINCIPAL
Re: NEXT YEAR'S BUDGET

I have been directed by the Superintendent to start the budget process as soon as possible. I guess that means NOW! I know how time-consuming the process will be for all of us, but I also know that we are fortunate in being able to make real contributions in terms of real needs as we know them. So let's start with our performance objectives. What do we need to achieve them—*really* need? State aid is being cut. We must be realistic. We cannot ask for anything simply because it would be nice to have. Here we go!

1. Please read *carefully* the instructions on every form. They vary.

2. Please inventory your equipment and *specialized* supplies. Remember: equipment lasts until it wears out or is broken, like a textbook or a barometer. Specialized supplies are white rats or litmus paper. General supplies like chalk, paper, etc., are inventoried in the supply room for the entire school. Use any system you desire as long as the item is described along with the amount *you now have.* I know the year has just started, but if we do this each year in September, it will give us a good rough idea of how much we need. Check with other department teachers to avoid gaps and duplication.

3. Include a justification statement for each program or group of items on the reverse side of the form. Your department head can help you with this. If a program or group of items

are included in several forms, it is unnecessary to repeat the justification. Merely cite the form on which the justification was written. Without this being done properly, the program items may be eliminated.

4. Include the cost for each program or item plus 5 percent for inflation and shipping and then round it off to the next higher five dollars (e.g., a $24.75 item plus 5% = $25.99; rounded off, this is $30.00).

5. Use a descriptive name for each item or program, such as "Athletic Equipment—hockey sticks," or "Film—Russia Today." Each of these would appear on a different form for a different budget category.

6. Do not include names of publishers or manufacturers. *This is not a requisition.* It is a request for money to be appropriated.

7. Be certain to include everything needed. Money not requested for typewriter covers will not be appropriated.

8. Turn in completed budget request forms to your department head by Monday, October 20.

9. After each request has been reviewed by your department head and by me, the total budget will be typed in book form. It will then be reviewed by the central office. The total district budget will then be submitted to the Board of Education, which, in turn, will scrutinize each category before it is approved. We can then start ordering approved items in April for delivery after July 1 of the new fiscal year.

10. Increased requests over last year's amounts must be thoroughly substantiated, *especially* if it appears that an amount will be unexpended in a given category at the end of the budget year.

. . .Soliciting Votes for

IF YOU HAVE A CHILD IN THE
ROCK TOWNSHIP SCHOOL SYSTEM

. . . you should know that we spend less than other districts to provide outstanding educational programs. We are very proud of this fact:

Rock Twp.	State Avg.	County Avg.	Similar Districts
$4,192	$4,601	$4,524	$4,551

We can keep providing QUALITY education for your children at reasonable cost ONLY if we have YOUR SUPPORT.

Rock Township votes for the school budget next Tuesday.

Keep educational quality high; keep costs low.

Vote YES!

BUILDING (See Also: CUSTODIAL SERVICES)

. . .Building Check

PROCEDURES FOR A "BUILDING CHECK"

Notification: All staff members will be notified via the public address system with the words "BUILDING CHECK."

Procedures:

1. *Teachers in all instructional rooms including the library:*

   a. Carefully check desks, closets, file cabinets, and so on.

   b. Send a student to the office with a note indicating the room number, the date, the teacher's signature and the words "All Clear."

   c. The office will check off these notes against a master list.

2. *Teachers on duty assignments other than the cafeteria:*

   a. Report to the office for assignment.

3. *Should a suspicious object be discovered:*

   a. Never touch or move the object.

   b. Evacuate the instructional area.

   c. Notify the office via a note that you have evacuated room #_____. This will be sufficient indication to the office that the entire school must be evacuated.

General Remarks:

1. Please remain calm under all circumstances. Failure to do so may result in student panic and possible physical injury to students or staff.

    2. "All Clear" or "I have evacuated room #_____" must be sent
       to the office immediately.

Evacuation:

    See Procedures for Fire Drill.

. . .Building Condition Report (Teachers)

BUILDING REPORT

ROCK TOWNSHIP HIGH SCHOOL

Date: _____   Room: _____

1. Physical condition of building needing attention:

Room # _____ | _____ Repairs _____

2. Any other circumstances that should receive the attention of the office,
   e.g., cleaning.

       Teacher Signature: _____

. . .Custodian's Building Condition Report

Building: _____

Head Custodian: _____

For the month of _____, 19_____

Conditions which have been corrected: _____

_____

_____

Conditions in need of correction: _____

_____

_____

Potentially dangerous situations: _____

_____

_____

Vandalism: _____

_____

    Signature of
    Head Custodian: _____

. . .Granting Request to Use Building

PERMIT FOR USE OF SCHOOL BUILDING AND GROUNDS

This is to certify that the _____

_____ has been reserved for

_____

From _____ Until _____

On the Date(s) _____

At a Total Charge of _____

CUSTODIANS ASSIGNED: REMARKS:

_____ _____

_____ _____

_____ _____

Board of Education
Rock Township

Date: _____ by: _____

NOTE:

The holder of this permit should read carefully all "Rules and Regulations."

There must be one uniformed person on duty for each 100 people present.

There must be sufficient fire and police protection to uphold law and order for special events.

Schools WILL NOT be available when school is in session, on Election Day, or during special school elections.

If a school function conflicts, school activities will have preference, and you will be notified.

When all-purpose rooms or auditoriums are requested, kindly notify the Board of Education if chairs will be required, et cetera.

Special service of custodians is not to be expected unless arranged at the time of the request.

No smoking in school buildings.

A CERTIFICATE OF LIABILITY INSURANCE must be filed before the building is used.

. . .Improvement to Building Form

ROCK TOWNSHIP HIGH SCHOOL

Improvement of Building for the Year July 1, 19_____ to June 30, 19_____

Your Name: _____ Room: _____

Department: _____ Date: _____

DIRECTIONS: Include repair or replacement items such as fan motors and drapes or repair and maintenance of the building itself, such as concrete work, windows, painting, etc., and renovations such as removal or addition of partitions.

PRIORITY CODE: VHP = very high   HP = high   MP = medium   LP = low

Priority	Program or Item	Quantity	Item Cost	Total Cost

. . .Letter on Condition of

(A) negative

Dear Sir:

We are all aware that the first thing about us that the public knows is our appearance. Often, we are totally judged by how we appear to the public. Whether or not this is right or wrong, it is, nevertheless, a fact of our existence.

That is why I am particularly anxious about the condition of this building as I have witnessed it lately. I have every confidence that bringing it to your attention is the quickest way to remedy the situation.

I have attached a list of concerns I have received from teachers and other staff members. I am certain that these oversights will be handled with your usual speed and dispatch.

Thank you so much for all your concern.

Sincerely,

J. Benson

(B) *positive*

Dear Danny,

Recently, I sent you a list of concerns from faculty and staff concerning the general condition of this building. When I did this, I knew that you would give them your prompt attention. However, the speed and efficiency with which they were handled has absolutely amazed me, and I want to thank you personally for doing such a magnificent job.

Danny, the place is gorgeous. Honestly, it looks better now than it did the day it opened, and I was there for that occasion, too.

Thank you, Danny, for the fine condition in which this building now stands. I do appreciate your hard work and concern.

Yours sincerely,

John Benson

. . .Refusing Request to Use Building

Date: _____

M _____

_____

_____

Dear _____,

Please be informed that your request to use (name of building)

_____ on (date) _____

has been denied because of the following reason(s): _____

_____

_____

We regret if this has caused you any inconvenience. If you have any questions or wish further clarification, please call me at 123-4567.

Sincerely,

. . .Requesting Use of Building

REQUEST TO USE SCHOOL BUILDING

Name: _____

Name of Group or Organization: _____

Building Requested: _____

Date Requested: _____ Time: From _____ to _____

Describe Activity: _____

_____

Approximate Number of People to Use Building: _____

Name and Address of Person to Contact Regarding the Disposition of This Request:

Name: _____ Telephone: _____

Address: _____

_____ Zip _____

   I hereby state that the information in this application is true and accurate and that, if approved, I will abide by the rules and regulations for the use of public school buildings as set down by the Rock Township Board of Education.

Date: _____ Signature: _____

BULLETIN (See Also: BULLETIN BOARD; HANDBOOK; NEWSPAPER; PUBLIC RELATIONS)

. . .Form for Placing a Notice on the Daily Bulletin

DAILY BULLETIN NOTICE

The following message is to be included in the Daily Bulletin on the following date(s):

_____ _____ _____ _____

NOTICE:

             Teacher's Signature: _____

Please place this form on Mrs. Bordon's desk BEFORE 1:30 P.M. of the day preceding publication.

. . .Memo of Criteria for Daily Bulletin

TO: Faculty
FROM: J. Benson, Principal
RE: Criteria for Notices on Daily Bulletin

I am sure that you are aware that our daily bulletin is an essential part of our functioning during the routine of the school day. As it is, Mrs. Borden takes on the task each day of compiling the next "issue" and does an admirable job of it. We can make her life a little easier and produce bulletins which are shorter, clearer and ultimately, more helpful, if we follow a simple guideline.

Here it is: Items on the daily bulletin must be those that pertain to the educational process and our school, for example, notice of meeting times for extracurricular activities, notice of deadlines for reports or grade lists, announcements of departmental meetings, and the like.

If you want to sell your car, rent a condo, or find out who's interested in playing bridge, use the faculty lounge bulletin board.

If we all abide by this criterion, I am certain that we will produce a succinct and useful bulletin and allow Mrs. Borden to retain her sanity.

. . .Memo on Use of

(A) curbing abuse

Dear Bill,

Just a memo to let you know that I have had several complaints from staff members lately that the daily bulletin seems to be full of lists of names of students whom your department members wish to interview. With these lists, there is the request that their teachers send them to your people at certain times during the school day. The staff seems reluctant to interrupt their lessons by having to keep tabs on the time and on certain students. In short, they resent doing it.

I feel that they may have a point. Certainly, student runners from your office could go to the teacher involved with a signed pass to request a specific student. Or the student to be interviewed could be given a pass the day before to leave class at a specific time. This would allow an overcrowded daily bulletin to have some "breathing room" and would take the pressure off the teacher.

What do you think? I'd be glad to talk to you about it as soon as possible in my office.

(B) *soliciting use*

To: FACULTY
From: J. BENSON
Re: USE OF DAILY BULLETIN

It has gotten back to me that my memo to you establishing the criterion for placement of a notice on the daily bulletin was an attempt on my part to curtail your use of the bulletin. Honestly, folks, I don't know where some people get this stuff, but that could not be further from the truth.

The only criterion established was that the message be related to the educational process of our school. You are the professionals, and, as I have frequently said, I am proud of the stature of this faculty. You know what type of notices should go on this bulletin. I ask that you use your professional judgment, that is all.

Please continue to use the daily bulletin to allow our school as a whole, and your class in particular, to function as the fine educational reality it is.

BULLETIN BOARD   (See Also: BULLETIN; CLASS; SCHEDULE; AND ALL THOSE ITEMS THAT WOULD BE POSTED ON A BULLETIN BOARD, SUCH AS HONOR ROLL, ETC.)

. . .Form for Placing Notice on Office Bulletin Board

OFFICE BULLETIN BOARD

Date of Request: _____

   I would like to place the following message on the Office Bulletin Board:

Dates of Placement: FROM _____   TO _____
                             Signature of Person
                             Making Request: _____
. . . .
Dear _____,

   Your request to place a message on the Office Bulletin Board from _____

_____ to _____ has been:

(   ) Granted   (   ) Denied for the following reason(s):

                             J. Benson, Principal

. . .Hall Bulletin Board Assignment List

To All Teachers:

Please fill in the form below as to which time you prefer to put up a display on the Front Hall Bulletin Board. It's strictly first-come, first-serve; so if you really have a preference, better sign up now. All assignments run from the 15th of one month through the 14th of the next month.

DATE	TEACHER	THEME OF BULLETIN BOARD
Sept.–Oct.		
Oct.–Nov.		
Nov.–Dec.		
Dec.–Jan.		
Jan.–Feb.		
Feb.–Mar.		
Mar.–Apr.		
Apr.–May		
May–June		

. . .Letter on Use of

To: ALL THOSE WONDERFUL, DEDICATED, OUTSTANDING EDUCATORS WHO WILL ENHANCE THE EDUCATION OF OUR CHILDREN BY CREATING A BRILLIANT BULLETIN BOARD FOR THE FRONT HALL THAT WILL ALSO ENHANCE THIS BUILDING AND MAKE THIS PLACE A BETTER PLACE TO BE AS WELL AS KNOCKING THE SOCKS OFF ANY VISITOR WHO SHOULD COME INTO THE BUILDING AND WHO PERFORM THIS INVALUABLE SERVICE WITHOUT BEING HERALDED AS THEY DESERVE OR EVEN A "THANK YOU" FROM THE SCHOOL'S ADMINISTRATOR WHO SHOULD REALLY BE THE MOST GRATEFUL OF PEOPLE FOR THESE EFFORTS.

From: JOHN BENSON

Re: BULLETIN BOARDS

Thanks, Guys! You do good work!

BUS (See Also: DISMISSAL PROCEDURES; FIELD TRIPS)

. . .Bus Card

ROCK TOWNSHIP HIGH SCHOOL

Name: _____ Grade: _____

Assigned Bus: _____

Bus Stop: _____

Date: _____ Signature: _____

. . .Bus Reassignment Notice

NOTICE OF BUS REASSIGNMENT

Dear _____,

This is to inform you that your son/daughter, _____,

a _____ grade student at _____ School,

has been reassigned to a new school bus effective _____,

19 _____.

OLD SCHEDULE:
     Bus Number: _____ Time: _____

     Bus Stop: _____

NEW SCHEDULE:
     Bus Number: _____ Time: _____

     Bus Stop: _____

This reassignment has been scheduled for the following reason(s):

_____

_____

Please call 123-4567 if you require any further information.

Sincerely,

. . .Notice of Possible Removal

_____, 19 ___

Dear _____,

This is to inform you that your son/daughter, _____,

a _____ grade student at _____ School,

is currently being considered for removal from bus transportation.

This review is being made for the following reason(s):

_____

_____

We urge you to discuss this situation with your child. If the situation continues, we shall have no alternative but to remove your child from school bus transportation for a specified amount of time.

You may call us at 123-4567 if you wish further clarification.

Sincerely,

. . .Notice of Removal

Date: _____

Dear _____,

We regret to inform you that your son/daughter, _____,

a _____ grade student at _____ School,

is suspended from the use of the school bus from _____ to _____

_____, 19_____.

This action is being taken for the following reason(s):

_____

_____

We notified you of the possibility of this action on _____, 19 _____. Unfortunately, the situation was not corrected, and the above action is taken.

If you should wish further clarification, please call me at 123-4567.

Sincerely,

. . .Request for Use of

Date: _____, 19____

School: _____

Name: _____

Grade and/or Subject: _____

I hereby request the use of the school bus(es) as follows:

Date: _____

Time: From _____ To _____

Number of Students: _____ Number of Teachers: _____

Place of Departure: _____

Destination: _____

Purpose of Trip: _____

Expenses to be borne by ( ) Group ( ) Board of Education

(Teachers are reminded that the trip must be directly related to the education of the students in order for the Board of Education to assume costs.)

. . .Statement of Bus Conduct

The importance of proper conduct while waiting for, boarding, riding or disembarking from a bus cannot be overemphasized. Any behavior that distracts the bus driver instantly endangers all. In the interest of safety, all students should understand, and parents are urged to impress upon their children, the necessity for strict compliance with the following rules:

1. Students are to remain well out of the roadway while waiting for the bus.

2. Getting on and off the bus should be done in an orderly manner.

3. Students are to remain seated while the bus is in motion.

4. No part of the body should ever be extended outside the bus.

5. Aisles should be kept clear at all times.

6. Conversations should take place in normal tones of voice. A sudden scream or yell is especially dangerous.

7. Nothing should be thrown either in or from the bus.

8. Smoking on the school bus is strictly forbidden.

9. Crowding, pushing, shoving, et cetera, are not only unnecessary, but dangerous as well.

10. Attitudes of helpfulness and cooperation will do much to insure safe and comfortable bus transportation for all.

    NOTE: Attention of students and parents is directed to the state school law, which states in part that, "A student may be excluded from bus transportation for disciplinary reasons by the principal, and his parents shall provide for his transportation to and from school during the period of such exclusion."

Buses will leave the school grounds shortly after dismissal. For those engaged in supervised after-school programs, late buses will be provided and are scheduled to leave the school grounds at 3:15 P.M.

Late buses will run every day, Monday through Thursday of each week.

. . .Supervision of Buses

SUPERVISION OF BUSES

The main goal of this duty is to provide a link to communicating with bus drivers and student riders so that a safe journey home for all will result. Teachers on bus duty are to be guided by the following instructions:

1. Bus duty teachers will be assigned three to four buses to monitor actively.

2. As often as possible, board each bus to let students/drivers know you are there and correct any situation you can.

3. The following steps are to be followed in the discipline process:

    a. *First offense:* assign student(s) a particular seat with a serious warning.

    b. Then, assign student(s) a Central Detention. Place name in Central Detention Book in the main office with your name in parentheses.

    c. Then, refer students to Mr. Jones for disciplining. Have bus driver write up a referral.

C

CAFETERIA (See Also: LUNCH)

. . .Cafeteria Supervision Assignment Sheet

CAFETERIA SUPERVISION

Five teachers are scheduled for each lunch period. One teacher will supervise tables 1, 2, and 3, and a second will cover 4, 5, and 6, and so on. One teacher will maintain general supervision and assist where needed. All rules of cafeteria behavior are in effect.

Lunch Period	Tables 1-2-3	4-5-6	7-8-9	10-11-12	General
A	Mr. Jones	Miss Hansen	Mr. Torun	Mr. Smith	Mrs. Kerr
B	Mrs. Eddy	Mr. Yost	Miss Kern	Mrs. Jerrod	Mr. Winter
C	Mrs. Kerr	Mr. Jones	Miss Hansen	Mr. Torun	Mr. Smith
D	Mr. Winter	Mrs. Eddy	Mr. Yost	Miss Kern	Mrs. Jerrod

. . .Letter on Quality of

Dear Mrs. Sage,

I have never been in a school where students have NOT complained about the food. That is almost as natural an occurrence as erasing the blackboards. That is to be expected, I suppose, and, for the most part, can be translated that we will not allow them to make a meal of potato chips and chocolate bars.

Therefore, when students come to me to request that "Mrs. Sage's stew" be served more often than once a week, that is something to note. I pass on the request, as I am certain that you will be happy to accommodate this request, to the benefit of us all.

I also want to commend and congratulate you for your fine running of this school's cafeteria. Thank you for your continuing efforts on behalf of our students.

Yours sincerely,

. . .Statement on Cafeteria Behavior

Rock Township High School has four lunch periods scheduled into its daily school program with approximately one quarter of the student body in attendance at each. Accordingly, during these lunch periods, Rock Township High School expects that all its students will conduct themselves properly, practice good table manners, and abide by the following rules:

1. Enter and leave the cafeteria at a walk.

2. Form and keep a single line at each service area.

3. Go through the serving line one time only. (The doors leading to the serving areas will be closed as soon as the last student in line has been served.)

4. Be seated and remain seated at your table until dismissed by the teacher in charge.

5. Leave the cafeteria during lunch period only with the permission of the teacher in charge.

6. Refrain from pushing, jostling, and asking luncheon neighbors for money.

7. Enjoy the conversation at your lunch tables. However, loud and boisterous talk, yelling, screaming, et cetera, are definitely not acceptable.

8. Special note is made of the rule that students are not to throw any object—no matter how small, for however short a distance.

9. Do not take food of any kind from the cafeteria.

10. Leave the table clean and suitable for luncheon use by other students.

. . .Supervision of Cafeteria

To: ALL TEACHERS ON CAFETERIA DUTY
From: J. BENSON, PRINCIPAL
Re: SUPERVISION OF CAFETERIA

Supervision of the cafeteria is far from an easy duty. It will go easier for all concerned, however, if we are all aware of certain requirements and regulations:

1. Cafeteria duty extends for the full period. Please be on time and stay until the bell ending the period rings. If you must be late, please inform an administrator.

2. Supervise all food lines. Insist that the line proceed in an orderly fashion without pushing, shoving, or "cutting in."

3. Actively supervise your assigned tables. This includes making certain that the tables are reasonably clean before students leave.

4. If a student misbehaves, deal with him or her immediately. Remove the student from the cafeteria at once. Stop any trouble before it begins.

5. Serious infractions such as fighting or the throwing of food should be referred to the main office immediately.

6. Be circumspect with lavatory passes. Use your own good judgment.

If we all adhere to these guidelines, I believe that we will survive, and our students will enjoy a pleasant lunchtime as well.

CHAIRPERSONS   (See Also: DEPARTMENTAL MEETINGS; UNIT COORDINATION)

. . .Evaluation of

EVALUATION

CHAIRPERSON: _____

DEPARTMENT: _____ DATE: _____

NUMBER OF TEACHERS IN DEPARTMENT: _____

FOR THE SCHOOL YEAR 19_____–19_____

Check YES or NO for each of the following. If NO is checked, explain on a separate sheet.

ITEM	YES	NO
Met all deadlines		
All reports completed		
All observations completed		
Budget adequately prepared		
Held all required meetings		
Requisitions and forms completed		

OBSERVED RAPPORT BETWEEN CHAIRPERSON AND MEMBERS OF DEPARTMENT: _____

_____

_____

WAYS IN WHICH CHAIRPERSON HAS MET PERSONAL OBJECTIVES: _____

_____

_____

OUTSTANDING ACTIVITIES OF THE DEPARTMENT: _____

_____

_____

PERSONAL COMMENTS: _____

_____

_____

Signature of Evaluator: _____

Signature of Chairperson: _____

. . .Job Description

(A) committee

MEMO

To: FACULTY
From: J. BENSON, PRINCIPAL
Re: COMMITTEE CHAIRPERSONS

From time to time it will be necessary to form committees and to appoint chairpersons of those committees. It shall be the duty of the chairperson to

1. Assume responsibility for steering the committee to the completion of its assigned task.

2. Assign meetings when necessary for work and study.

3. Assign tasks in the committee.

4. See to it that proper minutes are taken of each meeting.

5. Be responsible for providing informal reports of progress to the principal.

6. Prepare and present a final report in writing of the findings or results of the committee's work.

It is hoped that this delineation of duties will simplify and define the tasks of all committee chairpersons.

(B) department head

MEMO

To: ALL DEPARTMENT HEADS
From: J. BENSON, PRINCIPAL
Re: DUTIES

In reply to a number of requests, the following is a delineation of the duties of department chairpersons:

1. The chairperson shall prepare and submit to the principal the annual budget for the department and all teachers within that department.

2. Chairpersons shall observe and evaluate each member of the department as follows: tenured teachers once per semester; nontenured teachers twice per semester. A copy of each evaluation shall be submitted to the principal.

3. Chairpersons shall keep account of textbooks and equipment used within the department and shall be responsible for replacement, repair, and/or ordering.

4. Chairpersons shall conduct monthly departmental meetings to insure the implementation of curriculum.

5. Chairpersons shall keep those records as required by the main office including but not limited to percentage of promotion sheets, textbook usage forms, failure notices, etc.

6. Chairpersons shall distribute, collect and turn into the main office those forms, papers, cards, etc., as required.

7. Chairpersons shall receive and act upon complaints and suggestions of department members, immediately forwarding to the office any difficulties which cannot be amicably settled within the department.

8. Chairpersons shall submit an annual report of doings within the department.

. . .Letter to

(A) *outstanding*

Dear Marty,

As the school year draws to a close, it does me a great deal of good to close the door to my office and, as the song goes, "Count my blessings." When I do that, a name that keeps coming up is yours.

Here's what I mean: Not only are all reports, requests, budgets, and the like from your department in on time, but they are so accurately done that it is evident that hard and diligent work went into them. Add to this the outstanding activities both in and out of the classroom that your department has either run or sponsored over the past year, and I cannot help but understand that someone is doing something right, and that someone is you.

The teachers in your department are happy with their accomplishments, the students evidence learning at its best, and the "mechanical" side of it runs like the proverbial "well-oiled" machine. I believe this to be a reflection of the leadership you have provided.

On behalf of the students of this school and personally as well, I want to thank you and congratulate you on an outstanding job. Well done!

Yours sincerely,

(B) *poor*

Dear Mr. Wade,

It gives me no enjoyment to write this letter, but I have no choice. As chairperson of the XXXXXX department, you accepted certain responsibilities that went with the position. Over the past school year, and in spite of many notices advising you of the situation, you have not met those responsibilities.

Only three of the ten required monthly reports were ever turned in, and those were so unstructured as to be useless. Complaints and requests by members of your department were totally ignored by you to such a degree that those teachers had to come to me personally to handle situations which were within your purview as department head. Despite many efforts on the part of your teachers, ideas and suggestions died lonely deaths from your inaction. The job you were supposed to do did not get done.

Again and again you were offered aid in these tasks, and time after time you refused. Indeed, as of this writing, I still have no idea of what prevents the smooth operation of your department.

It is with deep regret that I must inform you that a copy of this letter is being sent to the superintendent, and I am asking for a review of your position within the limits of the present contract.

Sincerely,

CHILD STUDY TEAM   (See Also: CLASSIFICATION; LEARNING DISABILITIES; PSYCHOLOGICAL SERVICES; REFERRAL; SPECIAL EDUCATION; UNIT COORDINATION)

. . .Request for Services of

CHILD STUDY TEAM

Request for Services

DATE: _____

NAME OF CHILD: _____ BIRTHDATE: _____

ADDRESS: _____ PHONE: _____

SCHOOL: _____ GRADE: _____ TEACHER: _____

REASON FOR REFERRAL:

A. Describe the child's school behavior and academic functioning that are of concern to you (specific examples are more helpful than generalized statements).

B. What have you been trying so far in handling the problem(s)?

C. To what extent are the child's parents aware of the problem(s)?

SPECIALIZED SERVICES PROVIDED CURRENTLY OR IN PREVIOUS YEARS (e.g., speech therapy, specialized counseling, physical therapy, visual training, tutoring, individualized prescriptive, or supplemental instruction):

PERTINENT CUMULATIVE FOLDER INFORMATION (e.g., retention, persistent problems, strong points, etc.):

PERTINENT HEALTH INFORMATION (to be filled in by school nurse):
    Most recent screening (dates and results):
        Visual:
        Auditory:
    Other recorded medical information:

SIGNATURE OF PRINCIPAL: _____

. . .Status Report Form

STATUS REPORT

TO: _____ DATE: _____
             (Name of School)

FROM: _____
        (Team Member Sending Memo)

RE: _____
        (Student's Name and Grade)

Dear _____,

In response to your referral, I have been assigned to evaluate this student.

I shall try to keep you informed as to the progress of my evaluation.

If you have any additional information or any questions, please:

1. leave a message for me with your school secretary, and I will try to see you on my regularly scheduled day at your school; or

2. call me at 345-6789 and, if I am not in, leave a message with my secretary.

Thank you for you help.

              Signature: _____

CITIZENSHIP   (See Also: ACHIEVEMENT; AWARDS; COMMUNICATION; DISCIPLINE; LEADERSHIP)

. . .Award for Good Citizenship

Date: _____

To Whom It May Concern:

Be it known that

_____

a _____ grade student at
ROCK TOWNSHIP HIGH SCHOOL
is awarded this certificate for
OUTSTANDING CITIZENSHIP
and particularly for

_____

_____

Awarded by: _____

_____

. . .Letter of Appreciation for

Dear Monisha,

So, you won the award for outstanding citizenship, eh? Now, what could you have possibly done to deserve that? Just because you have served your school through four years on the student council; just because you have headed charity drives every Christmas that you've been here that gives much-needed comfort to the needy; just because you carry a straight A average and still manage to serve on dance committees, social organizations, and the like—are these reasons to give you a citizenship award?

Of course they are! And the faculty and I want you to know that we cannot remember when it has been better deserved.

We appreciate your efforts, and we are proud to have you as a student in this school.

Yours sincerely,

CLASS (See Also: ATTENDANCE; BULLETIN BOARD; CUTTING; LESSON PLANS; SUBSTITUTE TEACHER)

. . .Record Form

CLASS RECORD

Month: _____   Subject: _____

STUDENT	DAILY GRADE																							MONTHLY AVERAGE

. . .Rules of the Class

1. Students are to be on time for class or have a pass explaining their tardiness. Unexcused tardiness is not permitted.

2. Always be polite. Extend courtesy and aid to those around you. Use words like "Please" and "Thank you." Try never to embarrass anyone.

3. If you wish something, raise your hand and wait until you are recognized by the teacher. Then ask fully and completely.

4. Homework is due on the day for which it was assigned. Late homework will be penalized if there is no acceptable reason why it is late.

5. The bell does not dismiss the class—the teacher does.

6. Whenever there is a guest in our room, whether a teacher or student, that guest is to be treated with respect.

7. You are here to learn. If you do not understand something— ask.

8. It is your responsibility to make up work after an absence. The same goes for missed tests and assignments. I will not go to you—it is your responsibility to ask me.

9. Extra help will be available to anyone who wishes it. Please see me, and we will arrange a convenient time.

10. You are not likely to be allowed to throw things around or generally "mess up" your home. It is expected that you will take pride in your school as well. Before leaving the room, each student is responsible for cleaning the area around his or her desk.

11. The class will proceed in an orderly fashion. Consequently there will be relative quiet unless otherwise instructed. If you wish to speak, raise your hand, and you will be recognized.

12. If you need to use the lavatory or see the nurse, come to my desk and ask quietly.

13. Obscene, profane, or vulgar language, hitting anyone, mocking anyone, destroying property, cheating, and bad manners WILL NOT BE TOLERATED AT ANY TIME.

14. All the rules of the school apply.

IF EVERYONE COOPERATES, THERE IS NO REASON WHY WE SHOULD NOT HAVE A HAPPY AND PRODUCTIVE SCHOOL YEAR.

. . .Schedule of Student Assignments

(A) in class

CLASS ASSIGNMENT SCHEDULE

SUBJECT	MONDAY 22	TUESDAY 23	WEDNESDAY 24	THURSDAY 25	FRIDAY 26
Math	homework		homework		homework
English			composition		spelling
Science				report	
History		test			
Civics				debate	
Art		sculpture			
Music	report				

(B) out of class

OUTSIDE ASSIGNMENT SCHEDULE

STUDENT	MONDAY	TUESDAY	WEDNESDAY	THURSDAY	FRIDAY
Adams, Kelly	Office Aide 10–11:15		Office Aide 9–10		Office Aide 11–11:30
Carren, Tom		Trumpet Lesson 1–2		Trumpet Lesson 1–2	
Dorin, Bill	Reading Lab 2:15–3	Reading Lab 9:15–10	Reading Lab 10–10:45		
Lorsky, Mary	Nurse's Aide 9–10			Nurse's Aide 9–10	Nurse's Aide 10–11

. . .Student Work Assignment Sheet

WORK ASSIGNMENT SHEET

For the week of _____ to _____, 19_____

TASK	STUDENT	TASK	STUDENT
Windows	Bill Howard	Board	Sally Emmons
Paper	Jill Lacy	Art Supplies	Jack Kelton
Books	Mary Hunt	Monitor	Bobby Chorter
Homework	Tim Intor	Bulletin	Kelly Greene
Basket	Judy Rich	Milk	Stuart Lansley

Alternate (if any listed student is absent): Randy Maslow

CLASSIFICATION (See Also: CHILD STUDY TEAM; REFERRAL; PSYCHOLOGICAL SERVICES; SPECIAL EDUCATION)

. . .Classification Summary Sheet

CLASSIFICATION SUMMARY AND IEP

CONFERENCE PARTICIPANT SIGN-OFF SHEET

NAME: _____ DOB: _____

SCHOOL: _____ CONFERENCE DATE: _____

CLASSIFICATION AND IEP CONFERENCE PARTICIPANTS

TITLE	*NAME*	*SIGNATURE*
LDT/C	_____	_____
PSYCHOLOGIST	_____	_____
SOCIAL WORKER	_____	_____
SPEECH/LANGUAGE THERAPIST	_____	_____
PARENT	_____	_____
TEACHER/GUIDANCE COUNSELOR	_____	_____
_____	_____	_____
_____	_____	_____
_____	_____	_____
_____	_____	_____

After parent consultation, the Child Study Team has determined that _____ _____ should be classified as _____.

The IEP participants listed, having met and reviewed _____ current educational status, recommend that the following educational program be implemented: _____ as specified in the attached IEP.

I(We) the parent(s)/guardian(s) of _____ have reviewed this IEP and approve the recommendation for programming and placement.

X _____

PARENT'S SIGNATURE   DATE

. . .Letter to Parents

Dear Mr. & Mrs. Smith,

I'd like to take this opportunity to thank you for your time yesterday and the cooperation you gave us in discussing John's program. I know it was difficult to meet with the Child Study Team and all of John's teachers to discuss the many problems John is experiencing. I would like to summarize what we decided to do in an effort to find a more appropriate program for John so that he will have the opportunity to meet with more success in school:

1. I have processed the necessary request form for the neuropsychiatric evaluation.

2. Once this evaluation is completed, and we have the report from the doctor, we will schedule another conference to discuss the findings and possible classifications.

3. A recommendation will be made regarding an appropriate program for John for your consideration.

All of this was explained to you at the meeting, and we are in receipt of your signed agreement to these procedures. This letter shall serve as a confirmation of our understanding.

John's teachers are all very concerned about John and appreciate, as I do, your willingness to work cooperatively with all of us on John's behalf. As I said to you yesterday, please feel free to call me if you have any questions or concerns.

I will be in touch with you soon.

Sincerely,

Janet Jones, LDT-C

. . .Referral for Possible Classification Form

REFERRAL FOR POSSIBLE CLASSIFICATION

(Complete in triplicate. Forward all copies to Unit Child Study Team Administrator within seven (7) days of parental approval.)

Copy of In-School Intervention Plan Materials (Request for Prompt Services) must be attached.

Date _____

Student _____ Date of Birth _____

Address _____ Grade _____

Telephone _____ School _____

Parent/Guardian _____ Teacher/Guidance Counselor _____

Parent Notification of Referral

1. Conference with parent/guardian _____

2. Reasons for referral _____

   _____

   _____

3. A copy of the reasons given for referral and of due process procedures were discussed with the parent/guardian: Date _____

Signature of:
Classroom Teacher/Guidance Counselor _____

Principal _____

Date _____

____ I am aware of this request and have discussed and received a copy of the reasons for the referral and of my rights under due process.

____ I do not wish my child to receive this service.

Date _____ Parent/Guardian _____

Date Received: _____ Assigned to: _____

EVALUATION TO BE COMPLETED BY: _____
                                        (Sixty (60) Calendar Days from Referral)

_____
                    Child Study Team Administrator

CLERICAL SERVICES   (See Also: SECRETARY; SUPPLIES)

. . .Letter Concerning

(A) outstanding

Dear Betty,

Over the years that we have worked together, how many words have I dictated and you typed? Of course that's a question that neither of us can answer, but would you say a million was a close estimate? . . . two million? . . . three?

Whatever the answer, it has been a lot of words, and you have handled every one of them, and you have done so in a manner that has made me look good. That's no small task, and I am grateful to you for all your effort on my behalf, and I am especially grateful for your efficiency, your skill, and your concern for our school.

I am most fortunate to have someone of your caliber working with me, and I want you to know that your services are deeply appreciated.

Yours sincerely,

(B) *poor*

Dear Ms. Smith,

I am writing to you in regard to certain clerical services which you recently rendered at our school. As a member of the substitute secretary's pool you were assigned to our school on October 17, 19XX. At that time I dictated five letters to you early that day with the request that they be ready for signing and mailing by the end of the school day.

Not only were only four of the letters finished by the time you left, but those that were remain unusable. Clerical and typographic errors abound, words are misspelled, and several quotes were inaccurate, certainly NOT what I dictated to you.

You have been in our school five separate times prior to this incident, and on each occasion we have found it necessary to question the quality of your work. Each time, we have tried to effect a positive change which, on subsequent appearances, has NOT been evidenced.

I regret that I shall have to send a copy of this letter to the assistant superintendent for personnel along with a request that your name be dropped from the secretarial pool.

Sincerely,

. . .Request for

REQUEST FOR CLERICAL SERVICES

Name: _____

Date: _____ Grade or Subject: _____

I hereby request the following clerical service(s):
Nature of Service (Describe in Detail): _____

_____

_____

Date Service is Required: _____

Where Required: _____

Reason for Requesting Clerical Aid: _____

Signature: _____

. . .Requisition Form for Supplies and Equipment

REQUISITION OF CLERICAL SUPPLIES

Name: _____ Date: _____

School: _____ Position: _____

I hereby requisition the following supplies for clerical use:

ITEM #	QUANTITY	DESCRIPTION

Place of Delivery: _____

Date of Delivery: _____

Signature of Person Making Request: _____

CLOSING OF SCHOOL   (See Also: DISMISSAL PROCEDURES; FIRE DRILLS; VACATION)

. . .Emergency Closing

EMERGENCY CLOSING OF SCHOOL

The following procedures are to be followed in cases where the school is to be dismissed earlier than the regular time:

1. Students will be notified via the public address system to get their coats and report to their respective homerooms.

2. When students have reported to their homerooms, attendance is to be taken, and a list of students suspected of cutting is to be sent to the office.

3. Rooms will be dismissed in sections via the public address system.

4. Under no circumstances are teachers to dismiss their classes prior to notification from the office via the public address system.

5. During the homeroom period and throughout dismissal, the following teachers are assigned to direct students to their homerooms and to assist during dismissal inside and outside of the building.

OUTSIDE	*INSIDE*
Mr. James—front (buses)	Miss Jacobs—Area between 200–205
Mr. Lee— " "	Mrs. Stevens— " 206–210
Mr. Warren— " "	Mrs. Kelly— " 100–105
Mr. Harte—Jay Rd. (buses)	Ms. Lane— " 106–110
Mr. Calter— " "	Mrs. Hanks—West Wing Exit
Mr. Innis— " "	Mr. Wender—South Wing Exit
Mr. Thomas—Parking Lot	Mr. Lenk—West Wing Bathrooms
	Mr. Kern—South Wing Bathrooms
	Mr. Leon—Shop Area
	Mr. Petrov—Gym Area

6. Upon dismissal of a homeroom the teacher in charge will go to the bus loading areas and assist with supervision.

. . .End of School Year

CLOSING OF SCHOOLS
FOR THE SCHOOL YEAR 19XX–19XX

ALL SCHOOLS:

June 22—Last day of school for students. School will close at the regular time.

June 23—Last day for teachers. Procedures for the completion of all obligations will be made on a school level.

PRINCIPALS AND TEACHERS:

June 23—Each principal will bring the following to the Central Office as soon as possible:

> Registers
> Statistical Reports
> Enrollment Sheets (June)
> Failure Notices
> Tolls—Fines—All Other Reports

PAYDAYS:

The middle of June payday will be June 15. The final check will be presented at the school to each teacher who is present on June 23. Checks for teachers who are absent on June 23 shall be returned to the central office and will be mailed pending any necessary adjustment.

Those teachers on payroll deduction will make arrangements for summer payments by contacting the Teacher's Credit Union.

Home instructors are to get their time sheets and progress reports into Ms. Anderson's office by Tuesday, June 27, 19XX, at the latest in order for the sheets to be processed and charged to the 19XX–19XX Home Instruction account.

PROMOTION, FAILURE, AND RETENTION:

High School:

High school teachers shall fill out on a sheet of paper the names of the pupils in their assigned classes who have failed to pass, with explanation of the reason for such failure. The grade status of a high school student is determined by his success in passing certain numbers of points toward graduation.

Junior High Schools:

Junior high school teachers shall fill out on a sheet of paper the names of the pupils in their assigned classes who have failed to pass, with explanation of the reason for such failure. Promotion to the next grade level in the junior high school, if the pupil is a seventh or eighth grader, is determined by conferences between the various teachers of a given pupil and administrative officials in accordance with junior high school policy on retention.

Ninth grade students will have their status determined for the following year at the total number of secondary level credits they have passed. Ninth grade students are treated in the same way as senior high school students in this regard.

Elementary Schools:

Elementary teachers are asked to fill out only a list of pupils to be retained. Promotion lists or enrollment lists for the following year are filled out elsewhere. Promotion or retention at the elementary level is decided upon by the teachers, the principal, and the elementary supervisor, and often the parents of the child will be involved in this decision.

PERCENTAGE PROMOTION SHEET:

Each elementary school principal is to prepare a percentage promotion sheet for each grade level in the building, that is, Grade 5, enrolled 122, passed 116, retained 6—percentage 95%.

In the junior highs and in the high school, a percentage promotion sheet is to be made by subject rather than by grade level, that is, English 9B, enrolled 100, passed 90, failed 10—percentage 90%. This should be done by department heads in the high school and junior high schools.

ENROLLMENT SHEETS IN THE ELEMENTARY SCHOOLS:

Enrollment sheets for next year should be made up at this time and handed to the principal. The principal will keep these enrollment sheets available in his desk. If the principal wishes to change the makeup of certain classes, this can be done readily. If there is no change, the enrollment sheets are ready to be handed out next fall.

PERMANENT RECORD CARDS:

Elementary Schools:

The classroom teacher is responsible for bringing the Permanent Record Card for each of her pupils completely up to date by the year's end.

Junior High Schools:

At the 7th, 8th, and 9th grade levels, bringing the Permanent Record Card up to date by the end of the year is the responsibility of the Guidance Department.

High School:

At the 10th, 11th, and 12th grade levels, the responsibility for bringing the Permanent Record Card up to date by year's end is that of the Guidance Department.

BOOK RECORD SHEETS AND FINES:

The record of books should remain in the possession of the individual school. If this is done, and books on which fines have been paid are subsequently returned by pupils, refunds can be handled through the school.

When fines have been collected, the building principal should turn over the complete amount of the fines to the Office of the Secretary of the Board of Education. The principal will receive, from the Secretary of the Board, a receipt for all such fines.

FINANCIAL RECORDS:

Records of school funds, and all papers concerning school funds, are to be turned in by the building principal to the central office when other reports are turned in. Information connected with the receipt or disbursal of school moneys should be placed in an envelope correctly marked with the school name, so that this information will be available to the school auditor.

TEXTBOOKS—SURPLUS—REBOUNDS:

Please refer to Business Office Bulletin #126, dated June 8, 19XX.

SUMMER ADDRESSES:

An envelope is provided for every teacher who will be returning in September, for the purpose of mailing the assignment sheet about the middle of August. After the teachers have self-addressed them, the envelopes should be put in alphabetical order and returned to the central office.

FINAL REPORTS AND RECORDS:

Final reports and records must be up to date before teachers leave. The building principal will turn in to this office the reports and records due here and will keep all other records in his or her office.

TITLE I TEACHERS:

All Title I teachers will work in accordance with the schedule distributed by Mrs. Carlson.

Best wishes for a happy summer!

> Jonathan T. Cronin,
> Assistant Superintendent

. . .Inclement Weather

To: ALL PARENTS OF ROCK TOWNSHIP SCHOOL CHILDREN
From: OFFICE OF THE BOARD SECRETARY
Re: INFORMATION RELATING TO SCHOOL CLOSING AND
         TELEPHONE CALLING

This information on the subject of school closing due to weather or other conditions is intended to provide all parents with relevant information in this regard.

1. The decision to close school is made by 5:30 A.M.

2. The township fire sirens are set off at 6:30 A.M., 7:00 A.M., and 7:30 A.M.

3. The school closing announcement is broadcast by two radio stations:

   WUVW—1234 AM—81.2 FM
   KXYZ—1345 AM—82.1 FM

4. The switchboard of the Board of Education should not be called for confirmation of the closing. The decision to close is usually a day-to-day matter, so avoid calling for an answer on "tomorrow," as the switchboard when jammed (i.e., *200* calls an hour) restricts incoming and outgoing telephone calls.

5. Announcement or cancellation of nonschool-hour programs and athletic programs due to inclement weather or other reasons is announced over radio stations WUVW and KXYZ once the decision is made by the proper authorities.

6. ABOVE ALL—DO NOT CALL THE ROCK TOWNSHIP POLICE DEPARTMENT ABOUT SCHOOL CLOSINGS. THE POLICE SWITCHBOARD, WHEN TIED UP BY THESE CALLS, CANNOT HANDLE ITS OBLIGATIONS TO RECEIVE AND RESPOND TO POLICE EMERGENCY CALLS, FIRE EMERGENCY CALLS, AND FIRST AID EMERGENCY CALLS.

REMEMBER—Unnecessary calls prevent actual emergencies from being received.

. . .Letter on Time Lost

Dear Staff Member:

As you know only too well, March 6, 19XX was "one of those days." The snow that fell that day causing schools to be closed early and to remain closed the following day created a situation which has generated a great deal of concern. To meet the 180-day instructional requirement for students and maintain graduation at the Newton Field Arts Center, it has been determined that we will end this school year in the following manner:

SECONDARY LEVEL

March 6, 19XX will be considered a workday; therefore, June 21 will still be the last day for students, and graduation will take place that day.

Secondary teachers will report to work on June 22, which will be the last staff day for the 19XX–XX school year.

ELEMENTARY SCHOOL

March 6, 19XX will be considered a snow day; therefore, June 22 will be the last day for elementary students to attend to meet the 180-day requirement. This school day will be a half day for students. Staff will remain until the end of the regular school day, and this will be the last staff day for elementary teachers.

TEN (10) MONTH SECRETARIES

For ten-month secretaries, this would mean that the last day of work for the 19XX–XX school year would be Tuesday, June 27, 19XX.

While I realize that the resolution to the situation created by the March 6 weather emergency is not one that can make everybody happy, I feel that by closing the school year in this manner and releasing all staff from the previously scheduled June 23 workday is the best possible compromise.

Sincerely,

CLUBS   (See Also: EXTRACURRICULAR ACTIVITIES; LEADERSHIP; NEWSPAPER; YEARBOOK)

. . .Evaluation of

Name of Club or Activity: _____

Evaluator: _____ Date: _____

Number of Students Involved in the Activity: _____

From What Grade(s): _____ Faculty Advisor: _____

Nature of Club or Activity: _____

ITEM	NEEDS IMPROVEMENT	SATIS-FACTORY	GOOD	EXCEL-LENT
Rapport between advisor and student				
Student interest				
Involvement of most students				
Meeting needs of students				
Student loyalty to club				

COMMENTS: _____

_____

_____

Signature of Evaluator: _____ Date: _____

Signature of Advisor: _____ Date: _____

. . .Letter to Advisors

Dear Advisor:

It is the process and not the product that counts. That has been and continues to be our guiding philosophy here at Rock Township Middle School. It applies to our academics, and it applies to our extracurricular activities as well.

As a faculty advisor of one of our clubs, I know that you will implement this philosophy in the activity as well as you have in your classrooms. It is the student and the student's growth that counts, not whether the chess match is won or lost; not whether everyone remembers lines precisely; not whether you have the neatest room in school.

In the past, we have gone to great lengths to place the student first, and I know that you will continue to do this and continue to implement our child-centered philosophy throughout this school year.

Thank you for all you do each and every day.

Yours sincerely,

. . .Letter to Solicit Participation

AN OPEN LETTER TO ALL STUDENTS OF ROCK TOWNSHIP HIGH SCHOOL:

As we begin this school year I would like to remind you that a school is more than a building filled with classrooms, just as your education is more than a mark on a report card or a term paper. School is also the people who are in it, and your education continues with all the experiences you encounter in your school career.

Toward that end, I would like to draw your attention to the fine array of clubs and extracurricular activities which are provided for you. Participation in these clubs can open up worlds of pleasure and fulfillment for you.

Take advantage of what the school has to offer, and you will look back on these days as happy and profitable ones for all concerned.

With best wishes for a great school year,

J. Benson, Principal

COMMUNICATION (See Also: CONFERENCES; NEWSPAPER; PUBLIC RELATIONS)

. . .Between School and Parents

Dear Parent:

It is important for your child to derive maximum benefits from the educational program at our middle school. Cooperation between the home and school is essential if this goal is to be attained. Communication between you and your child's teachers is a necessary ingredient for the success of your child. The following is a brief explanation of various services offered by the guidance department.

Parental Conference

A parent/teacher and/or parent/student/counselor conference provides an excellent opportunity to discuss a child's achievement in school. Parents are encouraged to arrange such conferences with the guidance office so that a mutually convenient appointment can be arranged.

Student Conference

Guidance counselors are anxious to help students with school or personal problems. Students who desire to arrange a conference with their respective counselor (Mrs. Stone, 6th; Mr. Ray, 7th; Mr. Ely, 8th) should inform the guidance secretary.

Student Progress Reports

Parents who have a question about a child's achievement should not wait until report cards are issued but should consult with the student's counselor at the first indication of a problem.

Individual evaluations of a student's performance are obtained by consultation between the student and the student's teachers. A weekly progress report (Friday, or the last day of each school week) that provides an accurate evaluation of the student's progress should be picked up by the student, completed by the teachers, and brought home for parent review.

Warning Notices/Cluster Progress Reports

The purpose of a Warning/Cluster Report is to affect student behavioral change to prevent failure. A notice may also be sent when a student is doing passing work, but is capable and should be urged to do better. This can only be accomplished through teacher, guidance, and parental involvement, which will lead to a greater student awareness of responsibility. Warning/Progress reports are mailed during midmarking period. (Cluster may give a student a report to hand-carry home.)

Sincerely,

. . .Memo on Establishing

To: STAFF
From: J. BENSON, PRINCIPAL
Re: COMMUNICATION

As the school year begins, I again remind you that the home is our staunchest ally, IF we lay a proper foundation of trust, honesty, and efficient communication.

That begins as soon as possible into this new school year. Take or make an occasion to contact the home, even if it is just to introduce yourselves. Get in the habit of talking to the home. Insist that the home talks to you. Invite that communication.

Yes, you may be inviting a problem or two, but I can assure you from long experience that establishing a good line of communication with the student's home will pay you dividends in the classroom and in the progress of your students as well.

. . .Memo on Necessity of

To: STAFF
From: J. BENSON, PRINCIPAL
Re: WE NEED TO TALK!

It was brought to my attention recently by the parent of one of our students that several teachers in this building are unhappy about some recent decisions that I had to make. That does not upset me, since, as the saying goes, "You can't please everyone!"

What DOES upset me, however, is that I heard it from the outside rather than from those personally involved. That hurts. I have always stated that my door was open for anyone any time, and I have stood by that statement. If you have something to say, why don't you come to me and say it?

In a place this size, and especially in a place where we deal with the lives of developing students, we MUST have OUR "act" together, or we will all suffer. Communication is a necessity, for without it, we cannot succeed.

You know where I am. Let me hear from you. We need to talk!

COMPLAINTS (See Also: PARENTS; REPRIMANDS; SUGGESTIONS)

. . .Explanation of Procedures

MEMO

To: ALL STUDENTS AND FACULTY
From: J. BENSON, PRINCIPAL
Re: COMPLAINT PROCEDURES

In any institution the size of Rock Township High School, it is inevitable that there will arise complaints on a number of subjects. If and when these arise, part of their solution lies in following certain procedures in each case. Therefore, whenever a legitimate complaint arises, the following procedures are to be taken:

1. Those with complaints should go the the Main Office and obtain a Student or Faculty Complaint Form.

2. This form is to be filled out, describing the complaint in detail, signed (unsigned forms will NOT be considered) and returned to Mrs. Zeller in the Main Office.

3. Within a week you will receive a reply from me regarding the disposition of your complaint.

4. If you disagree with that disposition, you may arrange for a personal conference.

It is hoped that these procedures will help give every person at Rock Township High School the opportunity to be heard.

. . .Letter of Complaint

(A) to teacher

Dear Mr. Jones,

I read with some interest your "Letter to the Editor" in the November 16, 19XX edition of *The Rock Township Gazette*. In that letter, you openly criticize our school (of which you are a part) for lack of "foresight" in developing a curriculum to serve the needs of students in the twenty-first century. Although you were not specific, you indicated that this need was not being met here at Rock Township High School.

What I find incredible about that letter is not the fact that you have a negative view of our curriculum, but the fact that this is the first time I have ever heard about it.

Certainly, you have had every possible opportunity to express any view you wish to me on a personal basis, yet I was unaware of any discontent on your part, nor did you make it known to the vice-principal or the guidance people.

Rather, you chose to air your personal opinion in a public forum where the only result can be dissension and a negative view of our school and school system. I am deeply upset about this, and I want you to know that I feel you were completely unjustified in what you stated.

I might even have proven that to you, had you the courtesy to talk to me before going to the local press.

Sincerely,

(B) *to vendor*

Gentlemen:

Recently we received shipment from you of 60 gross of wooden pencils, every single one of them without erasers. The only difficulty is that we ordered them WITH erasers.

Our records show that we ordered catalog number AR1762A. These pencils are clearly marked as AR1762B both on the packing box and individually on each pencil.

We try to make as few mistakes as possible, gentlemen, but we still need those erasers the way we ordered them. We will keep the pencils you sent, and you can pick them up here at the school when you deliver what we ordered. Oh, that will be as soon as possible, right?

Yours sincerely,

. . .Reply to

COMPLAINT REPLY FORM

To: _____

From: J. Benson, Principal

I have read your complaint dated _____, 19_____

concerning _____

_____

The disposition of your complaint is as follows: _____

_____

_____

_____

I hope this meets with your satisfaction. If it does not, please arrange for a conference at a time of mutual convenience.

Date: _____ Signature: _____

CONFERENCES   (See Also: COMMUNICATION; COUNSELING; GUIDANCE; NEGOTIATIONS)

. . .Evaluation of

CONFERENCE EVALUATION FORM

DATE: _____

PEOPLE PRESENT: _____

_____

REASON: _____

_____

OUTCOME: _____

_____

RECOMMENDATIONS: _____

_____

. . .Notice of Upcoming

Dear Parents,

The Guidance Department of Rock Township Junior High School will be scheduling students for high school courses on Tuesday, Wednesday, and Thursday, April 21, 22, and 23, 19XX. On those evenings from 7:30 to 10:30 P.M., we shall be holding conferences with students and their parents. Scheduling will be done at these conferences in order to allow all questions to be answered and to assure that everyone is satisfied with the final schedule.

You and your son/daughter, _____, have been

tentatively scheduled for a conference with _____ on

_____, _____, 19_____ at _____ P.M.

If this time is inconvenient, please call the Guidance Department at 345-6789 and arrange for an alternate conference time or date. You may also inform us if you wish us to proceed with the scheduling without a conference.

We look forward to seeing you soon.

Sincerely,

. . .Request to Come for

Dear Mr. & Mrs. _____,

_____ to _____ on _____ has been set aside as the time I would like to confer with you concerning your child's progress. The conference will be held in the homeroom.

For scheduled conferences to be successful, the time limits set must be strictly adhered to. As the conference progresses, if you or I see that more time is necessary, we will arrange an additional appointment.

Sincerely,

_____: Teacher

. . . . . PLEASE DETACH AND RETURN PROMPTLY . . . . .

( ) We shall attend the conference as scheduled.

( ) The time is inconvenient. I shall call the school office at 234-3232 and request another time.

_____: Parent

. . .Role of Guidance in

The counseling process provides young people with a nonjudgmental professional who will listen sympathetically to their problems, offer possible alternative solutions, and, where appropriate, suggest sources of assistance or opportunities within the school setting. Counselors meet with students individually, in small groups if there is a common concern, or in large groups if there is a general concern. Counseling sessions may be initiated by the student, the parents, the principal, staff members, or the counselor.

The guidance department is also responsible for the coordination of all community-based programs which may be presented to the students.

CONFIRMATION   (See Also: MEMO; SIGN-IN SHEETS)

. . .Form for Multiple Uses

To: _____

From: J. Benson, Principal

Date: _____

This shall confirm our:

( ) conversation
( ) meeting
( ) correspondence
( ) appointment
( ) conference

on (Date): _____

at (Time): _____

Re: _____

_____

Comment: _____

_____

_____

. . .Letter of

Dear Mrs. Meyers,

This shall confirm that the cafeteria/all-purpose room has been reserved for your class during periods seven and eight on Friday, April 17, 19XX. It is further understood that the services of the custodian WILL be required following this time period, and it is further understood that you will be dismissing your class directly from the cafeteria.

Thank you for all that you continue to do for our children. This activity sounds as if it will be outstanding. Personally, I will make every effort to clear my schedule and be present for at least a part of it.

Again, everything you wished has been confirmed, and I look forward to joining you and your class.

Yours sincerely,

. . .Of a Conversation

Date: _____

To: _____

From: J. Benson, Principal

This shall confirm our conversation on _____, 19_____ at

approximately _____

In that conversation we discussed the following:

_____

_____

_____

Thank you for taking the time to talk.

CONGRATULATIONS (See Also: ACHIEVEMENT; BOARD OF EDUCATION; NATIONAL HONOR SOCIETY; AND ALL THOSE TOPICS WHERE A LETTER OF CONGRATULATIONS WOULD BE APPROPRIATE)

. . .To Faculty

Dear Faculty,

Well, you did it! You survived another school year none the worse for wear (well, maybe a *little* worn around the edges), and you have managed to aid our students through another school year of growth and development. That's no small accomplishment.

Yes, you are employees of the school system, and yes, you do get paid for what you do, but what I have seen and witnessed this past year cannot ever be recompensed in salary. I have seen you give of yourselves far beyond any written requirements; I have seen you fight for our kids with a fervor that cannot be bought; I have seen you do things and spend hours that are beyond counting. I know you as the dedicated individuals you are.

Therefore, I congratulate each and every one of you for all that you have given over this past year. Our students may not realize as yet, and the general public may not perceive, but we who are a part of that day-to-day quest known as education understand the hard work, the sleepless nights, and the sheer agony that go into the education of each child.

Congratulations, dear people . . . for those who cannot speak and for we who can . . . congratulations on a job well done!

Yours sincerely,

. . .To Students

Dear Students,

Recently, the majority of you attended a special program at the State Arts Center. As you are undoubtedly aware, that outing took a great deal of coordination, since the entire school had to be bused both to and from the Center, and that is neither a short nor an easy trip.

It is an understatement to say that your cooperation, attention, behavior, and general manner were outstanding throughout the entire day. You made it enjoyable — there is no other conclusion possible.

Therefore, on behalf of the entire faculty of this school as well as on the behalf of the Board of Education, I congratulate you all for the superb accomplishments in growth and maturity you made during this trip. I also add the congratulations of the students who will come after you and will participate in other activities such as this because YOU made it so successful.

Congratulations and thanks on their behalf as well.

Yours sincerely,

COUNSELING (See Also: CONFERENCES; GUIDANCE; INTERVIEW; REFERRAL; TUTORS)

. . .By Outside Agencies

Dear Dr. Mellinger,

We have been advised by the parents of Robert Henderson that he is currently undergoing psychiatric evaluation and counseling at your center pursuant to the conditions of probation set down by Juvenile Court Judge the Honorable Jamison T. Rath.

Also pursuant to that probationary order, a copy of your evaluation is to be sent to the Rock Township High School Guidance Department. Please address the report to

Mr. Howard K. Lennel
Guidance Office
Rock Township High School
Rock Township, _____

We would also appreciate it if you would place the word "CONFIDENTIAL" on the envelope.

We stand ready to offer you whatever assistance you may require.

Sincerely,

Howard K. Lennel,
Director of Guidance

. . .Contacting Counselors

HOW TO CONTACT COUNSELORS

Counselors meet with students routinely throughout the year to get to know them better, discuss educational plans, et cetera. Students who wish to see their counselors may come to the guidance office between classes or during lunch and make an appointment or sign the counselor's sign up sheet. The counselor will then send a pass to the student's class.

Students may also contact their counselors as they meet in the halls, cafeteria, classrooms, or other areas of the building.

Parents who wish to speak to the counselor, make an appointment for a cluster or a teacher conference, get homework for an absent child, request a progress report, et cetera should call the Guidance Office and arrangements will be made.

While it is customary for students to see their grade-level counselor, any other counselor is also available to be of assistance.

. . .Notification to Parents of

Dear Parents,

Rock Township High School, in an effort to meet the needs of its students, has a full staff of qualified and certified counselors in the Guidance Office who stand ready to aid students at any time with anything from personal and academic problems to scheduling and college placement.

An individual student may request counseling on his own or such counseling may be instigated by parental request. As a matter of policy, each student is counseled at least once during each school year.

If you have any questions or if you should wish counseling for your son or daughter, please call the Guidance Office at 234-5678, Extension 12. We will be very happy to speak with you.

Sincerely,

H. K. Lennel,
Director of Guidance

. . .Report on

REPORT ON COUNSELING SESSION

Person Counseled: _____

Session Number: _____ Date: _____

Place Held: _____

Counselor: _____

Persons Present: _____

_____

Problem(s): _____

_____

_____

Disposition: _____

_____

_____

Date of Next Counseling Session: _____

Counselor's Comments: _____

_____

_____

. . .Request for

Date: _____

I request that the following student be seen for a counseling session:

Name of Student: _____

Grade: _____ Home Room: _____

Reason for Referral: _____

_____

_____

Should a report be sent? ( ) YES ( ) NO

If Yes, to whom? _____

_____

Signature: _____

Relation to Student: _____

CUSTODIAL SERVICES (See Also: BUILDING)

. . .Letter of Thanks for

Dear Danny,

As you know, last night we held our annual Back-to-School night activities here at the school. It was a great success, and I feel that you must share in the credit for that success.

Not only was the school spotless, but everything, even those twenty-year-old walls and stairwells, seemed to gleam and shine. It was extremely obvious that a great deal of care had been exercised for this building. Indeed, throughout the evening, I received many comments on the outstanding condition of the physical plant.

Thank you for all you have done and continue to do. Please convey my feelings to your crew as well, and please understand how happy I am to be working with you here at Rock Township High School.

Yours sincerely,

. . .Request for

NAME: _____ DATE: _____

 I hereby request custodial services as follows:

LOCATION	CONDITION WHICH REQUIRES CUSTODIAL ATTENTION

                    Signature: _____

. . .Requisition Form for Supplies and Equipment

School: _____ Date: _____

Head Custodian: _____

 I hereby request the following supplies and equipment for custodial care:

QUANTITY	ITEM #	DESCRIPTION	DATE NEEDED

( ) will pick up supplies   ( ) please deliver to the school

                    Signature: _____

CUTTING   (See Also: ABSENCE; CLASS; DETENTION; REFERRAL; TARDINESS)

. . .Class Cutting Form

Teacher: _____ Date: _____

PERIOD	ROOM	SUBJECT	ABSENT
1			
2			
3			
4			
5			
6			
7			
8			

Teachers are to record the names of absent students, check against the absentee sheet, and circle those names not on the sheet. This form is due in the main office at the end of the teacher's school day.

. . .Letter to Parents

Dear Mr. and Mrs. Smith,

I must request that you call my office at your earliest convenience and make an appointment to come in to discuss the actions of your son, Adam, who is a student at the school.

Recently, Adam was referred to my office for cutting his gym class. That, in itself, would occasion some disciplinary action, but what made this so remarkable and convinced me that contacting you was the best course of action was that this was Adam's eighth referral for cutting in the last two weeks!

I am certain you realize how serious a problem this can be. I have enclosed a copy of Board policy on cutting. I discussed this with Adam, but he seemed unimpressed.

Perhaps in a conference together, we can come to an understanding of the causes of Adam's difficulty as well as coming up with a remedy for it, for his sake.

Please make the appointment as soon as possible, as we are all anxious to get to the bottom of this problem and help Adam continue his academic career.

Yours sincerely,

. . .Of Assigned Detention

Teacher Reporting: _____

Date: _____

   This is to report that _____,

Grade _____, was assigned detention on _____

for the following reason(s): _____

_____

_____

He/She did not report to this assigned detention although attendance records indicate that the student was present in school.

. . .Policy on

The following shall be the school's policy on and procedures for identifying and dealing with the wanton cutting of class:

1. Daily attendance is taken by the teacher.
2. Suspected cutters' names are submitted to the office on the daily absentee sheet.
3. The office will verify the cuts and publish a cut list.
4. The teacher will complete an office referral indicating date and period of cut and previous action taken (parent called 2/23; detention assigned 2/25; etc.).
5. The student should receive no credit for the day's work unless it is made up to the satisfaction of the teacher.
6. Three (3) demerits will be assigned by the office.
7. Possible action for repeated violations include

    a. Assignment to the Alternate School Program
    b. Five-day notice and a home visit by the truant officer
    c. Parent contact and conference in school
    d. Suspension from school in some instances

DEGREES (See Also: ACCEPTANCE; ACHIEVEMENT; CONGRATULATIONS; GRADUATION)

. . .Application for Acknowledgment of

Name: _____ Date: _____

School: _____ Grade and/or Subject: _____

Current Step on Salary Scale: _____

Current Salary: _____

Current Placement (i.e., BA, BA+10, MA+20, etc.): _____

New Degree Attained: _____

Date Presented: _____ Subject Area: _____

Institute Granting Degree: _____

Were Courses and/or Degree Approved by the
Board of Education Prior to Taking: ( ) Yes   ( ) No

New Placement on Salary Scale: _____

. . .Congratulations on Attaining

Dear Mr. Seidel,

It does not surprise me at all that you will be receiving your Master's Degree at the end of this month from State University. I say that, because it is evident to me as well as to all who know and work with you that you are an individual of great ability with an insatiable desire to learn and to pass on that learning to your students. It is no surprise, therefore, that your education continues formally.

I congratulate you on this fine achievement and wish you everything good that the future may have to offer. Knowing you, however, I believe that it will be you who will shape the future into something good for yourself and for each and every one of your students.

Again, my heartiest congratulations on this outstanding achievement.

Yours sincerely,

. . .Letter of Acceptance of Honorary Degree

Dear Dr. Pierce,

I am deeply honored that you and your Board would wish to bestow upon me an honorary Doctor of Human Letters degree at your commencement service to be held next month. Certainly, I, personally, am hardly worthy of such an honor. However, as a representative of hundreds of dedicated men and women who labor each day to provide quality education to the youth of our township, I most gratefully accept the degree in their name.

Please accept my deep thanks for this honor and please convey this message to your Board of Trustees.

Thank you again, and I look forward to meeting you at commencement exercises.

Yours sincerely,

DEPARTMENTAL MEETINGS (See Also: CHAIRPERSONS; FACULTY MEETINGS)

. . .Agenda for

ENGLISH DEPARTMENT MEETING
Thursday, November 14, 19XX

AGENDA

2:30–2:40—Minutes of last meeting, correspondence —Ms. Talman
          sent and received

2:40–2:45—Report of Textbook Committee   —Mr. Neri

2:45–3:05—Instructions for Budget Preparation;   —Mrs. Rassler
          New Budgetary Requirements;
          Explanation of New Budget Form

3:05–3:10—Questions and Answers   —All

3:10–3:15—English Department Holiday Party   —Mr. Harrington

. . .Evaluation of

ENGLISH DEPARTMENT MEMO

To: ALL DEPARTMENT MEMBERS
From: K. RASSLER, CHAIRPERSON
Re: EVALUATION OF DEPARTMENTAL MEETINGS

May I ask your help? I'd like you to fill out the following questionnaire and return it to my mailbox by Friday, June 16, 19XX. Please do not sign your name, and please be honest in your answers. It is my sincere hope that this evaluation will lead to improved departmental meetings in the future.

1. Using 1 as the worst and 10 as the best, how would you rate our meetings this year?   1. _____

2. Have the day and time of the meetings been convenient?   2. _____

3. Have the meetings been an aid to you in the running of your classes?   3. _____

4. Have the meetings been informative, providing insights you could not have gotten elsewhere?   4. _____

5. Did you have an opportunity to ask all the questions you wanted to ask?   5. _____

6. Did everything you wanted to discuss get covered?   6. _____

7. Did the chairperson monopolize the time or deny time to anyone?   7. _____

8. Was your "paperwork" made easier by our meetings?   8. _____

9. What one thing about our meetings would you improve? _____

_____

_____

10. Any comments? Anything: _____

_____

_____

. . .Notice to Department Members

ENGLISH DEPARTMENT MEMO

To: ALL MEMBERS OF THE ENGLISH DEPARTMENT
From: K. RASSLER, CHAIRPERSON
Re: DEPARTMENT MEETING

We will be holding our monthly departmental meeting on Thursday, November 14, 19XX, in Room 207 from 2:30–3:15 P.M.

This meeting is extremely important since it concerns our budget allotments. Since we are all interested in having enough supplies to last the year, I look forward to seeing you all this Thursday afternoon.

. . .Memo Concerning

To: ALL MEMBERS OF THE ENGLISH DEPARTMENT
From: K. RASSLER, CHAIRPERSON
Re: OPEN LETTER ON DEPARTMENTAL MEETINGS

There is not one doubt in my mind that the English Department of this school is the finest to be found—anywhere. I have often stated this publicly as well as telling each of you how I felt privately.

One of the things that keeps us sharp is our ability to communicate effectively. We know what's going on, we're in touch with one another, and we work together effectively and efficiently. This fact is a major joy of my academic life.

There can be no communication, however, where there is no knowledge—a fact of which I am certain you are aware. When a departmental meeting is called, it is done in order that we may ALL be made aware of information vital to our performance. It is also necessary in order that we may know each other's minds via the free exchange of ideas. None of this can take place unless you, ALL OF YOU, are present when these meetings are called.

In a separate memo, I gave notice of a departmental meeting to be held next Thursday.

I DO HOPE to see you ALL there.

DETENTION (See Also: CUTTING; DISCIPLINE; REFERRAL; TARDINESS)

. . .Letter Concerning

(A) changes in procedure

Dear Staff Member,

As was announced recently, there will be no late buses for the remainder of this year. Because of this, the following guidelines for our school have been established:

TEACHER DETENTION

There is no doubt that, at times, a teacher-assigned detention is a necessary step to be taken to convince students that consequences result for choices taken to misbehave. It becomes incumbent upon a parent to arrange for transportation whenever a teacher detention is assigned. However, let's face it, this is a NEW concept for our parents and requires CONSISTENCY on our part to make it work. Whenever a teacher detention is assigned, please follow these simple steps:

1. Give the student and parent at least 24 hours notice. (Do not assign detention to be served on the day it is issued.)

2. Fill out a DETENTION FORM that a student must take home, have signed, and returned to you. On it will be indicated name, date of detention, reason for, teacher name, and a reminder to parents to provide transportation. These forms will be available from the main office shortly.

3. Do not send to the office for discipline any student you would have assigned detention to before late buses were canceled. Again, the office should be used as a last resort, reserved for the most serious offenses.

EXTRA HELP

Whenever extra help is asked for, it is clearly the responsibility of the student to arrange for transportation.

AFTER-SCHOOL ACTIVITIES

In all cases of after-school activities, that is, sports practice, play practice, intramurals, and clubs, it is the students' responsibility to arrange transportation.

We've said before that promoting a wholesome and supportive atmosphere as well as effective discipline here at Rock Township requires support by everyone. We hope these guidelines help keep us on track in that matter.

(B) *to parents*

Dear Parents:

Being "kept after school" is a part of our folklore, our literature, and our culture. Invariably, it is associated in most minds with having "acted up" or misbehaved in school. This is not necessarily the truth.

While it is true that students may be detained for disciplinary reasons, this accounts for only a small percentage of those students who do remain after school is ended for the day. Students may also stay for extra help provided by our professional staff, to participate in extracurricular activities such as drama club or school newspaper, or to avail themselves of one of our many guidance functions. Far from a punishment, "staying after school" may be a richly rewarding experience.

This is the way we at Rock Township High view the subject, and we want to share these views with you. We care about your kids, and we are going to do everything within our power to see that they get a superior education—even if that means staying after school.

Sincerely,

. . .Notice to Home of Assignment

TEACHER DETENTION FORM

DEAR PARENT,

YOUR CHILD HAS BEEN ASSIGNED A TEACHER DETENTION. PLEASE ARRANGE TRANSPORTATION HOME AT 3:20 PM. LATE BUSES ARE NO LONGER RUNNING FROM THE SCHOOL. PLEASE SIGN BELOW AS YOUR CHILD MUST GIVE THIS TO HIS OR HER TEACHER. THANK YOU.

STUDENT _____

DATE OF DETENTION _____

TEACHER _____

PARENT SIGNATURE

_____

. . .Notice to Office of Assignment

NOTICE OF ASSIGNED DETENTION

_____, a _____ grade student has been

assigned detention by me on _____, 19_____

because _____

_____

_____

Date: _____ Signature: _____

. . .Notification of Parents

NOTICE OF INTENDED DETENTION

To the Parents of:

_____

HAS BEEN ASSIGNED DETENTION ON THE FOLLOWING DATE(S):

_____

DETENTION HAS BEEN ASSIGNED BY THE FOLLOWING TEACHER(S):

_____

DETENTION HAS BEEN ASSIGNED FOR THE FOLLOWING REASON(S):

_____

_____

If there is any difficulty with this detention, please call the school at 123-4567 and ask to speak to the teacher(s) involved. If there has been no parental contact, and the student does not attend the assigned detention, it will be entered as a cut and treated that way.

. . .Policy on

DETENTION

Students may be asked to stay after school for special help, to work off demerits, or for teacher and central detention. Students are expected to tell their parents twenty-four hours in advance of the date that they will be staying after school. All students are responsible for reporting at the time and place designated.

. . .Reminder Form

DETENTION REMINDER

This is a reminder that you have been assigned detention on _____

_____, 19_____ in Room _____

with _____.

Date of Reminder: _____

Student Signature: _____

Teacher Signature: _____

DISCIPLINE (See Also: BEHAVIOR; CITIZENSHIP; DETENTION; FAILURE; REFERRAL; REPRIMAND; SUSPENSION; VANDALISM)

. . .Code of Discipline

(NOTE: Under BEHAVIOR we have covered discipline procedures for behavior *within* a school. Discipline also extends to the school grounds and should concern itself with the safety of students coming to and going from school. The following discipline code is reflective of that latter philosophy.)

OUTSIDE SCHOOL RULES

Bicycles

Main Building

1. Walk bicycles inside the barricades
2. No DOUBLE riding
3. Ride bicycle on right sidewalk going toward Baily Street
4. Stop at Baily Street and obey the crossing guard
5. Bicycles going up Boulder Road stay to the right

Bicycles

Center

1. No DOUBLE riding
2. Park bicycles in racks along west wall of Center Building
3. NO foolish riding around Center Building Parking Lot

Walkers

1. Stay on cement walk coming out of the building
2. Walk on the left-hand side going to Baily Street
3. No running into streets
4. Stop and obey the crossing guard at Baily Street
5. Walkers going up Boulder Road cross by the barricade on Peter's Place and walk up the left-hand side of Boulder Road to Chamber's Drive
6. Only students living in Westwood Development are to go that way

Playground Rules

1. No throwing objects (such as tennis ball, football, etc.)
2. NO pushing or fighting
3. At the bell, line up quietly and obey the teachers and patrol on duty
4. No rough play or running on the playground

. . .Letter to Parents Concerning Infractions

DATE: _____

TO THE PARENTS/GUARDIANS OF: _____

Your child, currently a _____ grade student at Rock Township High School, has been referred to this office for disciplinary action on the following date(s) and for the following reason(s):

DATE	REASON
_____	_____
_____	_____
_____	_____
_____	_____

Of course you realize how serious this is and how important it is that we remedy this situation as soon as possible.

An appointment has been made for _____ at _____. If you cannot be present at that time, please call the school at 123-4567.

Yours sincerely,

. . .Notice of Improvement

DATE: _____

TO THE PARENTS/GUARDIANS OF: _____

Thank you for your recent cooperation involving your child and the disciplinary procedures of our school. We want you to know how important your understanding and support are to your child's growth. We thank you for your support, and we would like you to know that, by our observation, your child's behavior has improved in the following manner:

_____

_____

We feel that _____ should be congratulated for this improvement. If you have any questions, please call us at 123-4567.

Yours sincerely,

. . .Notice to Student

To: _____
From: Guidance Office
Re: Disciplinary Infractions

It has come to our attention that during the period _____ to _____, 19_____, you were referred to the main office for disciplinary action on _____ occasion(s). A meeting has been arranged with your guidance counselor, _____, for _____, _____, 19_____, at _____. Please drop into the guidance office prior to that time for a pass to Guidance on that day.

. . .Referral Form

DISCIPLINARY REFERRAL

Student's Name: _____ Date: _____

Grade: _____ Teacher: _____

NOTICE TO PARENTS

1. The purpose of this report is to inform you of a disciplinary incident involving the student.
2. You are urged to both appreciate the action taken by the teacher and to cooperate with the corrective action initiated.

REASON(S) FOR REFERRAL:

( ) Class Disruption   ( ) Inappropriate Language
( ) Cutting Detention   ( ) Smoking on School Grounds
( ) Cutting Class   ( ) Insubordination
( ) Lack of Cooperation   ( ) Safety Violations
( ) Fighting   ( ) Rude; Discourteous
( ) Destructive to School Property ( ) Misconduct in Cafeteria
( ) Unprepared for Gym   ( ) Truancy
    ( ) Other (Please Comment): _____
_____
_____

ACTION TAKEN PRIOR TO REFERRAL:
( ) Consulted Counselor   ( ) Held Conference with Parent
( ) Changed Student's Seat   ( ) Detained Student After School
( ) Telephoned Parents   ( ) Held Conference with Student
( ) Gave Corrective Assignment ( ) Other (Please Comment):
_____
_____
_____

PRESENT ACTION AND RECOMMENDATION(S) (For Office Use Only):
( ) Case Referred to _____ ( ) Student Will Make Up Time
( ) Student Suspended   ( ) Parent Conference Requested
( ) Placed on Restricted List   ( ) Talked to Student—Warned
    ( ) Other (Please Comment): _____
_____
_____

For Office Only—Number of Referrals for This School Year: _____

. . .Student Success Code

Dear Student,

The following code should be memorized by every student. It is your key to success. It is short and simple and will guide you through your academic career:

1. BE PRESENT AND ON TIME.

2. BRING BOOKS AND LEARNING MATERIALS.

3. DO ALL ASSIGNED WORK TO THE BEST OF YOUR ABILITY.

4. RESPECT THE RIGHTS, PRIVACY, AND HONOR OF OTHERS.

Adherence to this code of behavior will bring success—YOUR success.

DISMISSAL PROCEDURES (See Also: ABSENCE; BUS; CLOSING OF SCHOOL; VACATION; YEAR-END MATTERS)

. . .Early

EARLY DISMISSAL

In the event of early dismissal from school for whatever reason, the procedures for normal dismissal shall be followed with the following exceptions:

1. Teachers in Rooms 200–212 will proceed to the bus loading areas and supervise the leaving of all buses.

2. Teachers in Rooms 100–112 will supervise the halls and see to it that ALL students leave the building within five minutes of the dismissal.

3. Five minutes after the early dismissal, the custodians will lock all doors except the exit by the main office.

4. Teachers may leave five minutes after the last child has left the building.

. . .Final Day of School

MEMO

To: ALL FACULTY
From: J. BENSON, PRINCIPAL
Re: DISMISSAL PROCEDURES FOR THE LAST DAY
OF SCHOOL

To ensure a safe and rapid dismissal on the final day of school, the following procedures and assignments have been developed. The cooperation of the entire faculty is imperative for its success. I know that I can count on you.

1. General Information:
   a. No students are to be sent to the library or out of any classroom without a pass from the teacher.
   b. Lavatories will not be open during periods 7 and 8.
   c. Once students are outside, all interior doors (except for the door by the main office) will be locked.

2. From the beginning of period 8 until 15 minutes after dismissal, the following staff members are assigned as follows:

FIRST FLOOR:

Mr. Bartrum	Exit 11 (Near Shop Area)
Mrs. Colfax	Exit 10 (Near Nurse's Office)
Mr. James	Exit 7 (Gym Corridor)
Mr. Kerrington	Exit 8 (Near Side Parking Lot)
Mr. Lennel	Exit 1 (Main Door)
Mr. Hartnett	Exit 4 (Near Room 112)
Mrs. Wenz	Exit 2 (Across from Guidance)
Miss Johnson	Exit 3 (Near Room 108)
Mrs. Farrel	Exit 6 (Near Room 107)
Mr. Carlson	Exit 5 (Near Library)
Mrs. Houseman	Exit 12 (Near Room 101)

SECOND FLOOR:

Mrs. Marks	North Stairs Exit (Near Room 200)
Mrs. Geller	Center Stairs Exit (Near Room 205)
Mrs. Palusi	South Stairs Exit (Near Room 212)

OUTSIDE:

Mr. Quinn	Side Parking Lot
Mrs. Innes	Front Parking Lot

Mrs. Renner   Front Parking Lot
Mr. Dalton   Front of Building

3. Dismissal Procedures:
   a. On a staggered schedule, rooms will be dismissed via the public address system or in person by an administrator.
   b. Teachers are to ACCOMPANY their classes to the outer doors specified and then are to take their assigned bus duty posts.
   c. Once outside, no student will be permitted in the building.

4. Dismissal Schedule:

FIRST DISMISSAL:

Rooms 200, 201, 202,
       203, 204, 205,
       206   —Center Stairs ONLY to Exit 3 and Out

Rooms 207, 208, 209
       210, 211, 212   —South Stairs ONLY to Exit 4 and Out

SECOND DISMISSAL:

Rooms 100, 101, 102,
       103, 104, 105,
       106   —Exit 3 ONLY

Rooms 107, 108, 109,
       110, 111, 112   —Exit 2 ONLY

THIRD DISMISSAL:

Gyms, Shop Classes, and
All Activity Arts Rooms   —Main Door ONLY

5. Bus Duty Posts:

FRONT OF BUILDING: ROUND RIDGE ROAD:

Ms. Yarrow   Mr. Jacobs
Mr. Manners   Mr. Jordan
Mrs. Falthough   Mrs. Baily
Mr. Keats   Mr. Shelly
Mrs. Hunt   Mrs. Todd
Mrs. Melville   Mrs. Arran
Mr. Calle   Mr. Geld
Mr. Kranmer   Mrs. Lansing
Mr. Vickers   Mrs. Monk
Mrs. Tanner
Ms. Halley

. . .Normal

DISMISSAL PROCEDURES

1. The bell ending the school day shall ring at 2:45 P.M.
2. Bus Duty teachers will lock their rooms and report to their assigned bus loading areas where they will supervise until all buses leave.
3. After-School Hall Duty teachers will supervise in the halls. By 2:50 P.M. all students are to be either out of the building or engaged in extracurricular activities, detention, or extra help.
4. All teachers will help to supervise students leaving the building.

. . .Special

To: STAFF
From: J. BENSON, PRINCIPAL
Re: DISMISSAL PROCEDURES FOR FRIDAY,
          OCTOBER 23, 19XX.

As you know, October 23 is the date when we shall have our school-wide "CAREER CHOICE AWARENESS DAY." Certainly, this will be an exciting and enriching experience, but, at the time of normal dismissal, students will be scattered throughout the building. Therefore, the following "SPECIAL" dismissal procedures will be in force:

1. Hall Duty teachers will check all passes during period 8. Any student without a pass is to be escorted back to the room he or she came from.
2. After-School supervision teachers will leave period 8 five minutes prior to the end of the school day and will actively supervise the halls until all students have left the building.
3. Students will be advised to visit lockers prior to period 8. Therefore, students are to leave from the period 8 room and go directly to buses.
4. Since this is Friday, NO student will stay in the building for any reason. All students should be clear of the building by 2:50 at the latest.
5. If ALL teachers would lend a hand during this "special" dismissal, it would be greatly appreciated.

As in the past, I know that your competency and cooperation can be counted upon to make this a smooth and effortless dismissal. Thank you so very much!

DRINKING OF ALCOHOLIC BEVERAGES ON SCHOOL GROUNDS (See Also: BEHAVIOR; BUILDING; DISCIPLINE; REFERRAL)

. . .Notice to Parents

Dear _____,

   Please be informed that on _____, 19_____, your son/daughter _____, _____ grade student, was reported to the main office for the possession and/or consumption of alcoholic beverages on school grounds. Specifically:

_____

_____

_____

   As you may be aware, this is a violation of the policy set down by the Rock Township Board of Education.

   That policy sets a three-day suspension as punishment for the offense, and your son/daughter is hereby suspended from school on _____,

_____, and _____, 19_____.

   You are urged to discuss this matter with your child. If you have any questions, please call me at 234-5678.

Sincerely,
J. Benson, Principal

. . .Letter on Major Infraction

(A) to faculty member

Dear Mr. Majors,

   It is with deep regret that I must write this letter detailing an incident that occurred on Thursday, February 18, 19XX, at 8:15 A.M.

   At that time, I was called from my office to the first floor hall opposite Room 98, your homeroom. When I arrived, I found you sitting on the floor, resting against a wall. As I approached, I detected the strong odor of alcohol. When the chairperson of your department and I tried to talk to you, I observed that your speech was slurred. It was also apparent that your movements were curtailed, and, indeed, you made it to the main office only with physical assistance. At that point, you verbalized that you may have had a little "wake-up" drink, but you could not see what all the fuss was about. At this point you were driven home.

Only the fact that students had not yet entered the building kept this incident from becoming a tragedy. This was extremely unprofessional on your part, and a copy of this letter is being sent to the Board of Education with a recommendation for disciplinary action of the most serious type, since this is hardly the first time that something of this nature has happened.

Sincerely,

(B) *to student*

Dear Bobby,

How sad it was for me to have to visit you in the nurse's office on Wednesday, March 8, 19XX. I hate to see any of our students in a distressed situation. How sadder still that your distress was caused by your intake of alcohol here at school during the school day. Nothing is sadder than watching a young person throw away his or her future for something as meaningless as alcohol.

We want to help you, and unless you allow us to help you, we must see to it that you do not negatively influence the rest of our students. Therefore, I seriously urge you to cooperate fully during these next few days in what may be the best thing that has ever happened to you.

The future is bright; I want you to be a part of it.

Sincerely,

. . .Policy on

While the Rock Township Board of Education recognizes that alcoholic beverages may be a part of the social interaction of many adults, it is also aware that the students are not adults, and that the school building and grounds are public buildings. As public buildings they are subject to Rock Township Municipal Code 27:18–46. Therefore, the consumption and/or possession of alcoholic beverages on school grounds shall not be allowed. Adults who violate this policy shall be subject to the Municipal Code mentioned above; students will receive a three-day out-of-school suspension and parents will be notified of the reason for the suspension.

DRUGS   (See Also: BEHAVIOR; DISCIPLINE; MEDICAL; REFERRAL; SUSPENSION)

. . .Notice of Program on

ATTENTION!   ATTENTION!   ATTENTION!
PARENTS OF ROCK TOWNSHIP STUDENTS

Choose the correct answer to complete this statement:

DRUGS ARE . . .

   (a) destroying our youth, our homes, our communities.

   (b) a major cause of every type of crime and perversion.

   (c) everywhere; in every community.

   (d) all of the above.

If you chose "d" then you not only have some knowledge of this menace, but you will benefit from the

ROCK TOWNSHIP DRUG AWARENESS PROGRAM

Thursday, April 2, 19XX   8:00 P.M. at the school

You'll find that there is yet another choice, choice "E" if you will . . .

DRUGS ARE . . .

   (e) beatable!

   BE THERE . . . PLEASE . . . FOR EVERYONE'S SAKE.

. . .Notification of Parents

Dear _____,

   We regret the necessity of having to contact you on a very serious matter. On _____, 19_____, your son/daughter,

_____, a _____ grade student at our school, was referred to our office for the illegal possession and/or use of drugs. Specifically: _____

_____

_____

As we are sure you are aware, this is a violation not only of the Board of Education policy, but of civil law as well.

Your son/daughter is hereby suspended from school pending action of the Board of Education. You and your son/daughter have certain legal rights in these actions, and you are requested to call 234-5678 at your earliest convenience to arrange for a conference.

May we hear from you soon?

Sincerely,
J. Benson, Principal

. . .Policy on

The possession and/or use of a controlled dangerous substance, narcotic, and/or other illegal drug or drugs as defined by State Law 29:33–14 and 29:33–15 are illegal and therefore prohibited on school grounds. Students found in possession of, or using, the aforesaid substances shall be suspended forthwith from school until such a time as the Board of Education shall act upon the case. The parents of the offending student shall be notified of their legal rights, and due process shall be followed. The Board reserves the right to call in outside civil authorities where it deems it appropriate.

EDITORIAL   (See Also: NEWSPAPER; NEWS RELEASES; PUBLIC RELATIONS)

. . .Answering Editorials

(A) in local newspaper

Dear Sir:

In the Thursday, November 14, 19XX, issue of the *Rock Township Register,* your editorial entitled "Toward Tomorrow" called for increasing courses that were geared for "the needs of tomorrow's citizens," specifically the introduction of courses in computer technology and programming. Your editorial further stated that Rock Township High School must be "held accountable" for this "disturbing lack of foresight."

As principal of Rock Township High School, I feel that I would indeed be derelict in my duties if I did not answer your comments and clear the air of an obvious misunderstanding. Some four years ago the courses which you mention were proposed by curriculum committees and subsequently approved by the Rock Township Board of Education. The only obstacles were the hiring of qualified teachers and the purchase of a computer commensurate with the needs of the classes.

As you are undoubtedly aware, the budget has been defeated for the past four years running. Each defeat entailed a reappraisal of monetary allotments, and the outlay for the computer courses had to be weighed against possible cuts in the basic curriculum. Surely, your newspaper is not suggesting that we cut back courses in basic English and math. No one wants that. At the same time, the courses you suggest will be possible only when there is a sufficiency of funds to allow for their implementation.

I fail to see, therefore, how you can hold Rock Township High School responsible for not offering courses which are beyond our fiscal possibility to offer.

Sincerely,

J. Benson, Principal
Rock Township High School

(B) in school newspaper

I am happy to have this opportunity to answer the editorial in the last issue of "The Rocket." In that editorial it was charged that the administration of this school did not take student opinion into account when making decisions. I feel that it is my duty to answer this charge.

In making decisions relative to the good of Rock Township High School, it has always been the policy and the practice of the main office to solicit opinions from the students, to advise them of the situation requiring change, and to involve students in the decision-making process wherever possible. Toward those ends we have placed suggestion boxes in the main office and guidance office, and all signed suggestions are answered. We have a process for making a complaint as well. The student council (which represents the student body) has been consulted on all matters that include the students of this school. Moreover, there has been established a Student Advisory Committee whose functions include investigating student response to various suggestions and directives from the main office.

To me, all of this certainly spells involvement in every possible manner. If, however, there are other constructive suggestions that the editors of "The Rocket" have to offer, I always stand ready to discuss the matter with them.

J. Benson, Principal

. . .Principal's Editorial in Student Newspaper

It is a great pleasure to be able to write this editorial in the first issue of "The Rock Township High School Rocket" for this school year.

"The Rocket" is *your* school newspaper. As such it reflects and reports on the happenings at Rock Township High School over the school year. We are all a part of it, since it is a mirror of all that we do. Years from now, when we look back upon the hours and days spent here, it will be publications like "The Rocket" that will aid our memories and help us recall the activities, events, and functions, the happy and the sad, the troubles and the triumphs of our school careers.

Let us, then, do everything in our power to support "The Rocket" and its efforts on our behalf. Make sure you get every issue. Read it, contribute to its efforts, and if you should disagree with any of its opinions or editorials, there is an opportunity for you to answer those statements by writing letters to the editor.

I know that my office will always be open to members of "The Rocket" staff. I also hope that all students will cooperate and take advantage of all that is offered in this fine publication.

J. Benson, Principal

. . .Response to Negative Editorial

Dear Sir:

In your editorial of March 6, 19XX, you stated that the principal of Rock Township has "no respect for the students" of Rock Township High School, or for your newspaper, since no reply to your previous editorial had been forthcoming.

In answer, I would first say that I find your entire editorial to be highly offensive and insulting. It strikes me as incongruous that an editorial that starts out hailing "fairness" and "mutual admiration" as the *sine qua non* of effective human relations should relegate itself to name calling and unfounded accusation. Surely you are aware that respect is a quality gotten by giving it to others. I offered to meet with you; you refused. I offered to explain the situation to you; you refused. Had you allowed for that explanation, you might have had all the facts on which to base your editorial rather than half-truths and innuendo. If *this* is the criteria for "respect," I wonder who could ever achieve it?

Rather than strike out in a blind, haphazard, and potentially dangerous manner, I now, publicly, invite you to come to Rock Township High School at *your* convenience to ascertain some facts on which to base future editorials.

It is my sincere wish that you will seek out the truth soon, and I assure you that my only regret is that you refused to allow me to give you these facts prior to your editorial and the unwarranted damage it may have caused.

ENCOURAGEMENT (See Also: CONGRATULATIONS; RECOGNITION; THANKS)

. . .During Difficult Times

(A) to staff members

To: PROFESSIONAL STAFF
From: J. BENSON, PRINCIPAL
Re: CONCERNS ABOUT BUDGET CRISIS

As you are aware, I met with all department coordinators on Friday, March 3, 19XX, to discuss the continuing saga of our budget and the impact it will have upon our schools.

I will also be meeting with the superintendent later this week in order that I may have as much accurate information as possible.

Your coordinator will brief you in regard to our meeting, and please note that we will have a full faculty meeting on Thursday, March 16, to discuss the school budget.

In the meantime, please know that I continue to be a strong advocate of ALL the programs we offer here at Rock Township High School, and I am convinced that we need each and every teacher in order to continue to provide our students with a quality education. Please understand that I will continue to fight for the retention of all programs and all staff.

I would like to encourage you to see any member of the administrative team to discuss any of your concerns regarding teaching schedules and/ or assignments for the next academic year. You may see us in person or drop us a note in our mailboxes, as you wish.

Finally, please be assured of my personal gratitude for making Rock Township the outstanding school that it is. We have come through worse, ladies and gentlemen, and we will come through this as we always have— together.

(B) to students and parents

Dear Parents,

As I have often written, the Middle School is the most crucial educational period, as we must not only challenge students with an appropriate academic program, but we must meet their educational needs at the same time. Both content and the student must be valued.

A true Middle School must be able to point to its direct, intentional efforts designed to enhance the self-esteem of pupils. Enhancing self-esteem is a basic responsibility of middle-level education. Our students are persons first, students second. Even those educators whose nearly exclusive educational priorities center around the cognitive domain will find the achievement of their ends is most likely to be attained if the school gives direct attention to the business of helping "kids."

Even now, as we are in the midst of a swing toward more academic requirements and tougher standards, there is talk about improving self-esteem of young people.

Like everything else that is really worth doing, the matter of enhancing self-concept and self-esteem comes down to hard work over the long haul. It requires that we reconsider our curriculum plans, thinking about self-perception each step along the way. It requires that we consciously reexamine our teaching behavior and administrative procedures no matter how long they have been practiced. And it even requires that we continue to know our "kids" even better than we do now.

Beyond any doubt, we must continue to meet student needs or we will probably be unsuccessful in our teaching efforts. I want to say again that it is our professional job to help children to grow, to learn, and to mature, and we need the help and support of all parents and guardians.

As this is our third year as a Middle School I can, with great pride, state that we have moved from the transitional stages to the forefront of middle-level education. Needless to say, this is not enough as our entire staff has the common goal of making Rock Township an exemplary school. With your help and continued support we can make it!

. . .Message on the Need for

Let's face it, folks. We all like a pat on the back every now and then. Call it positive reinforcement, call it stroking, call it motivational technique—it feels good when somebody tells us we are doing a good job and encourages us to "keep up the good work."

If we, in our "advanced" (well, some of us, anyway) years, feel good about encouragement and compliments from our peers, how much more significant will such statements be to our growing, changing students?

Come on, folks. Certainly we can find the good if we look for it, and certainly we can afford to tell a kid how well he or she is doing; send home a note that is highly positive; take the time for a phone call to tell a parent (or a student) that you appreciate his or her efforts.

Believe me, we will reap benefits far beyond the immediate gratification of making someone happy.

I know you'll try it, for I know how positive you are. And, if along the way, as you're passing out the encouragement, you should think of me— well, I'll leave that to your imagination!

. . .To Entire Faculty

Dear Faculty,

"Now in these hot days is the mad blood stirring . . ."

No, that was NOT written about our students. It's from *Romeo and Juliet,* but as we all know, the sentiment applies, especially now as the school year draws to a close and our students grow more and more restless as the hot days of summer approach.

That's why I wanted to write to you to encourage you to "hang in there" as it were during these last two weeks. The more experienced teachers can tell you; this is the most difficult time of the school year, and the time that requires the most perseverance, the most attention to detail, and the most concentrated effort on your part.

Now, with our student's "mad blood stirring," our cool heads must prevail. So, hang in, hang tough, hang together, and we'll make it as we always have.

EQUIPMENT   (See Also: BUDGET; SUPPLIES; TEXTBOOKS)

. . .A-V Equipment Budget Form

BUDGET FORM FOR AUDIO-VISUAL MATERIALS

Name: _____

Department: _____ Room: _____

DIRECTIONS: Include the two general categories listed below. Do NOT
include film rentals, field trips, or maps.

I. RAW MATERIALS: Example: Unexposed film, flash bulbs, blank video tape, etc. Please include justification.

TOTAL COST	ITEM	QUANTITY

II. PREPARED MATERIALS: Example: Filmstrips, records, prepared cassette tapes, prepared transparencies, etc.

TOTAL COST	ITEM	QUANTITY

GRAND TOTAL (Parts I and II): _____

. . .Equipment Replacement Form

Replacement of Equipment for Year: _____

Name: _____ Room: _____

Department: _____ Date: _____

DIRECTIONS: Include replacement items of a permanent nature, usually costing above $25. A justification of need for each item or program must be written on the reverse side of this sheet. Absence of a justification statement or placement of an item on the wrong forms may result in the item being eliminated.

PRIORITY CODE: VHP = Very High   HP = High   MP = Medium   LP = Low

PRIORITY	PROGRAM OR ITEM	QUANTITY	ITEM COST	TOTAL COST
			Total This Page	
			Grand Total	

. . .Letter on the Use of

(A) *negative*

Dear Mr. Vickers,

As you are aware, your Community Children's Sports League has been given permission to use our school gymnasium on Tuesday nights. As you are also aware, I personally wrote a letter requesting that you be allowed to use the gym equipment during your meetings.

I am sorry to inform you that this arrangement does not seem to be working out. I was informed this morning that several items of equipment had been taken from storage in the gym area and left overnight lying on the gym floor. Moreover, one of the mats had a large rip in it and was lying stuck under the bleacher seats.

I wish you would contact me as soon as possible in order that this matter may be settled amicably on all sides.

Yours sincerely,

(B) *positive*

Dear Mrs. Barnes,

I think I may be able to help you.

You have been bringing your 4-H club into our school for some time now, and have been using our home economics rooms for your meetings. I will tell you frankly that at first, I was somewhat reticent about allowing anyone outside the school to use our equipment. In the days and months and years that followed, however, I have seen my concern vanish.

You and your club have always left those rooms and the equipment in them in pristine condition. When we enter a room and find it better than we left it, we know someone's doing something right. That someone is you, and we deeply appreciate it.

Therefore, we would like to offer you the use of some of the new equipment that has just come into the department. This would require a little training, and if you will contact me, I'll happily make arrangements.

Again, thank you for your years of care and concern—we look forward to many more.

Yours sincerely,

. . .New Equipment Requisition Form

New Equipment for Year: _____

Name: _____ Room: _____

Department: _____ Date: _____

DIRECTIONS: Include new equipment, both instructional and other, such as furniture, machinery, etc. EQUIPMENT is usually interpreted as items which cost $25 per item or more and will have a useful life of two years or more. A justification of need for each item or program must be written on the reverse side of this sheet. Absence of a justification statement or placement of items on wrong forms may result in the item being eliminated.

PRIORITY CODE: VHP = Very High   HP = High   MP = Medium   LP = Low

PRIORITY	PROGRAM OR ITEM	QUANTITY	ITEM COST	TOTAL COST
			Total This Page	
			Grand Total	

EVALUATION   (See Also: ACCOUNTABILITY; OBSERVATION; REPORT CARDS; SPECIAL EDUCATION; STUDENT TEACHER; YEAR-END MATTERS)

. . .Complete Procedures for (as per contract)

TEACHER EVALUATION

I. GENERAL ASPECTS

A. Foundation

To ensure agreement with and common understanding of the specific tasks and duties for which the teaching staff member is responsible, the written job description for the position held by the teaching staff member will form the foundation of the evaluation. The teaching staff member's performance will be assessed in terms of the degree of excellence with which he or she carries out the specific duties and responsibilities set forth in the job description and the individual professional improvement plan. The annual written performance report shall constitute the composite evaluation and shall summarize performance reports, incident reports, the revised individual professional improvement plan, and any other pertinent data that constitute the total performance.

B. Criteria

Explicit written criteria for determining the degree of excellence with which the teaching staff member performs will be developed by the professional staff and shall include, but not necessarily be limited to, relevant indicators of

Student progress and growth
Professional knowledge
Professional skills
Instructional effects
Professional activities
Behavior as an exemplar

C. Methods of Data Collection

Specific methods for collection of evaluation data will be developed for each position by the professional staff and shall include, but not necessarily be limited to

Observations
Review of personnel file, including a review of graduate courses, inservice courses, et cetera
Student progress
Participation on P.T.A. committees, inservices, curriculum committees, school committees, et cetera

D. Data Collection

The source of data may include professional staff, students, community members, and parents. The data obtained shall be collected and evaluated by properly certificated members of the professional staff.

E. Definition of Terms

1. *Teaching Staff Member* for the purposes of this policy, one who is part of the professional staff excluding supervisors.

2. *Appropriately Certificated Personnel (Supervisor)* staff member qualified to perform duties of supervision, which

include the superintendent, assistant superintendents, principals, assistant principals, and supervisors of instruction who hold the appropriate certificate and who are designated by the Board to supervise instruction.

3. *Indicators of Pupils' Progress and Growth*   results of formal and informal assessment of pupils as defined in N.J.A.C. 6:8–3.4.

4. *Individual Professional Improvement Plan*   written statement of actions developed by the supervisor and the teaching staff member to continue professional growth, time lines for their implementation, and the responsibilities of the individual teaching staff member and the district for implementing the plan.

5. *Administrative Professional Improvement Plan*   written statement of actions developed by the supervisor to correct deficiencies, time lines for their implementation, and the responsibilities of the individual teaching staff member and the district for implementing the plan.

6. *Job Description*   written specification of the function of the position, duties and responsibilities, the extent and limits of authority, and work relationships within and outside the school and district.

7. *Observation*   visitation to an assigned workstation by a certified supervisor for the purpose of formally collecting data on the performance of a teaching staff member's assigned duties and responsibilities and of a duration appropriate to same.

8. *Observation Conference*   meeting of supervisor and a teaching staff member to review a written report of the performance data collected in a formal observation and its implications for the teaching staff member's annual evaluation.

9. *Incident Conference*   meeting of a teaching staff member and an appropriately certified supervisor concerning a specific event. The conference is held to resolve the incident informally and shall be scheduled as soon as is practicable. If the incident is deemed serious, an incident report shall be placed in the personnel file.

10. *Incident Report*   formal written appraisal of the teaching staff member's performance during a specific event by an

appropriately certified supervisor. An incident conference must be held before an incident report can be placed in the personnel file.

11. *Performance Report*   written appraisal of the teaching staff member's performance prepared by an appropriately certified supervisor.

12. *Annual Summary Conference*   meeting between teaching staff member and appropriately certified supervisor to discuss the teaching staff member's total performance for the year cycle.

13. *Annual Written Performance Report*   written appraisal of the teaching staff member's total performance for the year cycle by a certified supervisor who has participated in the evaluation of the teaching staff member. The Annual Summary Conference must be held before the Annual Written Performance Report can be placed in the personnel file.

II. PROCEDURES

A. Notification

1. At the beginning of their employment, all teaching staff members shall be given a copy of the policy and procedures relating to staff evaluation by the assistant superintendent for personnel and/or principal.

2. Principals shall review with their staffs the policy and procedures on evaluation by October 1 of each year.

3. Amendments to the policy or procedures will be distributed by the administration within ten working days after adoption or acknowledgment by the Board of Education.

B. Observations

1. All teaching staff members, including those assigned to regular classroom duties and those not assigned to regular classroom duties, are subject to observations and performance reports.

2. Each observation shall be conducted for a minimum duration of one class period in a secondary school and for the duration of one complete subject lesson in an elementary school.

3. Observations need not be limited to the classroom, but may be made on any or all scheduled assignments.

C. Performance Reports

1. Each of the required minimum of one (tenured) or three (non-tenured) performance reports, as specified in II-D, shall be followed within three school days by a conference between the staff member and the supervisor to discuss the performance report and recommendations concerning the employee's total performance. All recommendations must appear on the written performance report.

2. All performance reports must be in written form and be made by appropriately certified personnel. The teacher's and supervisor's signatures must both appear on the performance report.

3. Immediately upon completion of the performance reporting process, copies of performance reports shall be distributed to the following:

   a. Assistant Superintendent (Personnel)
   b. Principal
   c. Teacher

4. The teaching staff member has the right to submit his or her written disclaimer of such performance report within ten days following the conference. Such disclaimer is to be attached to each copy of the performance report.

5. Report on Performance Reports forms shall be completed by each school principal monthly and must be received in the Office of the Assistant Superintendent (Personnel) with the monthly reports.

6. The superintendent of schools or his designee shall be notified immediately when formal action is under consideration (see Formal Action).

D. Schedule of Performance Reports

1. Nontenure

   a. New Jersey state law requires the Board of Education to complete performance reports for every nontenured teaching staff member at least three times annually and not less than once a semester. In addition, the three performance reports must be completed by April 30 of a staff member's first year, while the three performance reports must be completed from April 30 to April 20 of the second and third years. The number of performance reports may be reduced proportionally when an individual has been a staff member less than one year.

b. Each principal shall be responsible for meeting the following performance report schedule:

   (1) First: no later than October 31.
   (2) Second: no later than December 31.
   (3) Third:
       (a) If formal action is anticipated or recommended, no later than February 10.
       (b) If no formal action is anticipated, no later than April 30.

2. Tenure

   a. The Middletown Township Board of Education requires a minimum of one performance report for every tenured teaching staff member to be completed annually by May 15.

   b. Each principal shall be responsible for meeting the following evaluation schedule:

      (1) First: no later than May 15.
      (2) Others:
          (a) More than one may be completed as the need arises.
          (b) All evaluations must be completed by May 15.

E. Individual Professional Improvement Plan

   1. The individual professional improvement plan provides an opportunity to focus on specific aspects of the job description to continue professional growth. The plan is accomplished through a national process where the supervisor and staff member meet and set objectives designed to continue professional growth for the staff member while aiding the staff of the building to fulfill district and state goals. This process provides for teacher input in the objective(s), establishes a time frame, considers the ways and means of attaining objectives, and involves the means of assessing the results.

   2. The process is achieved through the following stages:

      a. Each staff member considers his or her objectives for the year. The objectives should center on teacher actions or behavior, not on personality factors. The objective or objectives under consideration should be measurable and/or observable to the extent that the supervisor and staff member should be able to agree that the objective was accomplished or was not accomplished.

b. The supervisor considers objectives for the year for the staff member, as outlined in (a).

c. The supervisor and teacher confer to determine the objectives and mutually agree on the measurable and/or observable objectives. If the supervisor and teacher cannot mutually agree to objectives, then the teacher selects an objective and the supervisor selects an objective until a reasonable number of objectives are reached. "Reasonable" is defined as the amount of work that is manageable within a specified time frame.

d. The teacher and supervisor then determine the implementation plan. This discussion considers the necessary materials, professional time, budgetary considerations, et cetera that are needed to accomplish the objectives and a time frame for the completion of the objectives.

e. The teacher and supervisor should agree on how the success in completing the objectives will be evaluated. This discussion should clarify what is to be accomplished, where this will take place, when the objectives will be completed, and how to determine clearly whether the objectives have been accomplished.

f. When the objectives have been defined, page 2 of the Annual Written Performance Report is completed. When complete, one copy will remain with the teacher, one will remain with the supervisor, and one will be sent to the assistant superintendent for personnel for the personnel file.

g. Data are gathered by the teacher and/or the supervisor throughout the year in the manner that was prescribed at the conference.

h. At the conclusion of the time frame, but in no event longer than one year from the setting of the objectives, the supervisor and the teacher meet to discuss the objectives.

The conference should have two outcomes:

(1) A determination of whether or not the objectives were met (May 1–June 30).

(2) The reestablishment of objectives that were not completed and/or the setting of new objectives for the following year between May 1 and June 30 or September 1 and September 15 for all teachers. Tenured teachers will work on a one- to three-year cycle.

NOTE: This process is more important than the outcome. It would be better to strive toward, but only partially complete, one challenging objective than to complete five less meaningful objectives.

i. The supervisor evaluates the Individual Professional Improvement Plan on the Annual Written Performance Report and discusses the evaluation at the Annual Summary Conference.

III. ANNUAL SUMMARY CONFERENCE

(To be held before the written performance report is formally filed in the personnel file.)

SHALL INCLUDE, BUT NOT BE LIMITED TO

1. Review of performance based on job description.

2. Review of progress toward objectives of the individual professional improvement plan developed at the previous annual conference.

3. Development of the objectives of the individual professional improvement plan for the next one- (1) year cycle for nontenured teaching staff members or for the next one- to three-year cycle for tenured teaching staff members.

4. Review of available indicators of pupil progress and growth toward the program objectives.

5. Review of the annual written performance report and the signing of said report within five working days of the review.

6. Relative to items 1 and 4—a discussion of (a) the evaluative procedure, (b) the evaluative criteria, and (c) the data collection methods to be followed in evaluating his or her performance.

IV. ANNUAL WRITTEN PERFORMANCE REPORT—PREPARED BY A CERTIFIED SUPERVISOR WHO HAS PARTICIPATED IN THE EVALUATION OF THE TEACHING STAFF MEMBER

The purpose of this report is to provide for the review of the total performance of the teaching staff member and shall include, but not be limited to

1. Performance areas of strength.

2. Performance areas needing improvement based upon the job description.

3. An individual professional improvement plan developed by the supervisor and teaching staff member.

4. A summary of available indicators of pupil progress and growth and a statement of how these indicators relate to the effectiveness of the overall program and the performance of the individual teaching staff member.

5. Provision for performance data which has not been included in the report prepared by the supervisor to be entered into the record by the evaluatee within 10 working days after the signing of the report.

PUPIL PROGRESS

The Annual Written Performance Report shall include a summary of available indicators of pupil progress and growth, and a statement of how these indicators relate to the effectiveness of the overall program and the performance of the individual teaching staff member. The answers to the following questions shall provide the data for the statements:

1. Are the intended outcomes for the student(s) clear? This refers to the students' understanding of the content they will study, their role during the learning process, and the behaviors that are expected at the conclusion of the activity.

2. Does the teacher monitor pupil progress and growth? This refers to the proper monitoring of task analysis devices, teacher-made evaluation devices, district monitoring devices, and state and standardized tests.

3. What does the teacher do with the information? This refers to analyzing the results of the student evaluation and implementing a program designed to provide for basics essential to continued student educational development in terms of student potential.

V. FORMAL ACTION—UNDER CONSIDERATION

The superintendent of schools or his or her designee shall be notified immediately when formal action is under consideration and the actions to be recommended are decided jointly with the administration of the school or schools to which the teaching staff member is assigned. Some of the possible results of "formal action" are certification of charges, nonrenewal of contract, withholding of an increment, and withholding of a part of salary for contracted services not performed.

A. Performance Reports

When a teaching staff member's performance report indicates one or more areas that are unsatisfactory, interim performance reports shall be made more frequently to monitor the implementation of suggested improvements.

B. Incidence Conference and Reports

Staff Actions Warranting Discipline—Should a member of the professional staff be involved in a situation which may warrant disciplinary action, his or her immediate supervisor or principal shall attempt to resolve the situation with a conference. The conference shall be held as soon as practicable. Following the conference, one or more of the following courses of action may occur:

1. The matter, if at all possible, shall be handled informally at the building level and closed without further action being taken.

2. A memorandum may be placed in the staff member's personnel file. The staff member may respond to the memorandum, in writing, if he or she so desires. The staff member's response will also be placed in the personnel file.

3. A letter of reprimand may be sent to the staff member and a copy placed in his or her personnel file. The staff member may respond to the reprimand in writing if he or she so desires. A copy of the response will also be placed in the personnel file.

4. The immediate supervisor or the principal may recommend to the superintendent or his designee that more severe disciplinary action be taken against the staff member. Should this occur, the superintendent or his or her designee may decide to hold a conference with the staff member involved and the staff member's immediate supervisor or principal. This conference shall be held as soon as practicable. Following said conference the superintendent or his or her designee may direct that any of the procedures set forth in paragraphs 1, 2, and 3 above be followed or in the alternative, he may recommend to the Board of Education that more severe disciplinary action be taken.

5. Should the latter occur, the Board or a committee of the Board may decide to hold a conference with the staff member, his or her immediate supervisor and/or principal and the superintendent and/or his or her designee. This conference shall be held as soon as practicable. The staff member and the Association shall be notified of said conference. The staff member and one representative of his or her own choosing shall be permitted to be present at the conference.

6. Following said conference, the Board may direct that any of the procedures in paragraphs 1, 2, and 3 of above be followed or in the alternative take the necessary statutory steps to withhold an increment or certify charges to the commissioner of education.

This section of the procedures has been added to overcome confusion regarding timing. If an incident arises, a conference should be held as soon as practicable and *not* held for one of the performance reports. These data should, however, be considered as part of the Annual Summary.

C. Administrative Professional Improvement Plan

If formal action is under consideration, it may be necessary to terminate immediately the mutually determined Individual Professional Improvement Plan and substitute the unilaterally determined Administrative Professional Improvement Plan. This should be officially acknowledged through a written letter to the teaching staff member which is placed in the personnel file. This plan will be designed to help the teaching staff member to overcome the deficiencies. Critical elements of the plan are

1. Time frames for overcoming the deficiencies.

2. Responsibilities of the teaching staff member and the supervisor for implementing the plan.

. . .Framework for

EVALUATION FRAMEWORK
BOARD POLICIES
(Continually Reviewed)

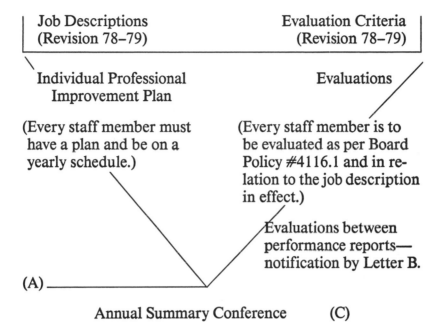

| Job Descriptions (Revision 78–79) | Evaluation Criteria (Revision 78–79) |

Individual Professional Improvement Plan

(Every staff member must have a plan and be on a yearly schedule.)

Evaluations

(Every staff member is to be evaluated as per Board Policy #4116.1 and in relation to the job description in effect.)

Evaluations between performance reports— notification by Letter B.

(A)

Annual Summary Conference   (C)

(Conference for each staff member to:
A. Evaluate Performance Reports, Incident Reports, etc.
B. Evaluate Individual Professional Improvement Plan)

Annual Written Performance Report

(Report for each staff member to be completed and signed within five working days of the review.)

A. If formal action is under consideration, the staff member is to be notified, in writing, that the Individual Professional Improvement Plan is being terminated and the Administrative Professional Improvement Plan activated. This plan is designed to help overcome the deficiencies.

B. This section of the procedures has been added to overcome confusion regarding timing. If an incident arises a conference should be held as soon as practicable and not held for one of the performance reports. These data should, however, be considered part of the Annual Summary Conference.

C. The Annual Summary Conference and Annual Written Performance Report does not eliminate the need to tie evaluations together by reference, example, citation, etc.

. . .Of Administrators

EVALUATION OF ADMINISTRATORS

It is the policy of the Board of Education that each employee of this system holding an administrative position shall be evaluated annually by his or her immediate supervisor.

The superintendent shall prepare an evaluation form and procedures for the conduct of all evaluations that are mutually agreeable to the administrators.

The superintendent shall report annually to the Board of Education on each administrator's performance.

. . .Of Self

SELF-EVALUATION

The following is an aid for self-analysis. Indicate by a check in the appropriate column that category which best describes you.

	NEVER	SELDOM	SOME-TIMES	OFTEN	ALWAYS
1. Possesses competence and knowledgeability in his or her field of work, and strives toward continued professional self-improvement.					
2. Maintains physical capability, alertness, and emotional readiness to teach.					
3. Exhibits high standards of moral and ethical conduct, and employs a wholesome sense of humor in dealing with people.					
4. Is fair and impartial in the treatment of pupils and recognizes the dignity of the child.					
5. Exhibits an understanding and acceptance of individual differences among students and provides for those differences.					

	NEVER	SELDOM	SOME-TIMES	OFTEN	ALWAYS
6. Works well in communicating with parents.					
7. Contributes significantly to the total functioning of the school.					
8. Explores and openly evaluates new approaches to teaching.					
9. Is receptive to suggestions for improvement.					

. . .Purpose of

TEACHER EVALUATION

The Board of Education believes that effective district staff evaluation results in improved instruction and learning opportunities for all students of the school district. Supported by a positive program of staff supervision, effective staff evaluation enables teaching staff members to continue their professional growth.

The Board of Education will endeavor to create and maintain a positive climate for staff members through a clearly defined and communicated evaluation system. A complete understanding of the evaluation system should minimize apprehension and maximize a positive, objective-oriented approach to the improvement of instruction. When formulating objectives designed to improve instruction, the district assignment and staff member's individual needs, abilities, and aspirations should be the determinants.

The purposes of teacher evaluations are

   a. To provide each teacher with an appraisal of professional strengths, weaknesses, and total performance as an employee of the Board of Education.

   b. To provide information that will aid the individual staff member and supervisor to devise a plan to reduce weaknesses and more effectively utilize strengths.

   c. To provide for the improvement of instruction and pupil achievement.

   d. To provide for the review of the total performance of teaching staff members.

The professional growth of the teaching staff member which results from participation in the evaluation process provides significance to the process itself. Evaluation shall be a continuous, constructive, and cooperative experience between the teaching staff member and the supervisor.

EXAMINATIONS   (See Also: FAILURE; GRADES; HONOR ROLL; REPORT CARDS; RETENTION)

. . .Letter to Parents Concerning

Dear Sixth and Seventh Grade Parents/Guardians,

It is truly hard to believe that our academic year is coming to a close. Despite the problems that our district has had, we can assure you of a very successful year at Rock Township Middle School.

Parental involvement in the schools is, perhaps, one of the most necessary characteristics of successful educational institutions. Please know that I have appreciated all your help and cooperation, and I again wish to remind you that my staff is totally committed to making Rock Township an exemplary middle school. We feel we are very close and now must work harder than ever before to achieve this goal.

For your information, please review the following schedule:

Friday, June 16	Periods 1 and 2 exam
Monday, June 19	Periods 3 and 4 exam
Tuesday, June 20	Periods 5 and 6 exam
Wednesday, June 21	Periods 7 and 8 exam

On the above days, there will be no cafeteria service for students and there will be early dismissal at approximately 11:15–11:30 A.M. Please know that Sixth Grade students do not have final examinations, only a cumulative learning experience. This is Board of Education policy.

May I extend to you every wish for a safe and happy summer.

Kindest personal regards.

Sincerely,

. . .Memo to Teachers on

MEMO

To: ALL TEACHERS
From: J. BENSON, PRINCIPAL
Re: UPCOMING EXAMINATIONS

As a very new teacher I was once expounding about a test I had constructed which would, I assured everyone, "keep them studying all night!" An older and considerably wiser colleague remarked that he was not aware that I was giving a test on the ability to memorize.

He was right, of course, and over the years I, like all of us, have come to know that a test should be a diagnostic tool used to find out where a student is academically. Indeed, we are all aware that an examination given to fail, or, for that matter, to pass, a student is as worthless as a test of someone's ability to memorize 20 facts in five minutes.

I know that I can count on you to make the upcoming exams incisive, meaningful, and truly reflective of the fine education that has been going on all year.

. . .Notification of Change in

Dear Teachers,

Please be advised of the following schedule of exams for eighth grade students only, necessitated by the June 20 graduation date:

Day	Date	Exam	Periods	Room
Wednesday	June 14	G/W	1 & 2	Cluster
		Span. I	7 & 8	116
		Span. B	7 & 8	112
		Fren. B	7 & 8	103
Thursday	June 15	Reading	1 & 2	Cluster
		Fren. II	3 & 4	116
		Span. II	3 & 4	112
		Fren. I	3 & 4	Cafe N.
Friday	June 16	Soc. Stud.	Exam 1	Cluster
		Science	Exam 2	Cluster
Monday	June 19	Math	Exam 3	Cluster

Because of this schedule, there is some impact on classrooms. Therefore, be advised of the following classroom changes:

Wednesday, June 14, Period 8
    Mrs. Marciani, Health to Cafe south
    Mrs. Finkelstein, 6 Consumer to Cafe north
    Mrs. Egglmann, Communications to Rm 106

Please check over this schedule carefully, particularly our I.A./Home Ec and Phys. Ed teachers, to be certain that if you plan a final project or test for eighth graders, it gets done before your students "mysteriously" disappear out of one of your final classes. I hope this notice takes the mystery out of it all.

. . .Notification to Students of

To: ALL STUDENTS
From: J. BENSON, PRINCIPAL
Re: FINAL EXAMS

Very soon you will be taking your final subject area examinations for the current school year. A schedule of the times and places will be given to you during homeroom period, and a master list will be placed on the bulletin board outside the main office as well.

I wish you well in your exams, and I'd like to remind you that if you have kept up with your classes all year long, you have nothing to worry about in your final exams. Review your notes and study for them by all means, but remember that what you have learned over this year has become a part of you, a part that you should be able to represent quite well in a final examination.

I am confident that you will all do extremely well.

. . .Policy Statement on

Examinations serve useful purposes, but there are many pitfalls in their use that we must attempt to avoid. They should not be threats held over the heads of the students to make them work. There are obvious reasons why examination marks must be consistent with the marks given for the marking periods.

Teachers are reminded that examination marks are but a part of the student's academic progress indicators, and that the whole picture must be taken into account when formulating a final grade.

EXCHANGE STUDENTS (See Also: LANGUAGE; MINORITIES)

. . .Letter of Farewell

Dear José,

How quickly a year has passed. It seems just yesterday that I was welcoming you to Rock Township High School, and here it is time to say goodbye.

You have been with us for a year, and in that time we have had the pleasure to get to know you well. We shall carry the memory of you with us through the years to come. We shall remember your kindness, your willingness to help, and your ability to put us all at ease. We shall remember your inquisitiveness, your sense of humor, and the general goodwill which has been felt by all of us who knew you.

We have lived, laughed, and studied with you; we have known you as our friend; we shall miss you greatly in the days ahead.

Remember us in future years as we shall keep your memory alive in our minds.

Our best wishes for your continued success in all you do.

With best wishes,

J. Benson, Principal

. . .Letter of Recommendation

To Whom It May Concern:

As principal of Rock Township High School, I was the chief administrator during the time that Erika Von Werner was a foreign exchange student at our school.

During the year that Erika attended our school, she distinguished herself both in academic and in social areas. She maintained an "A" average and was appointed a "Student Tutor" in all subjects, including English, her "second" language. Socially, she headed a student committee that performed many charitable acts for the school and community, and both students and teachers were quick to point out that it was Erika's enthusiasm that was the lifeblood of that organization.

Erika was extremely popular with faculty and students. Indeed, there is no one of whom I can think who had anything but praise for her. She is a credit to herself, her parents, and her country.

I recommend her to your attention without qualification.

. . .Letter of Welcome

Dear Manuel,

Welcome to the United States of America and welcome to Rock Township High School. For the next year you will be a guest in our country as well as a student in our school. We hope that the time you spend here will be a profitable time for all of us.

We have much to learn about your country and your people, and we look forward to an exchange of understanding. We hope that we, in turn, may be of service to you, and we invite you to call upon us if there is anything we can do to make your stay more pleasant.

My office is open to you at any time as are the complete facilities of Rock Township High School. Please make use of them, and please visit us and let us get better acquainted.

Please accept my very best wishes for a happy and successful school year.

Yours sincerely,

J. Benson, Principal

EXTRACURRICULAR ACTIVITIES (See Also: EVALUATION; NEWSPAPER; PUBLIC RELATIONS; SPORTS; YEARBOOK)

. . .Contract for

To: _____

From: ROCK TOWNSHIP BOARD OF EDUCATION

Re: EXTRACURRICULAR CONTRACT

The Board of Education has awarded you an extracurricular contract for the school year 19_____–19_____ as follows:

NATURE OF CONTRACT: _____

_____

SALARY: _____

Please fill out the form below, sign it, detach and return it to the Central Office as soon as possible. Thank you.

ROCK TOWNSHIP BOARD OF EDUCATION

· ·

( )   I hereby accept the extracurricular contract for the school year
      19＿＿–19＿＿ as follows:

NATURE OF CONTRACT: ＿＿＿＿＿＿＿＿＿＿＿＿＿＿＿＿＿＿＿＿＿＿

＿＿＿＿＿＿＿＿＿＿＿＿＿＿＿＿＿＿＿＿＿＿

SALARY: ＿＿＿＿＿＿＿＿＿＿＿＿＿＿＿＿＿＿＿＿＿

( )   I do not wish to accept this contract.

Date: ＿＿＿＿＿＿＿＿＿ Signature: ＿＿＿＿＿＿＿＿＿＿＿＿＿

. . .Letter to Advisor

Dear Jane,

I believe it was Thomas Gray who wrote:

"Full many a flower is born to blush unseen
And waste its sweetness on the desert air."

Now, while you are far from being a "blushing violet" as the saying goes, there is something that reminds me of you in those lines of poetry. To me, you are that rare and outstanding flower that blooms behind the scenes rather than strutting its beauty in the spotlight.

If I have mixed my metaphors, I hope you have taken my meaning. The work that you do on that Student Council is all behind the scenes. The students or the school gets the credit, but you are the heartbeat of that organization. Their names may appear in print, but your name is inscribed in every heart that knows of your unselfish devotion to these kids.

I just thought you'd like to know that there are many of us who know only too well all the work you do, and we want you to know that your "sweetness," along with your dedication, zeal, and great compassion are far from "wasted."

Keep blooming, flower—keep blooming!

. . .Memo to Participants

To: ALL MEMBERS OF THE DRAMA CLUB

Wow! What a performance!

I'd like you to know that last Friday night was one of the times when I was proudest of being principal of Rock Township High. Your performance of "Oliver" was so outstanding, so professional, and so downright enjoyable that I gleamed with pride for you from curtain to curtain.

Everyone from Mr. Donner, your advisor and director, to John who did a fine job pulling that curtain is to be congratulated. You have seen the result of your hard work, and it was delightful!

Again, I congratulate you all on a very fine, very professional performance. Next stop Broadway?

. . .Philosophy of

We believe that in considering the totality of an education there are certain aspects of personality development and social interaction which fall outside the realm of academic curriculum.

We further believe that extracurricular activities provide just such opportunities outside of the curriculum for meeting with a variety of situations requiring social interaction and engendering personality growth. Along with development of social and personal graces, involvement in wholesome activities guided by competent faculty advisors may often provide an opportunity for the development and nurturing of a sense of morality and justice that will stand the student in good stead in later life.

We, therefore, feel that the school should do all within its power to sponsor, promote, and encourage extracurricular activities and participation in them by the largest possible number of students.

FACULTY MEETINGS (See Also: ATTENDANCE; DEPARTMENTAL MEETINGS)

. . .Agenda for

To: FACULTY
From: J. BENSON, PRINCIPAL
Re: FACULTY MEETING AGENDA

When: Thursday, June 2, 19XX
Where: All-Purpose Room
From: 3:00 P.M. to: 3:45 P.M.

AGENDA:

       3:00–3:15—Schedule for Final Exams, Mr. Benson
       3:15–3:30—Status of Textbook Orders, Mrs. Howard
       3:30–3:40—Questions and Answers, All
       3:40–3:45—Your Education Association Business, Mr. Fenn

COMMENT: If we start on time, we *end* on time. It's up to you!

. . .Attendance at

During the course of the year it is necessary to have faculty meetings. These are usually (at least if I can help it) short and to the point, and when we call them, they *are* important. All teachers are required to attend. If any conflict arises and you feel that you will be unable to make the assigned meeting, please see an administrator prior to the meeting. Thank you for your cooperation in this most important matter.

. . .Letter on Performance in

Dear Mr. Pierce,

I find it regrettable that during the faculty meeting of Wednesday, October 17, 19XX, you took the time allotted to you to discuss departmental budgets to actively criticize members of your own and other departments in this school.

Whatever your private opinions, certainly you must realize that a faculty meeting is not the proper forum for the voicing of these opinions. I have had a number of comments as to how uncomfortable, unproductive, and even deleterious were your, as one of your colleagues put it, "attacks" upon your fellow teachers.

Please see me at once in order that we may have this matter settled once and for all in order that it may never be repeated.

Sincerely,

. . .Notification of Staff

To: FACULTY
From: J. BENSON, PRINCIPAL
Re: FACULTY MEETING

This is the one you won't want to miss! Not only will there be a few surprises from the discipline committee, but the results of the statewide test are in. If that isn't enough, Mr. Gianisi will be discussing next year's salary guide!

It's all happening on Wednesday, May 22, 19XX, at 3:15 P.M. in the library. See you there!

. . .Policy on

FACULTY MEETINGS

for the school year

19XX–19XX

Pursuant to the agreement between the Rock Township Board of Education and the Rock Township Education Association for the 19XX–19XX school year, the following policy on faculty meetings shall be followed:

1. There will be ten regularly scheduled faculty meetings for the school year with two additional meetings which may be called at the principal's discretion.

2. The meetings will take place on the last Wednesday of the month. Should this day not be available, the meeting will be held on the Wednesday preceding the normally scheduled meeting.

3. The meeting shall begin within ten minutes of the end of the school day and shall not exceed the length of a regular period of class instruction.

4. A portion of time shall be set aside in each meeting for RTEA business.

5. Personal problems or those more judiciously handled on a one-to-one situation shall not be the subject matter of a faculty meeting.

6. An agenda for each meeting shall be published at least two days prior to the meeting.

If this policy is understood and implemented by all, our faculty meetings, it is hoped, should continue to be both useful and dynamic.

. . .Report on

FACULTY SECRETARY'S REPORT

Faculty Meeting of May 22, 19XX

The meeting was called to order at 3:17 P.M. by Mr. Benson. He spoke of the results of the statewide testing program. He pointed out that Rock Township High School was in the top ten percentile for the state in overall standings and further elaborated on the composite scores of specific areas of instruction. Mr. Benson remarked on the fine showing of our students as being reflective of the quality of instruction.

At 3:33 P.M. Mrs. Harrington spoke of the pressure on the Guidance Office at this time of the year and the necessity of all teachers getting in the names of possible failures for the school year as soon as possible.

At 3:36 P.M. Mr. Kennert, chairperson of the Discipline Committee, reported that the new discipline referral form is proving effective in leading to quicker and more judicious handling of disciplinary cases. This is gathered from many teacher comments and the report of the vice principal. Mr. Kennert further reported that teachers would soon be receiving a questionnaire from the committee. He asked that this form be filled out and returned as soon as possible, as it would serve as one basis for the revision of the discipline code.

At 3:47 P.M. Mr. Gianisi, the faculty representative of the Rock Township Education Association announced the new salary scale as approved by the Board of Education and the RTEA. A question and answer session followed.

Mr. Benson adjourned the meeting at 4:02 P.M.

Respectfully submitted,

Marion R. Haines,
Faculty Secretary

FAILURE   (See Also: DISCIPLINE; EXAMINATIONS; GRADES; GRADUATION; REPORT CARDS; RETENTION)

. . .Failures for the School Year Form

Please fill in the form below and return it to the Guidance Office no later than Tuesday, June 20, 19XX at the end of the school day:

Name: _____ Date: _____

Grade: _____ Subject: _____

FAILURES FOR THE SCHOOL YEAR

STUDENT	GRADE FOR MARKING PERIOD				FINAL AVERAGE
	1	2	3	4	

REASON(S) FOR FAILURE:

Teacher Signature: _____

. . .Notice to Parents of Failure (Marking Period)

(A) *first form*

Dear Parent (or Guardian):

Your son/daughter, _____, Grade _____, is not

doing satisfactory work in (subject) _____ for the marking

period which ends _____.

The purpose of this report is to bring this situation to your attention in order that pupil, teacher, and parents, working together, may seek to remedy the situation.

We are checking below some of the causes which seem to be contributing to his/her present difficulties:

( ) Absenteeism   ( ) Poor attitude in class
( ) Unsatisfactory test scores   ( ) Work not done on time
( ) Inattention in class   ( ) Frequently comes to school
( ) Lessons poorly prepared or not done   without books, pencils, etc.
( ) Other (Please Comment): _____

_____

_____

In order to help the situation improve, a conference here at the school may be helpful. Please phone the school (758-0903) for a conference.

Teacher: _____

(B) *second form*

Marking Period Ends: _____

Dear Parents (or Guardian):

(Student) _____ Grade _____

( ) is in danger of failing (subject) _____

( ) is doing passing work in (subject) _____, but is capable
    of doing, and should be urged to do, better.

In order to improve the situation, he/she must:

( ) take responsibility for bringing all necessary materials to class.
( ) hand in assignments regularly and on time.
( ) improve the quality of assignments.
( ) take responsibility for finding out about and making up all assignments
    missed because of absence, trips, etc.
( ) give complete attention to the explanation and practice exercises in
    class.
( ) study more diligently and pass more tests.
( ) improve behavior in class.

( ) put extra effort into improving skills in _____.
( ) come for extra help.
( ) complete a major project.
( ) Other: _____

_____

_____

Would you please:

( ) telephone the Guidance Office (234-5678, Ext. 12) for an appointment in order to discuss this more fully. If you prefer, you may arrange for a telephone conversation.
( ) sign and return this sheet to me.

TEACHER'S SIGNATURE: _____

. . .Notice to Parents of Failure (School Year)

Dear _____,

We sincerely regret to inform you that your son/daughter, _____

_____, a _____ grade student at Rock Township High School, is in danger of failing the following subject(s) for the current school year:

SUBJECT	TEACHER

The teacher(s) involved have indicated the following as possible reasons for this situation: _____

_____

_____

We are as concerned as you must be about this very serious situation. If you would care to call me at 234-5678, Extension 12, I will be happy to set up a conference at your earliest convenience.

I do hope that we may be of service and can help to rectify this unfortunate situation.

Sincerely,

H. K. Lennel,
Director of Guidance

. . .Notice to Teachers on

To: ALL TEACHERS
From: GUIDANCE DEPARTMENT
Re: FAILURE NOTICES FOR FOURTH MARKING PERIOD

Warning notices will be mailed at the end of the school day on Monday, May 22. The preparation and sending of failure notices is as follows:

1. Teachers are to obtain failure notices from the **Guidance Office**.

2. Teachers are to fill out the form in duplicate—one white, one blue—for each student who is not doing passing or satisfactory work in their course.

3. Please write the student's homeroom number and the homeroom teacher's name at the top of the notice on both copies.

4. Turn in completed forms to Department Chairpersons as soon as possible.

5. Department Chairpersons will check for completeness, legibility, etc., and submit the forms to the Guidance Office by the end of the day on Thursday, May 18.

6. On Friday, May 19, the Guidance Office will forward the blue copies to the proper guidance counselor and will "homeroomize" the white copies. The completed white copies will then be placed in the homeroom teacher's mailbox.

7. Homeroom teachers are to collate the completed white copies, obtain a sufficient number of stamped envelopes from Guidance, address them to parents via information obtained from attendance cards, seal and return the envelopes to the Guidance Office as soon as possible on Monday, May 22. The Guidance Office will be responsible for mailing the envelopes.

8. The fourth marking period ends June 23 (April 21–June 23).

9. INCOMPLETE POLICY: An INC (incomplete) should be given when a student has not done the work for a period in which the grade is given because of one of the following reasons:

   1. Extended absence due to illness
   2. An emotional crisis (death-divorce)
   3. An extenuating reason which the teacher will discuss with Guidance and the Administration before giving the grade

. . .Of a Program

The Program to Increase Contemporary Knowledge (PICK), which was implemented last September in our school, has now had its trial period at our school. On the basis of reports from the teachers, observations by supervisory personnel, and test results of the students involved, it has been decided that the PICK program will not be a part of our curriculum in the fall.

While it is, perhaps, inevitable that people will be anxious to place blame, the failure of any program is hardly one-sided. Rather, it is invariably a combination of elements, not the least of which is the simple fact that the program did not benefit our students in the manner we originally assumed. Since our students are our number one priority, that alone will suffice as sufficient reason to terminate this program and seek other, more productive alternatives.

. . .Role of Guidance in

Counselors monitor all failing grades and incompletes, meeting with students, teachers, and parents to attempt to improve the situation.

Students who are absent toward the end of a marking period may be given an incomplete instead of a grade. The student must then make up the work. If the work is not made up within 4 weeks the incomplete grade is automatically changed to an "F."

FIELD TRIPS   (See Also: BUS; VOLUNTEERS)

. . .Application for

It is the belief of the Board that properly planned field trips which are an integral part of the program of classroom instruction are a valuable part of the learning experience. (Policy #109)

In concert with the above, the following field trip guidelines have been established:

Trip Application

1. Each cluster will discuss field trips for their students and limit them to *no more than three (3)*.

2. A list of proposed field trips will be submitted by each cluster leader to Ron Pietkewicz no later than Friday, September 30, 1988. (Forms will be given to cluster leaders.)

3. A list of proposed field trips will be compiled by the main office and give to the faculty at large so all are aware of trips that are planned.

4. Other departments such as *Physical Education* and *Activity Arts* which are not "clustered" as such will follow the same procedures, except the department coordinator will compile the list of proposed trips.

5. It is important to note that this form has absolutely nothing to do with trip approval. *Teachers in charge* of each trip must fill out the appropriate trip approval forms and turn them in to Ron Pietkewicz no later than three (3) weeks prior to the actual date of the trip.

. . .Budget Form for

NAME: _____ Room: _____

DEPARTMENT: _____

DIRECTIONS: Include all trips, local and out of district. Include justifications. Figure costs at _____ per mile and _____ per hour of waiting time; add 5% and round off to the next highest five dollars. Trips should be coordinated within a department.

EST. COST	NO. OF BUSES	NO. OF STUDENTS	DESTI-NATION	ROUND-TRIP MILES	DESTI-NATION	PURPOSE
		-TOTAL-				

. . .Evaluation Form

FIELD TRIP EVALUATION FORM

(This form is provided for the teacher's personal records as an aid in evaluating and planning Field Trips.)

Date of Trip: _____

Group Taken: _____

Teachers: _____

Nature of Trip: _____

Bus Carrier: _____

HOW WOULD YOU RATE:	LOW	2	3	4	5	HIGH
Bus Service						
Student Interest						
Simplicity of Arrangements						
Treatment at Destination						
Educational Value						

Would You Take This Trip Again?   ( ) Yes   ( ) No

Why or Why Not? _____

_____

_____

Overall Evaluation of Trip: _____

_____

_____

. . .Final Considerations

Final Considerations

1. No student may partake of any trip unless a properly filled out permission slip is turned in signed by a parent.

2. A list of students who are going on the trip along with the date of the trip is to be given to each faculty member before the trip. This would be appreciated no less than *five* (5) days before the trip so other teachers can plan properly for their own classes.

3. Any student who can be determined (using complete discretion) as unable to afford any trip, cannot be deprived of the opportunity. Somehow, we'll (the Main Office) cover the expenses.

4. No trips which in any way compromise the safety of any of our students can be approved by the Main Office. Unfortunately, trips to Great Adventure, fishing trips, and the like, now fall into this category.

. . .Memo to Faculty on

To: ALL PROFESSIONAL STAFF

As this year begins, I must bring up the unhappy fact that I have had to disapprove of a number of field trips last year. An analysis of these refusals might reveal the fact that the vast majority of them were refused because the people requesting the field trip simply did not follow directions.

In any district our size, there must be procedures and rules, or there is chaos. Also, there are no field trips for Board approval when some or most of the pertinent facts are missing.

I urge you, therefore, to read your teacher's handbook and comply with the very clear directions stated there for requesting a field trip.

Thank you for your cooperation.

. . .Request Form

REQUEST FOR FIELD TRIP FORM

Teacher Making Request: _____ Date: _____

Grade and/or Subject: _____

Date of Trip: _____

Itinerary: _____

_____

_____

Teacher and/or Adult Chaperones (Please list yourself first.): _____

_____

_____

Number of Students Going: _____ Have Dates Been Confirmed: _____

Transportation by: _____ Cost: _____

Dear _____,

Your request for a field trip has been:

    ( ) Approved
    ( ) Not Approved for the Following Reason(s): _____

_____

Date: _____ Signature: _____

FILMS   (See Also: REPRIMAND)

. . .Form for Approval of

All films shown to students must be approved by Administration. Please fill in the form below and return it to the proper administrator at least one week in advance of the proposed showing:

NAME OF FILM: _____

RATING: "G" ONLY (NO EXCEPTIONS) _____

PURPOSE OF FILM: _____

RELATIONSHIP TO CURRICULUM: _____

DATE FILM TO BE SHOWN: _____

   ADMINISTRATIVE APPROVAL: _____

                 DATE: _____

. . .Notice on the Showing of

To: ALL PROFESSIONAL STAFF

Please be advised that all movies/films that are shown to our students should be rated "G" and related to our middle school curriculum.

The name of the film should appear in your lesson plans, along with the reason why it relates to the curriculum.

All films that are part of the district-approved curriculum may, of course, be shown. If the film does not fit the criteria, please discuss this with an administrator *before* the film is shown.

                                 Administration

FINANCIAL   (See Also: BOARD OF EDUCATION; NEGOTIATIONS; SCHOLARSHIPS)

. . .Memo on Money for Trips

Trip Moneys

1. Whenever moneys are involved, each cluster will determine the best method of collecting funds from their students to cover the costs involved.

2. Cluster leaders or any one designated teacher per trip are urged to turn into Ron Pietkewicz moneys collected for safekeeping. This can be done at the end of each day of collection. These envelopes may be picked up by the cluster leader or designated teacher the following morning if need be. However, be advised that the main office will not count or open any envelope during collection time. Special interest trips, such as band, chorus, et cetera., will be handled by the teacher in the same way.

3. When and *only when all moneys have been collected* for each trip, the total deposit will be given to Mrs. Divis no later than three (3) days before the trip departs. Deposit slips for cash and checks are available from Mrs. Divis. We are asking that someone in cluster, possibly an aide, fill out these deposit slips. This would be a *tremendous* help to Mrs. Divis.

. . .Policy on Money in School

It is sometimes necessary for teachers to handle money in connection with some of the activities of the school. Moneys collected from students are to be placed in a suitably labeled sealed envelope and given to the office for safekeeping. Please do not leave funds unguarded AT ANY TIME and in no event overnight in your room or desk. Your own valuables should be handled accordingly.

In the collection of moneys, student treasurers are used for all regular activities according to school rules and regulations, but fines or payments for lost or damaged books, et cetera are handled directly by the teacher who must furnish an account of the reason the money was collected. Teachers are to hand in the cash; personal checks will not be accepted. Receipts should be given and required when the transfer takes place.

. . .Support

FINANCING EDUCATION

The school budget is prepared each year by the Board of Education and its chief administrators after a review of budget requests submitted by teachers, principals, special services personnel, and other professional staff members. The budget consists of three main segments: current expense, capital outlay, and debt service. The citizens of the township vote annually on all of these except debt service, which is a fixed charge on bond issues previously approved by the voters. The school budget election is held in conjunction with the school board election. Prior to the election, a public hearing on the budget must be held and the proposed budget advertised, both in local papers and the district's official publication.

If the proposed budget is defeated by the electorate, it falls to the Township Committee to certify the budget, making whatever changes they may decree. Normally, the Township Committee and the Board of Education meet to study the proposed budget before the public hearing. In the event of defeat, the two bodies must meet within two weeks to confer on proposed cuts. The Board of Education has the right to appeal any cuts made by the committee to the commissioner of education who may reinstate the appealed funds or a portion thereof.

FIRE DRILLS   (See Also: CLOSING OF SCHOOL; HANDBOOK)

. . .Evacuation Drill Report

FIRE DRILL REPORT

SCHOOL: _____

DATE OF DRILL: _____

START TIME: _____ FINISH TIME: _____

TOTAL TIME TO EVACUATE BUILDING: _____

SPECIAL CIRCUMSTANCES: _____

_____

_____

DATE: _____ SIGNATURE: _____

                                        TITLE: _____

. . .Memo to Faculty on

To: ALL PROFESSIONAL STAFF

It is a local and state requirement that during a fire drill in school, the entire building be evacuated. While I will not go into the reasoning for this mandated necessity, neither will I argue its rightness or wrongness. We must totally evacuate the building; this is the law; it must be done.

Therefore, when the fire drill alarm sounds, ALL professional staff as well as ALL students MUST (i.e., MUST) exit the building. There are to be no exceptions, nor does it matter whether it is during a person's professional period or not. We are ALL to exit.

Our next fire drill will be soon; that's a certainty. I know that I can be equally as certain of your cooperation and support.

. . .Procedures for a Safe Fire Drill

FIRE DRILL (EVACUATION) PROCEDURES

A. SIGNAL. Repeated ringing of the fire drill bells.

B. GENERAL INSTRUCTIONS

   1. Books are to be left in rooms. Only valuables (pens, purses, et cetera.) are to be taken.

   2. Under no circumstances are students to go to their lockers.

   3. All windows and doors are to be closed but not locked.

   4. All electrical and gas equipment should be turned off.

   5. Pupils with physical disabilities are to report to the main office.

   6. Teachers must take their roll books.

   7. Ignore any bells during the fire drill.

C. PROCEDURES

   1. At the sound of the alarm, students are to form a double line in the classroom and await instructions.

   2. The teacher will review the exit to be used and the line of march.

   3. Pupils are to walk quickly in double lines in a compact group. Teachers are to be at the HEAD of the line.

   4. The teacher and class are to proceed to the designated area.

5. ABSOLUTE SILENCE IS TO BE OBSERVED THROUGHOUT THE EVACUATION, THE WAITING IN THE DESIGNATED AREAS, AND THE RETURN TO THE BUILDING.

6. While waiting for the signal to return to the building, teachers are to SUPERVISE ACTIVELY their students who are to remain together in a double line.

7. Returning to the building, pupils are to maintain a silent double line until they are seated in their classrooms.

8. *SPECIAL NOTE:* NO children, parents, visitors, teachers, or other personnel are to remain in the building during a fire drill.

D. TEACHERS WITHOUT CLASSES. Personnel not specifically assigned an evacuation duty are to report to the outside main exit and await instruction.

. . .Procedures for False Fire Alarms

To: ALL PRINCIPALS
From: OFFICE OF THE SUPERINTENDENT
Re: UNSCHEDULED FIRE DRILLS (FALSE ALARMS)

In the event that the fire alarm shall sound at an unscheduled time, the following procedures shall be implemented:

1. The school shall be evacuated according to regular fire drill procedures.

2. The Rock Township police shall be called and advised that the alarm is unscheduled.

3. A representative shall be sent to the area in which the alarm originated (determined by the Fire Alarm Bell Code) and a determination made as to the nature of the alarm.

4. Upon the report of the representative, the police shall be informed as to the nature of the alarm and whether outside aid shall be needed.

5. If the alarm is a false alarm, students shall be returned to class.

6. If the alarm represents a true emergency, students are to be moved to such positions where they will be out of danger and will not interfere with firefighting or emergency vehicles and personnel.

7. Principal shall immediately take steps toward the implementation of the above procedures.

. . .Statement of Policy

FIRE DRILLS

The signal for a fire or a fire drill is the repeated ringing of the fire alarm bells.

Signs are posted near the doorway of each room indicating the proper route for leaving the building. In addition, students will obtain from their teachers information regarding other procedures to be followed.

Students are to remain orderly, keep moving quickly and quietly, and be prepared to follow any additional instructions that may be given to them by teachers during exit.

For safety reasons students are required to stand 300 feet from the building (so engines and hoses can get through).

Students will return to their classes when the signal has been given.

GIFTED STUDENTS (See Also: ACHIEVEMENT; GRADES; NATIONAL HONOR SOCIETY; SCHOLARSHIPS)

. . .Evaluation of

(A) *first form*

CONTRACT EVALUATION FORM

Your Name: _____

Contract Title: _____

Date Approved: _____

Date Completed: _____

Number of Weeks It Took and Why: _____

---

1. Where did you get the idea for the contract?

2. Did you plan well? Why or why not?

3. Did you enjoy this contract? Is there more to learn about this subject? Do you think you will ever return to it?

4. Did you encounter any problems in the contract? What were they? How were they solved or did you solve them?

5. Did you accomplish your objective? Why or why not?

6. Did you learn something new? About yourself? About others?

(B) *second form*

PROJECT EVALUATION FORM

Student: _____ Date: _____

Evaluator: _____

Please check below each statement the word, phrase, or space which most closely corresponds with your evaluation. If none of the available comments apply, please write your own comments. If you are unable to judge an item, make no marks.

* *

1. Interest level throughout the project:
   ( ) Consistently High   ( ) Improved   ( ) Sufficient
   ( ) Dropped   ( ) Low

2. Accepts responsibility for:
   a. Attendance and Punctuality
      ( ) Dependable   ( ) Improved   ( ) Sufficient   ( ) Decreased
      ( ) Undependable
   b. Maintaining project and room:
      ( ) Dependable   ( ) Improved   ( ) Sufficient   ( ) Decreased
      ( ) Undependable

3. States in writing the goals of study (check what applies):
   ( ) Challengingly ( ) Originally ( ) Realistically ( ) Specifically
   ( ) Measurably

4. Lists in writing the methods of doing study (check what applies):
   ( ) Clearly   ( ) Realistically   ( ) In Logical Order
   ( ) In Ample Detail   ( ) Vaguely

5. Locates pertinent information from a variety of sources:
   ( ) Most Ably   ( ) Improved   ( ) Sufficient   ( ) Least Ably

6. Organizes information and materials well:
   ( ) Consistently ( ) Improved   ( ) Sufficiently   ( ) Decreased
   ( ) Seldom

7. Organizes time wisely:
   ( ) Consistently   ( ) Improved   ( ) Sufficiently   ( ) Decreased
   ( ) Seldom

8. Analyzes and criticizes (such as compares viewpoints, questions, judges, evaluates information, solves problems, uses logic, corrects errors, etc.):
   ( ) Consistently   ( ) Improved   ( ) Sufficiently   ( ) Decreased
   ( ) Seldom

9. Creates; produces original product; thinks original thoughts:
   ( ) Consistently   ( ) Improved   ( ) Sufficiently   ( ) Seldom

10. Works with little or no supervision:
    ( ) Consistently   ( ) Improved   ( ) Sufficiently   ( ) Decreased
    ( ) Seldom

11. Amount of teacher guidance needed as project progressed:
    ( ) Less and Less   ( ) Same as When Started   ( ) More and More

12. Makes a final presentation which is (check what applies):
    ( ) Interesting ( ) Creative ( ) Well-organized ( ) Unimaginative

13. Demonstrates increased general knowledge of study:
    ( ) Most Increase   ( ) Moderate Increase   ( ) Little Increase

14. Demonstrates increased depth of understanding (example: learning a specialized vocabulary and adding own opinions):
    ( ) Most Increase   ( ) Moderate Increase   ( ) Little Increase

15. Submits a written bibliography of sources utilized (check any that apply):
    ( ) Complete   ( ) In Proper Form   ( ) Incomplete   ( ) None

16. Shares results with other students and teachers:
    ( ) Most   ( ) High Moderate   ( ) Low Moderate   ( ) Least

17. Submits, throughout the project, evidence and evaluation of work done:
    ( ) Consistently   ( ) Regularly   ( ) Improved   ( ) Sufficiently
    ( ) Irregularly

18. Demonstrates ability to evaluate how well the objectives were accomplished:
    ( ) Very Accurately   ( ) Improved   ( ) Sufficiently   ( ) Poorly

19. Looks into suggestions which are offered:
    ( ) Consistently   ( ) Sometimes   ( ) Seldom

20. In making decisions about the project, the advisor gave:
    ( ) Too Much Help   ( ) Sufficient Help   ( ) Too Little Help

21. More decisions about the work were made in:
    ( ) Independent Study   ( ) Regular Class

22. Regular class work has:
    ( ) Improved   ( ) Remained High   ( ) Remained Low
    ( ) Gone Down

23. Followed through to completion:
    ( ) No Pushing   ( ) Some Pushing   ( ) Much Pushing

I would evaluate this project as: ( ) Acceptable   ( ) Unacceptable

On a separate sheet of paper, list any strengths and/or weaknesses inherent in the project itself, any evaluation of goals and methods accomplished, or other comments.

. . .Notice to Parents of Placement

Dear Parents,

So often a letter from school brings either a reprimand or notice of some impending doom. That is why it gives me so much pleasure to write this letter.

Your son, Jason, has been identified as a student who would benefit from our school's Gifted and Talented Program. We know Jason as an outstanding student with very special qualities which we believe would be better served in a program where he will be challenged on his own level of achievement. Pending your approval, we are placing Jason in this program at the start of the next marking period.

I have congratulated Jason on his fine record and achievements, and I would like to congratulate you as well. The care, concern, and support that Jason receives at home is an obvious contributing factor to his success.

It is a pleasure working with you and your son.

Yours sincerely,

. . .Notice to Parents of Program

Dear Parents,

This January we are beginning to prepare for our new Gifted Student Program which is slated to start in September. The program is intended to allow our students to reach their full potential.

We will be using several different criteria for student selection:

1. IQ test results.
2. Report Card grades of past years.
3. Teacher recommendations.
4. Torrence Test of Creativity.
5. Metropolitan Reading Placement Test.
6. Parent recommendation.

Before any students are assigned to this new project, materials will have to be made ready for them. Besides the normal classroom supplies, we are asking for magazines, records and tapes of the classics, reading books, extra encyclopedias, et cetera from our community.

The formation of the program has taken into consideration many different ways in which our children learn as well as the deep impact of the home upon a child's education. Consequently, the time schedules within our program will be far different from what they have been in the past (see attached sample schedule). Also, because of the difference in class assignments, we will be asking for the total support of the home. Periodic letters of progress will be sent from the student's advisor with replies required. Your input is essential to the success of our project.

There will be a meeting on Friday, January 29, 19XX, in the school auditorium at 7:30 P.M. to explain all of the ramifications and goals of this project. All teachers, administrators, and advisors to the program will be present. You are cordially invited to attend.

We hope to see you there.

Sincerely,

J. Benson, Principal

. . .Philosophy of Education of

To educate the gifted and/or talented student fully, we believe that certain criteria are essential to leading the student toward the recognition of his or her full potential.

Toward that end, all work assignments, enrichment activities, and scheduling having to do with the Gifted Student Program must meet with the following criteria:

1. Enlarging their worlds.
2. Exploring and exercising their minds.
3. Bringing them new and meaningful challenges.
4. Pinpointing their fields of interest.
5. Allowing them to be creative.

. . .Withdrawal from Program

GIFTED AND TALENTED PROGRAM WITHDRAWAL STATEMENT

Student: _____

Date: _____

At this time, it is recommended that my son/daughter not continue in the Gifted and Talented Program.

This decision has been initiated by _____.
I have met with the guidance counselor and the teacher to discuss this matter.

COMMENTS FROM PARENTS:

COMMENTS FROM COUNSELOR:

COMMENTS FROM TEACHER:

COMMENTS FROM STUDENT:

_____	_____
Parent's Signature	Guidance Counselor's Signature
_____	_____
Parent's Signature	Teacher's Signature
_____	
Student's Signature	

GOALS   (See Also: CURRICULUM; OBJECTIVES)

. . .District Goals

The following are the goals identified by all the schools in the district:

1. To acquire basic skills in obtaining information, solving problems, thinking critically, and communicating effectively.

2. To learn to enjoy the process of learning and acquire skills necessary for a lifetime of continuous learning and adaptation.

3. To develop an understanding of a student's worth, abilities, potentialities, and limitations.

. . .For a Middle School

MIDDLE SCHOOL GOALS

The following goals support the philosophy statement. The goals are not in order of priority:

1. Provide a middle school experience which will nurture and promote positive self-concept and self-discipline.

2. Provide a strong and balanced comprehensive program which includes the following: basic communicative, mathematical, physical fitness and study skills competencies, growth in creativity through exploration, and a variety of learning experiences.

3. Provide specific programs needed by teachers to meet the needs of students and emphasize the goals, objectives, instructional processes, and evaluation procedures necessary to implement an effective middle school.

4. Provide enrichment and advisory programs to assist learners in their quest for personal identity and self-expression and to prepare them to make appropriate educational, career, consumer, and recreational decisions in the future.

5. Provide experiences designed to develop attitudes and beliefs necessary for functioning as part of a democratic society.

6. Provide processes whereby learners receive multiple services designed to enable them to acquire and apply transition from the elementary to the secondary school as well as from childhood to adolescence.

7. Provide experiences designed to develop skills in interpersonal relationships.

8. Provide a balance of stimulating and enriching programs and support systems for ALL students.

9. Provide cocurricular activities, including an enriched intramural program, as an instructional vehicle while deemphasizing interscholastic competition in athletics.

10. Provide a structure for ongoing communication between the home and school.

11. Provide opportunities for the development of problem solving and critical thinking skills and an awareness of information technologies.

12. Provide organization of students, teachers, and time into grade-level clusters.

. . .Letter on Attainment of

Dear Mrs. Miller,

As your supervisor and evaluator, it has always given me the greatest pleasure to visit your classroom and observe the fine work you do with your students. It is obvious that a great deal of hard work and preparation goes into each lesson.

Therefore, when we had our summary conference last year, and you outlined your goals for your department for this current academic year, I would have been reticent about sanctioning such an ambitious program for anyone but you. Now, at the conclusion of this current year, I see that my judgment was correct.

Certainly, your goals were ambitious; certainly you have attained them with distinction.

I shall, of course, be much more specific in my written evaluation and in our summary conference, but I wanted you to know ahead of time that you have done an outstanding job, that you have attained your goals in the most meritorious manner, and that I, for one, am proud to have you as a member of this staff.

Yours sincerely,

. . .Outcome Goals

The following are the outcome goals of education as identified by teachers, students, and parents:

1. To acquire basic skills in obtaining information, solving problems, thinking critically, and communicating effectively.

2. To acquire job-entry-level skills and, also, to acquire knowledge necessary for further education, so that it serves as basic universal application for ALL students: NO TRACKING OR BREAKDOWN INTO COLLEGE/NONCOLLEGE.

3. To learn to enjoy the process of learning and acquire skills necessary for a lifetime of continuous learning and adaptation.

. . .Process Goals

The following goals involve the process of education:

1. Teaching staff and administrative members of high quality.

2. Providing a stimulating environment that activates the student's interests in all aspects of the curriculum and motivates the student to seek his or her full potential.

3. Instruction which bears a meaningful relationship to the present and future needs and/or interests of pupils.

. . .Projected Goals for the School

The Board of Education sanctions and promulgates the following goals for education within the township as a guide for its policy and other determinations. The public schools shall help every person to:

1. Acquire basic skills in obtaining information, solving problems, thinking critically, and communicating effectively.

2. Acquire the knowledge, skills, and understanding that permit his or her participation in a satisfying and responsible role on the job and as a consumer.

3. Learn to enjoy the process of education and to acquire the skills necessary for a lifetime of continuous learning and adaptation to change, and wise use of leisure time.

4. Acquire a stock of basic information, covering the principles of physical, biological, and social sciences, the historical record of human achievements and failures, and current social issues, including knowledge of the environment.

5. Become an effective and responsible contributor to the decision-making processes of the political and other institutions of the community, state, country, and world.

6. Acquire the ability to form satisfying and responsible relationships with a wide range of other people, including, but not limited to, those with social and cultural characteristics different from his or her own.

7. Acquire the capacities for playing satisfying and responsible roles in family life and society, including social customs, manners, morals, ethics, and integrity.

8. Acquire the knowledge, habits, and attitudes that promote personal and public health in physical, mental, and emotional maturity.

9. Acquire the ability and the desire to express himself or herself creatively in one or more of the arts, and to appreciate the esthetic expressions of other people.

10. Develop an understanding of his or her own worth, abilities, potentialities, and limitations.

GRADES (See Also: EXAMINATIONS; FAILURE; GIFTED STUDENTS; PERMANENT RECORDS; REPORT CARDS; SCHOLARSHIPS; TUTORS)

. . .Letter on Outstanding Grades

Dear Jenny,

They lied to me! They told me somewhere along the line that it was impossible to have a straight "A" student who was also one of the most popular students in school, one of the most active socially, and one of the most talented as well. They said it simply could not happen.

Of course, they had never met you. When you graduate this June, it will be with a straight "A" average for your four years here at Rock Township High School. During that time, you have also been elected "Campus Queen" during your junior and senior years, voted "most popular" in the yearbook, and have been a mainstay of both the drama club and the student council. If "they" had met you, their entire definition of "brilliant student" would have changed.

I am most pleased and honored to have had you as a student. Congratulations on this outstanding achievement.

Yours sincerely,

. . .Notice to Teachers on Final Averages

The following information is intended to assist teachers in the determination of final averages:

1. The final average is to reflect the work done during the four marking periods. If a student entered our school late, please check with Guidance for the previous grades and incorporate them into the final average.

2. The letter grades given during each marking period are assigned the following numerical values:

    A = 8, B+ = 7, B = 6, C+ = 5, C = 4, D = 2, F = 0

3. Using these values, determine the final average by totaling the grades and referring to the table on the following page.

YEARLY TOTAL	FINAL AVERAGE	YEARLY TOTAL	FINAL AVERAGE
32		21	
31	A	20	C+
30		19	
		18	
29		17	
28	B+	16	C
27		15	
26		14	
25		13	
24	B	12	C or D
23		11	(teacher judgment)
22		10	
		9	
		8	D
		7	
		6	

4. For yearly totals of 5 and below, teachers are to exercise judgment based on individual student merit as to whether a grade of "D" or "F" is to be given.

5. Please refer any questions to the Guidance Office.

. . .Philosophy of Grading

Marks serve several legitimate educational purposes—to inform parents how their child is perceived in school, socially and academically, to help the student see himself or herself as a learner and set his goals for further areas of learning, to monitor the student for school placement, and to regulate the flow of pupils into various programs.

There are as many ideas about marks as there are students, teachers and parents. They are, at best, our only assessment of the achievement of the student.

Students are marked on recitations, tests, quizzes, papers, participation, and in some cases extracredit work. Parents often question a teacher's grades. For this reason, it is wise to have approximately two grades a week for each student which assesses his or her work in a specific area. Since students often have an "off" day, many teachers, when averaging a student's grades, drop the lowest one (provided it is not an important project).

Teachers may be asked for the reasons for the failures each marking period, and the steps the teacher took during the period covered to see that the failure was averted. This is not for the purpose of "checking up" on the teacher, but is primarily to help in the education of the pupil and to keep the parents informed of what they can do for their children in their school work.

Halfway through each marking period warning notices will be sent to the parents of all students in danger of failing a subject in that marking period. A grade of "F" cannot be given on the report card unless a warning notice has been sent to the parents at least two weeks in advance.

It should always be remembered that marks should be given in relation to the ability of the student who is being marked. Marks on efforts alone should not be above "C," but a pupil who does as well as he is able, regardless of his or her accomplishments, should be passed. In subjects such as algebra, geometry, foreign language, stenography, et cetera, the pupil without the ability to do the work should be transferred to another subject. In this connection, it is the responsibility of each teacher to know the approximate ability of each student. Past records, test scores, et cetera are available at the Guidance Office and should be used. Guidance Counselors are eager to assist with any problems of placement.

GRADUATION (See Also: ASSEMBLIES; DEGREES; FAILURE; PERMANENT RECORDS)

. . .Memo to Faculty Concerning

TO ALL MEMBERS OF PROFESSIONAL STAFF:

Well, we've made it through another year—almost. The only thing that remains is graduation. I know that most of us have been through that before, but a little reminder should help all of us, myself included.

ALL faculty should arrive at the field (auditorium if the weather doesn't cooperate) by 6:30 P.M. Please take seats in the special section of the bleachers marked "FACULTY." Since this is the culminating activity for the students you have nurtured over the past four years, I would think that you would wish to dress appropriately. I intend to introduce the faculty as a unit and have you all stand in unison during the ceremony.

In general, if you can help out in any way and are not already assigned a special task, it would be greatly appreciated if you pitched in. We can use all the help we can get.

Above all, you have earned this special time as much as our students who will be graduating. Enjoy yourselves!

. . .Notice of Nongraduation

Dear Mr. and Mrs. Brady,

It is my unhappy duty to inform you that your son, Adam, will not be graduating with his class in the June 19XX ceremonies.

It is our policy to give every consideration to senior students, but, as I advised you in letters dated January 17, March 21, April 12, and May 6, 19XX, Adam's steadfast refusal to participate in class, to take any tests, or to do any assigned work has led to such academic weaknesses that it is impossible for him to pass his required courses.

I hope that we will be able to help Adam to overcome this very serious situation. If Adam applies himself to summer school courses, he may be able to receive his diploma in September or sometime early next year.

We stand ready to provide whatever assistance we may. Please call upon us and advise us of your decision in this matter.

Sincerely,

J. Benson, Principal

. . .Procedures for

GRADUATION, 19XX

The following procedures for graduation must be followed by all students who intend to receive diplomas:

1. On Wednesday, June 16, 19XX, graduating seniors will report to the Guidance Office to pick up their caps and gowns. You must sign for these items before you receive them.

2. On Thursday, June 17, 19XX, seniors will report to the Girl's Gym by 6:30 P.M. Seniors are to bring their caps and gowns and be ON TIME. Anyone who is late will hold back procedures for all others. BE ON TIME!

3. Once in the Girl's Gym, students will change into their caps and gowns and line up as arranged at practice. Students are not to leave the gym.

4. Mr. Weldman will be in charge of graduation. All problems are to be referred to him, and the students are to follow his directions.

5. Upon Mr. Weldman's signal, students will proceed to the athletic field and proceed with graduation ceremonies as rehearsed.

6. Upon completion of ceremonies, students will report back to the Girl's Gym where they will return caps and gowns and have their names checked off.

7. Students not returning caps and gowns will be charged the full price for them.

8. In the event of rain, the same procedures will be followed, except that the ceremonies will be held in the auditorium.

GRANTS (See Also: BUDGET; FINANCIAL)

. . .Grant Application Form

This application form has been designed to be as simple as possible to encourage professional staff members to apply. Please review evaluation criteria on page two of the Information Bulletin. Be sure to read the Information Bulletin before completing this document.

_____   For Funding Period _____
Date   (Spring, Fall, or Winter)

_____
Applicant's Name

_____
Home Address

_____   _____
Home Phone   School Phone

_____   _____
Position   School
IDENTIFICATION NUMBER: _____
(For Office Use Only)

                                    _____
                                    Applicant's Signature

Forward Proposal to: Rock Township Education Foundation
                     123 Crescent Drive
                     Rock Township, State 00000

If you have any questions, please call Ms. Joan Fermatt (555-1234).

Note: Attach additional pages if necessary.

SUMMARY PARAGRAPH:

1. PURPOSE AND NEED: What is the purpose of the project? Why do you believe there is a special need for this project?

2. TRANSFERABILITY: Approximately how many students will be affected by this project? Is the project such that it can be used by other schools? Explain.

3. OBJECTIVES: List your specific objectives. Be sure to state your objectives so that they can be evaluated when your project is completed.

4. PROCEDURES/METHODS: What are you going to do and how are you going to accomplish your objectives? What materials will you need? Give a time schedule of events.

5. EVALUATION: How will you determine whether your objectives have been achieved or whether your project is successful?

6. BUDGET: Detail your budget request. Include specific information such as kinds of materials and equipment needed and costs. Categories to be used could be items such as materials, equipment, transportation, honorariums, food, etc. Stipends to the applicant(s) will not be approved.

ITEM	BUDGET AMOUNT
EX: two cassette tape recorders	$90.00

. . .Grant Information Sheet

PURPOSE

The purpose of these small grants is to assist classroom teachers to foster innovative instructional processes and programs and to provide the time, talent, and resources to motivate students to learn and to achieve.

ELIGIBILITY

Any professional staff member in the Rock Township Public School District is encouraged to apply for the grants which will be awarded on a competitive basis.

APPLICATIONS

Applications have been designed to encourage teachers to apply. Applications may be obtained from the principals offices or from the Rock Township Education Foundation, 123 Crescent Dr., Rock Township, State 00000.

DATES

There will be three funding periods during which applications will be reviewed and grants awarded. The funding timeline for each period is below.

SPRING   Applications due January 31. Awarded March 1. Funding period is from March 1 to May 31.

FALL   Applications due June 30. Awarded September 1. Funding period is from September 1 to November 30.

WINTER   Applications due October 31. Awarded December 1. Funding period is from December 1 to February 28.

Obtain your applications now and submit them to Rock Township Education Foundation, 123 Crescent Dr., Rock Twp. The amount of the grant request should not exceed $500, and stipends should not be included.

AWARDING PROCESS

Proposals will be reviewed by the Allocations Committee of the Rock Township Education Foundation. Proposals will be evaluated on a competitive basis using a "blind" evaluation approach (neither the school or person submitting the proposal will be identified to the Allocation Committee). Checks will be issued to the person receiving the grant. Final awarding of all grants will be made by the Rock Township Education Foundation.

EVALUATION CRITERIA

The purpose of the grants is to foster innovative instructional process and programs and to provide the time, talent, and resources to motivate students to learn and to achieve. The general nature of the purpose of the grants is designed to be broad in order to encourage a wide variety of proposals. Examples of ideas for proposals which were funded by other educational foundations are available for your review from the Rock Township Education Foundation.

The minigrant proposals will be evaluated by the Allocations Committee on the following criteria:

1. *Purpose and need.* Is the statement of the purpose clear? Is there a need for the project?

2. *Transferability.* Does the project have the promise of benefiting students in the school in which it is being conducted or the Rock Township schools as a whole?

3. *Objectives.* Are the objectives clearly stated? Are they realistic and worthwhile? Are the objectives innovative? Are the objectives stated in such a manner that they can be evaluated?

4. *Procedures/Methods.* Are the procedures to be followed clearly described? How are you going to accomplish your objectives? What materials are needed? What resource personnel are needed? How will they be used? What is your timeline for completion?

5. *Evaluation.* Are the plans for evaluating the project suited to the nature of the project?

6. *Budget.* Is the budget request reasonable and sufficiently detailed?

Based on the Allocations Committee review, the Allocations Committee will (1) recommend approval by the Rock Township Education Foundation, (2) return the application with suggestions for resubmitting, or (3) disapprove the application.

Any applications which are not approved must be resubmitted if the applicant desires future consideration.

A brief evaluation report and a detailed report of final expenditures should be submitted to the Foundation at the end of the grant, indicating how your objectives have been met and how your funds have been spent. The report must be submitted thirty (30) days after the completion of the project.

GRIEVANCE PROCEDURES   (See Also: EVALUATION; REPRIMANDS)

. . .Principles of

8.7 A grievance to be considered under this procedure shall be presented by the grievant or his or her representative not later than (15) calendar days following its occurrence. The number of days allotted at each step of the grievance procedure is to be considered as a maximum time limit. Every attempt should be made to resolve the grievance as quickly as possible. A grievance which occurs near the end of the school year shall be presented on or before June 30th of the school year in which it occurred.

8.8 A grievant may present and process his or her grievance personally or through an appropriate representative. Should a grievant want to process his or her grievance personally or through an appropriate representative of his or her own choosing, he or she may do so; however, the majority unit shall be so notified and shall have the right to have its own representative present.

8.9 No reprisals shall be taken by the Board or Administration against any employee because he or she utilized the grievance procedure.

8.10 Should a grievance result from action by the Superintendent or the Board, a grievant may present his or her grievance initially as provided in 8.19.

8.11 Unless mutually agreed upon between the parties, no grievance shall be processed at a time when the grievant has regularly assigned duties.

8.12 Grievances arising from actions other than those of the immediate superior (administrator) or where such action is a public action of the Board may be initiated and processed with the Board as provided in 8.19.

8.13 If the alleged violation of the agreement is attributable to concerted action of the administrators in the district, or attributable to an administrator not limited to functioning in one building, or to the office of the superintendent, or to the Board directly, then the Association shall have the right to grieve under this article and any and all of its provisions to seek relief from the alleged violation.

8.14 The Association's right to grieve provides for the enforcement and administration of its agreement with the Board and does not intend violation of the individual's rights under law.

. . .Procedures for

8.15 A grievant may initially discuss the matter, identified as a grievance, with his or her immediate superior in an attempt to settle the grievance informally. This is not intended to extend the time limitation as set forth in 8.7.

8.16 A grievant may file a grievance in writing by presenting the written grievance to his or her principal and forwarding copies to the superintendent and the Professional Rights and Responsibilities Committee. The written grievance shall indicate the interpretation, application, or violation of policies, agreements, or administrative decision that the grievant believes adversely affects him or her.

8.17 The grievant and his or her principal shall meet in an attempt to resolve the grievance not later than five (5) school days following the date on which it was filed.

8.18 The principal shall communicate his or her decision in writing to the grievant not later than five (5) school days following their meeting. A copy of the decision shall also be forwarded, at the same time, to the Superintendent and the Township Education Association.

8.19 If the grievance has not been resolved at the initial step (principal–immediate superior), the grievant may request a hearing with the Board or its representatives. The request shall clearly explain the grievance and be made in writing not later than five (5) school days following the principal–immediate superior's decision, or if no such decision has been communicated, then not later than five (5) school days following the expiration of the five (5) school days period provided in 8.18. The grievance procedure for secretaries shall commence with the Board or its designee.

8.20 The grievant and the Board or its representatives shall meet in an attempt to resolve the grievance not later than ten (10) school days following the date on which the hearing was requested. The grievant may have up to three (3) representatives present when his or her grievance is reviewed by the Board or its representatives.

8.21 The Board shall communicate its decision in writing to the grievant not later than fifteen (15) school days following the hearing. A copy of the decision shall also be forwarded, at the same time, to the superintendent and the Township Education Association.

8.22 Should the Association decide that based on the Board's decision the grievance is satisfactorily adjusted, then the Board's decision shall be binding on all parties.

GUIDANCE (See Also: COUNSELING; PERMANENT RECORDS; REPORT CARDS; UNIT COORDINATION)

. . .Contacting Counselors

HOW TO CONTACT COUNSELORS

Counselors meet with students routinely throughout the year to get to know them better, discuss educational plans, et cetera. Students who wish to see their counselors may come to the guidance office between classes or during lunch and make an appointment or sign the counselor's sign-up sheet. The counselor will then send a pass to the student's class.

Students may also contact their counselors as they meet in the halls, cafeteria, classrooms, or other areas of the building.

Parents who wish to speak to the counselor, make an appointment for a cluster or a teacher conference, get homework for an absent child, request a progress report, et cetera should call the guidance office and arrangements will be made.

While it is customary for students to see their grade-level counselor, any other counselor is also available to be of assistance.

. . .Definition in Student Handbook

GUIDANCE DEPARTMENT

Each student in Rock Township High School will be assigned to a guidance counselor who will be more than willing to try to help the individual student with any personal or academic problem which may arise in school. Educational or vocational planning, course selections, and improvement of study habits are examples of some of the many areas with which counselors are glad to assist students.

Students who have appointments with their counselors will be given a "guidance slip" which is to be shown to the teacher when going to and returning from the Guidance Office.

Students (and their parents) are encouraged to use the facilities of the Guidance Department. Whenever a need arises, they should feel free to request a conference with a counselor and may arrange to do so through the Guidance Office secretary.

The Guidance Office publishes a special booklet annually, detailing their services. It is given to each student.

. . .Middle School Guidance Philosophy

MIDDLE SCHOOL GUIDANCE PHILOSOPHY

At no time in a student's life is there a greater need for guidance and counseling than in the middle grades. The guidance program is designed to help the middle-grade student to become a more effective student, to improve problem-solving and decision-making skills, and to become a more effective group member.

Through the application of individual and group counseling techniques, the student is encouraged to recognize his or her capacity for achievement, to develop a positive self-concept, and to grow in self-discipline.

The middle school counselors assume the role of facilitators in staff and curriculum development. They serve as resource people in helping the faculty to integrate into the curriculum the skills related to enhancing students' self-esteem and self-concept.

Each student is encouraged to recognize his or her capacity for achievement, to develop a positive self-concept, and to grow in self-discipline and social consciousness. Beyond providing academic, social, and living skills, the curriculum seeks to develop an appreciation of the ongoing quality of all learning experiences.

We hope the implementation of this philosophy challenges our children to reach their greatest potential so they will become productive, creative, responsible members of society in a changing world.

. . .Notice to Parents of Services

Dear Parents,

The services of the Guidance Department are available to all students and their parents.

A number of counselors are assigned to each grade level, and they remain with the same students throughout their high school years. This is in keeping with the developmental approach to guidance which emphasizes the growth of the individual student. Counseling services are available on an individual and group basis both upon request and according to need.

The duties of the counselor fall into three areas: working with students, working with the professional staff, and working with parents. Working with students includes counseling students on a referral or self-referral basis, administering and interpreting tests, planning and conducting orientation programs, and counseling students in selecting courses for the following year.

The counselor holds conferences related to student needs with the Child Study Team as well as with appropriate staff members. Each counselor consults with teachers to evaluate student progress, appropriate placement, and individual needs. The counselor works closely with curriculum committees, department chairpersons, liaison committees as well as with psychologists, physicians and such community agencies as the Division of Childhood and Family Services, the Commission for the Blind, Teenage Psychiatric Center, et cetera. Counselors provide supportive services to the entire staff whenever appropriate.

The counselor participates in student-teacher-parent conferences and arranges meetings between parents and members of the Child Study Team. The counselor is available to interpret test results and review school records for parents in an attempt to help them make realistic educational and vocational plans for their child. Counselors also provide career and educational information and arrange for home instruction and tutoring.

It is our sincere hope that all students and parents will take advantage of these services.

Sincerely,

H. K. Linnel,

Director of Guidance

HALL DUTY (See Also: ASSEMBLIES; BEHAVIOR; LOCKERS)

. . .Guidelines for

HALL DUTY

Teachers on Hall Duty are to be guided by the following instructions:

1. Each student in the halls during the time when classes are in session must have in his or her possession either a Hall Pass or a Library Pass.

2. Students found in the halls without a proper pass are to be escorted back to their classroom.

3. Check the boys' or girls' rooms at least twice each period and more frequently if conditions warrant.

4. Patrol the assigned area at irregular intervals.

5. Become acquainted with any classroom situation where a substitute is teaching and offer cooperation and assistance if such seems desired and/or indicated.

6. Refer all visitors to the office for a visitor's pass and assist them if possible.

7. Assist those teachers who have special activities in progress—for example, Field Trips, Health Examinations, Student Photographs.

8. Students requiring disciplinary attention are to be referred to the main office.

9. Be available to substitute briefly for any regular classroom teacher who may find it necessary to leave the classroom.

10. Teachers are expected to be on duty during the entire period of assignment and are responsible for any activity that occurs in the hall during that time.

. . .Memo to Teachers Concerning

To: ALL MEMBERS OF THE PROFESSIONAL STAFF:

The proper supervision of student traffic in the halls does much to assure the proper conduct and deportment of our students in school. Teachers on hall duty are to be guided by the following instructions:

1. Challenge each student for a proper pass signed by a teacher.

2. If any student does not have a proper pass, immediately send/escort that student back to class—no questions asked.

3. If the student is late to class, send that student to class where he or she will explain the reason for lateness to the teacher. The student will be admitted to class. (A teacher detention should be assigned for unacceptable excuses.) No students will receive a late pass from the main office.

4. No running, pushing, or shoving or any behavior which compromises safety or the maintenance of a learning atmosphere is to go uncorrected.

. . .Policy for Teachers on

GENERAL HALL SUPERVISION

Hall supervision is the responsibility of the entire staff. Each time that the student body is in the hall in the morning visitation period, between periods, or at the end of the school day, it is imperative that all staff members assist in hall supervision. Each staff member should be at the door to his or her room or at a lavatory if one is nearby. Students should be allowed to converse freely with their friends, but certain rules should be enforced:

1. Stay to the right when walking in the halls.

2. No loud talking or yelling.

3. No running.

4. No pushing or shoving.

5. No destruction of school property.

6. Any other discipline rules that apply to the movement of student traffic in the halls.

In addition, when the warning bell rings in the morning, all staff members should be sure that any students in their immediate area move to homeroom quickly and quietly.

HANDBOOK   (See Also: ANY ITEM THAT MIGHT BE INCLUDED IN A STUDENT OR TEACHER HANDBOOK SUCH AS ARE REPRESENTED IN THE SAMPLE TABLE OF CONTENTS, THE LAST ITEM IN THIS ENTRY)

. . .Guide for Handbook Use

(A) by students

Welcome to Rock Township High School. We are glad to have you here. This handbook answers many of the questions you may have about the rules and activities here at Rock Township High. We hope that this will be helpful to you throughout the year. We are looking forward to helping you have a good school year, and we're always open to any suggestions you might have.

(B) by teachers

The purpose of this compilation of suggestions and regulations is to aid new teachers in adjusting themselves to the policies of the school; and to enable all teachers to have, in concise and readily available form, answers to those questions which come up each school year. Undoubtedly those rules will be changed from time to time as circumstances change, and as we improve by discussing our problems and by experimenting with new ideas.

. . .Principal's Message in

(A) student's

WELCOME! Whether you are a newcomer to our school or an "old-timer," we hope you will find this school year to be a memorable and exciting one. Cooperation is, of course, the key, and toward that end we suggest that you read this handbook thoroughly. It will tell you exactly what we expect of you and what services and benefits you may expect from the school. We hope that you will take both messages to heart.

May this year be one of the most rewarding in your school career.

J. Benson, Principal

(B) *teacher's*

May we extend to you a warm welcome back to school. . . . It only seems a short time ago when we said good-bye. After consulting with our coordinators/cluster leaders we have developed a brief manual with the intent purpose of helping all teachers. We think it will help as it continues to further the communication and the respect that we have for each other.

Rock Township is a "special" place, and we have already *earned* the respect and admiration of the entire township's educational community. We all know that education at this level is the most difficult and challenging because it must deal forthrightly with the basics, but not omit esthetics and attitudes. Both content and the student must be valued.

Rock Township should evidence warmth, caring, and respect. Our school should be like a good family . . . composed of persons of different ages, but all respected and all with particular rules and responsibilities.

Needless to say, we are here to help you do what you do best, and no one does it better than Rock Township: T.E.A.C.H.

Have your *best* year *this* year!!! Please continue to help us on our journey to exemplary status.

. . .Sample Table of Contents

TABLE OF CONTENTS

HOMEROOM   (See Also: ASSIGNMENTS; CLASS; FAILURE; GRADES; PERMANENT RECORDS; REQUIREMENTS)

. . .Homeroom Attendance Procedures for First Day of School

HOMEROOM ATTENDANCE PROCEDURES

1. Send one (1) student to the office with attendance *by 8:20 A.M.*

2. Have office check off each homeroom as attendance comes in to be sure all forms have been collected.

3. All students arriving after attendance has been sent down *must report to the main office.*

4. If bus is late and attendance has already been taken in homeroom, but not sent to the office, homeroom teacher is to *remove students' names* from the absentee sheet *and* do not add to tardy sheet *since* it is not their fault that the bus was late.

5. If bus arrives after homeroom period, all students on the bus must report to the main office before entering period 1 class.

6. For attendance purposes, homeroom lists with students' names will be used for the first four (4) days of school: September 6, September 7, September 8, and September 9.

   Teachers: On September 6, September 7, and September 8 attendance sheets, please add names if not on sheet, or mark AB for absent after name if student does not appear. On September 9 attendance sheet, please write "delete" after the name of student(s) who have been marked AB by you on September 6, September 7, and September 8. If they appeared on any of the latter dates, DO NOT DELETE. *This is an extremely important* procedure to follow since it will be used for the September register to see exactly which students are actually enrolled and which ones did not appear.

7. Beginning on September 12, you will receive a standard attendance form to be used for the remainder of the school year.

8. Students who were absent must bring in an absence note signed by a parent and turn it into their homeroom teacher the next day. This note is to be placed in the teacher's attendance envelope.

9. This procedure will continue to be timesaving, convenient, and easy for all involved.

. . .Memo on Procedures

RE: *HOMEROOM PROCEDURES*

We want to bring the following information to your attention:

ENROLLMENT

Enrollment sheets for your classes are to be turned in to the main office for the first four days of school, that is, September 6 through September 9. On these sheets, please enter the class title and the number of students who actually appeared in your class each period. These are to be turned in to the main office at the end of each day.

LOCKER ASSIGNMENT

Attached please find a homeroom list with locker numbers and combinations for each of your students. When lockers are issued, please make a "big to-do" about locker combinations. Students must be convinced that if they choose to give their combination away to anyone, they are giving away any security attached to that locker. Because we have constraints on the number of lockers we have, we cannot be expected to change any locker for any reason, except an emergency. Quite frankly, if a student gives another student a combination, then that student must live with the consequences of that action.

While simple directions on how to open lockers have been enclosed, sixth grade teachers especially should plan some time to assist students in opening lockers since it is an extremely confusing task for these students.

Once individual lockers and combinations have been issued, please return the locker/combo/master sheet to Mr. Pietkewicz. After issuance, no changes can be made except by Mr. Pietkewicz since every locker issued must correlate with Rock Township's master.

To avoid confusion when students arrive, we strongly recommend that each homeroom teacher try the combinations of their students and report any problems to Mr. Pietkewicz before the end of the day, Friday, September 2.

Students with special needs (N.I.) have been included in regular homerooms this year. Homeroom teachers will note that the lockers of these students *are not* in the same location as the lockers of your homeroom students. Their lockers are situated next to their regular self-contained classroom. However, please issue a locker and combination to these students when others receive theirs. The special attention these students need in opening lockers will be given by their regular self-contained classroom teacher.

INSURANCE FORMS, FREE-LUNCH APPLICATIONS, EMERGENCY INFORMATION CARDS

These forms and two emergency information cards must be returned Wednesday, September 7. Again, please alphabetize them and return them to the main office by the end of the day.

HOMEWORK   (See Also: CLASS; GRADES; GUIDANCE; PERMANENT RECORDS; REPORT CARDS; REQUIREMENTS)

. . .Helpful Hints for Parents

Middle school presents a challenge for students in terms of increased amounts of homework, longer-term assignments, and individual responsibility for getting the work done and meeting deadlines.

Most clusters provide homework calendars on which students must write their assignments for each class. Each page has one week's assignments and should be kept in the student's notebook.

Students should have the telephone numbers of one or two reliable students who are in their classes so that they can call them for the assignments if the students are absent. If the absence will be for three or more days, parents should call the Guidance Office for assignments. Twenty-four hours' notice is required so teachers can prepare assignments.

When students are absent from school or a class for any reason, it is their responsibility to check with their teachers and arrange to make up the work that was missed.

. . .Notice of Incomplete Homework

Date: _____

Student: _____

Dear _____,

    I would like you to be aware that _____ presently has _____ incomplete _____ assignments. It is important for _____ progress that all work be completed on time.

    Your cooperation in this matter would be greatly appreciated. Kindly sign and return this notice. Should you have any questions, you may contact me at school.

Yours sincerely,

Teacher's Signature: _____

Parent's Signature: _____

. . .Weekly Planning Calendar

SUBJECT	MONDAY	TUESDAY	WEDNESDAY	THURSDAY	FRIDAY
Grammar					
Math					
Reading					
Science					
Soc. St.					

HONOR ROLL   (See Also: AWARDS; CITIZENSHIP; EXAMINATIONS; NATIONAL HONOR SOCIETY; PERMANENT RECORDS)

. . .Application for Inclusion

HONOR ROLL APPLICATION FORM

NAME: _____   DATE: _____

GRADE: _____   HOME ROOM: _____

MARKING PERIOD (Circle One):   1   2   3   4

I AM APPLYING FOR PLACEMENT ON THE ( ) HONOR ROLL
                                   ( ) HIGH HONOR ROLL

Please fill in the following for the Marking Period:

SUBJECT	TEACHER	GRADE

UPON CHECKING THE ABOVE INFORMATION, YOUR NAME WILL BE PLACED ON THE APPROPRIATE HONOR ROLL.

. . .Explanation to Parents

To qualify for honor roll, a student must have a 6.0 average or better with no grade lower than a "C" in any subject. To qualify for high honor roll a student must have a 7.6 or above average with no grade lower than a "B." To arrive at the number of quality points a student has received, add the quality points for each letter grade and divide by the number of subjects the student is taking. The number of required quality points are listed below.

A student is not eligible for honor roll with a failing grade in any subject. To arrive at the number of quality points a student has received, add the quality points for each letter grade and divide by the number of subjects the student is taking.

Letter Grade	Quality Points
A	8
B+	7
B	6
C+	5
C	4
D	2
F	0

. . .Policy on

Students will be named to the Honor Roll if:

A. They have at least a six-point average in all of their subjects. To compute this, please note the following numerals for letter grades.

$$A = 8; B+ = 7; B = 6; C+ = 5; C = 4; D = 2; F = 0$$

For example, if a student received A (8 points) in social studies, A (8 points) in English, B+ (7 points) in science, B (6 points) in math, C+ (5 points) in physical education, B (6 points) in Spanish, then his or her total would be 40 points. Divided by the number of subjects (6), it would equal 6.66 or a 6.7 average or a B+.

B. They pass ALL subjects.

C. An "Incomplete" is made up within 10 school days.

D. They meet the behavior requirements of nothing lower than a 3 in work habits or social attitudes. (These will be checked in special cases by Guidance.)

Marks in work habits and conduct are given according to a numerical system:

    1—Excellent   3—Improvement Made
    2—Satisfactory   4—Improvement Needed
           5—Parental Conference Requested

IDEAS   (See Also: PHILOSOPHY; SUGGESTIONS)

. . .Acknowledgment of a Good Idea

Dear Mrs. Thomas,

I just finished reading the note you left for me. May I say that I think your idea is outstanding.

We have been looking for a solution to the study hall problem for some time, and it looks as if you have provided us with the answer. Your suggestions are not only sensible, but perfectly within the realm of realization as well.

Please set up an appointment with me so that I may thank you personally and further discuss your excellent idea.

Thank you for sharing your thoughts with me.

Sincerely,

J. Benson, Principal

. . .Compiling Good Ideas

Dear Faculty,

I had a good idea recently. I know, I know—some of you are thinking that it may be time for a celebration. There, I said it first!

Seriously, my good idea is that this faculty is filled with good ideas. Indeed, as I have traveled through this building and stopped in your classrooms, I have been privileged to witness some fine ideas put into action. In fact, I am so impressed by you that I want to share what we have.

Could each of you take a moment, right now, to write down ONE new idea or novel method or something that has worked well for you in your day-to-day teaching? It will only take a few moments. When you're finished and those marvelous ideas I witnessed are finally written down, give them to me.

What I intend to do is to compile an "in-house" book of good ideas that I will share with each of you and give to new teachers next year.

How about it? Would you be willing to share? The ones who will benefit will be our students.

Come on, do it now!

Yours sincerely,

. . .Gentle Denial of a Poor Idea

Dear Mr. Bernard,

I have read with great interest your suggestions on improving the physical education facilities of our school. It is evident that a great deal of thought went into them and that you have the welfare of our students in mind. They are clear, precise, and do you a great credit.

This makes it all the more difficult for me to tell you that it is not possible to implement your suggestions at this time. Recent budgetary cutbacks, of which you may be aware, have necessitated a hard look at each dollar spent, and our prime concern must be for the maintenance of the academic curriculum. Consequently, it would not be possible to go ahead with the plans you have suggested.

I want to thank you, however, for sharing your ideas with me. I hope I will be hearing from you again in the near future.

Thank you for being so interested in the good of our school.

Sincerely,

J. Benson, Principal

. . .Soliciting New Ideas

To: ALL MEMBERS OF THE PROFESSIONAL STAFF

If you stand in pitch blackness and hold a match in your hand and NEVER STRIKE IT, you will never get out of the dark. I doubt that there is anyone who would care to argue that point.

If you have a good idea, and it stays in your head and is never shared with anyone, that idea, however bright, will die the death of the unstruck match in the dark. In my mind, there is no refutation of this point either.

Ideas, like matches, need to be struck against something in order to take light.

May I suggest that I would very much like to play the role of that striking stone. If you have an idea about this school, the administration, the kids, our curriculum, the cafeteria—I want to hear about it; I want to share your enthusiasm; I want to help you if I can see that idea spread.

Drive back the darkness—use me!

IEP (INDIVIDUALIZED EDUCATIONAL PRESCRIPTION)
(See Also: INSTRUCTION; SPECIAL EDUCATION)

. . .Coding Sheet

1. First Name: _____   7. Town: _____

2. Full Name: _____   8. School: _____

3. Birthdate: _____   9. Current Place: _____

4. Sex: M   F   10. Teacher/G.C.: _____

5. Phone: _____   11. Case No.: _____

6. Address: _____   12. Parent's Name: _____

DATES: AR Conf.: _____   Initial IEP Conf.: _____   Reevaluation Due: _____

ANNUAL REVIEW PARTICIPANTS

CST Member: _____   Teacher: _____

Principal: _____   Teacher: _____

Parent: _____

OTHER PARTICIPANTS:

Title: _____   Name: _____

Title: _____   Name: _____

Title: _____   Name: _____

Title: _____   Name: _____

Classification: _____   Rationale for Placement: _____

_____

_____

CIRCLE SPECIAL ED. PROGRAM:

1. Supplemental Instruction
2. Resource Room
3. Perceptually Impaired Class
4. Neurologically Impaired Class
5. Emotionally Disturbed Class
6. Multiply Handicapped Class
7. Trainable Mentally Retarded Class
8. Educable Mentally Retarded Class
9. Communication Handicapped Class
10. Preschool Handicapped Class
11. _____

CIRCLE SUBJECTS:

1. All Subjects
2. Acad. Mainstreaming When Possible
3. Nonacad. Mainstream. When Possible
4. _____
   _____

CIRCLE RELATED SERVICES:

1. Speech
2. Adaptive Phys. Education
3. Transportation
4. In-school Counseling
5. Occupational Therapy
6. Physical Therapy
7. _____

Regular Program: _____

Dates of Program: _____

Monitoring Schedule: _____

Case Manager: _____

Primary Language: English   Spanish   _____

CIRCLE EXEMPTIONS: §
1. Not Applicable
2. Alternative Standardized Testing
3. Modified HSPT Testing as per IG
4. Ex. HSPT Exam—Proficiencies not in IEP
5. Ex. HSPT Exam—Student adversely affected
6. Ex. HSPT Reading—Proficiencies not in IEP
7. Ex. HSPT Reading—Student adversely affected
8. Ex. HSPT Math—Proficiencies not in IEP
9. Ex. HSPT Math—Student adversely affected
10. Ex. HSPT Writing—Proficiencies not in IEP
11. Ex. HSPT Writing—Student adversely affected
12. Ex. from District Discipline Policy
13. Ex. from District Attendance Policy
14. _____
15. _____

CIRCLE RATIONALE FOR EXEMPTIONS:
1. Not Applicable
2. Emotional and Behavioral Diff.
3. Intellectual Deficiencies
4. Chronic Illness
5. Orthopedic Handicaps
6. Neurological Difficulties
7. Perceptual Difficulties
8. _____

§   MOST of these exemptions require alternatives to be specified in the IEP Goal and Objectives or IG Sections

Program Code: _____	Race: WH BK HS (Cir. one) AS Oth

CURRENT EDUCATIONAL STATUS: _____

_____
_____
_____
_____
_____
_____
_____
_____
_____

. . .Letter to Parents Concerning

Dear Mr. & Mrs. Jones,

As you are aware, Darren has been working under an Individualized Educational Prescription (IEP) in order to aid his individual growth and development this year. The year is almost over, and we would like to meet with you for a summary conference concerning Darren's progress over this time.

We have tentatively scheduled a conference for Thursday, June 7, 19XX, in the Guidance Office at 9:45 A.M. If this is NOT convenient, please contact the school as soon as possible and arrange for an alternate date.

We look forward to sharing with you some of the positive aspects of Darren's educational progress over the past academic year.

Yours sincerely,

. . .Role of Guidance in

The Guidance Counselor sits in with parents and the Child Study Team at IEP meetings to ensure that they understand the student's needs and to provide information to the team and parents about the student's educational progress and adaptation to his or her classes, teachers, and peers.

ILLNESS   (See Also: MEDICAL; PERMANENT RECORDS;
TARDINESS)

. . .Infectious Situation Report

To: J. D. HATCHER, ASST. SUPT.
From: HARRIET BYRNE, R.N.
Re: POSSIBLE INFECTIOUS SITUATION

Please be advised of a potentially infectious situation that exists at
Spaulding Elementary. On May 2, 19XX, I was called there to investi-
gate a case of head lice that had been reported by the school nurse.

Subsequent investigation uncovered the fact that the child in question
did, indeed, have head lice. Her parents were notified, educational materials given, discussion conducted, and the proper prophylaxis begun.

Further investigation of the children in the subject's class indicated that
three out of twenty-four children shared the problem. These three were
isolated, and procedures as indicated above were followed in each case.

It is my intention to conduct a follow-up investigation not only of the
primary subject's classmates, but of the entire school as well. Upon
completion of that examination, I shall issue a more complete report and
inform you of the extent of the problem, if any. In the meantime, I felt
you should be made aware of the possible ramifications of this situation.

. . .Letter of Concern Regarding

(A) for a student

Dear Robbie,

We were all upset to hear of your recent illness, and we were also
saddened to hear of the recuperative period you'll be spending at
home. I must admit that part of this concern is selfishness on our
part, for we will certainly miss someone who has been so active in
our school, so dynamic a force among students and faculty alike, so
popular and needed here at Rock Township High School. Your
absence shall be felt most deeply.

The one positive thing about the situation is the fact that you *are*
healing and getting stronger every day. That gives us hope that the
time shall pass swiftly and you will soon be back where you belong—with us.

Until then, know that our prayers and best wishes for your swift recovery are with you.

Yours sincerely,

(B) *for a teacher*

Dear George,

How happy we are that you are finally on that elusive road to recovery! We are overjoyed at the prospect that you will soon be back among us. We have missed you greatly, and if your absence has proven anything, it is that you are an essential part of this school and, quite simply, we need you!

Therefore, make certain that you take your time and get well completely before you come back, but please do come back! We miss you; the school functions better with you than without you; I could use your advice and good humor, and—most importantly—your students NEED you!

Our prayers and good wishes are with you.

Yours sincerely,

. . .Sick Leave Record Sheet

To: SPEARS, GEORGE W.
Location: ROCK TOWNSHIP HIGH SCHOOL
Re: AVAILABLE SICK AND PERSONAL DAYS
           FOR 19XX–XX.
Date: 7/8/XX

The following number of sick leave days will be available to you for the 19XX–XX school year, without loss of salary, in accordance with the Board of Education policy on absences.

19XX–XX	
Number of sick leave days accumulated	11.0
Unused personal days	1.0
19XX–XX (current year)	
Sick leave allowance	10.0
TOTAL NUMBER OF SICK LEAVE DAYS	22.0
TOTAL PERSONAL DAY ALLOWANCE	3.0

Should you have any questions regarding your sick leave time, please call Mr. Richard Ballester at 123-4567, Ext. 22.

INQUIRIES (See Also: MEDICAL; PROFESSIONAL ASSOCIATIONS; ZONING)

. . .Into Job Possibilities for Students

Dear Member of the Business Community,

There are many fine students at Rock Township High School who are honest, industrious, and capable. Many of these teenagers are anxious and willing to join the working people of our community on a part-time basis. Jobs for these young people would not only provide them with additional income, but would give them experience, direction, and responsibility that would become a valuable part of their education.

We were wondering if you, as a functioning member of the business community of Rock Township, had any part-time jobs in your establishment which might be filled by these young people? Not only would you be contributing to the growth of future citizens, but I am certain that you would find their performance satisfactory.

If you have any such positions available, we would appreciate hearing from you. Please call me at 234-5678, Ext. 12, and we can discuss whatever you have in mind. I am certain we can find the right applicant for you.

In the name of our students, I thank you for any and all considerations.

Sincerely,

H. K. Lennel,
Director of Guidance

. . .Into Position Availability

Dear Dr. Smith,

I have been a teacher in Rock Township for the past six years. During that time I took particular interest in improving the reading skills of my students. This, in turn, led me to graduate studies in the field of reading, particularly in the instruction of those students who are drastically below grade level.

Recently, I received my Master's Degree in Reading from Fairmont University. My concentration was in remedial reading instruction.

I am anxious to serve the needs of the students of Rock Township in this regard, and I was wondering about the possibility of utilizing my knowledge on a full-time basis.

I would greatly appreciate it, therefore, if you would be kind enough to inform me if you anticipate any openings in my particular field in the near future. Needless to say, I would be more than willing to fill out any applications required, come for interviews, or present any credentials you may deem necessary.

Thank you for your many past kindnesses and for all future considerations.

> Very truly yours,
>
> Mary D. Rodner

. . .Response to Inquiry

Dear Ms. Rodner,

Thank you for your letter of January 30, 19XX, inquiring into the availability of positions in the field of remedial reading instruction in the Rock Township public schools.

I would like to congratulate you on attaining your Master's Degree and tell you that we are well aware of your fine record as a teacher in our school system.

We anticipate one opening in remedial reading for the 19XX–19XX school year. It will be on the junior high school level. As you are aware, in the interests of fairness, we must advertise the availability of this position and invite applications for it. Undoubtedly, there will be a number of applicants.

We shall, however, be very happy to consider your candidacy for the position. Please fill out the enclosed application and return it to the Central Office. Also, please call and arrange for a personal interview at your convenience.

Thank you again for your interest.

> Sincerely,
>
> Thomas Smith,
> Superintendent of Schools

INSTRUCTION   (See Also: LESSON PLANS; STUDENT
TEACHER; SUBSTITUTE TEACHERS)

. . .Improving the Quality of

The following is the policy of the Board of Education relative to staff development in order to improve the quality of instruction:

"Today's dynamic and rapidly changing society, with its tremendous accumulation of new knowledge and the attending obsolescence in some areas of practice, makes it imperative that all staff members be engaged in a continuous program of professional and technical growth in order that they may provide a quality educational program for all students being served by the Rock Township public schools.

"It is the policy of the Board of Education that a program of staff development be established to provide an opportunity for the continuous professional and technical growth of the staff through a program designed to meet documented needs.

"As a result of the operation of this policy, participants will have the opportunity to learn of developments and changes which will improve, expand and renew their skills, knowledge, and abilities."

Following this policy, the Staff Development Committee has been meeting to determine its long-term objectives. It is our intent to keep you informed of our progress.

This fall we will be surveying the staff in order to determine our priorities and directions. The following explanation of the scope and purpose of staff development is designed to give you some "food for thought" prior to our survey.

WHAT ARE SOME OF THE REASONS FOR A STAFF DEVELOPMENT PROGRAM?

1. District policy
2. District and building goals
3. Individual training desires
4. Individual objectives
5. New skills for new programs
6. Professional renewal

WHAT ARE THE COMPONENTS OF STAFF DEVELOPMENT?

I. Institutional

The type of training or research necessary to meet the district or building goals to introduce new programs or otherwise serve an institutional need would be required, and in accordance with contractual arrangements. These activities might include

1. Inservice training
2. Visits in and out of district
3. Workshops
4. Conferences
5. Internships

II. Individual

To meet individual training desires either during nonschool hours or during school hours with approval of the building administrator, programs would be voluntary and pursued independently. These might include

1. Visits
2. Workshops
3. College or university courses
4. Teacher centers

If you have any thoughts you wish to contribute, would you please direct them to a member of the Staff Development Committee.

. . .Individual Instruction

(A) attendance record

INDIVIDUAL INSTRUCTION—ATTENDANCE RECORD

MONTH _____ 19 _____

NAME OF PUPIL _____ SCHOOL _____ GRADE _____

ADDRESS _____ PARENT'S NAME _____

SIGNATURE OF INSTRUCTOR _____ SUBJECT OR SUBJECTS _____

INSTRUCTOR'S ADDRESS _____

TIME SCHEDULE

WEEK Beginning Sunday	Date	Monday Date	Hrs.	Tuesday Date	Hrs.	Wednesday Date	Hrs.	Thursday Date	Hrs.	Friday Date	Hrs.	Total Hrs.

TOTAL NUMBER OF HOURS FOR THE MONTH:

When listing the hours under "Daily" and "Total" hours, please be sure that you show no fraction other than 1/2. If the fraction involved is 1/4, please save it until you can show a fraction of 1/2 hours.

This report must be accurate. Please check your calendar for all dates to be listed under "Time Schedule."

Important: Mr. Frank Grimes, c/o Chris Clifford,
                                                              Administration

Attendance and Progress forms must be submitted, each in DUPLICATE. DO NOT HOLD forms for several months. In order to meet the payroll deadline, it is necessary that you have this two-page form in the office of the Supervisor of Special Services by the last working day of the month. To accomplish that, you must have the form in the interoffice mail by 8:00 A.M. three work days prior to the last working day of the month. Please include completed work only for this month and any unreported work for the preceding month.

(Note—The same procedure can be followed on the 15th of the month if payment is desired on the 30th.)

NOTE:

(B) *progress report*

INDIVIDUAL INSTRUCTION
PROGRESS REPORT

MONTH _____ 19_____

NAME OF
PUPIL _____ SCHOOL _____

ADDRESS _____
SIGNATURE OF   SUBJECT OR
INSTRUCTOR _____ SUBJECTS _____

EACH AREA BELOW SHOULD BE COMPLETED IN DETAIL:

SUBJECT: Reading, arithmetic, etc.—pg. #s and skills being worked on, etc.

TEACHER'S PROCEDURES: Teacher-made materials, methods and tech-
                                            niques used and which work best with
                                            student, tests given, and items of interest

STUDENT'S PROGRESS: Academic progress, attitude, and physical condition

FURTHER RECOMMENDATIONS:

GRADE FOR MONTH:

TERMINATION: Date of return to regular classes, or moved, or date when instruction terminated, reason for, etc.

. . .Letter Concerning

Dear Mrs. Pearson,

I am pleased to inform you that your son, Harold, currently a sixth grade student at Hanson Middle School, has been approved for individualized instruction in the subjects of English and math for the 19XX–XX academic year. His teacher will be Mrs. DiSalvo, and the individualized instruction will begin on September 6, 19XX, the first day of school of the upcoming academic year.

Should you have any questions regarding this arrangement, please feel free to call me at 123-4567, Ext. 21, during regular school hours.

Yours sincerely,

INTERVIEW (See Also: CONFERENCES; COUNSELING; GUIDANCE)

. . .Interview Evaluation Sheet

INTERVIEW EVALUATION

Candidate: _____ Date: _____

Interview for the position of: _____

Interviewer: _____

Please check the appropriate category:

ITEM	HIGH	VERY HIGH	SATIS-FACTORY	LOW	UNACCEPT-ABLE
1. Credentials					
2. Knowledge of subject area					
3. Reflects philosophy of district					

ITEM	HIGH	VERY HIGH	SATIS-FACTORY	LOW	UNACCEPT-ABLE
4. Enthusiasm					
5. Originality of ideas					
6. Apparant affinity for students					
7. Innovative ideas					
8. Receptiveness to suggestions					
Overall impression: _____					
Comments: _____					
Recommendation(s): _____					

. . .Report on

REPORT ON THE INTERVIEW OF: _____

FOR THE POSITION OF: _____

DATE HELD: _____ WHERE: _____

INTERVIEWER(S): _____

_____

SUBJECTS DISCUSSED: _____

_____

STRONG POINTS OF CANDIDATE: _____

_____

AREAS OF CONFLICT: _____

_____

COMMENTS: _____

_____

RECOMMENDATION(S): _____

_____

Signature of
Head Interviewer: _____

Please attach Interview Evaluation Sheet.

. . .Request to Come for

Dear _____,

Your application for a position in the Rock Township public school system is currently under review. We have arranged for a personal interview as follows:

INTERVIEW FOR THE POSITION OF: _____

INTERVIEWER: _____

DATE: _____ TIME: _____

PLACE: _____

COMMENTS: _____

_____

If this is inconvenient for you, please notify us at least 48 hours in advance at 123-4567, Ext. 17.

INTRODUCTION   (See Also: NEWSLETTER; NEWS RELEASES; PUBLIC RELATIONS; VOLUNTEERS)

. . .Of a New Administrator

To: THE FACULTY OF ROCK TOWNSHIP HIGH SCHOOL
From: THOMAS SMITH, SUPERINTENDENT OF SCHOOLS
Re: YOUR NEW PRINCIPAL

I would like to take this opportunity to introduce Mr. John T. Benson, the new principal of your high school.

Mr. Benson was selected from a number of highly qualified candidates. He has taught for eight years, holds an M.A. in Administration and Supervision from Fairmont University, and has served as vice-principal of Talburg High School for the past seven years. He is an energetic, vital human being with a background of practical experience in education. I am certain that, with your cooperation, he will do an exemplary job.

. . .Of a New Faculty Member

Dear Faculty,

I'd like to introduce myself. My name is Mary Rodner, and I am the new remedial reading teacher here at Miller Junior High School. I have a Master's Degree in reading from Fairmont University with a concentration in the instruction of remedial reading. Before coming to this position, I taught right here in Rock Township for six years.

Believe me, I know the time-consuming work that goes into effective teaching. I also know firsthand the exasperation and frustration involved in dealing with the student who is drastically below grade level in reading. In fact, it was just that feeling which led me into the study of reading.

Perhaps, in some small way, I may be of help. If you have any students who you feel could use my services, please refer them to me. I am in the process of reviewing records now, and very shortly I shall start a schoolwide testing program. I want to work with you as a partner in the education of our students.

I am anxious to get started, and I look forward to getting to know you on a professional and on a personal level.

I'm glad to be here,

Mary D. Rodner

JOB (See Also: WORKING PAPERS)

. . .Example of Job Description

JOB DESCRIPTION

Title:	Teacher
Alternate Title:	Resource Teacher, Speech, Audio-Visual, Media Specialists, Learning Consultants, Social Worker, Guidance Counselor, Nurse, Psychologist
Qualifications:	Holds or is eligible for a New Jersey Instructional Certificate with the appropriate teaching endorsement.
Immediate Responsibility:	Appropriate administrator
Overall Job Goal:	To implement Board policy regarding educational philosophy/curriculum under the direction of the administration through planning; organizing, managing; interacting with students; establishing rapport with students, staff, parents, and community; and continuing professional development.
Functions:	1. Plans instructional objectives and activities consistent with the curriculum guides.
	2. Directs and supervises learning activities.
	3. Implements the disciplinary procedures of the district.
	4. Supervises behavior in the school environment to maintain the safety and well-being of the students and staff.
	5. Selects material suitable to the educational objectives.

6. Utilizes a variety of analytical and evaluative techniques suitable to the curriculum content.

7. Communicates a positive support of the students in their educational development.

8. Recognizes the exemplary influences of the educator over the student.

9. Relates with staff, parents, and community through positive professional cooperation.

10. Suggests positive recommendations for the continuing review and development of curriculum.

11. Remains abreast of current developments and contemporary interpretations of subject matter and teaching methodology consistent with the professional assignment.

12. Actively participates at scheduled staff meetings and serves on educational committees.

13. Assumes responsibility periodically for conferences with parents.

14. Recognizes the extracurricular program as integral development of the child.

15. Performs other duties within the scope of employment and certification as assigned by the appropriate administrator.

Terms of
 Employment: Ten-month year.

Evaluation: According to state statute and rule and Board policy and procedure.

. . .Letter on Job Well Done

Dear Mr. Gerren,

Recently, you were hired by our student council to perform your Magic Clown act as part of our benefit carnival in support of our Children's Hospital Fund. If your performance had not been satisfactory, I would have told you so. It is only right, therefore, that I commend you for a job well done when that is the case, as it most certainly was.

Not only was your performance flawless, but you evidenced a keen understanding of and love for children. Your material was funny, age appropriate, and of such a nature that everyone could enjoy the entire performance without offense. We were impressed.

We shall be happy to recommend you in the future. Thank you again for doing such a marvelous and entertaining job.

Yours sincerely,

. . .Request for Summer Job

SUMMER WORK REQUEST

STUDENT: _____ DATE: _____

HOME ADDRESS: _____

_____ ZIP: _____

HOME TELEPHONE NUMBER: _____ GRADE: _____

I hereby authorize the Rock Township High School Guidance Department to inform me of any available summer jobs.

I AM WILLING TO WORK DURING THE SUMMER: ( ) FULL TIME

( ) PART TIME

DATES AVAILABLE: FROM _____ UNTIL _____

I WILL WORK: ( ) DAYS ONLY   ( ) NIGHTS ONLY   ( ) EITHER

I HAVE:
( ) OWN TRANSPORTATION   ( ) TRANSPORTATION AVAILABLE
( ) PUBLIC TRANSPORTATION   ( ) BICYCLE   ( ) NONE

MINIMUM ACCEPTABLE HOURLY WAGE: _____

I HAVE: ( ) DRIVER'S LICENSE   ( ) WORKING PAPERS
( ) SOCIAL SECURITY CARD

IS THERE ANYTHING THAT WOULD PREVENT YOU FROM WORKING THROUGH THE SUMMER (e.g., family vacation, etc.): _____

IF "YES" EXPLAIN AND GIVE DATES UNAVAILABLE: _____

_____

ANY COMMENTS YOU WOULD CARE TO MAKE: _____

_____

DATE: _____ STUDENT'S SIGNATURE: _____

. . .Schedule of Jobs

School: _____

Head Custodian: _____

JOB SCHEDULE OF

Custodian: _____

From: _____ To: _____

AREA	TASK	TIME
_____	_____	_____
_____	_____	_____
_____	_____	_____
_____	_____	_____
_____	_____	_____
_____	_____	_____
_____	_____	_____

Special Duties: _____

_____

_____

Special Instructions: _____

_____

_____

Break Times: 1st Half of Shift: _____ 2nd Half of Shift: _____

Lunch: From: _____ To: _____

Date: _____ Signature of Head Custodian: _____

Signature of Custodian: _____

JOURNALS (See Also: CONGRATULATIONS; NEWS RELEASES; PUBLIC RELATIONS)

. . .Congratulations on Publication in

Dear Harry,

Last night I had the pleasure of reading your article, "Getting to the Gifted Child," in the May 19XX issue of the State Education Association *Journal.* The insight which you possess into the problems of the gifted child coupled with your highly readable, conversational style makes for an enjoyable, informative article which will surely benefit every educator.

Please accept my congratulations on the publication of your article and let me also say how fortunate it is for me and the students that you are a part of our school.

Please keep writing—we need you!

Best wishes for continued success,

John Benson

. . .Inquiry Letter About an Article

Dear Editor,

In the May 19XX issue of the State Education Association *Journal,* Volume XXII, Number 9, on pages 43–45, you published an article entitled "Getting to the Gifted Child" by Harold Thompkins.

Mr. Thompkins is a teacher in Rock Township High School of which I am the principal. I was very impressed with Mr. Thompkins' article, and I am certain that members of our Parent-Faculty Organization would appreciate reading it.

I was wondering if reprints of the article are available and, if so, what the costs involved would be? We would be ordering at least 200 copies. I would appreciate any information you would have on this possibility.

Thank you for your consideration.

Sincerely,

J. Benson, Principal

KEYS (See Also: HANDBOOK; LOCKERS; VACATION)

. . .List of Key Assignments

(A) *individual*

NAME: _____

The following key(s) has/have been assigned to you for the 19____-____ school year:

KEY SERIAL NUMBER	KEY OPENS
_____	_____
_____	_____
_____	_____

This is to verify that I have received the key(s) listed above, and it/they is/are now in my possession.

SIGNATURE: _____

DATE: _____

(B) *master*

KEY ASSIGNMENTS

ROOM	LOCKERS From	To	DOOR SERIAL NO.	CLOSET SERIAL NO.	TEACHER
105	170	205	G287609A	K988975A	Mr. Marsden

. . .Procedures for the Collection of

To: ALL HOMEROOM TEACHERS
Re: COLLECTION OF LOCKER KEYS

On Monday and Tuesday, June 21 and 22, 19XX, locker keys will be collected during homeroom period by homeroom teachers. The following is offered as a guide for that collection:

1. Distribute the white key tags to all students in your homeroom. Have the students write the locker number on one side of the tag and the serial number of the key on the other side.

2. Call each student individually. Check to see that the correct locker and serial numbers are recorded on the tag. Place the key, properly tagged, into the manila envelope provided by the office and check off the student's name from your locker list.

3. If a student, for whatever reason, has not returned his or her locker key by the end of homeroom period on Tuesday, June 22, place the name of that student, the locker number and the serial number on a separate sheet along with your name and homeroom number and send that list to the office immediately. The office will handle collection of fines.

4. Return the manila key envelope with all tagged keys to the main office by the end of the day on Tuesday, June 22.

THANK YOU FOR YOUR COOPERATION.

. . .Procedures for the Distribution of

LOCKER KEY PROCEDURES

1. Issue one key for each student without charge. (Keys will be handled the same as textbooks.) If the key is lost during the year, $1.00 will be charged for a new key. If it is not returned at the end of the year, a $1.00 fine will be charged before the issuance of a report card.

2. Before issuing a key, record in DUPLICATE the locker number, serial number of the key, and the name of the student to whom it is issued. Keep one copy for your records and return the original to the main office.

3. Remove identification tags from issued keys.

4. Return all extra keys on the third day school is in session in the original envelope with your name and room number. PLEASE LEAVE IDENTIFICATION TAGS ON ALL KEYS RETURNED TO THE OFFICE.

5. If a student forgets or loses his key, he may have his locker opened by reporting to the hall locker duty teacher during homeroom period. At this time the student should remove all necessary material for the school day. Lockers WILL NOT be opened at any other time by the hall locker duty teacher. At the end of the day, the student may again have the locker opened at 3:00 P.M. by reporting to the main office at 2:10 P.M.

6. Students are to check on lost keys only through the homeroom teacher and not through the main office. If the key is located and returned to the office, it will be returned to the student via the homeroom teacher's mailbox.

7. Any key found not to be in working order should be so indicated by the locker number in the envelope when returning extra keys.

KINDERGARTEN   (See Also: CONFERENCE; SPECIAL EDUCATION; VOLUNTEERS)

. . .Notice to Parents

Dear Parents,

On _____, _____, 19_____, your child will be starting kindergarten classes at our school. We hope that your child will find this a happy and enjoyable experience. We have taken the liberty of preparing this list of suggestions which have worked well in the past. We hope they will be helpful to you as well.

1. Come to school a little early and let your child explore the playground area. Show your child EXACTLY where you will be waiting after school. Repeat this several times.

2. When you are met at the door by your child's teacher, please remain cheerful and happy, say good-bye, and leave promptly. It has been our experience that any tears disappear quickly as the day's activities begin.

3. At dismissal time, please wait outside the building at the spot you pointed out to your child earlier. The children will be brought to

you and released only to you. (If someone else is to pick up your child, you must notify the school.)

4. Please remember that children are quick to pick up attitudes from adults. If you, personally, are enthusiastic and happy and keep emphasizing how enjoyable school will be, your child will be also and will have no trouble adjusting to school.

5. This is a milestone in your child's life. Enjoy it.

We look forward to working with you in the coming school year.

. . .Parental Expectation Form

NAME OF PARENT (GUARDIAN): _____

ADDRESS: _____ TELEPHONE: _____

_____ ZIP: _____

NAME OF CHILD: _____

IN WHAT SKILL(S) DO YOU FEEL YOUR CHILD NEEDS THE MOST HELP: ___

_____

WHAT PROGRESS WOULD YOU LIKE TO SEE YOUR CHILD MAKE IN KIN-DERGARTEN: _____

_____

_____

WHAT IS YOUR BEST TIME FOR A CONFERENCE: _____

COULD YOU HELP SUPERVISE CLASS TRIPS AND ACTIVITIES: _____

WOULD YOU BE AVAILABLE TO HELP IN CLASS WITH SUCH ACTIVITIES AS STORY TELLING, SPECIAL ART PROJECTS, ETC.: _____

IF YES, WITH WHAT ACTIVITIES: _____

ANYTHING WE SHOULD KNOW ABOUT YOUR CHILD: _____

_____

COMMENTS: _____

_____

. . .Preentry Criteria Sheet

NAME OF CHILD: _____

DATE OF BIRTH: _____

PLEASE CHECK WHAT APPLIES:

( ) Toilet trained   ( ) Speaks understandably
( ) Feeds self   ( ) Seldom speaks
( ) Needs help feeding self   ( ) Speaks in sentences
( ) Eats almost all foods   ( ) Does not speak (Explain on back.)
( ) Eats very few foods   ( ) Speech impediment (Explain.)
( ) Has temper tantrums   ( ) Initiates own actions
( ) Teases other children   ( ) Follows requests
( ) Overactive   ( ) Cares for own property
( ) Highly excitable   ( ) Is attentive
( ) Timid and/or shy   ( ) Has many interests
( ) Plays well with others   ( ) Few interests
( ) Is 'picked on' by others   ( ) Has many fears
( ) Overly aggressive   ( ) Cries easily

MY CHILD NEEDS TO:

( ) Adjust to other children   ( ) Relax
( ) Become less active   ( ) Get interersted in something
( ) Become more active   ( ) Acquire manual/motor skills
( ) Become cooperative   ( ) Become self-reliant
( ) Other: _____

_____

COMMENTS: _____

_____

_____

. . .Progress Report

(A) first form

NAME OF CHILD: _____ DATE: _____

KINDERGARTEN TEACHER: _____

SOCIAL ASPECTS: _____

_____

PHYSICAL COORDINATION: _____

_____

SKILL DEVELOPMENT: _____

_____

READING AND MATH PROGRESS: _____

_____

OUTSTANDING ACTIVITIES: _____

_____

NEEDS IMPROVEMENT IN: _____

_____

SPECIAL PROBLEMS: _____

_____

COMMENTS: _____

_____

TEACHER'S SIGNATURE: _____

PARENT'S SIGNATURE: _____

(B) *second form*

NAME OF CHILD: _____ DATE: _____

TEACHER: _____

REPORT FOR THE PERIOD FROM: _____ TO: _____

ITEM	EXCEL-LENT	GOOD	AVER-AGE	POOR	IMPROVEMENT NEEDED
Recognizes letters					
Pronounces letters					
Names letters					
Recognizes numerals					
Counts					
Tells time					
Knows shapes and colors					
Knows home address					
Knows telephone no.					
Gets along with other children					

ITEM	EXCEL-LENT	GOOD	AVER-AGE	POOR	IMPROVEMENT NEEDED
Cooperation					
General behavior					

Special Problems: _____

_____

Overall Progress: _____

_____

General Comments: _____

_____

Teacher's Signature: _____

Parent's Signature: _____

LANGUAGE (See Also: EXCHANGE STUDENT)

. . .Foreign Language Night

Dear Parents,

On Thursday, April 29, 19XX, at 8:00 P.M., the Foreign Language Department will be holding its annual Foreign Language Night presentation. This event, which will be held in the cafeteria, involves students from the French, Spanish, and Russian classes of Rock Township High School presenting sketches, songs, and folk dances —all in the various foreign languages. For your refreshment, authentic dishes representing many foreign lands will be served by our students.

This event gives our students an opportunity to practice the languages they have studied so hard to learn. It also is a very entertaining evening which many parents have praised highly in past years. All we need for its success is your attendance.

We look forward to meeting you.

Sincerely,

(Mrs.) M. Parone, Chairperson
Foreign Language Department

. . .Letter on

(A) inappropriate

Dear Mr. & Mrs. Brady,

I regret that I must contact you to report on a very distasteful incident involving your son, Adam.

This morning an assembly was held in our auditorium. As the speaker concluded and asked if there were any questions, Adam shouted an obscene phrase loudly enough for the entire assembly to hear. I wish to make it clear that the words were not merely vulgar, but of the vilest and most obscene nature; so much so, that I feel it inappropriate to repeat them in this letter. There was no doubt that it was Adam, and, indeed, he admitted the outburst to me in my office.

Obviously, we cannot and will not tolerate language of this sort under any circumstances. Adam has been informed of this, and he is hereby suspended until such time as we may all meet with appropriate personnel to settle this matter once and for all.

Please call the school as soon as you receive this to make arrangements for our interview. Obviously, we wish as little disruption of Adam's education as possible, but we also need to provide an atmosphere of education for all of our students, free from obscene outbursts such as Adam evidenced this morning.

May we all meet at the earliest possible time.

Sincerely,

John Benson, Principal

(B) selection of

Dear Parents,

That the world is shrinking should come as no surprise to anyone. Each night, the TV news brings foreign lands right into our living rooms. We regularly visit other lands, and the citizens of those countries regularly visit us. People half a world away are suddenly our neighbors.

Perhaps this is as it should be as we begin to grow closer and strive toward universal understanding that transcends borders. And, if understanding is one of our goals and one of our necessities, in commerce and industry as well as in human relations, then the ability to speak to others from different cultures and different lands is a must for the citizen of the future.

Since our children ARE the future, it makes sense, therefore, that they be prepared for it by taking one or more of the foreign languages offered at Rock Township High School. We offer comprehensive courses in French, Spanish, German, and Russian, and we emphasize communication skills in these languages. The benefits of a second language are tremendous, and we wish you would speak to your son or daughter about the selection of one of these when the scheduling session is held next week.

We believe that the better we can communicate with our fellow human beings, the better we will all be for it. We wish to give this opportunity to your children. It is worthy of your consideration.

Thank you for your concern.

Yours sincerely,

(Mrs.) M. Parone, Chairperson
Foreign Language Department

. . .Policy on Appropriate Use of

We believe the old saying that "there is a time and place for everything." We especially apply this standard to the use of language by students in the school and classroom.

While certain language, whether it be termed "vulgar" or "obscene," may be used with impunity in private conversations, we feel that such language is inappropriate for use in a public situation where individuals who are offended by such language are not at liberty to absent themselves from the situation.

Consequently, the use of vulgar, obscene, or profane language is expressly forbidden, and any student who shall use such language shall be subject to the disciplinary code of the school.

LEADERSHIP   (See Also: CITIZENSHIP; CLUBS; EXTRACURRICULAR ACTIVITIES; NEGOTIATIONS; RECOMMENDATIONS)

. . .Guidelines for

LEADERSHIP

A LEADER is someone who:

ACCEPTS RESPONSIBILITY for his or her own actions and decisions.

INITIATES ACTIONS for the good of the group without being told.

MAKES DECISIONS logically and calmly, having weighed all the evidence.

STAYS CALM in the face of adversity or turmoil.

GETS OTHERS TO WORK because they want to work, not because they fear the consequences of not working.

GIVES ENCOURAGEMENT to others, spurring them to their best efforts.

GAINS RESPECT through his or her own actions, without demanding it.

IS KIND to all and tolerant of new and different ideas or opinions.

BE A LEADER!

. . .Letter Concerning

Dear Fred,

Now that the recent "budget crunch" has settled itself, I am taking the luxury of looking back at the past year, and I begin to see many things from a fresh perspective.

Chief among the "shining moments" of this past year has been your leadership as vice principal of this school. At a time when heads grew hot because of lack of funds, you provided the cool breeze to calm and soothe the situation. Certainly, your insight, compassion, and proficiency provided the very model we all needed to get through a year filled with cuts in allocations and all but depleted budgets.

Most noticeable of all was the fact that you lead by example. Instead of saying "do this," YOU did it. So to speak, you didn't order the troops to attack; you, personally, were the first one over the barricades. This is leadership at its finest, and the positive responses you got in terms of cooperation more than evidence its success.

Thank you on behalf of the entire school. It is a pleasure working with you.

Yours sincerely,

John Benson

. . .Student Evaluation Form

STUDENT'S NAME: _____

GRADE: _____ HOMEROOM: _____

ACTIVITY: _____ DATE: _____

EVALUATOR: _____

POST AND/OR POSITION OF STUDENT IN ACTIVITY: _____

Please check the appropriate category:

QUALITY	FREQUENTLY	SOMETIMES	NEVER
Initiates own actions			
Accepts responsibility			
Admits mistakes			
Responsiveness to others			
Makes logical decisions			
Handles pressure well			
Gains approval of peers			
Follows through on decisions			
Displays conscientious behavior			

COMMENTS ON OVERALL PERFORMANCE: _____

_____

_____

RECOMMENDATIONS: _____

_____

SIGNATURE OF EVALUATOR: _____

LEARNING DISABILITIES

(See Also: ACCOUNTABILITY; CHILD STUDY TEAM; IEP; MAINSTREAMING; PERMANENT RECORDS; PSYCHOLOGICAL SERVICES; SPECIAL EDUCATION; TUTORS)

. . .Identification of

Name of Student: _____

School: _____ Grade: _____

Date: _____ Evaluator: _____

PERSONAL AND HEALTH INFORMATION:

Date of Birth: _____ Sex: ( ) Male ( ) Female

Child living with: ( ) Both Parents   ( ) One Parent   ( ) Guardian(s)

Vision: _____ Hearing: _____

Health in General: _____

TEST INFORMATION:

Test Used: (1) _____ (2) _____

Results: (1) _____ (2) _____

Other: _____

ACHIEVEMENT RECORD:

Grades: _____

_____

Tests: _____

_____

Observation: _____

_____

DIFFERENTIAL BETWEEN ABILITY AND ACHIEVEMENT:

( ) Reading Basics   ( ) Mathematical Calculation
( ) Comprehension   ( ) Math Reasoning
( ) Written Expression   ( ) Listening Skills
( ) Oral Expression   ( ) Logical Reasoning

Explain: _____

_____

RECOMMENDATIONS: _____

_____

_____

_____

SIGNATURE OF EVALUATOR: _____

TITLE: _____

. . .Letter to Parents Concerning

Dear Mr. & Mrs. Jenkins,

Recently, your son, Barry, was referred to the Child Study Team for evaluation regarding the possibility of a learning disorder that might be keeping Barry from reaching his full academic potential.

His teachers are concerned, and so are we, about Barry's declining classroom grades, and we shall be attempting to determine if there may be some cause that is prohibiting Barry from learning as he should.

You will be a very necessary part of this evaluation. We shall be contacting you shortly to set up an interview where we may freely discuss Barry's progress. Throughout the entire process, we will keep you totally informed, and, of course, no final disposition will be made without your insight and consent.

We are all concerned about Barry's future. Working together, we can strive to make certain that that future is a bright and happy one.

Yours sincerely,

. . .Referral for

TEACHER: _____ DATE: _____

SCHOOL: _____ GRADE AND/OR SUBJECT: _____

I have reason to believe that the following student may have a learning disability, and I hereby tender his/her name for evaluation:

Student: _____

Age: _____ Grade: _____

Reason(s) why you believe this student may have a learning disability:

_____

_____

_____

_____

SIGNATURE OF TEACHER: _____

LESSON PLANS (See Also: CLASS; INSTRUCTION; OBSERVATION; STUDENT TEACHER; SUBSTITUTE TEACHER)

. . .Daily

Every teacher must prepare a written lesson plan for each class, sufficiently clear so that in a crisis another teacher could follow it. Each department has a lesson plan format which is to be used in the preparation of the plans. A copy of the lesson plan should be given to any administrator who observes a class.

Nontenure teachers are to hand in lesson plans as indicated every Monday morning before school starts:

Activity Arts, Physical Education	Mr. H. Johnson
English, Foreign Language, Social Studies	Mrs. B. Harrington
Math, Science and Specials	Mr. K. Warren

Tenure teachers will be notified via the Daily Bulletin when their lesson plans are due. They will turn them in as indicated above.

. . .Emergency

When a teacher is out of the building, that teacher's substitute will be directed to the department coordinator for appropriate plans and schedules of classes and duties. Therefore, teachers are asked to confer with their department coordinator for more definite procedures along these lines. However, one (1) emergency plan and one (1) schedule must be kept on file in the Main Office. Be advised that this plan will only be used as a last resort—probably when both teacher and department coordinator cannot be contacted for plans. This plan must be filed with Mrs. Pedersen on or before Friday, September 9.

. . .Letter to Teacher

(A) commending

Dear Mr. Rennel,

As you know, it has been my duty to check your lesson plans for this current academic year. Now that the year is all but over, I'd like to take this opportunity to tell you how pleasant you made that duty for me.

Looking over your lesson plans for this past year makes me wish that I could be a student in your class. Your care, concern, obvious expertise, and genuine love of your students literally leap off the page at every turn.

Please accept my heartiest commendation for your extremely professional approach.

Yours sincerely,

(B) reprimanding

Dear Mrs. Gordon,

Please allow me to bring to your attention a matter of concern in hopes that it may be quickly remedied.

One of my duties is to check your weekly lesson plans. I remind you that the preparation of these plans is part of your job description and that they play an important part in effective teaching. Therefore, I am upset with what I have witnessed in your plans over the past several months.

On seven occasions your lesson plans were late, and on five occasions, I did not receive them at all. I have notified you on all of these occasions. Moreover, the lesson plans I have received seem "sketchy" at best. A lesson plan that merely states "see book" could not possibly be followed by a substitute teacher or a colleague in an emergency situation. Indeed, when you were absent on April 17, 19XX, there were no lesson plans to be found, and your department coordinator was required to make special plans for you for that day.

It is my sincere hope that bringing this to your attention will be sufficient to ameliorate this situation, because if this continues, I see no other course than to begin action as prescribed in the existing contract between the RTEA and the Rock Township Board of Education.

I sincerely hope that this will not be necessary.

Sincerely,

LOCKERS   (See Also: HALL DUTY; KEYS)

. . .Assignment of

LOCKERS

At the beginning of the school year, each student will be assigned an individual hall locker and will be issued a numbered key for it by the homeroom teacher. At the end of the school year, the student is to return the key or be charged one dollar. Fines will also be assessed for willfully damaged keys.

Students are held responsible for the cleanliness of their lockers and are not to share them with other students.

To replace a key if it is lost, duplicate locker keys may be obtained from the office upon payment of $1.00. Should the original key be found later, the duplicate key may be returned for a refund of 50 cents—the remainder of the fine being charged for materials and labor.

. . .Letter on Abuse of

Dear Mr. & Mrs. Waring,

This morning, as I was walking down the halls of this school, I witnessed a most distasteful sight. I saw your son, Robert, kicking his locker. By the time I got to him, he had vigorously kicked his locker an estimated twenty times, and the door to the locker was not only discolored and badly chipped but had several deep scratches and dents in it as well.

As I am certain you realize, a locker is lent to a student during the school year, but it remains the property of the township, and any abuse of that property may result in required compensation for that abuse. I have informed Robert of this, and I hope that you will reinforce this at home as well.

Robert will receive three days of central detention for his action, and I certainly hope that this will end all future outbursts against his locker or other school property.

Sincerely,

. . .Locker List

LOCKER LIST

NAME OF TEACHER: _____

Homeroom: _____ School Year: _____

LOCKER KEY NUMBER	LOCKER NUMBER	ASSIGNED TO

LUNCH (See Also: CAFETERIA; WASTE)

. . .Duties of Supervisors

The supervision of the cafeteria during lunch periods is a full-time responsibility and a difficult one. Therefore, it is imperative that assigned teachers report to this duty on time.

While specific duties shall be assigned to individual teachers, it is the duty of ALL supervisors to see to the safety and well-being of the students in the lunch period. Moreover, supervisors shall be responsible for the maintenance in good condition of school property. Offending students are to be immediately removed from the situation and referred to the office for disciplinary action.

A properly functioning lunch period is only possible when ALL people cooperate.

. . .Rules for Outside Lunches

When the weather permits, students may eat their lunches in the outside student lunch area located to the north of the school. This area, which was created by the Student Council, is for the use and enjoyment of all students at Rock Township High School. Because it is for the enjoyment of all, certain rules and regulations for its use are necessary.

1. All refuse is to be discarded in the trash cans provided for this purpose. These cans are emptied after each lunch period, so there will be sufficient room for the disposal of all waste.

2. Students are expected to clean up the table or area in which they have eaten. Remember that other students will be using the area after you. Provide them with a clean area.

3. Willful destruction of or damage to school property in this area is forbidden as it is throughout the school.

4. Smoking and/or the use of alcoholic beverages in this area are forbidden.

5. All the rules of the school apply.

This is your area. Let us all do our best to make it a pleasant place which may be enjoyed by all. Your cooperation is essential.

M

MAINSTREAMING (See Also: ACCOUNTABILITY; CHILD STUDY TEAM; LEARNING DISABILITIES; PSYCHOLOGICAL SERVICES; SPECIAL EDUCATION; TUTORS)

. . .Guide to Teachers

To: FACULTY
From: J. BENSON, PRINCIPAL
Re: MAINSTREAMED STUDENTS

In keeping with state mandates, a number of our special education and handicapped students are being mainstreamed in our school. If one of these students is assigned to your class, you might find the following suggestions helpful.

1. Treat the student as you would any other member of your class. Do or say nothing that would single out or embarrass the student, but accept no behavior you would not accept from any other student.

2. In the case of some handicapped students it may be necessary to allow them to leave class a few minutes prior to the normal passing time. A separate sheet will be issued by the nurse identifying these students.

3. As you would in any normal classroom, try to suit your academic work to your student's abilities. Mrs. Framton, director of special services, will be happy to confer with you about any academic problems.

4. Understand that these students, no less than any others, are entitled to the best education you can give them. I know that you will do everything in your power to deal in a meaningful and effective manner with each and every one of your students.

. . .Letter to Parents of Mainstreamed Child

Dear Mr. & Mrs. Blunt,

I am overjoyed to be writing you on a happy note. As you know, Sandra was mainstreamed into English and social studies classes approximately a month ago. In that time, all reports that I have received indicate that Sandra is making a satisfactory adjustment and is progressing nicely.

I am particularly pleased with what seems to be happening to Sandra personally. Subsequent interviews with Sandra have encouraged me to believe that this mainstreaming has done much to enhance her self-image and her confidence. I am certain that you must have noticed this at home as well.

We will continue to monitor Sandra's progress and send you periodic reports. In the meantime, however, I was certain you would want to share this good news.

Yours sincerely,

. . .Philosophy of

We believe that every student in our school system is entitled both by law and by natural right to the best education we can offer. Toward that end, we believe that, wherever possible, all students should be a part of the normal school society, and that certainly no child should be set apart or excluded from that normal school society solely on the basis of a handicap.

Therefore, it is our policy that a thorough study shall be made of each child who is classified as handicapped or mentally retarded. This study shall be for the purpose of determining whether or not the child is capable of functioning in a normal school society and if such a placement would be to the benefit of the student. If, indeed, such placement would be beneficial, then such placement shall be made under the direction and supervision of the Department of Special Services.

MEDICAL (See Also: EMERGENCY; NURSE; X-RAYS)

. . .Medical Excuse Form

SCHOOL: _____ DATE: _____

STUDENT: _____

GRADE: _____ HOMEROOM: _____

THE ABOVE-NAMED STUDENT IS EXCUSED FROM PHYSICAL EDUCATION

FROM _____ UNTIL _____, 19_____.

REASON: _____

CONFIRMED BY DR. _____

STUDENT ASSIGNED TO: _____

GUIDANCE COUNSELOR: _____

SIGNATURE OF SCHOOL NURSE: _____

OTHER INFORMATION: _____

_____

. . .Medication Form

SCHOOL: _____ DATE: _____

STUDENT: _____

DIAGNOSIS: _____

MEDICATION: _____

DOCTOR IN CHARGE: _____

DIRECTIONS FOR ADMINISTERING (e.g., one tablet, q.i.d.): _____

_____

SIGNATURE OF DOCTOR: _____

SIGNATURE OF PARENT: _____

. . .Request for Medical Information

(A) *for students*

Dear Parents (Guardians),

We are always anxious to keep your child's health records up to date. This is particularly important in the case of an emergency. Could you take some time to help us? Please fill out the following form and have your child return it to his or her homeroom teacher.

Thank you for your cooperation.

NAME OF STUDENT: _____ GRADE: _____

DISEASES OR ILLNESSES DURING THE PAST YEAR: _____

_____

_____

SERIOUS INJURIES, FRACTURES, OPERATIONS: _____

_____

_____

ADDITIONAL MEDICAL INFORMATION SINCE LAST UPDATE: _____

_____

_____

SIGNATURE OF PARENT (GUARDIAN): _____

(B) for teacher candidate

NAME OF CANDIDATE: _____

ADDRESS OF CANDIDATE: _____

_____ ZIP: _____

DATE OF PHYSICAL EXAMINATION: _____

WEIGHT: _____ HEIGHT: _____

LUNGS: _____ HEART: _____

BLOOD PRESSURE: _____ GENERAL CONDITION: _____

IS THE CANDIDATE CURRENTLY BEING TREATED? _____ IF YES,
FOR WHAT: _____

_____

( ) TINE TEST   ( ) CHEST X-RAY   DATE: _____ RESULT: _____

ANY CONDITION OR DEFECT WHICH WOULD PREVENT CANDIDATE
FROM PERFORMANCE OF DUTIES? _____ IF YES, EXPLAIN: _____

_____

CAN YOU RECOMMEND THIS CANDIDATE FOR EMPLOYMENT WHICH
INVOLVES CLOSE CONTACT WITH SCHOOL-AGE CHILDREN: _____

IF NO, EXPLAIN: _____

_____

NAME OF DOCTOR: _____

ADDRESS: _____

_____ PHONE: _____

DATE: _____ SIGNATURE OF DOCTOR: _____

. . .Thanks to Medical Personnel

Dear Dr. Payne,

On behalf of our entire school, I wish to thank you and your staff for the highly efficient, effective, and professional way in which our annual school physicals were conducted. With a minimum of disruption to regular school routine, you were able to examine our entire student body and identify many areas of concern before they became critical. Those students who are now receiving the care and help they needed may well be thankful for your expertise and skill.

Most of all, I wish to commend you on the caring, warm, and, yes, loving attitude you manifested during these examinations. I have had many, many positive comments about your obvious kindness and concern, and that is an intangible quality that students are quick to pick up.

In short, Doctor, we were overjoyed to have you in our school, and we do hope that we may have the pleasure of seeing you again next year.

Yours sincerely,

MEMO   (See Also: SUGGESTIONS; THANKS)

. . .Checklist Form

DATE: _____

TO: _____ FROM: _____

( ) PLEASE SEND ME   ( ) LET'S DISCUSS
( ) PLEASE REVIEW   ( ) PLEASE ADVISE
( ) FOR YOUR APPROVAL   ( ) PLEASE INITIAL AND RETURN
( ) PLEASE CIRCULATE   ( ) PER YOUR REQUEST
( ) FOR YOUR ACTION   ( ) FOR YOUR INFORMATION
( ) RETAIN FOR YOUR FILE   ( ) MAY I HAVE YOUR OPINION?
( ) WOULD YOU PLEASE TAKE CARE OF THIS?
( ) OTHER (COMMENT): _____

_____

_____

. . .Short Message Form

TO: _____ DATE: _____

FROM: J. Benson, Principal

RE: _____

MESSAGE: _____

_____

_____

_____

_____

. . . . please detach and return . . . .

I have read your memo dated: _____

COMMENT: _____

_____

_____

Date: _____ Signature: _____

MIDDLE SCHOOL (See Also: ALL TOPICS THAT WOULD APPLY TO THE MIDDLE SCHOOL. FOR EXAMPLE, UNDER GOALS YOU WILL FIND THE GOALS OF THE MIDDLE SCHOOL LISTED.)

. . .Example of Middle School Curriculum

MIDDLE SCHOOL CURRICULUM

Grade 6	Grade 7	Grade 8

REQUIRED SUBJECTS FOR ALL STUDENTS

Grade 6	Grade 7	Grade 8
Science	Science	Science
Social Studies	Social Studies	Social Studies
Mathematics	Mathematics	Mathematics
Language Arts or	Language Arts or	Language Arts or
Language Arts (G/T)	Language Arts (G/T)	Language Arts (G/T)
Physical Education	Physical Education	Physical Education

Grade 6	Grade 7	Grade 8
Keyboarding (1/5)	Art 7 (1/5)	Art 8 (1/5)
Industrial Arts 6 (1/5)	Industrial Arts 7 (1/5)	Industrial Arts 8 (1/5)
Home Economics 6 (1/5)	Home Economics 7 (1/5)	Home Economics 8 (1/5)
Study Skills (1/5)	Intro. to Typing (1/5)	General Music (1/5)
Expl. Foreign Lang. (1/5)	Computers 7 (1/5)	Computers 8 (1/5)
Art Design (Thompson Only)		

ELECTIVE SUBJECTS

Choose Only One	Choose One Full Year	Choose One Full Year
Band	Band	Band
Chorus	Chorus	Chorus
Life Skills: consisting of one quarter year of Communications, Consumerism, Our Environment, and Media	Foreign Language I (French/Spanish) Foreign Language A (French/Spanish)	Foreign Language II (French/Spanish) Foreign Language B (French/Spanish) Foreign Language I (French/Spanish)

	Or Two Half Years	Or Two Half Years
	Drama Arts	Drama Arts
	Creative Writing	Creative Writing
	Media/Communictions	Media/Communications
	Art	Art
	Home Economics/Crafts & Leisure	Home Economics/ Culinary Arts
	Industrial Arts/Metal	Industrial Arts/Wood
		Personal Typing
	Industrial Arts/Graphics– Bayshore Only	Technology Education

. . .Philosophy of

MIDDLE SCHOOL PHILOSOPHY

Emerging adolescents have special characteristics and needs that identify them as a unique group. The middle school will provide a balanced program and environment to meet these needs in terms of learning styles and social development, and will provide for individual differences. Students will be encouraged to be independent and self-directed, not only through classroom instruction, but also by guidance counseling, a choice of extracurricular activities, and leadership opportunities appropriate for this age. The result will be a school sensitive to the needs of students in this period of change in their lives, an articulated program to facilitate a smooth transition from elementary to high school, and opportunities to develop their potential.

Each middle school in Rock Township will be organized to maximize flexibility, individuality, variety, and a strong instructional program that provides interdisciplinary learning and decisionmaking.

The middle school's uniqueness is not primarily that of the organization of courses, grouping, schedules, staffing, or materials; it is a matter of the focus and spirit of the whole operation.

Each student will be encouraged to reorganize his or her capacity for achievement, to develop a positive self-concept, and to grow in self-discipline and social consciousness. Beyond providing academic, social and living skills, the curriculum will seek to develop an appreciation of the ongoing quality of all learning experiences.

We hope the implementation of this philosophy will challenge our children to reach their greatest potential so they will become productive, creative, responsible members of society in a changing world.

. . .Principal's Message on

Every school is a training ground, but the middle school is much more than that. With its complement of pre- and early adolescents, it is also the field upon which learning and abilities are tried, tested, and perfected; personalities formed and honed; and the patterns of a lifetime established. For the student, it is a time of tears and laughter, assurance and vulnerability, clumsiness and grace all wrapped into one package and existing side by side.

It is up to us, therefore, to provide guides to aid them through this time of transition and afford them every opportunity to grow, to develop, to be children, to be young adults. We are implementors, guides, teachers, surrogate parents—we discipline, we encourage, we praise, we cry with them, and we rejoice with them.

We are a middle school, and we will help our children grow.

. . .Request for Learning Strategies

Dear Teachers,

As you are aware, I have been very impressed with the implementation of our middle school philosophy into our instruction. I can attest to this because of my walk-through observations and my own school visibility.

I now need your help! In order that everyone gains from this experience I would very much appreciate it if you would list your best teaching strategy, motivational technique, or any educational strategy that you feel can help students. I will compile a list so all of us can implement these techniques. For example, homework passes, exemption from tests, bonus points, throwing out a student's worst grade, T.E.S.A. strategies, assertive discipline procedures, parent contact, building student confidence/self-esteem, etc.

If you wish to remain anonymous (why would you?) that is of course up to you. Isn't it time to give ourselves the credit we have earned? Simply write it down and place it in my mailbox. We all will benefit.

Sincerely,

MINORITIES   (See Also: ACCOUNTABILITY; EXCHANGE STUDENTS; PUBLIC RELATIONS)

. . .Letter on Chauvinism

Certainly, we are in this together. As educators we carry a greater burden of responsibility than the "average" citizen. We are expected to care more, know more, and see more when it comes to our students. We have the charge of preparing them for "life," whatever that may entail.

This applies not only to academic matters, but to interpersonal relationships as well. If we wish to be part of a joyous future, we must begin today to prepare our students for it.

If you truly believe that we are "in this together," then we must act that way. We must see to it that *every*one has *every* opportunity to become *every*thing he or she is capable of becoming, and we must do this without regard to such society-imposed barriers as race, nationality, or sex. Do we assign a task only to boys, because "the gals" wouldn't be interested? When something to do with art or design comes up, do we naturally assume a young lady will take charge of it, because "those girls" just naturally are artistic. As innocent and apparently harmless as these attitudes may seem, they are part of a chauvinistic approach that limits individuals because of who they are rather than what they are, and that's bad for everyone, and particularly for the future of our children.

Let us examine ourselves in all honesty and rid ourselves of our own chauvinistic and prejudicial attitudes and then proceed toward helping our students face tomorrow steadfast and unafraid and with the knowledge that we are truly "all in this together!"

. . .Literature Concerning

MEMO

To: ALL DISTRICT LIBRARIANS
From: THOMAS SMITH, SUPERINTENDENT OF SCHOOLS
Re: MINORITY LITERATURE

America has been described as "A Nation of Immigrants." Certainly we can all agree with this, because we are all aware that it was the cooperative effort of people of ALL races, ALL religions, ALL nationalities that made our country great. Indeed, each group has contributed to America's growth and has a rich heritage to share with us.

Consequently, it is not only desirable, but essential, that the libraries of our schools contain literature reflective of the efforts of all Americans, their contributions, and their heritages. We may be justly proud of the contributions made to our society by all its members, and we want our students to have ready access to information on each group.

We are directing, therefore, that all librarians take this into account when ordering materials and books for the library. It must be the effort of every librarian to provide an accurate and balanced reference source representing all Americans.

. . .Philosophy of Education Regarding

Education in a democracy is for everyone. The children in our schools are representative of a wide variety of ethnic, racial, and religious groups. These groups have all made a contribution to both the building of our nation and the "American way of life" as it has been termed. Consequently, in a democratic education the contributions, efforts, and cultures of all groups should be stressed and the students made aware of the contributions and cultures of all.

. . .Policy on Dealing with Prejudice

Prejudice exists. That is an unfortunate fact of life. Prejudice is detestable in society and unforgivable in an American classroom. Teachers are, of course, to take particular pains to rid every vestige of personal prejudice from themselves or their classrooms. Should an incident of prejudice occur in a classroom, teachers should not allow the incident to go by unnoticcd. This would only lend a degree of passivity to the incident. Instead, the incident must be handled and every effort made to point out the unfairness and irrationality of prejudice and to insure that every effort be made to see that the incident NOT be repeated.

MONTHLY REPORTS   (See Also: YEAR-END MATTERS)

. . .Administrator's Form

SCHOOL: _____ DATE: _____

ADMINISTRATOR: _____

REPORT FOR THE MONTH OF: _____ 19_____

AVERAGE DAILY ATTENDANCE: _____

NUMBER OF SUSPENSIONS: _____ NUMBER OF TRUANCIES: _____

NUMBER OF DISCIPLINARY REFERRALS TO ADMINISTRATIVE ACTION: ___

NUMBER OF PLACEMENTS IN ALTERNATE SCHOOL PROGRAM: _____

NUMBER OF NEW STUDENTS: _____ NUMBER OF STUDENTS LEFT: _____

PROBLEMS AND DIFFICULTIES: _____

_____

_____

OUTSTANDING EVENTS OR ACTIVITIES: _____

_____

_____

COMMENTS: _____

_____

_____

SIGNATURE OF ADMINISTRATOR: _____

. . .Of Tutoring

TEACHER: _____ DATE: _____

NAME OF PUPIL BEING TUTORED: _____

GRADE: _____ SCHOOL: _____

REASON FOR TUTORING: _____

IN WHAT SUBJECT(S): _____

THIS REPORT COVERS TUTORING FOR THE MONTH OF _____, 19____

LIST DATES WHEN STUDENT WAS TUTORED: _____

_____

_____

TIME PER TUTORING SESSION: _____

TOTAL TIME FOR THE MONTH: _____

TEXTBOOK(S) USED: _____

_____

PAGES COVERED IN TEXTBOOK(S): _____

PLEASE DECRIBE THE PROGRESS OF THE STUDENT: _____

_____

_____

ANY PROBLEMS: _____

_____

COMMENTS: _____

_____

SIGNATURE OF TEACHER: _____

. . .Teacher's Form

SCHOOL: _____ DATE: _____

TEACHER: _____

SUBJECT(S): _____ GRADE(S): _____

ROOM(S) USED: _____

OUTSTANDING EVENTS OR ACTIVITIES: _____

_____

ANY CONDITION OF THE ROOM OR SCHOOL WHICH REQUIRES
ATTENTION: _____

_____

_____

ANY STUDENT(S) WHO REQUIRE SPECIAL SERVICES: _____

_____

SPECIAL PROBLEMS: _____

_____

COMMENTS: _____

_____

SIGNATURE OF TEACHER: _____

NATIONAL HONOR SOCIETY (See Also: ACHIEVEMENT; AWARDS; CONGRATULATIONS; HONOR ROLL; PERMANENT RECORDS; SCHOLARSHIPS)

. . .Letter of Congratulations

(A) *to parents*

Dear Mr. and Mrs. Williams,

I have already spoken to your daughter, Judy, and offered her my congratulations upon her election to the National Honor Society. I would like to extend those congratulations to you as well. If ever the word "honor" could be extended to describe an individual, it would be proper and fitting in Judy's case. Her high academic record, as well as her record of care and concern for the good of others, mark her as an individual truly worthy of this distinction. I know you must be justly proud of her as we are at the school.

I look forward to meeting you at the induction ceremonies later this month. I just wanted you to know how highly we regard your daughter and how pleased we are that she is receiving recognition for her continuing expressions of excellence.

Sincerely,

(B) *to students*

To: ALL NATIONAL HONOR SOCIETY CANDIDATES

For better or for worse, an institution is often judged by the caliber of its members. Quite often, we hear groups of people derided and chastised because of the negative actions of some members of the group. Perhaps this is natural, since we tend to judge on that which is known to us, and the negative is often that which is splashed across newspaper front pages and made lead stories on the TV news.

But, let us not concentrate on the negative. Let us instead go searching for the positive. It isn't that difficult to find if we make up our minds to see the total picture. We will then see the fine young men and women present on this stage tonight. Then, we will see the record of their achievements, a bright and shining record of academic achievement and personal service to others. Then, we will see a positive future, filled with hope because they will be a part of it.

I extend my congratulations as well as that of the entire faculty and staff of our school to the inductees along with our sincere and fervent hope that this will be the beginning of continued success throughout their years as productive citizens of a better tomorrow.

. . .Media Announcement of

Barry Bennett, a junior at Rock Township High School, has been elected to the National Honor Society at the school according to Principal John Benson.

Bennett carries an "A" average, is president of the Junior Class, president of the Student Welfare League, a member of the Student Council, a member of the debating team, and plays first-string football at the school.

According to Rock Township High School principal, John Benson, election to the National Honor Society is made on the basis of an evaluation of the student's academic record, moral integrity, and general school citizenship.

Barry Bennett will be inducted into the National Honor Society during a ceremony to be held later this month at the school.

NEGOTIATIONS   (See Also: BOARD OF EDUCATION; FINANCIAL; LEADERSHIP)

. . .Letter Suggesting Meeting Schedule

Dear Mr. Trumbull,

The Rock Township Board of Education would like to propose the following schedule of meetings for this year's negotiations for consideration by you and your negotiating team. Please inform us at your earliest convenience if this schedule is agreeable to you and your team.

1. Regular meetings shall be held on Wednesday evenings starting Wednesday, October 17, 19XX, and continuing until the successful conclusion of negotiations.

2. Meetings will take place in the Board Room of the Board of Education Office, 123 Round Ridge Road, Rock Township.

3. Meetings shall begin promptly at 8:00 P.M. and conclude no later than 11:00 P.M.

4. Additional meetings and/or extension of meeting times may be scheduled by mutual consent of all parties.

We hope this schedule is agreeable to you. Please let us know your feelings as soon as possible.

Sincerely,

Jonathan B. Tanner, Secretary
Rock Township Board of Education

. . .Letter to Confirm Representation

Dear Mr. Sarenen,

As the date approaches for the first negotiations session between the Rock Township Board of Education and the Rock Township Education Association, it is only fitting that we begin to detail certain procedural elements of those negotiations. We are in possession of your letter of October 10 in which you name the representatives of the Association who will constitute the negotiations committee for your side. The Board has no objections to anyone named on that list.

On behalf of the Board, the following individuals shall represent the Board during these negotiations:

Mrs. Estelle Waverley, Negotiations Committee Chairperson
Dr. George Bailey, Assistant Superintendent of Schools
Mr. Harold Daniels
Mrs. Mary Martinsen
Mr. James Oliver

If there is any objection on the part of the Association to any of these representatives, please let us know within ten (10) days of the receipt of this letter.

All else being equal, the Board looks forward to meeting with you at the agreed location of the Board of Education office on Thursday evening, November 4, at 7:30 P.M. for the first negotiations session.

On behalf of the entire Board of Education, may I extend our sincerest wishes that the negotiations into which we are about to enter may run smoothly and prove amicable for all concerned.

Yours sincerely,

. . .Memo on Negative Publicity

To: ALL MEMBERS OF THE NEGOTIATING TEAM

Newspapers are in business to sell newspapers, and this means touting the sensational and, quite often, the negative. It is a sad but true commentary that people buy the negative and quite often leave the positive by the wayside.

We are in the midst of critical negotiations. As we progress towards a settlement that is amicable to all sides, these negotiations will have their "ups and downs." This is understandable and a part of the process itself. We can minimize the tensions, however, by keeping this as it should be—a private affair.

Let us, therefore, be extremely circumspect in what we say to anyone outside of negotiation chambers. Particularly, let us NOT give the press an opportunity to create a conflict where one does not exist. "NO COMMENT!" should be our watchword until such time as negotiations are over and the master contract signed.

. . .Memo on Record Keeping

To: ALL BOARD AND TEACHER NEGOTIATION TEAMS
From: THOMAS SMITH, SUPERINTENDENT OF SCHOOLS
Re: RECORD KEEPING DURING NEGOTIATIONS

The keeping of accurate records of all meetings is an essential developmental process. Nowhere is this more true than in the upcoming negotiations between the Rock Township Board of Education and the Rock Township Education Association. There must exist accurate records of negotiations in order that all parties may refer to them and receive pertinent and exact information.

Consequently, it is my suggestion that the first item of negotiations be the appointment of a secretary mutually agreeable to each party. I further suggest that the minutes of each meeting be reviewed by the chief negotiators for each party and signed by them as an indication that the minutes are accurate and truly reflect what has occurred at the meeting.

In this way, there should be no contention as to the representative nature of the records.

. . .Setting the Ground Rules for

Dear Mr. Trumbull,

We should like to propose to you and your negotiating team the following procedures for this year's negotiations.

1. The schedule of meetings shall be that suggested in the Board's letter of October 1, 19XX, which has been approved without changes by the Rock Township Education Association.

2. Whenever possible, informal discussion shall obtain. In any case of disagreement, however, procedures from Robert's Rules of Order shall apply.

3. The chairing of meetings shall alternate between the head negotiator for the Rock Township Board of Education and the Rock Township Education Association.

4. Visitors including, but not limited to, the principals of various schools in Rock Township may be present at negotiating sessions with the consent of both parties or at the specific request of the head negotiator of a party in order to testify to or clarify a point of negotiations. It is understood that these visitors shall take no part in direct negotiation procedures, but they shall act solely as observers or witnesses.

5. Expenses incurred during negotiations shall be equally divided between the Rock Township Board of Education and the Rock Township Education Association.

We hope that these procedures meet with the approval of your negotiating team. Please inform us as soon as possible of your decision.

Sincerely,

Jonathan B. Tanner, Secretary
Rock Township Board of Education

NEWSPAPER (See Also: BULLETIN; EXTRACURRICULAR ACTIVITIES; NEWS RELEASES; PUBLIC RELATIONS)

. . .Guidelines for Public Relations

To: ALL PRINCIPALS
From: JAMES NORRIS, DIRECTOR OF PUBLIC RELATIONS
Re: PUBLIC RELATIONS AND NEWSPAPERS

Recently, with a change in editorial policy at our local newspaper, we have been fortunate to receive increased coverage of school events. With this increased coverage, we have an excellent opportunity to present ourselves to the general public of Rock Township. While the majority of news releases have come and will continue to come from this office, principals are increasingly being called upon by the local press to provide stories and articles of interest.

Consequently, I thought it might be of interest to you if I offered a few suggestions for your consideration:

1. EMPHASIZE THE POSITIVE. We have many outstanding students and activities in our schools. The public should be aware of this.

2. DON'T HIDE THE NEGATIVE. If something unfortunate has happened, do not try to cover it up. Present it honestly. State your opinion of the incident in a positive manner.

3. TELL THE WHOLE STORY. Make certain that you present all sides of an issue. If, for instance, 50 students stage a demonstration, be certain you mention that the other 500 students stayed in class and did not join them.

4. IF YOU ARE IN DOUBT, a phone call to this office will receive immediate attention.

Remember, we don't have to manufacture news. There are enough positive, energetic, and fine activities going on in our schools to supply many news stories. Let's let the public know the good things that are going on in our schools.

. . .Letter to Local Newspaper

Dear Editor,

Quite often, letters to the editor are filled with anger, frustration, and even righteous indignation. That is why it is so great a pleasure to write you on a very positive note.

Recently, your newspaper devoted an entire section to what is going on at Rock Township High School. As principal of that school, I was delighted to see the many efforts of our students and faculty finally being given the recognition that they have earned with their tireless work and dedication. Your emphasis upon the positive actions of our students is a fresh and welcome change from the sensationalism one often sees regarding youth and education.

On behalf of our faculty and student body, I commend you for your positive approach. We hope to see more of the same in the future.

Yours sincerely,

John Benson, Principal

. . .Philosophy of the School Newspaper

A school newspaper exists for the students of the school. While it cannot help but be reflective of the quality of life at a school and, consequently, serves as a public relations vehicle, it is primarily intended for the growth, entertainment and information of the school's students. Students who participate in the production of the school newspaper should learn the practices of good journalism. They should be involved in the actual production of the paper and through that involvement learn the intricacies of production and preparation. Students who receive the school newspaper should obtain from it accurate, unbiased, and unprejudiced reporting, reflective of the events and activities that are so much a part of their school lives.

. . .Policy on Content

The school newspaper is a public vehicle intended for the students of the school and also intended to be reflective of school life. Consequently, the following guidelines for the content of the school newspaper are offered:

1. Language of an obscene, profane, or vulgar nature is to be avoided at all times.
2. All reporting is to be accurate. Any story that appears in the paper must be checked for accuracy. This applies to all direct quotes as well as any description of policy or events.
3. Criticism is an editorial prerogative. News stories should be factual, without prejudice, bias, or commentary.
4. Editorials should be positive in nature. Anyone can find fault. Any editorial of a critical nature should be accompanied by suggestions for positive improvement.
5. Personal invective has no place in any newspaper.
6. All sides of a story must be told. One-sided reporting must never be allowed.
7. News should be reflective of the efforts of our school and its students. The use of the names of *all* participants in an event or activity is encouraged.

NEWS RELEASES   (See Also: JOURNALS; NEWSPAPER; PUBLIC RELATIONS)

. . .Checklist for Newsworthiness

To: THE FACULTY

Is your story newsworthy?

Many teachers have stories concerning their classes or extracurricular activities which they feel are worthy of release through our school system's Public Relations Office. Before you submit such a story, it would be appreciated if you could fill in the following checklist. If you can answer "Yes" to any seven questions, we would like to see it. If not, perhaps you might like to rethink it.

Thank you for your cooperation. This process will save us many hours of valuable time.

OFFICE OF PUBLIC RELATIONS

YES NO

( ) ( ) Does your story concern something that goes beyond the day-to-day operation of the school?

( ) ( ) Does your story emphasize positive interaction of students, students and faculty, or students and the community?

( ) ( ) Does your story emphasize positive aspects of school life?

( ) ( ) Does your story contain any unusual aspects which take it out of the realm of the mundane?

( ) ( ) Would anyone besides the parents of the students involved need or want to know about the story?

( ) ( ) Does the story have any humorous or heartwarming qualities?

( ) ( ) Have all the facts of the story been checked for accuracy?

( ) ( ) Does your story contain aspects with which a significant number of the general public could identify?

( ) ( ) Could you provide black-and-white photographs if needed?

. . .For Parents

That's right, parents! A first in the Rock Township Middle Schools. A science festival for students and parents alike! A chance for you to share a day to remember with your kids—our students.

Come join with us in making this day something special. Simply stated, we expect to "showcase kids." We want to provide a forum for kids to express themselves and "show" the great work they can do when given the chance.

On this day, students from our three middle schools will reinforce concepts they've learned in school or perhaps have researched themselves in the broad arena of science. Your child may participate by designing a project that demonstrates some scientific principle, or planning an exhibit, or joining with another or more students in presenting a minilesson on one of our "stages."

Many prizes for participating will be awarded to students by random selection. There will be no competition between students for prizes. The only requirement to win one of the many prizes is to participate.

Your child's science teacher will provide you with information and further details at appropriate times throughout our planning stages. That information will come to you via your child. Watch for it!!!

Parents, there's no doubt that you can make a difference! We need you to encourage your child to participate and help your child prepare for this event. Again, it's a first for Rock Township. It's a chance for all our students to come together, to break whatever barriers artificially exist between schools, to share, to learn, to be part of a unique experience!!!

Mark your calendar for Saturday, March 18! The exact times and place will be announced in the near future. Have your child complete the required sign up sheet that must be returned before the holidays.

Thank you for your time. We can only hope for your support!!

Sincerely,

The Middle School Science Committee

. . .Good News Form

SOME GOOD NEWS FROM SCHOOL
Bradford Middle School

TEACHER: _____ DATE: _____

MESSAGE: _____

_____

_____

_____

. . .Model News Story

A group of students at Rock Township High School have been roaming the halls interrupting classes lately, and the faculty and administrators are delighted.

It began in the social studies class of teacher Mary Norris. "We were discussing the plight of the people in Costa Grande, who had been devastated by a hurricane followed by an eruption of a volcano," Mrs. Norris reported. "My class was shocked and moved by the suffering of these unfortunate people."

"We felt we had to do something," Tom Barron, a member of the class, recalls, "but we had no idea of how to go about it."

Mrs. Norris arranged for a visit by Mr. Frank Callerton, associate director of the American Relief Society. "I spoke to them of the urgent need for food, clothing, and medical supplies," stated Mr. Callerton, "and these great kids did the rest."

After that, Mrs. Norris and her students went into action. During each class period for the next week, students visited other classes in the school informing others of the desperate need of Costa Grande residents and asking for donations of food and clothing.

"They were marvelous," Mrs. Norris remembers. "The entire school reacted so well that we had a real problem of where to store the materials that were coming in."

"In all," reports Rock Township High School Principal John Benson, "our students raised over seven thousand dollars worth of supplies. We are proud of them and their actions which bespeak the fine character of our students and community. They are a credit to the school and themselves."

The accumulated materials will be accepted by the American Relief Society at a schoolwide assembly to be held next Monday morning at 10:00 A.M.

. . .Policy on

The superintendent and staff shall decide upon and follow a continuing program of information designed to acquaint the citizens of the community and the public generally with the achievements and the needs of the schools. The superintendent shall be responsible for

1. News releases and the publication of educational reports
2. The photographing of school activities for publication

3. Information liaison between the school system and the community at large

News releases by the Board are to be considered official Board releases only if approved by a majority of the members prior to release, either in a meeting of the Board or verbally to the secretary/business administrator. The superintendent shall approve for release all staff-prepared statements for publication regarding districtwide concerns. Staff members submitting to any publication articles in which the public schools are mentioned are also requested to show these to the superintendent for clearance.

NONRENEWAL OF CONTRACT (See Also: REPRIMANDS)

. . .Of a Nontenured Teacher

Dear Mrs. Smith,

At the February 21, 19XX meeting of the Rock Township Board of Education it was determined that your teaching contract will not be renewed for the school year 19XX–19XX.

In accordance with the current contract between the Rock Township Board of Education and the Rock Township Education Association, you may, within thirty (30) days of this notification, request in writing from the assistant superintendent in charge of personnel a written statement of reasons. Such statement shall be supplied within fifteen (15) days of receipt of such request.

You may also, within five (5) days of receipt of such statement, request and receive an interview with the superintendent and following such interview, may request, within five (5) days, an informal appearance before the Board of Education. You may be represented by counsel or one individual of your choosing. You also have the right to present persons to the Board who will make statements on your behalf. Such persons shall be called into the meeting to address the Board one at a time and shall be excused from the meeting after making their statements.

Such informal appearance must be scheduled within thirty (30) calendar days of receipt of such request and the Board shall notify you, in writing, of its final determination within five (5) days following the informal appearance.

Sincerely,

James T. Shannon,
Assistant Superintendent

. . .Of a Tenured Teacher

Dear Mr. Jones,

It is with sincere regret that we must inform you that at the February 21, 19XX meeting of the Rock Township Board of Education it was determined that your teaching contract will not be renewed for the 19XX–19XX school year.

The reasons for this action are as follows:

1. During the period May 1, 19XX, through February 15, 19XX, you were late to school an average of 55 minutes on 83 school days and late to your assigned classes an average of 7 minutes on no fewer than 194 occasions.

2. During the period May 1, 19XX, through February 15, 19XX, you refused to prepare and/or submit lesson plans, emergency lesson plans, cumulative records, reports, and other written materials required by the main office.

3. During the period mentioned above, you appeared at school under the influence of alcohol to such an extent that you were unable to perform your professional duties on 21 separate occasions.

4. Classroom observations by qualified and certified supervisory personnel during the aforesaid period indicated several areas in which improvement was needed. Subsequent observations revealed no effort toward correction on your part and indicated a continuing decline in performance.

5. You were advised of the above situations in letters dated May 15, June 10, June 30, September 15, October 5, October 31, November 14, November 31, December 3, and December 17, 19XX, and January 10, January 28, and February 14, 19XX. In each of these letters we advised you of the seriousness of the situation, advised you of possible consequences if these situations were not corrected, and offered aid and direction in helping you overcome any difficulties which might be engendering these situations. None of these letters was answered.

You are advised that you are entitled to all the rights and procedures as outlined in Article 19 of the current contract between the Rock Township Board of Education and the Rock Township Education Association. It is the purpose and intent of the Rock Township Board of Education that due process be followed in all situations.

Please be advised that if it is your intent to appeal this decision of the Board of Education, we must receive written notice of that intent within thirty (30) days of the receipt of this letter.

Sincerely,

James T. Shannon,
Assistant Superintendent

. . .Policy on

(A) general

The contract for each full-time professional employee not under tenure shall specify that sixty (60) days' notice shall be given by either party prior to unilateral termination of the contract. In addition, the superintendent shall submit to the Board of Education a written evaluative summary for all professional employees recommended for employment in their tenure year.

It shall be the policy of the Board that personnel covered by special contracts, for which special state certification is not required, are employed on an annual basis with the proviso that continuation of employment is a prerogative of the Board. Special contracts are listed in the current agreement. It is not the intent of the Board to provide tenure status to any employee in these categories.

(B) grounds for

It is the duty of the Board to protect the pupils of this district from the classroom influence of inefficient staff members.

For a tenured staff member of this system to be charged by the Board with inefficiency, the following conditions must be demonstrated by the superintendent:

1. The staff member was aware of the terms and conditions expected of him or her at the start of his or her assignment.
2. The staff member was found to be wanting by evaluators certificated to perform evaluations using generally endorsed professional methods.
3. The staff member was given written notice by the superintendent upon order of the Board of the alleged inefficiency, specifying the nature thereof with such particulars as to furnish him or her an opportunity to correct and overcome the same.
4. The staff member was found at least ninety (90) days after being given notice (but less than 135 days) still to be inefficient in the performance of his or her duties.

Upon the demonstration of the preceding conditions by the superintendent and following the determination by the Board in accordance with statute that the charge and the evidence in support of the charge are sufficient, if true in fact, to warrant a dismissal or withholding an increment, the Board shall certify the charge of inefficiency to the commissioner.

NURSE (See Also: MEDICAL; PERMANENT RECORDS; PHYSICAL EDUCATION)

. . .Daily Record Form

See sample form on page 257.

. . .Disease Report

REPORT ON COMMUNICABLE DISEASE TO HEALTH OFFICER

School _____ Month _____ Nurse _____

Disease	Total	Disease	Total
Chickenpox	_____	Strep throat	_____
Measles	_____	Whooping cough	_____
Mumps	_____	German measles	_____
Scarlet fever	_____	Hepatitis	_____
Meningitis	_____	Encephalitis	_____

NAME	AGE	ADDRESS	SUSPECTED DISEASE

. . .Students Going to Nurse

STUDENTS GOING TO THE NURSE

Any student may request a pass to the nurse which *must be granted.* Students should inform the teacher of this necessity unless an emergency arises. Abuses of this should be discussed with the nurse, guidance counselor, or administration. A list of students with special ailments and problems is published and distributed in the fall. Please check this and keep it readily available for reference.

HEALTH DEPARTMENT—Nurse's Daily Record

Date _____   School _____

TIME IN	NAME OF PUPIL	GRADE	COMPLAINT	TREATMENT	RETURN TO CLASS	TAKEN HOME	BY WHOM	ACCIDENT REPORT

O

OBJECTIVES (See Also: GOALS; PHILOSOPHY)

. . .Examples of Schoolwide Objectives

Rock Township High School will provide every student with the opportunity to:

Acquire a stock of basic information covering the principles of the physical, biological, and social sciences; the historical record of human achievements and failures; and current social issues, including knowledge of the environment.

Acquire the knowledge, understanding, and skills that permit his or her participation in a satisfying and responsible role in contemporary society.

Learn to enjoy the processes of learning, and to acquire the skills necessary for a lifetime of continuous learning and adaptation to change, and to use leisure time constructively.

Acquire basic skills in obtaining information, solving problems, thinking critically, and communicating effectively.

Acquire the ability to form satisfying and responsible relationships with a wide range of people, including those with social and cultural characteristics different from his or her own.

Acquire the ability and the desire to express himself or herself creatively in one or more of the arts, and to appreciate the esthetic expressions of other people.

Acquire the capacities for assuming satisfying and responsible roles in family life and society.

Acquire the knowledge, habits, and attitudes that promote personal and public health and well-being.

Become an effective and responsible contributor to the decision-making processes of the community, state, nation, and world.

Develop an understanding of his or her own worth, abilities, limitations, and potential.

. . . .Guidelines for Writing Behavioral Objectives

STATING BEHAVIORAL OBJECTIVES FOR CLASSROOM INSTRUCTION Major Categories in the Cognitive Domain of the Taxonomy of Educational Objectives (Bloom, 1956)	USING THE TAXONOMY OF EDUCATIONAL OBJECTIVES Examples of General Instructional Objectives and Behavioral Terms for the Cognitive Domain of the Taxonomy	
Descriptions of the Major Categories in the Cognitive Domain	*Illustrative General Instructional Objectives*	*Illustrative Behavioral Terms for Stating Specific Learning Outcomes*
Knowledge. Knowledge is defined as the remembering of previously learned material. This may involve the recall of a wide range of material, from specific facts to complete theories, but all that is required is the bringing to mind of the appropriate information. Knowledge represents the lowest level of learning outcomes in the cognitive domain.	Knows common terms. Knows specific facts. Knows methods and procedures. Knows basic concepts. Knows principles.	Defines, describes, identifies, labels, lists, matches, names, outlines, reproduces, selects, states.
Comprehension. Comprehension is defined as the ability to grasp the meaning of material. This may be shown by translating material from one form to another (words to numbers), by interpreting material (explaining or summarizing), and by estimating future trends (predicting consequences or effects). These learning outcomes go one step beyond the simple remembering of material, and represent the lowest level of understanding.	Understands facts and principles. Interprets verbal materials. Interprets charts and graphs. Translates verbal materials to mathematical formulas. Estimates future consequences implied in data. Justifies methods and procedures.	Converts, defends, distinguishes, estimates, explains, extends, generalizes, gives examples, infers, paraphrases, predicts, rewrites, summarizes.

Application. Application refers to the ability to use learned material in new and concrete situations. This may include the application of such things as rules, methods, concepts, principles, laws, and theories. Learning outcomes in this area require a higher level of understanding than those under comprehension.	Applies concepts and principles to new situations. Applies laws and theories to practical situations. Solves mathematical problems. Constructs charts and graphs. Demonstrates correct usage of a method or procedure.	Changes, computes, demonstrates, discovers, manipulates, modifies, operates, predicts, prepares, produces, relates, shows, solves, uses.
Analysis. Analysis refers to the ability to break down material into its component parts so that its organizational structure may be understood. This may include the identification of the parts, analysis of the relationships between parts, and recognition of the organizational principles involved. Learning outcomes here represent a higher intellectual level than comprehension and application because they require an understanding of both the content and structural form of the material.	Recognizes unstated assumptions. Recognizes logical fallacies in reasoning. Distinguishes between facts and inferences. Evaluates the relevancy of data. Analyzes the organizational structure of a work (art, music, writing).	Breaks down, diagrams, differentiates, discriminates, distinguishes, identifies, illustrates, infers, outlines, points out, relates, selects, separates, subdivides.
Synthesis. Synthesis refers to the ability to put parts together to form a new whole. This may involve the production of a unique communication (theme or speech), a plan of operations (research proposal), or a set of abstract relations (scheme for classifying information). Learning outcomes in this area of stress creative behaviors, with major emphasis on the formulation of new patterns or structures.	Writes a well-organized theme. Gives a well-organized speech. Writes a creative short story (or poem or music). Proposes a plan for an experiment. Integrates learning from different areas into a plan for solving a problem. Formulates a new scheme for classifying objects (or events, or ideas).	Categorizes, combines, compiles, composes, creates, devises, designs, explains, generates, modifies, organizes, plans, rearranges, reconstructs, relates, reorganizes, revises, rewrites, summarizes, tells, writes.

Evaluation. Evaluation is concerned with the ability to judge the value of material (statement, novel, poem, research report) for a given purpose. The judgments are to based on definite criteria. These may be internal criteria (organization) or external criteria (relevance to the purpose) and the student may determine the criteria or be given them. Learning outcomes in this area are highest in the cognitive hierarchy because they contain elements of all of the other categories, plus conscious value judgments based on clearly defined criteria.	Judges the logical consistency of written material. Judges the adequacy with which conclusions are supported by data. Judges the value of a work (art, music, writing) by use of internal criteria. Judges the value of a work (art, music, writing) by use of external statements of excellence.	Appraises, compares, concludes, contrasts, criticizes, describes, discriminates, explains, justifies, interprets, relates, summarizes, supports.

OBSERVATION   (See Also: EVALUATION; LESSON PLANS; STUDENT TEACHER; VOLUNTEERS)

. . .Form for Targeted Needs Improvement

TEACHER: _____ DATE: _____

SUPERVISOR: _____

This is to certify that we have met and discussed needs improvement relative to classroom instruction. The following have been mutually **agreed** upon as targeted needs improvement for the 19____–19____ school year:

SIGNATURE OF TEACHER: _____

SIGNATURE OF SUEPRVISOR: _____

. . .Of Behavioral Patterns

(A) anecdotal record

I observed Adam Brady on Monday, May 7, 19XX, during his senior English class from 10:30 A.M. until 11:15 A.M. It was Adam's first day back from a five-day out-of-school suspension.

Adam entered the room one minute after class had begun. The teacher said, "Adam, you're late; please see me after class." Adam answered, "Yeah," and walked slowly to his seat. Adam carried no books or supplies. A pencil was stuck behind his right ear. At his desk, he sat with his shoulders back, arms crossed, his left foot and leg out in the aisle. His eyes were on the window. He continued in this position while the teacher covered material relevant to the composition to be done that day in class. Paper was passed out. Adam received it from the boy in front of him, took none for himself, and tossed the paper over his head to the girl behind him. The paper scattered over the floor. Adam smiled and resumed his former position.

Some ten minutes later the class was working and Adam had not changed his position. The teacher went to Adam and spoke to him in a low voice. I could not hear what the teacher said, but Adam's answers were, "So what?" "Yeah," "Right," and "Yeah." The teacher left and Adam placed his head in his arms folded on his desk. He remained in this position for 17 minutes.

At the end of this time, he raised his head, stretched, yawned, took the pencil from behind his ear, and began to write on the desk. Shortly thereafter the bell rang, and Adam left the room quickly, pushing a student out of his way.

COMMENT: This is the fifth observation of Adam Brady. His attitude and behavior have not changed throughout the period.

(B) social interaction observation report

SOCIAL INTERACTION OBSERVATION

STUDENT: _____ DATE: _____

CLASS OBSERVED: _____

TIME OBSERVED: FROM: _____   TO: _____

1. Number of contacts with teacher: _____

   a. Contacts initiated by teacher: _____

   b. Contacts initiated by subject: _____

2. Number of contacts with other students: _____

   a. Contacts initiated by other students: _____

   b. Contacts initiated by subject: _____

3. With whom were most student contacts made: _____

   a. How many contacts: _____

   b. How many contacts initiated by student: _____

   c. How many contacts initiated by subject: _____

4. Names of students surrounding subject's desk: _____

   a. _____   e. _____

   b. _____   f. _____

   c. _____   g. _____

   d. _____   h. _____

5. Nature of subject-initiated contacts: _____

_____

_____

_____

6. Observer's comments: _____

_____

_____

_____

SIGNATURE OF OBSERVER: _____

OFFICE   (See Also: FINANCIAL; VOLUNTEERS; XEROX)

. . .Memo on Student Aides

To: ALL MEMBERS OF THE OFFICE STAFF

It is only right and proper that we afford some of our students the experience of being office aides. Quite frankly, it also allows us to function much more smoothly with these aides taking over certain functions of a functioning office.

We must be careful, however, to follow some commonsense guidelines concerning them:

1. Student aides come from study hall and activity arts classes only. Under no condition is a student to miss an academic class to function as an office aide.

2. Student aides are *never,* that's NEVER, to handle student records or confidential files of faculty or staff. Moreover, student aides are *not* permitted to run off tests or to handle tests and/or examinations into or out of the main office, even if a teacher gives permission.

3. Student aides may be used as initial contact for people coming into the school only if, in the opinion of the office staff, they present a positive image of the school and have been trained by the office staff in the proper procedures for greeting someone who comes into our school on outside business.

4. Needless to say, student aides should be instructed in their duties, and their time in the office should be relegated to the performance of these duties. We may not share coffee, opinions, or any confidential information with any student aide under any circumstances.

These guidelines, it is hoped, will keep everything running smoothly while providing our students with a positive learning experience that will help them in life as well as in school.

. . .Memo on Students in

To: ALL MEMBERS OF THE OFFICE STAFF

I have received many comments lately from members of the office staff regarding the large number of students in the office, particularly in the morning and late afternoon, and the subsequent distress that seems to be causing. Indeed, one person called it "Mass Confusion"!

To help alleviate this situation, I am initiating certain procedures which, I hope, will make for much smoother functioning of our main office.

1. All students coming into the main office will stay in the reception area *in front of* the main counter. Unless specifically

directed by office personnel, students are not to proceed beyond that main counter. If that reception area becomes too crowded, students are to be directed to wait in the hall until called by someone in the office.

2. Hereafter, all matters of notes explaining absence of students will be handled by homeroom teachers. Homeroom teachers will send to the office ONLY those students who have NOT returned notes explaining absence after three days or those with notes requesting a student to be excused early.

3. Teachers will ascertain the reason for a student request to go to the office. Other than for disciplinary reasons, difficulties with absences and/or excuse from school, and emergency medical reasons, students should NOT be sent to the office during prehomeroom, homeroom, and period 1. All other student business (i.e., purchasing a parking permit) can be handled during study hall, lunchtime, et cetera. The same goes for the last period of the day.

I hope that these changes will help alleviate the "overcrowding" issue during those normally hectic periods of our school day. If anyone has any questions, concerns—or better ideas—please see me at any time.

. . .Memo on Use of

To: ALL MEMBERS OF THE PROFESSIONAL STAFF

Certainly, the main office is at your disposal. In a very real sense, we exist to aid you to function properly in your job. It is also OUR job to see to it that the school functions as smoothly as possible in order that education may continue uninterrupted for everyone.

Toward that goal, it seems necessary to establish some guidelines whereby both the office and the classroom may function to the best of their abilities.

1. If a student is sent to the office for disciplinary reasons, the reason MUST be of the type that requires the action of an administrator. In other words, if a student hit another student or used obscene language, send him or her to the office; if the student didn't do his or her homework, and you want him or her to meditate upon the error of his or her ways in a quiet place, DON'T send him or her to the office (maybe a detention?). The office should not be used as a "cooling-off" room.

2. Materials to be duplicated must, *must, MUST* be given in at least 24 hours in advance of the time needed. Folks, we can't—we simply CANNOT—receive a test from you this morning and have 50 copies ready for first period. Please be considerate of our hard-working office staff and try to give as much lead time as possible.

3. Please don't send students to the office just because they asked you to go. Find out why and make an advised judgment. Sending a student to the office "to find out if I made the cheerleaders" is not only a waste of time, but it is a definite contributory factor toward tying up the office. Students should come to the office for important school business that CANNOT BE HANDLED ELSEWHERE.

4. As much as it is reasonable and prudent for you to do so, avoid sending students to the office during homeroom and periods 1 and 8, as these are peak times for "office traffic" and that place can get very full very quickly. If it can wait until some other time, please let it.

Under no circumstances should this memo be construed as a directive to NOT use the office. We are here for you; we exist to serve you; if you need us, use us. All that we ask is that you use some prudence and understanding in allowing us to function in an efficient manner which is to everyone's benefit.

Thank you for your understanding.

OPEN COMMUNICATIONS (See Also: PUBLIC RELATIONS; SUGGESTIONS; THANKS)

. . .Administrator's Message to Staff and Students

MEMO

To: ALL FACULTY AND STUDENTS
From: J. BENSON, PRINCIPAL
Re: COMMUNICATIONS

I honestly believe that it is only through talking honestly to each other that people achieve an open, truthful relationship in which they may work productively for the good of all.

I hope we can establish, right here at Rock Township High School, just such an atmosphere of open communication. I ask you not to hide your concerns. My office will always be open to every member of our school, and I invite your comments. I stand ready to discuss all points of view.

Remember, this is your school, and you have a stake in its future. Let us keep our communications open and work together for our school's ultimate good.

. . .Letter Concerning Poor Communications

Dear Mr. Kendricks,

I believe it was the movie, *Cool Hand Luke* that immortalized the line, "What we have here is a failure to communicate." Nowhere could that line be better applied than in our relationship this past week.

Your letter advising me that you intend to take legal action against the school if our students do not cease from "destroying your property" came as a complete surprise, since I neither know what you mean by that phrase nor was I aware that any problem existed between us. Certainly, this was the first time you had ever brought anything of this nature to my attention.

Obviously, we cannot work out solutions unless we both understand the problem, and we can't do that if we don't communicate.

Therefore, I invite you to call or visit the school and we will set up a mutually agreeable time to communicate and fully discuss this situation. I am certain that we can arrive at a solution that will benefit everyone.

I hope to hear from you soon.

Sincerely,

. . .School Policy Statement to Parents

Dear Parents,

I have just issued a memo to the faculty and students of Rock Township High School stating my belief that open communications among all levels are essential for the peak functioning of our school. I have invited everyone at the school to share his or her concerns, ideas, and suggestions with me. I have stated that my office is open to them at all times.

I would like you to know that these same sentiments are extended to you, the parents of our students. This school belongs to you as much as to your children. You have their best interests at heart and want what is best for them. Consequently, I would be eager to share your thoughts.

Please feel free to contact me at any time.

Sincerely,

J. Benson, Principal

OPEN HOUSE   (See Also: BACK-TO-SCHOOL NIGHT; ORIENTATION; PUBLIC RELATIONS)

. . .Handout to Those Attending

WELCOME TO ROCK TOWNSHIP HIGH SCHOOL

We are very pleased that you could visit us. We hope that you will enjoy your stay and will want to come again. The school is open to you, and we hope that you will take this opportunity to observe our facilities and the process of continuing education going on in our school.

When visiting classes, we ask that you take seats in the rear of the room. Not only will this afford you observation of the entire class, but the students will be less distracted by your presence, and you will get an accurate picture of a classroom session.

Should you wish a student guide to aid you in your tour, please ask in the main office, and a member of the Student Council will be happy to assist you.

For your convenience, a bell schedule for change of classes is attached. The main office will gladly answer any questions.

This is your school. Enjoy your stay.

J. Benson, Principal

. . .Invitation to Parents

Dear Parents,

On Wednesday, November 16, from 8:30 A.M. until 3:00 P.M., we will be holding an open house at Rock Township High School.

On that day, parents and community members are invited to visit our school, tour our facilities, sit in on classes, and see for themselves the educational process at work in Rock Township. We can promise no special activities geared for one day only, but we can promise that you will see the day-to-day operations of the place that occupies such a vitally important part of your son's or daughter's life.

The only thing we need to make the day a success is YOU. You are most welcome, and we look forward to seeing you on that day.

Please stop by the main office that I may meet you personally and welcome you to our school.

Sincerely,

John Benson, Principal

. . .Message to Teachers About

MEMO

To: FACULTY
From: J. BENSON, PRINCIPAL
Re: OPEN HOUSE

On Wednesday, November 14, 19XX, from 9:00 A.M. to 3:00 P.M. we will be holding an open house at our school. All members of the community will be invited to visit our school and observe our facilities and classes. I know we will all want to make this day an enjoyable one for our visitors, and toward that end, I'd like to offer some suggestions:

1. Provide directions where needed. If visitors are unaccompanied by a student guide, be prepared to direct them to their destinations. Assign one of your students to help if necessary.

2. Include visitors in your class. If you are giving a quiz, let them take it as well. Ask their opinion, if possible. Make it clear that you welcome their participation.

3. Do not discuss an individual student. It would be unfair to hold up your classes for discussion with a parent. I know you wish to be courteous, so suggest to such a parent that you set up a conference at a convenient time.

4. Be yourself. I AM VERY PROUD OF THE QUALITY OF EDUCATION IN OUR SCHOOL. We have no need to "show off." Conduct your normal classes, and I know that our visitors will be as impressed as I am.

I am certain that, with your help, this will be a profitable and enjoyable day for all.

ORIENTATION   (See Also: BACK-TO-SCHOOL NIGHT; OPEN HOUSE; PUBLIC RELATIONS)

. . .Function of Guidance in

ORIENTATION

1. Fifth Grade

Since a counselor is assigned a sixth grade class and stays with it through the eighth grade, the eighth grade counselor visits the fifth grade classes starting in February. The counselor meets the students, explains the guidance role, and introduces the middle school program and activities. Course selection sheets are distributed and the choices are explained. Students are urged to ask questions and express their concerns. The counselor visits the fifth grade classes at various times during the remainder of the year. If they are needed, individual conferences are held with students who have special needs.

Counselors coordinate a visit to the middle school by the fifth grade classes in the Spring. The visit provides an opportunity for students to familiarize themselves with the layout and operations of the school. It serves to reassure them about the transition to the middle schools.

2. Sixth Grade

Sixth grade counselors will notify the students that they are to report to their homerooms or to a central location on the first day of school. Schedules are distributed in the homerooms.

In coordination with the cluster teachers, counselors present further orientation activities. There is reintroduction of the counselor and the guidance role. Schedules, and how to read them, are explained. The need for good organization and study skills are stressed.

Throughout the first week of school the physical plant and school routine are explained.

3. Seventh and Eighth Grade

Seventh and eighth grade students require less by way of orientation than the sixth grade students. However, the counselors and cluster teachers review the school handbook, explain how to read the schedule, review the need for good organization and study skills, and explain the school routine.

4. New Students

Counselors enroll new students throughout the year. During registration, they gather pertinent information, review previous test results, prepare an appropriate schedule, and arrange for a tour of the building and introduction to the student's cluster section.

Small-group meetings are held with new students to improve their transition to a new school.

5. Ninth Grade

Middle school counselors arrange for and facilitate orientation activities involving the high school counselors and the eighth grade students prior to the beginning of scheduling activities.

* * * * * * * * * * * * * *

ORIENTATION

Parent orientation meetings are hosted by counselors at the beginning of the scheduling process. The various offerings and procedures are explained to help parents make informal choices with their children.

Counselors are also available at "Back to School Night" for a brief interchange. Should parents wish a more detailed discussion, it would be best to call for an appointment.

. . .Welcoming of Parents and Students

Dear Parents & Students:

Welcome to Rock Township Middle School's orientation. Please fill out registration papers. We will be requesting records from the student's sending school; however, any report cards, test scores, et cetera, you may have with you will be helpful in scheduling your student.

We have set aside two testing dates for any additional information we may need, please discuss this with the counselor before leaving.

Please stop at Mrs. Zappala's desk (in the guidance office) on your way out so she may review the registration papers and/or testing date reservation.

A tour will be given to your student at the end of this orientation to help familiarize your student with Rock Township.

Sometime during the summer you will receive your child's bus pass. If you have any questions regarding the bus transportation please contact Mr. Genovesse at 555-5111. Transportation is determined by his department.

If you have any questions, you may call the guidance office at 123-4567.

Sincerely,

P

PARENTS (See Also: COUNSELING; DISCIPLINE; SPECIAL EDUCATION; SUSPENSION; THANKS; TUTORS; VOLUNTEERS)

. . .Introduction to Handbook for

INTRODUCTION

We are most happy to be able to send you this *Handbook for Parents.* All too often the home and the school are looked upon as two functioning entities separated by a student. Sadly, this is quite often true. It is with the hope of bridging this gap that this handbook was prepared.

Within these pages you will find the rules of our school, an explanation of the services we offer and our expectations for the education of your child. You will also find specific directions for implementing any of the procedures necessary for your involvement in our school. We hope you will find this information useful.

We look forward to serving you and your children throughout the coming year. If we may be of service, please contact us at the numbers you will find within this, your *Handbook for Parents.*

. . .Invitation to Parents

Dear Parents of Ninth Grade Students,

You are cordially invited to hear about your child's secondary education.

On Thursday, May 15, 19XX, from 8:00 P.M. until 10:00 P.M. at the Rock Township High School Auditorium, Mrs. Janet Talmann, 10th grade guidance counselor, will discuss what will happen to your child when he or she enters Rock Township High School. She will cover the 10th grade curriculum, sports activities, and extracurricular programs. She will also answer any questions parents may have.

I shall be there, and I look forward to meeting you.

Sincerely,

J. Benson, Principal
Rock Township High School

. . .Letter on School Procedures

Dear Parents,

During any given academic year it is only natural that certain points or questions may arise that will require clarification. Certainly, it is our desire to keep you fully informed about every policy and procedure of this school.

Therefore, the very first thing about which we wish to inform you is how to get to the right person to answer you question. Here are some useful numbers:

IF YOU ARE ASKING ABOUT:	CALL, AND ASK TO SPEAK WITH:
Grades, averages, scheduling, conferences, counseling, records, placement	123-4567, Ext. 22, counselor
Absence, excuse from school, attendance	123-4567, Ext. 24, Mrs. Davis
Homework, class work or project	123-4567, ask for teacher
Disciplinary action, suspension, punishment	123-4567, Ext. 21, Mr. Greer
Anything to do with money	123-4567, Ext. 25, Mrs. Sanderson
Social/volunteer, P.T.A., aides, etc.	123-4567, Ext. 26, Ms. Williams

Thank you, and we hope this will be of service to you.

PERMANENT RECORDS (See Also: GRADES; GRADUATION; GUIDANCE; HONOR ROLL; LEARNING DISABILITIES; NATIONAL HONOR SOCIETY)

. . .Of Faculty

(A) address cards

Date: _____

Name (Mr., Mrs., Miss, Ms.): _____

Present Address: _____

_____ Zip: _____

Telephone: _____

Permanent Address: _____

_____ Zip: _____

Telephone: _____

Person to Notify in Event of Emergency:

Name: _____ Telephone: _____

Relationship: _____

(B) assignment record

ASSIGNMENT RECORD

NAME: _____ page _____ of _____

DEGREE(S): _____

CERTIFICATION: _____

DATE FIRST EMPLOYED: _____

DATE OF TERMINATION: _____

DATES		SCHOOL	DESCRIPTION OF DUTIES (Include Grade Level and Subject(s) Taught)
From	To		

(C) guidelines for review of personal file

Every employee of Rock Township has the right to review his or her personal file which is kept in the Central Administration Building. The following are guidelines for such a review:

1. Review of a personal file shall be by appointment only. Such an appointment should be made at least 24 hours in advance.

2. An employee has the right to be accompanied by a person or persons of his or her choosing. The names of such person or persons must be registered at the time of review.

3. An employee has the right to make copies of material in his or her personal file, but no material may be removed from the file without specific written permission of the Board of Education.

4. A member of the Board of Education or a person or persons designated by the Board may be present during the time of review.

5. An employee has the right to make written comments on any material in his or her personal file. These written comments shall be attached to the material commented upon and become a permanent part of the employee's personal file.

6. An employee may review his or her personal file twice in any one calendar year.

. . .Of Students

(A) academic record card

Student's Name: _____

Student's Address: _____

_____ Zip: _____

Parent or Guardian: _____ Telephone: _____

Date Entered School System: _____ Date Left: _____

GRADE: _____ School Year 19_____–19_____

| SUBJECT | GRADES | | | | | TEACHER |
	1	2	3	4	Final	
English						
Phys. Ed.						

Extracurricular Activities, Awards, etc.

_____

_____

(B) notice of right to review

Dear Parents,

As parents of a student in the Rock Township School System, you have the legal right to review the permanent record folder of your child. This folder contains the academic and social record of your child's progress in the school system. It is kept on file in your child's school.

You have the right to review this folder in person either alone or in the company of a person or persons of your choosing, including legal counsel. You may make copies of any material in the file, but no material may be removed from the file without specific permission of the Board of Education.

If you have any questions regarding this procedure, please call the Central Administration Building at 123-4567 or your child's school.

Sincerely,

Thomas Helms,
Assistant Superintendent of Schools

(C) parental release form

Student's Name: _____ Grade: _____

Student's Date of Birth: _____ School: _____

I hereby authorize the Rock Township Board of Education to release copies of permitted records checked below to:

_____

_____

_____

( ) Observations and ratings by professional staff members acting within their sphere of competency.

( ) Samples of pupil work.

( ) Information obtained from professionally acceptable standard instruments of measurement such as inventories, aptitude tests, vocational preference inventories, achievement tests, standardized intelligence tests, PSAT, ACT, and SAT scores.

( ) Authenticated information provided to a parent or adult pupil concerning achievements and other school activities which the pupil wants to make a part of his or her records.

( ) Verified reports of serious or recurrent behavior patterns.

( ) Extracurricular activities and achievements.

( ) Rank in class and academic honors earned.

( ) Other: _____

Signature of Parent/Guardian
or Adult Student: _____

Address: _____

_____

Relationship to Student: _____

Date: _____

(D) record release

RECORD RELEASE

PREVIOUS SCHOOL _____

PLEASE FILL OUT PROPERLY TO ENSURE CORRECT ADDRESS.

STREET ADDRESS: _____

TOWN, ZIP: _____

DEAR SIR:

RE: _____ DATE OF BIRTH: _____

Please forward all mandated records for the above-named student who has enrolled in the _____ grade of ROCK TOWNSHIP MIDDLE SCHOOL.

In addition, we would appreciate receiving copies of all permanent records to include HEALTH RECORDS as per parent request below.

Sincerely,

Head Counselor

I authorize the release of all permanent records of the above-named student to ROCK TOWNSHIP MIDDLE SCHOOL.

_____   _____
SIGNATURE OF PARENT   DATE

(E) *request for*

SCHOOL: _____ DATE: _____

ADDRESS: _____

_____

Dear Sir:

RE: _____ D.O.B.: _____

ADDRESS: _____

_____

Please forward all mandated records for the above-named student who has enrolled in the _____ grade of the Rock Township public schools. In addition, we would appreciate receiving copies of all permitted records as per the parent release below.

Thank you for your prompt attention to this matter.

DIRECTOR OF GUIDANCE: _____
. . . .

Please check the appropriate response:

I ( ) DO ( ) DO NOT authorize the release of all permitted records of the above-named student to the Rock Township public schools:

SIGNATURE OF PARENT/GUARDIAN OR ADULT STUDENT: _____

ADDRESS: _____

_____

RELATIONSHIP TO STUDENT: _____

DATE: _____

PHILOSOPHY (See Also: CURRICULUM; GOALS; IDEAS; OBJECTIVES)

. . .Of a School System

It is the educational philosophy of the Rock Township public schools to provide quality education that will give special emphasis to the basics and provide a comprehensive education to meet the demands of our complex society. It is important to recognize the sanctity of the home and hold in high regard the traditional family unit and to emphasize its importance as the basic unit of our American society. The educational program shall encourage loyalty to the United States and emphasize the teaching of our heritage and the responsibilities of good citizenship.

The general philosophy is to provide a broad and balanced curriculum, but the study of the basics of reading, writing, and arithmetic shall be presented as worthwhile academic pursuits essential for communication and development of functional individuals in our society. Profanity, immorality, illegal use of drugs and alcohol, and other such practices shall be represented as unacceptable behavior.

It is the responsibility of the Rock Township public school system to respect the rights of all individuals and to provide for every student regardless of race, creed, or sex, the opportunity of a successful learning experience by giving the students the highest quality of professional instruction, the best materials, and the greatest motivation we can provide.

. . .Of an Individual School

Rock Township High School is organized for the purpose of educating young people for a satisfying and productive life. The challenge of the school is to recognize each student as an individual and to help the student develop a feeling of self-worth. Education should stimulate the student to develop those attitudes, skills, ideals, and appreciations which help him or her to become a useful and knowledgeable citizen. The school affirms high moral and ethical standards.

As part of a total community, the school should seek to cooperate with the community, recognizing that this relationship contributes to the development of its youth. The school encourages parents to play a significant role in this cooperative effort.

Because the development of society is an ongoing process that cannot be separated from the past, and because the preservation of our past achievements and failures can make it possible to enhance our present and future conditions, it is necessary to preserve and transmit the heritage of our society.

The past does not provide all the answers, however, and today's world is characterized by change. Because change is inevitable, because it can be beneficial, and because it necessitates major adjustments for society, it is essential to provide our students with the learning tools with which to meet successfully the challenge of change.

As students respond to the educational experience provided for them, it is the expectation that they will recognize that school is a challenge, a privilege, a responsibility, a right, and an opportunity.

. . .Of Education

We believe that a public school system anywhere in the United States exists to serve all the children of all the people as best it can. From the age of 5 to 20 each child has the right to attend the public schools. From the age of 6 to 16 each child is compelled by law to be enrolled in school.

We believe, therefore, that those involved in education must make every effort to meet the needs of all students in granting them the fullest possible educational opportunities.

PHOTOGRAPHS   (See Also: FINANCE; PERMANENT RECORDS; PUBLIC RELATIONS)

. . .Memo to Students on

To: ALL STUDENTS OF ROCK TOWNSHIP HIGH SCHOOL

As you are probably aware through the number of posters on the walls, this Friday, September 23, 19XX, is "SCHOOL PICTURE DAY."

Now, whatever you may personally think about school pictures, they do serve a very important purpose. They are your ID pictures on your student ID, they enter into your permanent records, and they are YOUR photo in the yearbook. As that alone, they are the way in which you will be remembered by your classmates.

Let's make every effort, therefore, to present as positive an image as we are capable of presenting. Remember that date and also remember that in a very real sense, you are NOT taking a photograph—you are creating a memory.

. . .Notice of School Photos

SCHOOL PICTURE NOTICE
ROCK TOWNSHIP HIGH SCHOOL
PICTURE DAY: FRIDAY, SEPTEMBER 23, 19XX

Because it is the most efficient system in school photography, we are using a satisfaction guaranteed prepay plan of purchase. PACKAGES WILL ONLY BE PRINTED FOR THOSE STUDENTS WHO ORDER AND PAY FOR THEIR PACKAGES ON PICTURE DAY. If you are not satisfied with the finished package, we will promptly refund your money, in full, with no hassles upon return of a complete package of pictures to the studio.

Select one or more of the packages listed below. YOUR CHILD WILL HAVE A PICTURE TAKEN FOR EACH PACKAGE YOU ORDER. If paying by check or money order, *please make payable to: Ace Photos. Please note on check: student name, grade, and homeroom #.*

We are pleased to advise that Ace Photos is contributing services and financial support for your school activities. Ace Photos takes pleasure in being able to help your school this way.

* *

PACKAGE A	PACKAGE B	PACKAGE C
1—8 × 10	1—5 × 7	2—3 × 5
1—5 × 7	2—3 × 5	4—2 × 3 wallets
2—3 × 5	4—2 × 3 wallets	8—1 × 2 wallets
4—2 × 3 wallets	16—1 × 2 wallets	
8—1 × 2 wallets		
$10.00	$8.00	$6.00

PACKAGE D	PACKAGE E	PACKAGE F
1—8 × 10	1—5 × 7	2—3 × 5
1—5 × 7	2—3 × 5	4—2 × 3 wallets
2—3 × 5	4—2 × 3 wallets	24—1 × 2 wallets
4—2 × 3 wallets	32—1 × 2 wallets	
24—1 × 2 wallets		
$12.50	$10.50	$8.50

All pictures are in color and all prices include tax.

* *

. . .Special Letter to Parents

Dear Parents,

"Mem'ries," so the song goes, "of the way we were." Well, that aside for a moment, the memories of those "dear old golden school days" (I'm full of quotes today) come in wallet-size and 5 × 7 color photos that are cherished, treasured, admired, honored, and a whole lot of other adjectives, by grandparents, parents, pals, and aunts and uncles. In short, folks, it's school picture time again. In fact, it's this Friday, September 23, 19XX.

I have already informed our students of the time and place of picture taking, and they have been given a notice about prices and packages that might be ordered. This notice should arrive hand in hand with this one. It will inform you what to pay and how to pay depending on the number and kinds of photos you'd like.

I thought I'd inform you of all this in case you'd like your son and/or daughter to "dress up pretty," so to speak, on that day. That, of course, is up to you. All student photos will be used in the school yearbook.

These are your memories; we hope you'll enjoy them.

Yours sincerely,

PHYSICAL EDUCATION   (See Also: MEDICAL; PERMANENT RECORDS; SPORTS)

. . .Eligibility Requirements

ATTENTION: ALL MIDDLE SCHOOL FALL ATHLETES:
    CHEERLEADERS, PARENTS, AND COACHES

1. To be eligible for fall activities, you must pass the equivalent of 35 credits. This includes all 8th graders entering high school.

2. All permission slips must be returned no later than June 9, 19XX, to your coach or school nurse.

3. Physicals will be given at High School North gym area from 8:00 A.M. to 11:30 A.M.

4. Physical dates for all middle schools:

    August 22—8:00 A.M. to 9:30 A.M. Boys' Soccer *A to J*
        9:30 A.M. to 11:30 A.M. Boys' Soccer *K to Z*

August 23—Girls' Soccer, Field Hockey, Cheerleaders *A to J*

August 24—Girls' Soccer, Field Hockey, Cheerleaders *K to Z*

Physicals must be administered after July 1, 19XX, to be valid for the 19XX–XX season.

. . .Course Objectives

PHYSICAL EDUCATION

The Physical Education course objectives are

1. To develop vigor, endurance, good health habits, strength and body control, motor skills, relaxation, and agility to maintain a state of "physical fitness."

2. To develop an appreciation of physical activities.

3. To develop skills of team work, good citizenship, and a wise use of leisure time.

HEALTH

The Grade 6 Health Curriculum unit includes drug/alcohol education, chemical use/abuse, responsible decision making, wellness, diseases including references to sexually transmitted diseases, and fitness.

The Grade 7 Health Curriculum unit includes drug/alcohol education, chemical use/abuse, responsible decision making, dealing with life, sexuality—including sexually transmitted diseases—and family living.

The Grade 8 Health Curriculum unit includes first aid, drug/alcohol education, chemical use/abuse, and AIDS education.

. . .Typical Newsletter Release

PHYSICAL EDUCATION AT WORK

Rock Township students recently completed the President's Challenge, a fitness test designed to measure a student's level of physical fitness.

The test consisted of five tests: (1) pull-ups, (2) curl-ups, (3) sit and reach, (4) shuttle run, and (5) mile run. The test measures upper-body and abdominal strength, speed and agility, flexibility, and endurance.

Presidential awards are given to those students who achieve 85% on all the test items. Last fall there were eight Presidential winners.

National awards are given to those students who achieve 50% in all events. The national awards are new this spring.

Last fall 579 students were tested. This spring all classes including health classes were tested (over 750 students). I am proud to say that the Rock Township students rose to the occasion. Of the 579 students tested, 500 improved, 63 went down, and 16 stayed the same. This equates to an 86% improvement from last fall. We went from eight Presidentials in the fall to 89 in the spring and will be awarding 255 National awards.

Credit can be given to the P.E. staff for their commitment to this program and to the kids for their desire to do better. Congratulations to all for a job well done!

PROFESSIONAL ASSOCIATIONS (See Also: EVALUATION; OBSERVATION; RETIREMENT)

. . .Memo on Membership in

To: FACULTY
From: J. BENSON, PRINCIPAL
Re: MEMBERSHIP IN PROFESSIONAL ASSOCIATIONS

Mr. Joseph Leighton of our Science Department has been appointed faculty representative for the current school year. Besides the tasks of that office, he will be responsible for handling membership in professional organizations.

It is my hope that when Mr. Leighton sees you regarding membership, you will want to join ALL the associations from the local to the national. We live in a world that is constantly changing, where new ideas and new methods are being developed every day. Especially in education must we strive toward relevance and innovative methods to meet the needs of today's students. There is no better way to share, express and learn about these concerns than in joining with your fellow educators throughout the state and nation. Moreover, these organizations have worked in the past and will continue to work in the future for the betterment of educators and education.

I sincerely urge that you consider joining all professional associations.

. . .Seeking Information from

Dear Mr. Harrison,

I am currently enrolled in a doctoral program at Fairmont University. As part of my doctoral thesis, I would like to include some statistics on the rise in membership in your association in relationship to the rise in the number of teachers over the period from 1961–1970.

Perhaps you might be able to help me. If at all possible, I would like your membership figures for that time period. Also, I believe that you possess the figures on the number of actively employed teachers during each year of that time period. I would appreciate those as well. Moreover, any comments which you might care to make would be most beneficial to me.

PROGRESS   (See Also: CHILD STUDY TEAM; EVALUATION; PERMANENT RECORD; REPORT CARD)

. . .Form for Student Progress

PROGRESS REPORT

In my opinion _____ has been doing approximately as well as he is able to do and has been showing a proper attitude in his work for the week ending (date) _____.

Period	Subject	Teacher's Signature	REMARKS: If the teacher cannot conscientiously sign the above statement, please state the reason.
1	_____	_____	_____
2	_____	_____	_____
3	_____	_____	_____
4	_____	_____	_____
5	_____	_____	_____
6	_____	_____	_____
7	_____	_____	_____
HR	_____	_____	_____

Homeroom Teacher's Signature: _____

Students should present these forms with name, date, and subjects properly filled out and ready for the teacher's signature each Friday.

* *

I have examined the above form for the week ending Friday, _____

    Parent's Signature: _____

I understand that the student is fully responsible for

1. Presenting these forms to the teachers on Friday during his or her class periods.
2. Bringing these forms to me, properly filled out, every Friday evening.
3. Returning these forms to the Guidance Office on Monday morning.

    Parent's Signature: _____

. . .Handbook Explanation of Progress Report

PROGRESS REPORTS

1. Midway through each marking period a student's progress report is mailed to the parents of students who are failing a course. A progress report may also be sent to summarize performance in the cluster subjects.

2. A weekly progress report may be carried by the student. On this form teachers indicate the student's progress for the preceding week.

   Parents must take responsibility for receiving and acting upon the information that is given. They must set up consequences for failure to have the weekly progress report signed by the teachers and brought home.

PSYCHOLOGICAL SERVICES   (See Also: CHILD STUDY TEAM; LEARNING DISABILITIES; MAINSTREAMING; MEDICAL; REFERRAL; SPECIAL EDUCATION)

. . .Diagnostic Services Referral Form

DIAGNOSTIC SERVICES REFERRAL*

1. All referrals are to be submitted to the director of special education.
2. All referrals are to be approved by the building principal as recommended by the resource teams.

3. Please attach copies of Request for Resource Team Meeting form and Resource Team Meeting Minutes with this referral.

Name of Student: _____ Building: _____

Date of Birth: _____ Grade/Classroom: _____

Reason for Further Evaluation: _____

_____

_____

_____

Has the evaluation consent form been signed by the student's parents? _____

Check type of diagnostic evaluation requested:

_____ Psychological   _____ Vision

_____ Social History   _____ Hearing

_____ Physical Therapy   _____ Medical

_____ Occupational Therapy   _____ Complete diagnostic team evaluation (psychological, speech, language, academic, social, medically related consultation, etc.)

_____ Other (please specify): _____

_____

_____
Principal's Signature

*Place one copy in special services file and give one copy to director of special education.

. . .Notice to Parents of Referral to

Dear _____,

Our aim within the Rock Township School System is to provide every child with the best education possible. Consequently, we try to take all steps necessary for insuring that each child is performing at his or her maximum capabilities. This is why we are notifying you.

Your son/daughter, _____, a _____ grade student at _____ School, has been referred to our Child Study Team for psychological evaluation. The reason(s) for this referral follow: _____

_____

    The member of the Child Study Team in charge of your child's case is: _____. He or she may be reached at _____. You may direct all inquiries to this person who will be glad to answer any questions you may have.

    We sincerely hope that we may be of service to you and your child.

Sincerely,

Barbara H. Yarrow, Coordinator
Child Study Team

. . .Record of Special Services

RECORD OF SPECIAL SERVICES AND LOCATION OF FILES*

Name _____ Date of Birth _____

The intent of this record is to provide a sequential description of a student's special services and the location of files. Entries should be made whenever a child is placed in a special education program.

Service Area	Date Initiated	Date Terminated	Personnel	Location of File

*Place this form in the student's cumulative file.

P.T.A. (See Also: PARENTS; PUBLIC RELATIONS; THANKS; VOLUNTEERS)

. . .Administrator's Message in P.T.A. Bulletin

To: MEMBERS OF THE ROCK TOWNSHIP HIGH SCHOOL P.T.A.

    I am happy to be able to include this personal message in the first Parent Teacher Association Bulletin of the school year. In the past, the Parent Teacher Association has served the students of our school in an exemplary manner, and I am certain that this year will be no different.

The energy, enthusiasm, and concern evidenced by the members of our Parent Teacher Association are welcome and beneficial adjuncts to Rock Township High School and our children's education.

I look forward to this year and the positive involvement of the Rock Township High School Parent Teacher Association.

J. Benson, Principal

. . .Sample Goals of

P.T.A. goals for the current school year shall be:

1. Increase P.T.A. membership and expand the base of participation in P.T.A. activities.

2. Provide forums for the exchange and discussion of ideas on issues and topics of current interest.

3. Improve communications between faculty, parents, and students.

4. Enhance the image of our school throughout the community.

5. Provide support for the leadership at our school and throughout the district.

6. Establish incentives for excellence in performance by both faculty and students.

. . .Soliciting Participation in

(A) *helping*

Dear Parents,

The Rock Township High School Parent Teacher Association invites you to become a member for the 19XX–19XX school year. Let us strive for 100% membership. The money from your dues is used for the benefit of your children.

Dues are $1.00 per year per person. Please indicate below the names of the people joining and the amount remitted. This tear-off sheet should then be returned by your child to his or her homeroom teacher whether or not you wish to join.

Yours sincerely,

Ellen Narnel,
Membership Chairperson

.... TEAR-OFF HERE ....

NAME OF STUDENT (1) _____ GRADE _____ H.R. _____

(2) _____ GRADE _____ H.R. _____

I ( ) DO   ( ) DO NOT wish to join. NAME: _____

ADDRESS: _____

PHONE: _____ AMOUNT ENCLOSED: $ _____

Our special activities are only as successful as our parent participation. Please indicate areas in which you would be willing to help this year.

( ) Tutoring Math   ( ) Teacher Aide
( ) Tutoring Reading   ( ) Typing
( ) Tutoring Grammar   ( ) Reading Aide
( ) Nurse's Office Aide   ( ) Refreshments
( ) Dance Chaperone   ( ) Homeroom Telephone List
( ) Student Clubs   ( ) Special Projects
( ) Other: _____

(B) volunteering

P.T.A. VOLUNTEERS NEEDED

The P.T.A. of Rock Township High School once again needs the support of all parents. If you would like to help in any of the areas listed below, please indicate your choice and interests and return this form to your child's homeroom teacher. Please consider participating in some way. The P.T.A. needs your help!

1. DANCE CHAPERONES (Parents to chaperone one or more school dances) ( )

2. LIBRARY (one hour per week: 2:15–3:05 P.M.) ( )

3. PUBLICITY (newspaper articles, posters, etc.) ( )

4. NURSE'S OFFICE (two hours per week typing and/or clerical) ( )

5. TUTORING (as a helper or aide to a department head) ( )

   A. Math ( )   B. Reading ( )

6. REFRESHMENTS (baking for school functions) ( )

7. P.T.A. NEWSLETTER (to help with typing, etc.) ( )

8. TELEPHONING (occasional phoning if necessary) ( )

9. PEP CLUB (to help promote school spirit) ( )

10. OTHER (all time, talents, and ideas welcome) ( )

NAME: _____

TEL. #: _____

GRADE OF CHILD IN SCHOOL: _____

COMMENTS: _____

PUBLIC RELATIONS (See Also: NEWS RELEASES; OPEN COMMUNICATIONS; AND ALL TOPICS THAT MIGHT BE CONSIDERED PUBLIC RELATIONS EVENTS, SUCH AS BACK-TO-SCHOOL NIGHT, OPEN HOUSE, ETC.)

. . .Guidelines for Administrators

To: ALL ADMINISTRATORS
From: WILLIAM SMITH, SUPERINTENDENT
Re: PUBLIC RELATIONS AND OUR SCHOOLS

Public relations serve a useful purpose in today's society on all levels. We in education as well should take advantage of public relations methods in informing the public of what is going on in our schools and presenting our side of what is going on in education. An informed public cannot help but be well disposed toward our school system when they are aware of the fine activities and outstanding education that are taking place.

As an administrator, you are the singular person most aware of what is happening in your building. Let's make certain that we inform the public of all that is going on.

Is there a new program? A class doing something special? A teacher or administrator who has distinguished himself or herself in some way? A student who has some unusual or outstanding characteristics, abilities or accomplishments? An activity that would be of interest to the community? A speaker invited to the school who might be of special interest? All of these and more are fit topics for public relations releases.

Please take some time to compile these releases and send them to this office. Make certain you identify the school and the person issuing the release. It would also be appreciated if you would check the spelling of all names used in an article.

It is up to you to keep the public informed. I have confidence that you will do the job completely and efficiently.

. . .Guidelines for Teachers

To: FACULTY
From: J. BENSON, PRINCIPAL
Re: PUBLIC RELATIONS

I have been informed by the superintendent that we should become aware of public relations in regard to the community we serve. "An informed public," Dr. Smith stated, "cannot help but be well disposed toward our school system when they are aware of the fine activities and outstanding education that are taking place." I think we can all agree with that statement.

Are you doing something with your class that might be of public interest? Do you sponsor an extracurricular activity that is engaged in a special project? Do you have a student who is in some way "special?" What about you? Will you be receiving a graduate degree? Published anything lately? Doing some unusual public service?

These are just some ideas, and I am certain you can think of many more. Don't let potential stories go by unnoticed.

Mr. Peter Connors of the Science Department has agreed to act as public relations coordinator for our school. If you have any ideas for public relations releases, please see Pete as soon as possible.

I know that you will cooperate as you have in the past, and I am certain that our school will be brought forward in the best possible light.

QUESTION (See Also: BULLETIN; NEWS RELEASES)

. . .Organization by Question Form

NOTE: Since administrators must often conduct workshops, give speeches, and prepare all sorts of written materials, the following questionnaire is invaluable. Whatever the topic, applying these questions will allow you to formulate a new approach to even the oldest topics.

1. How was it in the past?
   How is it now?
   How may it be in the future?
2. How does it appear?
   What is it really like?
   Why is there a difference?
3. What does society think?
   What does a smaller group think?
   What do I think?
4. What is one type?
   What is another type?
   What is a third type?
5. What is its most obvious characteristic?
   What is its least obvious characteristic?
   Why is the most (or least) obvious characteristic so significant?
6. What is its best quality?
   What is its worst quality?
   What conclusion can be drawn?
7. When did it happen?
   Why then?
   Could it happen again?
8. How can it be done?
   Steps A, B, C.
   What is the result?
9. My first impression.
   My later view.
   My present evaluation.
10. A notable mistake.
    Efforts to adjust, correct.
    The outcome.
11. One way to get there.
    An alternate way.
    Why one is better.
12. The theoretical approach.
    The practical approach.
    The difference between them.
13. How is A like (unlike) B?
    Why is A like (unlike) B?
    So what?

. . .Rhetorical Question Approach

ARE YOU A PARENT OF A HENDRICKS MIDDLE SCHOOL STUDENT?

WOULD YOU LIKE TO LEARN ABOUT YOUR CHILD'S FUTURE?

WANT TO MEET THE PEOPLE WHO SPEND MOST OF THE DAY WITH YOUR KID?

WANT TO KNOW WHAT THE TEACHER *REALLY* SAID ABOUT HOMEWORK?

WOULD YOU LIKE TO FIND OUT IF YOUR CHILD'S TEACHER *REALLY* HAS TWO HEADS?

CAN YOU FIT INTO YOUR CHILD'S DESK?

DO YOU ENJOY DRINKING COFFEE FROM STYROFOAM CUPS?

If you can answer YES to all (or even almost all) of the above, then you are cordially invited to the fourteenth ANNUAL

HENDRICKS MIDDLE SCHOOL

BACK-TO-SCHOOL NIGHT!!!

RECOGNITION (See Also: EVALUATION; OBSERVATION; THANKS)

. . .Memo Concerning

To: STAFF, ADMINISTRATORS, PARENTS, AND RESIDENTS
From: SELECTION PANEL
Re: GOVERNOR'S TEACHER RECOGNITION PROGRAM

We are going to participate in the governor's Teacher Recognition Program. Governor Florio and the New Jersey legislature initiated a program to recognize our teachers. The guidelines indicate that Rock Township school district can have a teacher selected from each building for a maximum of seventeen teachers. Those teachers who are selected from the building really represent the very fine individuals in that building. In turn, the recipients of the award represent all the many fine teachers in the district.

Teachers must be selected by a panel composed of teachers, administrators, and parents. Teachers selected by the panel must have distinguished themselves during the previous school year through exceptional contributions in the following:

> Use of effective instructional techniques and methods

> Establishment of productive classroom climate and rapport with students

> Development of feelings of self-worth and love of learning in students

The panel will select one teacher for each building and forward the names of the individuals to the Board of Education. The Board will certify the district's selections to the commissioner of education.

Attached is a form for the nomination of teachers for the governor's Teacher Recognition Program.

. . .Nominating Form Memo

To: ADMINISTRATORS, PARENTS, AND TEACHERS
From: SELECTION PANEL
Re: NOMINATIONS FOR GOVERNOR'S TEACHER
RECOGNITION PROGRAM

The members of the Selection Panel are seeking recommendations for the governor's Teacher Recognition Program. Those teachers who are being recommended to the panel must have distinguished themselves during the previous school year through exceptional contributions in the following areas:

Use of effective instructional techniques and methods

Establishment of productive classroom climate and rapport with students

Development of feelings of self-worth and love of learning in students

Those teachers selected by the panel and forwarded to the commissioner will receive a Certificate of Recognition for their achievements. The local district will receive a check in the amount of $3,000 for each nominated teacher, to be used for an educational purpose designated by the teacher.

If there are/is teacher who you believe should be considered for recognition under this program, please complete the bottom of this form and return it in a sealed envelope to: Selection Panel, _____(address)_____. This form is to be returned no later than February 6, 19XX.

THE FOLLOWING INDIVIDUAL SHOULD BE CONSIDERED FOR THE TEACHER RECOGNITION PROGRAM:

NAME: _____ SCHOOL: _____

THIS PERSON IS WORTHY OF RECOGNITION BECAUSE_____

_____

_____

_____

_____

_____

. . .Memo Soliciting Selection Committee

To: All Members of the Professional Staff
From: Assistant Superintendent for Personnel
Re: Governor's Teacher Recognition Program

As you know, Governor Florio has initiated a Teacher Recognition Program that will provide the local district with a check for three thousand dollars . . . for each teacher nominated . . . to be used for any educational purpose designated by the teacher. The provision of the Teacher Recognition Program indicates that district teachers are to be on the selection panel. The selection panel is the group that nominates a teacher from each school and submits the list of teachers to the Board of Education.

We are requesting that staff members volunteer to serve on the selection panel. If you are interested in serving on the selection panel that nominates a teacher from each school in the district, please contact me by Monday, February 6, 19XX.

PLEASE PROVIDE INFORMATION BELOW:

NAME: _____

SCHOOL: _____

RECOMMENDATIONS (See Also: LEADERSHIP)

. . .Of an Administrator

Dear _____,

I am in possession of your recent letter requesting a recommendation for Mr. Harold Wainsford whom you are considering for the post of principal in your district.

I take the greatest personal and professional pleasure in recommending Mr. Wainsford to you without qualification. For seven years he has served as vice principal of our school, and I have found him to be a highly responsible and competent individual who has performed above and beyond the call of his duties. He accepts responsibility squarely and always goes that "extra inch" with the good of the students and the school in mind. If our school enjoys a reputation for academic excellence, an enthusiastic and cooperative faculty, and a student body filled with positive spirit, it would only be stating the truth that it is due, in large part, to the efforts of this man.

I sincerely believe that Mr. Wainsford would make an invaluable contribution to your school system, and I recommend him to your serious consideration. My only regret will be the effort I will have to put in trying to find someone to fill his shoes. It will not be an easy task.

Sincerely,

. . .Of a Student

Dear Sir:

I am quite happy to recommend Jason Banner for admittance to your college in September 19XX. As principal of Rock Township High School, it has been my pleasure to be associated with Jason for the past three years. Since you are in possession of his records, you are already aware of his outstanding academic record. I am also in a position, however, to be aware of Jason's record of personality development and community involvement.

Whether as an elected officer of the Student Council, editor of the yearbook, editor of the school newspaper, or organizer of myriad school activities, Jason has always been a responsible, enthusiastic, and competent young man, anxious to help, of high moral principles, and one with the unique ability to admit his mistakes and learn from them.

Perhaps it is an indication of his personality and proficiency that he is respected and popular with faculty and students alike.

I am happy to recommend Jason Banner to your institution without qualification.

Sincerely,

J. Benson, Principal

. . .Of a Teacher

Dear _____,

I take great pleasure in responding to your request for a recommendation for Mr. Thomas Giger, who has applied for a teaching position in your district.

Mr. Giger has taught in my school for the past seven years. During that time, his record has been impeccable, his knowledge and expertise unquestioned, and his capabilities as a teacher and leader of youth have been an inspiration to us all. He is respected by his colleagues (teachers and administrators alike) and literally loved by his students. The school system that employs Mr. Giger will benefit beyond question.

While I deeply regret the loss of Mr. Giger from our school, I can only envy the administration and staff of the school to which he will go. Without qualification, I recommend him to your attention.

Sincerely,

REFERRAL (See Also: CHILD STUDY TEAM; COUNSELING; DISCIPLINE; DRUGS; PSYCHOLOGICAL SERVICES; SPECIAL EDUCATION)

. . .All-Purpose Form for

NAME OF PERSON MAKING REFERRAL: _____

SCHOOL: _____ DATE: _____

PERSON BEING REFERRED: _____

GRADE: _____ AGE: _____ DATE OF BIRTH: _____

HOME ADDRESS: _____
_____ ZIP: _____

REFERRAL TO WHAT PROGRAM OR AGENCY: _____

REASON FOR REFERRAL: _____
_____
_____

WHAT HAVE YOU TRIED PRIOR TO MAKING THIS REFERRAL? _____
_____
_____

WHY DO YOU FEEL THAT REFERRAL TO THIS PROGRAM OR AGENCY WILL BE BENEFICIAL TO THE PERSON BEING REFERRED? _____
_____
_____

YOUR SIGNATURE: _____

POSITION: _____

. . .Memo to Faculty on Student Referral

To: All Members of the Professional Staff
From: Office of the Superintendent
Re: Office Referrals

It is generally agreed that teachers should be responsible for discipline in their own classrooms. This is the case at North High School. Under certain conditions it may be necessary for the teacher to refer a student to the office. Examples of this would be

1. When the teacher has lost control and cannot regain it without help.

2. When the disturbance, such as a mental disturbance, stems from a cause that requires special attention.

3. When the teacher feels that a student must be removed temporarily from the class. In this case he or she may prefer to deal with the case himself or herself at a later time and will indicate this by note or telephone call to the office. In any case where a student is sent to the office, a message should follow immediately.

4. When a teacher has exhausted his or her resources and feels that a case must be turned over to the administration. In this event the teacher should feel that decisions as to punishment also be referred. The principal or his or her assistant will not assign punishment in terms of the student's total school record and should not be expected to avenge the teacher's injured feelings. It is reasonable to expect that a recommendation from the teacher be considered, but with the referral of the problem should go the referral of the judgment. Otherwise, the principal's role would be merely that of executioner.

5. If a student is asked to leave class, the assistant principal's office will be notified immediately by a discipline referral and the student will be sent to the office at once.

6. The principal and/or his or her assistant principal will be available at any time to discuss any problem with you. We are most eager to help. If you see difficulties on the way, tell us about them. We may be able to help keep them from materializing.

LENGTH OF REFERRAL

Truancy: (An unexcused absence before or after reporting to school)
          3 days

Smoking: (Outside designated area or at undesignated time)
          3 days
Fighting: 3 days
Severe Cases of Fighting: (With use of weapon or when student's presence may cause further disruption in school)
          Up to 10 days
Other Offenses or an Accumulation of Offenses: Up to 5 days
                                                Up to 10 days extreme
                                                situations

If, after three referrals, cooperation with school personnel is not obtained, legal action will be taken against the student through the court. A conference with the parent, student, alternative school counselor, and the secondary supervisor is mandatory after these referrals before the student can be readmitted to the regular school.

RELATIONSHIPS   (See Also: BACK-TO-SCHOOL NIGHT; DISCIPLINE; PUBLIC RELATIONS)

. . .Community

COMMUNITY RELATIONSHIPS

Each teacher should always remember that he or she is a member of the community and should participate in community activities.

1. Use cooperative school-community planning.

2. Utilize advertising media such as TV, radio, and newspaper.

3. Be a public relations agent to give information to the public about the functions and needs of the school.

4. Use resource specialists.

. . .Professional

PROFESSIONAL RELATIONSHIPS

In our professional relationships we should be

1. Ever mindful of the requirements of our profession.

2. Operate by the Code of Ethics.

3. Belong to and participate in the activities of local, state, and national education groups.

4. Keep up an effective inservice program.

. . .Student-Teacher

STUDENT-TEACHER RELATIONSHIPS

In a student-teacher relationship, the teacher should make a study of the whole child, including his or her physical, social, intellectual, and emotional needs.

You will be a more effective teacher if your actions speak acceptance rather than mere tolerance. You don't have to accept the child's standards for yourself, but you should accept the child's standards as his or her own.

Your role is to teach ALL children, not merely those with clean shirts, quick minds, or good manners.

A good way for a teacher to win the loyalty of students is to show them he or she is truly concerned about them, individually and as groups. Demonstrate, for example, your interest in the athletic events, plays, and dances. The important thing is not to *pretend* you are interested in these things. Actually get interested in them.

WHEN IT BECOMES NECESSARY TO REPRIMAND AN INDIVIDUAL, REMEMBER TO REPRIMAND IN PRIVATE, PRAISE IN PUBLIC.

REPORT CARDS   (See Also: EVALUATION; EXAMINATIONS; GRADES; GUIDANCE; PERMANENT RECORDS)

. . .Message to Parents Concerning

Report cards are prepared for every child each nine weeks. Wednesdays will be the day for sending home notices, news, and other forms of information with your children.

Parent-teacher conferences will be scheduled twice during the school year near the end of the first and third nine-week periods. However, you are invited and urged to contact the teacher, the principal or any other school official at any time to discuss your child's welfare.

Satisfaction in learning should be encouraged. The report card recognizes competition, but stresses self-improvement and self-achievement.

The grading scale is as follows:

Grades 1–3	Grades 4–6
+ Above average	A Excellent
✓ Satisfactory	B Very good
N Needs improvement	C Average
	D Below average
	F Unsatisfactory

We recommend that you make appointments for after-school visits with your child's teacher whenever you have a question about your child's progress.

. . .Policy Statement on

It shall be the policy of the Rock Township school system that every pupil enrolled in the system shall receive an evaluation of his or her progress four times each school year. Such evaluation shall be in writing, indicating the pupil's progress during the preceding 45 school days. This written report shall be signed by the pupil's parent or legal guardian and returned to the school following the first three marking periods.

In addition to these written reports of progress, elementary schools shall hold parental conferences twice a year, in the fall and spring, during which a child's progress may be discussed by the teacher and the child's parents or guardians.

. . .Sample Statements on

REPORT CARDS

Report cards are sent home with the student in November, February, and April. They are mailed home at the end of the fourth marking period.

Counselors monitor the marks report sheets which are then sent to Data Processing. When the report cards are prepared, they are distributed to the students to take home, have signed, and returned to homeroom teachers.

Counselors monitor the report cards conferring with students and/or parents as needed.

*   *   *

REPORT CARDS

Report cards will be issued to parents four times during the school year. If you or your parents have any questions regarding your achievement, an appointment to discuss your report card with your teacher or counselor can be arranged by calling the guidance office.

Interim reports, warning of unsatisfactory work, are mailed to parents halfway through each marking period.

*   *   *

REPORT CARDS

Report cards are issued every nine weeks. Two parent-teacher conferences are held each year at the end of the first and third nine-week periods. Scheduling for the conferences is done through the office.

The report card is reviewed by the Report Card Curriculum Committee. Changes may be suggested to the representatives on the committee—two from Rock Township Elementary School.

Two types of report cards are issued—one in the primary grades and a slightly different one in the intermediate grades. The system uses "S," "N," and "I" at the present time with letter grades given in the academic subjects of the intermediate grades.

Further information on the report cards is available in the Curriculum Guide and will be given out as the time approaches for the first report cards.

REPRIMANDS   (See Also: BEHAVIOR; DISCIPLINE; SUSPENSION)

. . .Of Support Staff Personnel

Dear Mr. Cogins,

I regret having to bring to your attention an unpleasant incident that happened last Thursday, March 21, 19XX. At that time, several students came to me to report that there was a man smoking openly in one of the halls. I personally escorted those students to the place they had indicated, and there we came upon you, brushing up a floor while smoking a cigar. Indeed, the smoke was clearly visible and several students were commenting and crudely joking about it.

I am certain that you are aware that your master contract states that all custodial personnel will abide by the rules of the school and the township. I respectfully remind you that smoking is against the rules of this school, and, since this school is a public building, it is contrary to the civil laws of Rock Township as well.

I hope that this reminder will be sufficient to keep the incident from repeating itself. I am certain that you will cooperate in this matter.

Sincerely,

. . .To a Faculty Member

(A) *for a minor infraction*

Dear Mr. Hyers,

I regret having to bring to your attention certain recent events, but I feel that the situation warrants it. On Monday, Wednesday, and Thursday of last week you were over half an hour late to school. This resulted in your missing your homeroom assignment and necessitated having one of your colleagues cover your assignment. This is not the first time this year that something of this nature has happened.

I am certain that you will wish to remedy this situation immediately. If there is any way in which I may help, I shall be happy to do so. Please feel free to contact me at any time.

Sincerely,

J. Benson, Principal

(B) *for a serious infraction*

Dear Mr. Smith,

I sincerely regret having to write this letter. For the good of our school and the profession of education, however, I feel that it is necessary to bring to your attention a most serious matter.

On Thursday, October 21, 19XX, during period 1 of the school day, it was brought to my attention that you had been brought to the nurse's office by one of your colleagues. When I visited you there, it was readily apparent that you were heavily under the influence of alcohol. In fact, you were indisposed to such a degree that you had to be driven home.

I am certain that you must realize how serious something of this nature is. It was only through the concern and good graces of your colleagues that you were saved from an embarrassing situation in front of your classes.

Your personal life is, of course, your own. When it interferes with your professional duties, however, it becomes the concern of every educator.

This is the second time in two years that such an incident has occurred. It must not, and it shall not, happen again.

A copy of this letter is being sent to the superintendent to be placed in your personnel file. If an incident of this nature should again occur, we will have no recourse but to recommend to the Board of Education your immediate dismissal.

We sincerely regret the necessity of this action. If there is any way in which we may help you overcome this problem, we stand ready to offer any assistance you may require. Please feel free to seek our aid at any time.

> Sincerely,
>
> J. Benson, Principal

. . .To a Student

(A) for a minor infraction

Dear Robert,

On Tuesday, November 17, you were referred to the main office for running in the hallways to such an extent that another student was knocked down and narrowly escaped serious injury.

I sincerely urge you to consider fully the consequences of your actions in the future. Part of maturity is learning to consider the rights, safety, and feelings of others. Had the other student been injured as a result of your impetuous actions, you would have been faced with a situation with serious consequences.

I know that you will understand the purpose of this letter, and make every effort to see that the situation does not occur again. I am sending a copy of this letter to your parents, and I look forward to contacting you for happier reasons in the future.

> Sincerely,
>
> J. Benson, Principal

(B) *for a serious infraction*

Dear Adam,

I find it necessary to write to you about a most serious matter. On Wednesday, January 18, you were referred to my office for striking another student with a window pole. The student required emergency treatment and stitches.

This is not the first incident of this nature in which you have been involved. In fact, during your two years at Rock Township High School you have been referred to the office for fighting or hitting other students no fewer than 16 times. This is a most serious record, and one that must be dealt with immediately.

Society will not tolerate belligerent behavior of this nature, and neither will we. A student in our school is expected to display a mature and cooperative attitude. This you have not manifested. If you wish to remain a student in our school, you must manifest a drastic and immediate change in your attitude and behavior.

You are currently on a nine-day suspension. When you return to school, I personally expect that an incident of this nature will not occur again. Indeed, it must not. If it does, the very next incident will necessitate a recommendation to the Board of Education for your immediate expulsion from our school system.

Let me reiterate, we will not tolerate any displays of overtly aggressive, belligerent or antisocial behavior. Such behavior will be dealt with swiftly and to the fullest extent of the powers of the Board of Education.

A copy of this letter is being sent to your parents and the superintendent of schools.

Sincerely,

J. Benson, Principal

RESIGNATION   (See Also: RETIREMENT; THANKS)

. . .Acceptance with Regret

Dear Mr. Rentmann,

I am in possession of your letter of May 23, 19XX, in which you state your intention to resign your position as teacher in the Rock

Township school system. I accept your resignation but only with the most profound regret.

Most certainly, I understand your position. Given the state of today's economy and the needs of a growing family, it is only natural that we seek the most advantageous financial position. I only wish that I could match the salary offer you received.

When I say that WE shall miss you, I refer to myself, personally, the faculty and administration of Rock Township High School, and the students you have served so well for the past six years. Having served with you on various committees and having reviewed the observations of the high school administrators, I can only conclude that the students who have been fortunate enough to be in your classes over these years have benefited immensely from your professionalism, concern, and genuine love for those under your charge.

If we may be of any assistance to you in the years to come, we hope you will seek us out.

Please accept my best wishes for continued success in all your future endeavors.

Yours sincerely,

. . .Sample Letter of

Dear Dr. Smith,

Please be advised that it is my intention to resign my position as a teacher in the Rock Township school system at the end of the current academic year.

Please know that I have enjoyed my seven years of teaching in Rock Township, and I have the highest personal regard and respect for my colleagues and the entire educational staff of this system.

I am leaving only because my husband has received a considerable promotion in his job which necessitates our moving to another state. Indeed, I know I shall miss my colleagues and my students. I shall also miss working with people the caliber of yourself and the other members of the professional staff.

Thank you for all you have done for me in the past, and know that I shall always remember my days in Rock Township.

Very truly yours,

(Mrs.) Gloria Kramer

RETENTION   (See Also: CHILD STUDY TEAM; EXAMINATIONS; GUIDANCE; SPECIAL EDUCATION; YEAR-END MATTERS)

. . .Form for Review of

STUDENT PROMOTION REFERRAL FORM

A. BACKGROUND:

Student: _____   Teacher: _____

Grade: _____   Date of Birth: _____

Previous School

Retentions: _____   Year: _____

B. STUDENT PROGRESS:

Subjects: Grades: Final Avg.:   Citizenship: Work Habits:

C. REASONS FOR QUESTIONING PROMOTION:

D. PARENT COMMENTS:

E. TEACHER COMMENTS:

F. COMMENTS OF TEAM:

G. ADMINISTRATIVE DISPOSITION AND REASONS:

. . .Policies and Procedures for

NONPROMOTION OF STUDENTS TO NEXT GRADE LEVEL

The teacher has primary responsibility to evaluate student efforts and achievements. Furthermore, the teacher is accountable for the accuracy and recording of the grades on the student's permanent record.

Nonpromotion of a student to the next grade or failure of a specific subject is the responsibility of the teacher with the concurrence of the principal.

Notification of the parents/guardian of nonpromotion or failure is the responsibility of the teacher and principal.

Parents and students will be given due process by the teacher, principal, superintendent, and Board of Trustees if the nonpromotion or failure is challenged.

The teacher in consultation with the counselor will take into consideration, in addition to academic attainment, such factors as the student's chronological age, mental age, social growth, attendance pattern, physical development, emotional status, effort, and purpose, in determination of nonpromotion or failure of a student.

Individual conferences are scheduled during the month of November following the first quarter report card. These conferences provide an opportunity for parents and teachers to discuss a child—his or her problems, weaknesses, and his or her particular strengths. Suggestions for helping the child at home and at school can be mutually shared and a course of action can be planned. Individual conferences are scheduled for about 15 minutes. The school staff will contact parents regarding a time and date which is convenient.

Children are dismissed during the time that the conferences are held. Other written communications and parent-teacher conferences may be used to inform parents about pressing problems which arise through the year.

When a teacher has determined that a student will not be promoted, the teacher will discuss the situation with the counselor. The counselor will then schedule a session with the student.

Any inquiries from parent or student challenging a grade or nonpromotion will be referred to the teacher involved.

Names of any students failing a course for the semester must be referred to the principal.

Prior to the end of the third quarter, the principal will notify, in writing, the parent that the student is not expected to be promoted to the next grade level. At this time a meeting will be scheduled with the principal, teacher, and parent to discuss the situation. This meeting will be documented in writing. A meeting may be held during the fourth quarter if necessary or if requested by the parents.

. . .Sample Statements on

If you, as a junior high school student, fail the equivalent of two full-year subjects, you will be transferred, rather than promoted to high school, or you can be retained by your principal.

If you fail the equivalent of three, four-year subjects and/or both math and English, you will be retained.

If you fail ninth grade English and are transferred into tenth grade, you must take both basic skills and regular English classes. However, if you fail ninth grade math you must take basic skills math in tenth grade, and may opt to take an additional math course. If you choose another math elective, you will still be required to take basic skills math.

Your parents will be notified if you are doing unsatisfactory work and you may not be promoted to senior high.

*   *   *

PROMOTION-RETENTION

1. Any student who fails the equivalent of two full-year subjects is to be transferred rather than promoted, and may possibly be retained at the discretion of the principal in conference with guidance.

2. Any student who fails the equivalent of three full-year subjects is to be retained.

3. Any student who fails both mathematics and English is to be retained.

These regulations apply to seventh, eighth, and ninth grades.

RETIREMENT   (See Also: RESIGNATION; THANKS)

. . .Form for

RETIREMENT APPLICATION

NAME: _____ SOCIAL SECURITY NO.: _____

SCHOOL: _____ POSITION: _____

AGE: _____ DATE OF BIRTH: _____

NO. OF YEARS TEACHING: _____ DATE FIRST EMPLOYED: _____

YEARS IN TOWNSHIP: _____ DATE FIRST EMPLOYED IN TWP: _____

STATE EDUCATION ASSOCIATION MEMBERSHIP NUMBER: _____

PENSION AND ANNUITY FUND NUMBER: _____

CURRENT SALARY: _____ EMPLOYEE NO.: _____

TEACHING EXPERIENCE (List positions held in chronological order, addresses of schools, and dates of employment):

_____

_____

_____

_____

PERSONAL INFORMATION:

ADDRESS: _____ TELEPHONE: _____

_____ ZIP: _____

WHEN DO YOU WISH TO RETIRE: _____

. . .Letter to Retiree

Dear Mr. Sloan,

I have been advised that you will be retiring at the end of the current school year. May I be the first to wish you a happy and peaceful retirement. It is my sincere hope that the years ahead will be a time of joy and accomplishment for you.

Over the years I have worked with you, it has been my honor and pleasure to get to know you both professionally and on a personal basis. On both accounts, I hold you in the highest esteem. Indeed, you are not only an outstanding human being, but the epitome of the professional educator.

I know that the faculty and students will miss you, as will I. You have left behind you a rich legacy of competence and affection, the memory of which shall stand us in good stead in the years to come.

Again, best wishes on your retirement, and please remember to visit us frequently.

Sincerely,

J. Benson, Principal

. . .Memo Concerning

To: ALL MEMBERS OF THE PROFESSIONAL STAFF

I have been advised by central administration that a "Retirement Workshop" will be given at our school on the afternoon of Thursday, April 2, 19XX, in the library. The workshop will begin at 2:50 P.M. and will last about an hour, depending on questions. The workshop will cover the procedures you will need to know about the actual process of retirement as well as giving you specifics on how to get the best possible retirement benefits given your age and employment status.

Obviously, this workshop does not apply to ALL personnel, but if you are "young at heart" (and, of course, we all fit that category) but are nearing retirement, this might be a worthwhile activity. Even if retirement is five or more years down the turnpike, it certainly won't hurt to know what we'll find when we arrive.

Personally, I intend to be there, and I know that you'll find it worthwhile if you come.

SCHEDULE (See Also: BULLETIN; PERMANENT RECORDS; SUBSTITUTE TEACHER)

. . .Change of Schedule Form

SCHEDULE CHANGE

Name: _____ Grade: _____ Date: _____

OLD SCHEDULE

Period	Subject	Room	Teacher	Initial
1				
2				
3				
4				
5				
6				
7				

NEW SCHEDULE

Period	Subject	Room	Teacher	Initial
1				
2				
3				
4				
5				
6				
7				

HOME ROOM #: _____

. . .Faculty Scheduling Preference Memo

To: FACULTY
From: ADMINISTRATION

Please list the courses you would prefer to teach next year. If you have
requested to move to another school, we will try to honor this request,
but please complete this list as well.

1st Choice: _____

2nd Choice: _____

3rd Choice: _____

Please return this sheet to Mrs. Daniels in the main office by April 4,
as we will need it for scheduling.

. . .Letter to Parents on

Dear Parents,

During the 19XX–XX school year, seventh grade students will
take an eight-period daily schedule at Rock Township. In addition
to the seven required subjects, students may select one elective from
the following offerings:

FULL YEAR COURSES	HALF-YEAR COURSES (CHOOSE TWO)
Chorus	Drama Workshop
Band	Art Workshop
French I	Home Ec.—Crafts and leisure
Spanish I	Industrial Arts—Metal
Spanish A	

Foreign Language: French or Spanish I is the traditional first year of
language study, identical to that taken in grades 9, 10, or 11. Students
who would benefit from a slower-paced program could elect the
two-year program known as French or Spanish A, B. While foreign
language taken in grades 7 or 8 does not meet college admission requirements, it does provide five to six years of language study in high
school. Levels four, five, and six are designated as honors courses and
are appropriately weighted in computing high school rank.

The student who starts a language in seventh grade should present
the following characteristics:

1. An interest in a language and willingness to spend twenty
   minutes per night on homework.

2. Good study skills.

3. Above-average competence in all other subjects.

4. Reading and Language Achievement scores.

| Level I | 90% or above |
| Level A | 50% or above |

Workshops: Two half-year workshops may be combined for the eighth period elective. The courses described in the "Curriculum Guide" provide a hands-on, more indepth experience in the practical or fine arts.

Music: Both Chorus and Band are offered for a full year in grade 7. They develop musical background and the opportunity to perform as a group.

After reviewing the course descriptions in the "Curriculum Guide," please circle the course you wish to have included in your son/ daughter's schedule for next year and return to the homeroom teacher by Wednesday, January 18.

. . .Memo on Exam Schedule

To: ALL MEMBERS OF THE PROFESSIONAL STAFF

Midterm examinations are scheduled for January 26, 27, 30, and 31. Please be advised that this year the examination grade will be a separate grade on the student report card. The examination schedule for the four days is as follows:

8:10–8:20	Homeroom
8:25–9:55	Examination
10:00–11:30	Examination
11:30	Dismissal

There will be no cafeteria service for students. There will be no late buses on these days. The last bus will depart by 11:40 A.M.

Sixth grade students do not have a midterm examination. They may have a cumulative learning experience.

We are asking the following professional staff to relieve all examination teachers for 10 minutes. Hall duty assignments will be in effect during examinations.

AREA	ROOMS	STAFF MEMBER
I. A. WING	90–94	MR. TOMO
SCIENCE WING	95–100	MR. JOHNSON
GUIDANCE WING	101, 103, 105, 107	MR. KELLY
	102, 104, 106, 108	MRS. SULLIVAN
	109, 110, 112, 116	MR. KURZ
UPSTAIRS WING	200, 202, 204, 206, AND 208	DR. SEARES
	201, 203, 205, 207, AND 209	MRS. ABBOT
	211, 212, 213, 214, 215, AND 217	MRS. DOUGLAS

THANK YOU for your cooperation with this exam schedule. As always, if you have any questions with this, please feel free to speak to an administrator.

. . .Student Schedule Form

NAME: _____
         Last   First   Middle Initial

ADDRESS: _____ PHONE: _____

            _____ ZIP: _____

I wish to have a SIX/SEVEN period day. (Circle One)

    REQUIRED: **1.** Physical Education

                 2. English

    ELECTIVE: **3.** _____

                4. _____

                5. _____

                6. _____

                7. _____

      STUDENT SIGNATURE: _____

      PARENT SIGNATURE: _____

The completed schedule is to be handed in to your English teacher no later than Wednesday, March 22, 19XX.

. . .Student Scheduling Explained

SCHEDULES

On the first day of school, students find schedules awaiting them in their homerooms. Much work has gone into the preparation of these schedules. In the middle of the preceding year counselors meet with their students' teachers and get their recommendations for placement. These recommendations and general knowledge of the students are all considered by the counselor in determining the placement that would be most advantageous to each student. Counselors then visit classrooms to explain course offerings and distribute course selection sheets. These sheets are taken home and discussed further with parents. Both students and parents sign the course selection sheets which are returned to the teacher and then to the counselor. Counselors review the selections and then meet with each student to discuss the choices, possible revisions, educational or career plans, et cetera. Sometimes extensive revisions to the master schedule are made necessary as the counselor seeks to develop the most advantageous schedule for each student.

At the end of the year many revisions must be made because scores on standardized tests require inclusion in or removal from basic skills classes. Changes are also required because of failure or changed performance in one or more subjects.

After the school year begins, schedule changes may be required because it becomes apparent that some other placement might be more advantageous. However, these changes are made only for good cause, not for frivolous reasons.

. . .Teacher Schedule Form

19XX–19XX
TEACHER SCHEDULE

TEACHER: _____

SCHOOL: _____

PERIOD	ASSIGNMENT	ROOM NUMBER
1.		
2.		
3.		
4.		
5.		
6.		
7.		

Homeroom Assignment: _____

Duty Assignment: _____

SCHOLARSHIPS   (See Also: AWARDS; FINANCIAL; GRADES; NATIONAL HONOR SOCIETY)

. . .Announcing Availability of

To: ALL SENIORS
From: J. BENSON, PRINCIPAL
Re: COLLEGE SCHOLARSHIPS

Please be informed that there are two college scholarships available exclusively to seniors at Rock Township High School.

The first is a five-thousand-dollar scholarship presented by the Rock Township Education Association. It is awarded on the basis of a competitive examination which will be held on Saturday, March 30, at 10:00 A.M. in the cafeteria. While there is no fee for taking this examination, seniors must register for it at the main office prior to that date.

The second is a four-thousand-dollar scholarship presented by the Rock Township Art League to a senior student who intends to pursue a career in the arts. It is awarded on the basis of evaluation of an art portfolio. Interested students should see Mrs. Wilson for details.

I sincerely hope that many of you will wish to try for these valuable scholarships.

. . .Application for

STUDENT'S CONFIDENTIAL STATEMENT

(All applications must be submitted to the Guidance Office by April 15.)
College students must submit a transcript of work done.

Name _____

Living with: ☐ Parents ☐ Father
☐ Mother ☐ Other _____
(Please explain.)

Are parents: ☐ Divorced? ☐ Separated?

Check if living: ☐ Father ☐ Stepfather
☐ Mother ☐ Stepmother

College or school you expect to attend:

Name _____ Check year ☐ Fr. ☐ Soph. ☐ Jr.

Tuition $_____ Room and Board $_____ Incidental Expenses $_____

Have you applied for any other scholarship award? _____ If yes, please state name and amount. _____ _____

Do you contribute any part of your earnings to help defray household expenses? _____ If yes, please state amount. $_____

Describe briefly your proposed major field of study and the reason for selecting this major. _____

_____

_____

_____

_____

_____

_____

Date _____ Student's Signature _____

. . .Letter on Awarding of

Dear Miss Jarret,

Congratulations! This letter is to inform you that you have been chosen as this year's winner of the Rock Township Art League Scholarship. Your outstanding performances in *Dames at Sea, Kismet,* and *The Glass Menagerie* have shown this committee not only your great versatility as an actress, but also the high degree of dedication and integrity which you bring to each of your roles.

Your extensive participation in community theater also came to our favorable attention: the stunning costumes you designed and executed for Elsa in *The Sound of Music,* Dolly in *Hello, Dolly* and Anita and Maria in *West Side Story.* All of them showed your masterful grasp of theatrical style and sensibility.

It is our deepest wish that you use the $4,000.00 Rock Township Art League Scholarship in your continuing study of the performing arts.

Congratulations and best wishes for what we are certain will be a very promising theatrical career.

Sincerely,

Joan Sullivan Atwater,
President of Scholarship Fund,
Rock Township Art League

SECRETARY   (See Also: APPRECIATION; REPRIMANDS; THANKS)

. . .Dismissal of

Dear Ms. Gerald,

We regret the necessity of informing you that your employment by the Rock Township Board of Education as a secretary will be terminated at the end of the working day on Friday, April 16, 19XX.

During your four months of employment, we have found it necessary to send you letters of reprimand on nine separate occasions. We have brought to your attention your continued lateness, the general poor quality of work processed through your desk, the loss by you of three very important letters which occasioned serious consequences through your lack of delivery, your taking of Board property for your personal use, and much more. In our last letter we advised you that a repeat of any of these actions would necessitate reappraisal of your employment by the Board.

To date no improvement has manifested itself, and recently, you were responsible for losing important budget forms which will mean that necessary supplies will be drastically delayed. Moreover, you refused to admit the mistake, which further added to the delay until responsibility was definitely established.

Therefore, we feel that the action of the Board is more than warranted. You will receive your final paycheck in the mail on Friday, April 23, 19XX.

Sincerely,

. . .Note of Appreciation to

Dear Mrs. Goldman,

Now that the school year is almost over, I'd like you to know how much I appreciate the myriad ways in which you have helped me during the past months.

I speak not only for your excellence in secretarial matters, but of all those ways in which you go above and beyond your duties. Your foresight, diligence, and concern are not only appreciated, they are essential to me.

Thank you again for your help. It is a pleasure working with you.

Cordially,

J. Benson, Principal

. . .Outline of Duties

1. Office management
   a. Plans and coordinates clerical operation of the school office.
   b. Instructs, reviews, and grades work of office training students.
2. Principal's office
   a. Schedules appointments for the principal and vice principals.
   b. Handles principal's correspondence and maintains files of correspondence, reports, and records.
3. Payroll
   a. Keeps attendance record of total staff and submits payroll.
   b. Maintains sign-in sheets for all personnel.
   c. Secures leave of absence forms from personnel.

    d. Submits payroll for special programs (Driver Training, Lay Reader, Athletics, Classroom Cleaners, Overtime, Language Drillmaster, etc.).

4. Personnel records (total staff)

    a. Yellow Jackets (certificated)

    b. Blue Jackets (classified)

    c. Classification records

    d. X-ray certificates

    e. Other personnel records as required

5. Substitute teachers

    a. Calls substitute teachers when necessary.

    b. Submits payroll.

6. Worker's compensation—prepares claims in case of injury for staff and students. Keeps updated log of injuries and submits quarterly and annual OSHA reports.

7. Responsible for bell schedule of school

8. Responsible for Daily Bulletin

9. Responsible for the message center facilities

    a. Receives and distributes mail with student help.

    b. Reviews incoming correspondence, reports and other material for dissemination and administrator's attention.

    c. Teachers' mailboxes.

    d. Serves as "general information" to the public.

    e. In charge of switchboard and instructs students in operating it.

10. Has charge of official duplicating and mimeographing work

11. Serves as custodian of keys

12. Responsible for checking out teachers at the close of the school year

13. Coordinates school calendar

14. Screens Free Lunch applications

15. Assists typist in screening School Bus Transportation applications

16. Issues parking stalls to faculty, staff, and students

17. Performs other duties as required

SIGN-IN SHEETS (See Also: ABSENCE; SUBSTITUTE TEACHER)

. . .Checklist Form

SIGN-IN SHEET FOR THE MONTH OF

September

Date

TEACHER	6	7	8	11	12	13	14	15	18	19	20	21	22	25	26	27	28	29					

. . .Letter on Abuse of

Dear Mr. Patterson,

This may seem like a very small matter, but I assure you that, as the first grade teacher said after the math lesson, "It's the little things that count."

Here it is: You have not been signing in to school each morning, or, rather, you have done so on so erratic a basis that it is impossible to tell if you are in the building without making a physical check of your presence.

On several occasions, the last being just this morning, there have been telephone calls for you. These calls have been from various sources, and that's not important. What is important is that we have no other way of knowing if you are in the building. A check of the sign-in sheet is sufficient for most people, but when it is ignored, it imposes a difficulty on our office staff, and it certainly does not overwhelm the caller with our efficiency.

Therefore, I am asking you to start using the sign-in sheet on a regular basis. Since this is Board of Education policy and part of the master contract, it is perfectly logical to require this action of you.

Should you have any difficulty with this, please feel free to see me at any time.

Sincerely,

. . .Policy on

The teachers in each building are provided with time sheets in the office of that building. The newly agreed-upon system as negotiated between the Board of Education and the R.T.E.A. requires merely the placing of a check mark and the teacher's initials in the appropriate box after the name of the teacher and on the appropriate date. When the agreed-upon time for signing in each building has come and passed, this time sheet will be withdrawn by the principal or his or her representative, and a different time sheet provided which will require the signature of the employee and his or her time of arrival.

Time sheets shall be checked by the principals of the buildings and turned into the administration office at the conclusion of each month. Should a principal observe habitual tardiness on the part of a teacher in his or her building, this problem should be attacked via a principal-teacher conference. Should such a conference between principal and teacher be unsuccessful, the matter should be reported to the office of the superintendent. If habitual tardiness is not then curbed, salary deduction may be ordered by the superintendent.

SMOKING   (See Also: BEHAVIOR; DISCIPLINE; DRUGS; SUSPENSION)

. . .Letter on Violation

Dear Mr. and Mrs. Razner,

This is to inform you that on Monday, November 2, 19XX, at approximately 9:30 A.M. your son, Robert, was referred to this office for smoking in the second floor boys' lavatory.

As you may be aware, it is the policy of the Board of Education that students are not allowed to smoke on school grounds. The Board has set an automatic suspension of three days as the penalty for the violation of this rule.

Consequently, your son is suspended from school on November 2, 3, and 4, 19XX. He may return to regular classes on Thursday, November 5, 19XX. It is sincerely hoped that in the future Robert will appreciate and cooperate with the rules established for the successful operation of the school.

Thank you for your cooperation.

Sincerely,

Howard A. Kelly,
Vice-Principal

. . .Memo Concerning

To: ALL MEMBERS OF THE PROFESSIONAL STAFF

I doubt that we can call it a "smoking controversy" any longer. The proof is too conclusive for "controversy" to exist. Smoking leads to illness and death; it IS a drug that addicts its users; it is NOT beneficial to growing things like people and particularly children.

Therefore, smoking by students is ABSOLUTELY forbidden ANYWHERE on school property. You are to report anyone caught smoking.

As for the faculty itself, I am advised that the Board of Education is expected shortly to write a policy that prohibits smoking anywhere on school property by anyone. This would, of course, apply to faculty lounges and rest areas.

We teach by example as well as by word. When this new policy becomes effective, perhaps we can all consider setting the example that will become the standard for our "smoke-free" school.

. . .Procedures for Enforcing Smoking Rules

The following procedures will be applied in enforcing the smoking rules.

1. All school personnel shall report to the administrator all students observed smoking on school premises.

2. First offense—a parent-student-administrator conference shall be held. The number of days suspended will be determined by

    a. student attitude and behavior at the time of apprehension (insubordination, etc.)

    b. the extent of student and parental understandings and commitments reached

3. Second offense—A parent-student-administrator conference shall be held and the penalty imposed will not be less than the one imposed on the previous offense. Serious discipline may be administered. A student may be directed to attend a stop smoking clinic if it is available in the district.

4. Third offense—Serious discipline shall be administered. A contractual agreement between student-parent-administrators will be signed by all parties agreeing to the student's dismissal from school on the next offense.

If you have any reactions to the above penalties, please contact one of the administrators at the school.

SPECIAL EDUCATION (See Also: CHILD STUDY TEAM; EVALUATION; KINDERGARTEN; LEARNING DISABILITIES; MAINSTREAMING; PARENTS; PSYCHOLOGICAL SERVICES; REFERRAL; RETENTION; TUTORS)

. . .Consent for Placement in

STUDENT: _____ DATE: _____

The above-named student has been classified in the following areas:

( ) MENTALLY RETARDED   ( ) LEARNING DISABILITIES

( ) EMOTIONALLY DISTURBED   ( ) SPEECH HANDICAPPED

( ) VISUAL IMPAIRMENT   ( ) HEARING IMPAIRED

              ( ) PHYSICALLY HANDICAPPED

SIGNATURE OF ADMINISTRATOR: _____

* *

DATE: _____

I, as the parent or guardian, hereby

        ( ) give   ( ) do not give

my consent for the placement of _____
in the special education classes of the district.

SIGNATURE OF PARENT OR GUARDIAN: _____

ADDRESS: _____

_____ ZIP: _____

. . .Evaluation Form for Student

STUDENT: _____ DATE: _____

ADDRESS: _____ TELEPHONE: _____

_____ ZIP: _____

NAME OF PARENT OR GUARDIAN: _____

TEACHER: _____ SCHOOL: _____

REASON FOR REFERRAL: _____

_____

PERSON MAKING REFERRAL: _____

SPECIFIC PROBLEMS OF STUDENT IN CLASSROOM: _____

_____

STEPS TAKEN TO REMEDY PROBLEMS AND RESULTS: _____

_____

RESULTS OF PARENTAL CONTACTS: _____

_____

GENERAL COMMENTS: _____

_____

Please attach pertinent health information.

. . .Explanation of Special Services

SPEECH THERAPY PROGRAM

A speech therapist is assigned to Rock Township on a scheduled basis each week.

Referrals for speech therapy are made to her and those children in need of help are scheduled for classes. These children will need to leave the classroom for this help period, usually from about 20 minutes to half an hour.

The speech room is located in the new room in the basement. Please refer questions about students to the therapist. The most serious needs get first priority and others are placed on the waiting list. These students are then included as soon as possible.

SPECIAL LEARNING DISABILITY PROGRAM

A special learning disabilities teacher is available to give the classroom teacher help with students who have special problems.

The main duties of this person are the testing, evaluation, and remediation procedures necessary to help correct student problem areas and promote progress. The work with the student will take on different dimensions depending on the problem and the need. In some cases it may involve work in the room; other cases may necessitate taking the child from the room for special help.

After testing and evaluation, conferences will be held with the teacher and with the parent.

. . .Letter to Parents on Due Process

Dear Parents of Special Education Students,

In a recent letter we informed you of your legal rights regarding the placement and education of your child. One of those rights was the right to request a hearing if you should disagree with the classification and/or placement of your child.

You should be aware that, if you request such a hearing, you have certain rights during that hearing. You have the right to

1. Be represented by legal counsel.

2. Request a closed hearing.

3. Request the presence of school personnel.

4. Cross-examine all witnesses.

5. Present your own witnesses.

6. Request and obtain a record of the hearing.

7. Determine whether the child should be present.

8. Obtain an independent evaluation.

Moreover, interpretation for the deaf and/or translation into languages other than English shall be provided.

We hope that this information shall be beneficial to you should you require it.

Sincerely,

Maria Adams Hartmen, Director
Office of Special Education

. . .Policy on

It is the desire of the Board to make available the best possible services for the identification, evaluation, and educational placement and programming for all students between the ages of 5 and 20 who are residents of the district and are not attending nonpublic schools, who need special help or placement. Toward this end, the Board directs that basic child study teams consisting of a psychologist, a learning disability teacher-consultant, and a school social worker be employed as an integral part of the professional staff.

Children so identified by district personnel, medical and health professionals, parents, or agencies concerned with child welfare shall, after approval by the respective school principal, be referred to the child study team for examination in accordance with the rules and regulations of the State Board of Education. This examination shall be completed within 60 days of the referral.

Classifications and educational placements and programming shall be approved by the director of special services and discussed with the parent or guardian of the child prior to their implementation and, whenever possible, shall be implemented within the facilities of the district. When the needs of a child require special educational facilities not available in the district, recommendation for outside placement shall be made to the Board by the superintendent.

All records and reports relating to special education, identification, evaluation, classification, and placement shall be regarded as confidential, and access shall be limited to those personnel and approved agencies directly concerned with determining the classification or the making of recommendations for placement, and those directly involved in the educational program of the child. No records, except in the case of a court subpoena, will be sent to any outside source without the written authority of the parent or guardian.

Handicapped children less than 5 years of age will be considered for a program of special education at district expense only upon the recommendation of the superintendent that such a program would benefit both the child and the district.

Names of children involved will be reported to the Board in executive session and will be recorded in the official minutes.

. . .Request for Special Services Policy

REQUEST FOR CHILD STUDY TEAM SERVICES

Requests for assistance from the Child Study Team, or an individual member of the team, are typically initiated by the classroom teachers who have identified academic, emotional, or social problems that interfere with a student's ability to learn. Requests may also be initiated by parents, guardians, outside agencies concerned with the welfare of the student, and the student.

1. Request for Consultation

Consultative services will consist of a request to the Child Study Team, or an individual member of the team, to discuss a student's problems and to utilize their fields of expertise in exploring possibilities of handling the problem within the school situation. Prior to requesting consultative services, school personnel should have tried to remediate the problem using resource personnel available to them in the general education setting. Permission of the parent, guardian, or adult student shall be obtained in writing.

"Request for Consultation" should be completed by school personnel and two copies forwarded to the unit Child Study Team administrator, who will assign the case to the appropriate team member.

2. Referral for Possible Classification

Based on observations and information obtained during the consultation period, the Child Study Team may, after discussion of the case with school personnel and as a team, recommend that a comprehensive evaluation is necessary as the student:

   a. Is potentially handicapped under the criteria established by law.

   b. If classifiable, needs special education and/or related services that cannot be provided to the general school population.

"Referral for Possible Classification" should be completed by school personnel upon the decision of the Child Study Team that a comprehensive evaluation is necessary. A parent conference must be held by the principal at which time the "Parental Permission for Formal Referral" must be completed. A copy must be attached to the referral form.

NOTE: TIME IS OF THE ESSENCE.

1. THIS MUST BE FORWARDED TO, AND RECEIVED BY THE UNIT CHILD STUDY TEAM ADMINISTRATOR WITHIN SEVEN CALENDAR DAYS OF THE DATE THE PARENT AGREED TO THE EVALUATION.

2. THE EVALUATION HAS TO BE COMPLETED WITHIN SIXTY CALENDAR DAYS OF THE DATE OF REFERRAL.

SPORTS (See Also: AWARDS; EXTRACURRICULAR ACTIVITIES; PHYSICAL EDUCATION; PUBLIC RELATIONS; THANKS)

. . .Game Report Form

GAME REPORT

_____ vs. _____   Date _____

Score: We _____ They _____   Sport _____

Officials: _____   Transportation: (Briefly describe any
_____   problems; if OK please mark so.)

_____

_____

Rating of Officials: (Brief)

Injuries: Game Problems:

To be turned in to athletic director via interoffice mail after each and every game (all levels). Please include vouchers for home games.

. . .Letter of Requirements for Participation

Dear Parents,

For your information we have prepared the following guidelines for all students who intend to participate in organized sports activities at our school.

1. Students and their parents are expected to read the rules pertaining to his or her sport and return a form stating that the parent and student have read the rules and understand their responsibility.

2. A student dropping out of a sport has the obligation to confer with the coach prior to leaving the team. He or she may not, during the same season, leave one team for another without both coaches being in agreement. The student also may not participate in a new season until his or her participation in the preceding season is officially completed.

3. A student must attend classes on days when practice or games are scheduled unless the student has been given an excuse to be absent from a school administrator. Illness shall be reported to the school office and coach by telephone.

4. A student suspended from school or enrolled in the Alternate School Program (ASP) may not participate in any athletic contest until the suspension is lifted.

5. A student must observe all training rules set down by the coach. Repeated offenses against rules pertaining to the use of drugs, alcohol, and tobacco will result in a student being dismissed from the sport.

6. Attendance at all practice sessions is obligatory unless the student has a valid excuse for his or her absence.

7. Coaches are to set the standards and example for student conduct during practice sessions, while traveling to away contests, in the locker room, on the bench and on the playing fields.

8. Since transportation to and from games is provided by the Board of Education, students may not use their own transportation to any contests. If a student wishes to return home from a contest other than by bus, he or she must present written authorization from his or her parent or guardian.

It is our hope that these regulations will be of service to you in understanding the functioning of our sports program.

Sincerely,

William Moone, Head Coach

. . .Permission Form for Participation in

(A) complete form

PERMISSION TO ENGAGE IN (Name Sport) _____

Name _____ Grade _____ Birthdate _____

Address _____ Telephone _____

MEDICAL HISTORY (Please give dates of following:)
Any serious accidents and/or injuries (type) _____

Surgical Operations (type) _____

Allergies _____

Hernia _____

Serious Medical Diseases (type) _____

Chest Diseases _____

Diabetes _____

Convulsive Seizures _____

Eyes (vision) _____

Ear, Nose, and Throat _____

Cardiac (heart defects) _____

Hypertension (High Blood Pressure) _____

Orthopedic _____

Present Medication _____ REASON _____

ANY PREVIOUS REJECTION FROM COMPETITIVE SPORTS (Date and Reason)

Girls: Menstrual Difficulties _____

PARENT'S FORM

The answers to the above are correct. I understand that any misrepresentation of any of the information contained herein will result in the student being denied the opportunity to participate. I hereby give my consent to the participation of

_____ IN _____
(Full Name)   (Sport)

conducted by the school against other schools and within the school. I shall assume all responsibility and expense for any injury received in practice or participation. I give my permission for my son/daughter to be diagnosed and treated by the team physician should such services be necessary.

_____   _____
Date   Parent's or Guardian's Signature

PHYSICIAN'S SIGNATURE

_____   _____
         Date   Medical Inspector's Signature

Height _____ Weight _____ Blood Pressure _____
This form must be turned into the School Nurse one week before Physical
Examination. Parents will be notified if rejected and a statement from the
student physician certifying his/her physical ability to participate will be
necessary. Final decision, however, will be made by the School Medical
Department.

(B) *short form*

I hereby grant permission for my son/daughter, _____,

to participate in the sports activity _____.
I further grant permission for a physical examination of my son/daughter. I
have read the rules and regulations of the sport and understand them and
the responsibilities of myself and my son/daughter.

I relieve the school of all responsibility beyond that of normal supervision.

SIGNATURE OF PARENT: _____

DATE: _____

. . .Sample Team Rules

SOCCER RULES AND REGULATIONS

All players are required to follow the team rules outlined below. The
breaking of these rules will be dealt with seriously. All players must
know these rules. Ignorance is no excuse. Failure to follow them will
result in a suspension from the team. If the infraction is considered
serious enough, the suspension will become permanent. Above all, each
player must understand that playing soccer for Rock Township High
School is a privilege and not a right. All soccer participants are subject to
S.I.A.A. rules and regulations.

SQUAD MAKEUP

1. Making the team is based on 3 A's: ABILITY, ATTITUDE,
   and AGGRESSIVENESS.

2. Cuts from the squad are at the discretion of the coaching staff.

3. Players may be removed from the squad by the coach for
   disciplinary reasons.

4. If a player quits the team, it is his or her responsibility to notify the coaches that he or she is doing so.

PRACTICE

1. Practice is essential for success. You are expected to attend *every* practice, do what is asked of you, and give your best.

2. Practice begins at the time scheduled by the coach and you are expected to be on time.

3. The only excuse for missing practice is absence from school. If you work, schedule your hours around soccer practice. If you can't, you must make a decision as to whether to work or play soccer. Special circumstances require prior approval by coaches.

4. If you are absent from school, you cannot practice or play in a game on that date.

5. Practice is held rain or shine, unless otherwise noted by the coach. Do not go home "thinking" practice has been canceled unless you know for sure.

INJURIES

1. All injuries of *any nature* must be reported to the coach at the TIME THEY OCCUR.

2. After the coach has been notified, you *must* report the injury to the nurse's office at the beginning of the next school day.

3. If a player sees a physician for treatment of an injury, he or she will not be permitted to return to the team to practice or play until he or she presents to the coach a note signed by the doctor, stating that he or she is physically able to play soccer.

PERSONAL CONDUCT

1. Do your school work and stay out of trouble in school. We cannot bail you out of detention, special classes, or A.S.P. (Alternate School Program, In-school Suspension). Let the faculty and administration know that soccer players are caring people and good students.

2. If you are assigned to A.S.P. for any reason, or suspended from school, you may not practice or play until you return to school. Then you will have the coaching staff review the reasons for your transgressions. Don't get into a bad situation to begin with.

3. On the day of a game, you will dress for gym class, but DO NOT PARTICIPATE. If you encounter difficulty with your gym teacher, notify a coach and let him or her take care of the problem.

4. You are responsible for all equipment issued to you.

5. Smoking, drinking, or the abuse of drugs are totally inconsistent with your participation in the sport of soccer and you will refrain from their use. Failure to do so will result in the most serious consequences.

6. Coaches and fellow players are to be treated with respect at all times.

7. Hustle all the time. Be serious about exercises, drills, and practices. They will be used as the basis by which the coaches will judge your suitability to participate in games.

8. Team members are expected to conduct themselves in a courteous manner on all bus trips and at away contests.

If you have any questions concerning these rules, consult your coach.

I have read the attached rules and regulations and agree to comply with them during the current season.

I understand the consequences of failure to comply with these rules and regulations.

Student's Signature	Date

Parent's Signature	Date

STUDENT COUNCIL   (See Also: APPRECIATION; THANKS)

. . .Letter of Appreciation to Faculty Advisor

Dear Mrs. Burnes,

As the school year draws to a close, I have been thinking of the many fine activities that have taken place which have been sponsored by our Student Council. Not only have these activities been highly successful and enjoyable, but the growth in maturity and civic consciousness of the Student Council members has been manifest.

I feel that a large share of the credit for that growth must go to you. Your fine personal example, combined with your dedication and unselfish devotion to the highest ideals of the educational profession, has been a vital, driving force in molding an outstanding Student Council that has literally become a training ground for future leaders.

My deepest thanks and appreciation for your fine efforts.

Sincerely,

J. Benson, Principal

. . .Letter of Appreciation to Members

Dear Jim,

As this current school year draws to a close, I would like to express to you my thanks for your participation in the Student Council this year and my appreciation for your services to our school.

As a member of the Student Council you have the satisfaction of knowing that you have served your fellow students by formulating policies and arranging activities that have benefited the entire school.

Again, my thanks and my appreciation for a job well done.

Sincerely,

J. Benson, Principal

. . .Message in Student Handbook

STUDENT COUNCIL

Both the junior and senior high schools have student councils, each with its own constitution. Participation in student council activities provides each student with an opportunity to offer valuable service to the school and to develop those characteristics of leadership so vital to the American way of life.

. . .Nominating Petition

**ROCK TOWNSHIP HIGH SCHOOL
STUDENT COUNCIL**

NOMINATING PETITION FOR HOMEROOM REPRESENTATIVES

TO THE STUDENT: This form is to be completed by each of your teachers
for his or her approval and returned to your homeroom teacher no later
than FRIDAY, SEPTEMBER 30, 19XX.

| (Name of Student) | (H.R.) | (H.R. Teacher) |

To Teachers: Please check the appropriate place, indicate any comments
and initial. When making your decision, please keep in mind the
following: Positive Leadership, Citizenship, Punctuality, etc.

TEACHER	INITIAL	SUBJECT	YES	NO	COMMENT

STUDENT COUNCIL ADVISOR: _____

ASSISTANT PRINCIPAL: _____

. . .Statement Concerning

It is important in the maintenance and improvement of democratic
institutions that students have the opportunity to participate effectively
in the decision-making process necessary for developing responsible and
productive citizens. Toward the attainment of this end, students shall
have the right to organize and conduct student council or government
association activities which contribute to the understanding and functioning of the objectives of the school system.

The objectives of the student government organization shall be to
improve the quality of the educational program, to provide to the administration suggestions in that respect, and to assist students in processing
grievances.

It shall be the policy of the Board that one student representative to the
Board be elected annually from the sophomore and junior classes to
serve the following terms of office:

Sophomore Class   1 year
Junior Class   2 years

The Board will officially accept these representatives at the annual organization meeting.

The organization, operation, and scope of each student government organization shall be defined in a written constitution developed through effective student participation with the school administrators and approved by the Board.

STUDENT TEACHER (See Also: CLASS; EVALUATION; LESSON PLANS; OBSERVATION)

. . .Evaluation Sheet

STUDENT TEACHER: _____

THIS IS MY _____ EVALUATION.   DATE: _____

AREAS IN WHICH IMPROVEMENT HAS BEEN NOTED: _____

_____

_____

AREAS IN WHICH IMPROVEMENT IS NEEDED: _____

_____

_____

OVERALL PROGRESS TO DATE: _____

_____

_____

SPECIAL AREAS OF PRAISE OR CONCERN: _____

_____

_____

GENERAL COMMENTS: _____

_____

_____

SIGNATURE OF COOPERATING TEACHER: _____

. . .Guidelines for

The steady increase in the number of young men and young women who come to the Rock Township Public Schools to do their student teaching and the high importance of the experience itself necessitate the following memorandum which will set forth some basic operational suggestions for a school district policy.

The student teaching experience serves as the culmination of the future teacher's college preparatory program. The goal of the school district is to provide an environment that will encourage the maximum growth of the teacher candidate. All activities of the school relative to student teaching must be implemented only after a thorough consideration of the effect on its primary objective, that of guaranteeing the best possible education for the children of the district.

Additionally, the responsibilities and rights of the cooperating teacher should be considered in the organization of the student teaching program.

It is not the intent of the school district to dictate the teacher education program of the preparatory institutions. Rather, the district is attempting to work with the college in the fulfilling of the responsibility for teacher preparation.

. . .Letter to

Dear Ms. Hanson,

On behalf of the faculty and staff of Rock Township High School, I welcome you to your student teaching experience. I sincerely hope that the time you spend here will be happy and pleasant as well as informative and helpful to you in your career as a professional educator.

Naturally, I am somewhat prejudiced in the matter, but I truly believe that this school and this faculty are the finest in the state, and as such you have a unique opportunity to "tap into" their perceptions, their experience, and their expertise in teaching. I strongly suggest that you do just that—allow them to teach you in order that you may teach others. It will be a powerful and beneficial experience.

If I or any of the administrators may be of service to you during your stay with us, please do not hesitate to see us.

Welcome!

Yours sincerely,

. . .Statement on

The student teaching experience serves as the culmination of the future teacher's college preparatory program. The goal of the school district is to provide an environment that will encourage the maximum growth of the teacher candidate. Any activities of the school relative to student teaching may be implemented only after a thorough consideration of the effect on its primary objective, that of guaranteeing the best possible education for the children of the district. Additionally, the responsibilities and rights of the cooperating teacher should be considered in the organization of the student teaching program.

Student teachers shall be selected and assigned by the administrative staff with the consent of the principal and supervisor and the cooperating teacher. In the case of candidates with unusual qualification, that is, from unaccredited institutions or programs, from foreign institutions, from special programs of an exceptional or sectarian nature, et cetera, special approval from the Board is required prior to selection. Student teachers selected to practice in this district shall comply with the Board's policy for employee physical examination.

While serving in the schools, student teachers shall be responsible to the principal through the professional to whom they are assigned for their conduct, and to their college supervisor for their classroom performance. Student teachers shall be allowed to participate in school activities where their contributions would be appropriate to the educational program of the school.

It is not the intent of the school district to dictate the teacher education program of the preparatory institutions. Rather, the district is attempting to work with the college in the fulfilling of the responsibility for teacher preparation.

SUBSTITUTE TEACHER (See Also: CLASS; EVALUATION; LESSON PLANS)

. . .Letter to

(A) for outstanding service

Dear Mrs. Panelli,

I wish to thank you and compliment you for the outstanding job you did in our school during your substituting assignment last Thursday, March 12, 19XX.

As you know, on that day we had a small fire in the cafeteria which necessitated the students being evacuated from that area due to smoke. You were on "Lunch Duty" during that time and aided in that evacuation. Reports that I have received both from students and teachers indicate that you were not only a real help during this emergency, but that your calmness, authority, and ability to work under pressure were responsible for the fact that no one in your section suffered injury of any type. Moreover, the caring and nurturing attitude you displayed toward some of our students who became extremely upset by the incident was deeply appreciated not only by us, but by several parents who have called to compliment and thank you for the concern you manifested toward their children.

On behalf of the entire student body and faculty, I thank you for action "above and beyond" your regular duties. I wish to thank you personally as well.

A copy of this letter is being sent to the director of personnel and the Board of Education.

                                    Yours sincerely,

(B) *for poor service*

Dear Mrs. Smith,

On Wednesday, April 8, 19XX, you substituted in our school, taking over the classes of Ms. Hall, who was ill.

During the course of that day, I received a number of complaints that the noise from your room was so loud that nearby classes could not be conducted. On three occasions you let your class go approximately five minutes before the bell. The nurse had to be sent to your room to treat a young man who had injured himself when he fell from the window ledge where he was walking at the time. The department coordinator, at my request, checked the room and Ms. Hall's plans later in the day, and not only did it appear that Ms. Hall's plans were not followed, but a check of supplies seems to indicate that several reams of paper and various other supplies are missing.

This is not the first time you have been in our school, nor is this the first time that something of this nature has occurred while you were substituting. On each prior occasion you were warned about the behavior exhibited, informed as to correct procedures, and given all help possible. In spite of this, the difficulties continue.

I am sending a copy of this letter to the director of personnel as well as to the Board of Education. I am recommending to them that you be dropped from our substitute list. I really feel that would be the best solution for everyone.

Sincerely,

. . .List of Substitute's Responsibilities

SUBSTITUTE TEACHER'S GUIDELINES

To enable each child to pursue his/her education as smoothly and completely as possible in the absence of the regular teacher, the substitute's responsibility is to

- ☐ Notify the office immediately should a student become ill or an accident occur.
- ☐ Notify the office immediately if disciplinary assistance is needed.
- ☐ Consult the secretary for supplies not available in the room.
- ☐ Become familiar with audio-visual materials and machines.
- ☐ Report damage of equipment or materials to the office.

At the end of the teaching day, the substitute should

- ☐ Leave the teacher's desk and room in order.
- ☐ Return equipment to the proper place(s).
- ☐ Turn off lights, close windows or doors.
- ☐ Leave keys and materials in the office.
- ☐ Check with the secretary to see if services will be needed the next day.
- ☐ Make certain time sheet has been signed.
- ☐ If possible, leave comments and record of day's progress and assignments completed.

A substitute teacher whose services will extend more than ten (10) days should attend faculty meetings.

A substitute teacher should recognize that he or she will benefit by

☐ Considering all records confidential.

☐ Avoiding discussion and comparison of situations in one school while serving in another.

☐ Avoiding comment on the progress of pupils or the work of the teacher.

☐ Making all observations, suggestions, or criticisms to the principal of the school involved.

☐ Using discretion in expressing personal reactions and opinions about what is seen and heard in a classroom.

. . .Substitute Report Form

SUBSTITUTE REPORT TO THE TEACHER

Date(s) of Work: _____

Teacher's Name: _____

Substitute's Name: _____

	Old Assignments Collected	Current Assignments Collected	Pages of Classwork Completed	Names of Disruptive Students
Per. 1				
Per. 2				
Per. 3				
Per. 4				
Per. 5				
Per. 6				
Per. 7				

Comments:

Please leave all work collected, this form, and any other materials in the department office prior to leaving the building. Thank you.

. . .Teacher Evaluation of Substitute Form

TEACHER REPORT ON SUBSTITUTE

Date(s) of Absence: _____

Teacher's Name: _____

Substitute's Name: _____

Period	Subject
Period	Subject
Period	Subject
Period	Subject
Period	Subject

Were the lesson plans followed?   ( ) YES ( ) NO

Was the class work completed as assigned?   ( ) YES ( ) NO

Did you find the condition of your room satisfactory?   ( ) YES ( ) NO

Did the substitute leave a report for you?   ( ) YES ( ) NO

Were you pleased with the work of the substitute?   ( ) YES ( ) NO

COMMENT:

Please turn in this form to the main office by the end of the day on which you return to school.

SUGGESTIONS (See Also: IDEAS; OPEN COMMUNICATIONS; THANKS)

. . .Faculty Suggestion Form

NAME: _____

DEPARTMENT: _____ DATE: _____

SUGGESTION FOR IMPROVEMENT

The following suggestion is for the improvement of our school within the limits of financial and legal responsibility and within the boundaries of practicality:

. . .Letter on Outstanding Suggestion

Dear Naomi,

I should be furious with you! You keep coming up with better suggestions than I do! I ask you, is this any way to run a school?

Seriously, Naomi, what a wonderful, thoughtful, and practical suggestion you submitted regarding the problem of activity arts scheduling. The suggestion you handed to me was one that not only solves the problem, but shows such obvious concern for the good of our students that one knows immediately how fortunate your students are to have you as a teacher.

Please be assured that your suggestion will be implemented to the benefit of all. Personally, I thank you for always caring about this school and its students.

A copy of this letter is going to central administration to be included in your file.

Yours sincerely,

. . .Student Suggestion Form

SUGGESTION FORM

NAME: _____ DATE: _____

HOMEROOM: _____ H.R. TEACHER: _____ GRADE: _____

I think that the following suggestion would really help our school:

_____

_____

SUPPLIES (See Also: EQUIPMENT; SECRETARY; TEXTBOOKS)

. . .Budget Form for

BUDGET FORM FOR GENERAL SUPPLIES

NAME: _____ ROOM: _____

DIRECTIONS: Include all instructional supplies except audio-visual, paper, and desk-top items. These items are to be included on separate forms by the subject coordinator. A supply item is usually expendable and usually costs under $25.00 per item. Examples include workbooks, prepared ditto masters, and minicourse and gym supplies.

AMOUNT	ITEM	QUANTITY	UNIT COST
		GRAND TOTAL	

. . .Inventory of Supply Room Memo

To: MS. HARRIET DONNER
From: J. BENSON, PRINCIPAL
Re: SUPPLY ROOM INVENTORY

We are starting the budget process in our school this week. I would like you to be ready for a complete supply room inventory by October 1. As usual, we will assign two teacher aides and four seniors from the business and commercial department.

We need, of course, the amount on hand of each item and the amount used since last year's inventory. I realize that general supplies constitute a relatively small share of our total budget. Strangely enough, it is an item which seems to be most closely scrutinized each year. It is particularly embarrassing in the final budget review to have large amounts of any item still on hand as the fiscal year comes to an end. Try to substitute paper that is in great supply for requests for another, less plentiful paper.

I'm certain that you will do a great job, as usual. Thank you.

. . .Memo on Availability of

To: ALL MEMBERS OF THE PROFESSIONAL STAFF

We are all aware that there are certain "signs of spring" such as birds and leaves on trees and little flower buds pushing their heads out of the cold ground. Well, folks, there's another sure sign of spring that I've discovered—one that states in no uncertain terms that spring is here and the school year has entered the home stretch—SUPPLIES ARE RUNNING LOW!

As you well know, we will not get our new order of supplies until August, far too late to do you any good here and now. I have been advised that if we wish to finish the year using composition paper rather than the inside of lunch bags, we had better start conserving NOW.

Therefore, PLEASE don't use two sheets of paper where one will do, etc., etc., etc. You know the drill—only too well.

Seriously, I know that we will do what we have done in the past—work together, conserve together, and get through this together.

'Nough said!

. . .Requisition of

SUPPLY REQUISITION FORM

NAME: _____ DATE: _____

HOMEROOM: _____ DEPARTMENT: _____

I hereby request that the following supplies be sent to my room:

QUANTITY	ITEM (give supply numbers where applicable)

This is my _____ request of the current school year.

SUSPENSION   (See Also: BEHAVIOR; DRUGS; PARENTS; REPRIMANDS; SMOKING; VANDALISM)

. . .Follow-up to Enlist Parental Aid

Dear Mr. and Mrs. Brady,

As you are aware, your son, Adam, is currently on suspension from Rock Township High School for an incident in which he struck another student with a window pole, injuring the other student. As you are also aware, this is only one of a number of incidents involving violence in which Adam has participated.

Soon, Adam will be returning to school, and we are most anxious that an incident of this nature does not again occur. We are deeply concerned for Adam's future, as we are certain you must be. Therefore, we are anxious to cooperate with you for Adam's ultimate benefit.

We would like to invite you to come to school and arrange for a conference with myself and Adam's guidance counselor. It is not our intent to dwell on the past, but rather to formulate a program of positive involvement and improvement for Adam's future school career.

Won't you please contact us, and let us see if we can work together for the good of your son.

Your sincerely,

J. Benson, Principal

. . .Letter on Lengthy and Serious Suspension

Dear Mr. and Mrs. Andersen,

We regret to inform you that your daughter, Kelli, is herewith suspended from school for a period of fifteen days. We have taken this action in accordance with the disciplinary policy established by the Rock Township Board of Education.

On Wednesday, February 17, 19XX, your daughter was referred to my office for selling marijuana to other students. The sale was witnessed by two teachers, further attested to by the student who purchased the marijuana, several packets of the substance were in your daughter's hands when the teachers interrupted the incident, and Kelli has admitted this and several other sales.

We are certain that you realize how extremely serious this situation is. This is not only a violation of school rules but of civil and federal law as well.

The reporting of this incident to the civil authorities is the prerogative of the Board of Education. A meeting will be held in my office on Tuesday, February 23, 19XX, at 10:00 A.M. Present at that meeting will be the assistant superintendent of schools, the legal counsel of the Board of Education, a representative of the Board, and myself. You are most seriously urged to attend this meeting for a disposition will be made at that time as to the further handling of your daughter's case. For your information, a statement of your legal rights in this matter has been enclosed.

We are most anxious to arrange an equitable solution to this most serious problem. I shall look forward to seeing you on the 23rd. Meanwhile, should you have any questions, please do not hesitate to call.

Sincerely,

J. Benson, Principal

. . .Policy Statement on

The Public School Board, through formal action, has adopted a Student Suspensions and Expulsions Policy. This policy provides a code prohibiting student misconduct in the following areas:

1. Disruption of school

2. Damage or destruction of school property and stealing or attempting to steal school property

3. Damage or destruction of private property and stealing or attempting to steal private property

4. Assault on a school employee

5. Physical abuse of a student or other person not employed by the school

6. Weapons and dangerous instruments

7. Narcotics, alcoholic beverages, tobacco, and stimulant drugs

8. Repeated school violations (failing to comply with directions of teachers, student teachers,. substitute teachers, teacher aides, principals, or other authorized school personnel)

A procedural code for dealing with alleged violations is also adopted. The school district has a short-term suspension (suspends students up to ten school days) and a long-term suspension or expulsion (decision to seek suspension over ten days or expulsion).

Any chronic offender who has been suspended for a total of 10 school days during a semester by the principal shall appear for a hearing as soon as possible.

. . .Procedures for

SUSPENSION POLICY

1. Students will be advised that they are in jeopardy of being suspended, and parents may be notified by phone or mail. The counseling department, principal, and dean of students or vice principal will make efforts to counsel the students for the purpose of adjusting the problem before a suspension will be imposed.

2. Flagrant defiance of and disrespect for school regulations, such as fighting or smoking in or around the building, may result in an immediate suspension of up to 10 days with only an informal hearing. A letter

stating the offense, the results of the hearing, and the disciplinary action taken will be mailed within 24 hours to the parents.

3. The form below will be completed in the presence of parents, students, and administration before suspensions will be imposed.

JUNIOR HIGH SCHOOL

Record of hearing on ....

Date _____ Student_____

A hearing is used at the Junior High School when a student's repeated violations of school rules indicate that his parents may be asked to withdraw him from school.

On the above date, the parents and student were called in for a hearing with school personnel. This was done with a sincere desire on the part of the school to keep the student in school if possible and to make sure that all the pertinent facts concerning the problems were carefully reviewed and discussed by all parties before making a decision on future attendance.

The decision reached by school officials as a result of this hearing is as follows:

( ) Student suspended from school for a period of

_____

( ) Student allowed to remain in school on a probationary status with the following agreement signed and agreed to by the parties involved.

AGREEMENT

Due to repeated violations of the rules and regulations of the Junior High School by

_____

this agreement will make it understood between student, parent(s), and school authorities that any further infractions of rules and regulations will be cause for suspension from attendance at the Junior High for ten school days.

Other parties present at hearing:

_____ Student_____

_____ Parent_____

_____ School Official_____

4. Upon parental request, assignments will be provided for any student on suspension out of school.

PURPOSE OF SUSPENSION

When a pupil is suspended, the school seeks the aid of the parents to help adjust the problem. The school and the parents can then work together cooperatively to adjust the problem.

All students are given informal hearings for any suspensions up to ten days' duration. Longer suspensions require and are given formal hearings.

FORMAL HEARINGS

Parent is requested to bring lawyer and/or anyone he/she wishes to a meeting in the principal's office. The results of the formal hearing places students on probationary status (one chance) or on suspension out of school.

SYMPATHY   (See Also: ILLNESS; MEDICAL; RESIGNATION)

. . .Letter on the Death of

(A) *an administrator*

Dear Mrs. Sumner,

I feel I cannot adequately express my sympathy on the passing of your husband. George and I worked together for many years, and it was my honor to count him among my friends. He was a man of exceptional warmth and wisdom, and his loss leaves a void that will not be readily filled.

I knew George as an outstanding administrator, a man whose natural abilities of leadership inspired and enlivened those under his purview to their finest achievements. He was universally liked by the teachers throughout the township as well as by his fellow administrators. Moreover, he earned the respect of all who came in contact with him.

I wish you would do me a favor. Please contact me and tell me what I can do at this time. Please believe that it will be my honor to render whatever assistance I may.

Again, my sincere condolences.

Sincerely,

Thomas Smith, Superintendent

(B) *a student*

Dear Mr. & Mrs. Perez,

It is at times such as this that I wish I had the skill of a poet in order that I might adequately express what is in my heart. I would tell you of the deep sense of loss and the emptiness that is there and that now fills the halls of this school with the news of Jimmy's death.

Jimmy was a fine student, well liked and respected by both his teachers and his fellow students. I got to know him personally through his work on the student council, and I can assure you that he was a credit to himself and to you, his parents.

He shall be deeply missed, and our hearts go out to you in this most difficult of times.

Please call upon us, as it will be our honor to help you in whatever way we are able.

With deepest sympathies,

(C) *a teacher*

Dear Mrs. Franklin,

How saddened we were to hear of Greg's passing. I know I speak for the entire faculty as well as myself when I tell you that his death has left a very real void which can never be entirely filled. The student body, the faculty, and I cannot help but sense this to our abiding sorrow.

Our only consolation is the knowledge that we were privileged to know and work with Greg over the years. During that time we came to know him as a person of intelligence and integrity, always anxious to help, whose life and career were an inspiration to us all.

We also take comfort in the fact that a part of him will continue to live, reflected in the lives of the students he has instructed and guided. As a teacher, he gave of himself (perhaps the greatest gift of all), and those students who were fortunate enough to fall under his tutelage will carry his ideals, his knowledge, and his moral principles into the world, and the world cannot help but be a better place for it.

Our hearts are with you at this most difficult of times.

With deepest sympathy,

John Benson, Principal

. . .Letter upon Tragedy

Dear Mr. & Mrs. Hansen,

All of us at school were devastated to hear the tragic news of Brian's accident and then to be told that he has been left a paraplegic. Certainly, our hearts go out to you and to Brian, as we are aware that this must be the most difficult of times. You have our hopes and our prayers.

I am loathe to write to Brian at this time, as I understand the difficulties an adjustment of this magnitude must entail. We wanted you to know, however, that we are here for you and for Brian should you need us.

Again, you have our sympathy, but you also have our support. We hope you will use us; it will be our pleasure.

                                        Yours sincerely,

T

TARDINESS (See Also: ABSENCE; CUTTING; DETENTION)

. . .Message to Staff Concerning

To All Staff,

Please, may we remind you to continue to call and speak with an administrator if you are going to be late for any professional responsibility.

We certainly realize that emergencies do happen and we are always willing to help. Needless to say, students may never be left unsupervised in a classroom.

If you cannot make a duty or are going to be late because of an emergency or unanticipated circumstance, please let us know so we can ask another teacher to substitute for you.

Thank you.

Sincerely,

Administration

. . .Message to Students Concerning

When you are tardy, it will be necessary to secure an admit slip from the dean of girls or the vice principal. Tardies should be covered by a written excuse on the day you are tardy or on the following day. The parents of a pupil who is frequently tardy without apparent excuse, will be notified that if the unexcused tardies persist, the pupil will be placed on special detention.

Students who get up too late or who miss the school bus or their ride are to report to school late. Late students are not penalized if they bring an excuse the following day.

Students who stay home for the above reasons will be counted as truant. Students who are late for class during the day are placed on detention. One night of detention is given each time you are late. If you are a bus student, you must report to the vice principal or dean of girls for a report topic instead of taking detention.

. . .Notice to Parents

Date: _____

Dear _____,

This is to inform you that your son/daughter, _____,

was late for school on _____. This is the

_____ time that he/she has been late this year. Let us make every effort to impress upon him/her the importance of getting to school on time. Please sign this form and return it to me.

TEACHER: _____

PARENT: _____

. . .Policy on

The following shall be the policy and procedures for handling lateness to class by students:

1. Students who arrive late to class should be challenged and asked for a written pass.

2. In the absence of a written pass, the student must be admitted to the class. He or she is not permitted to be sent to the office or to any teacher to obtain such a pass.

3. Teacher action for lateness is imperative (e.g., reduction of citizenship grade, parent conference, and detention are some of the possibilities which are left up to the discretion of each teacher).

4. Teachers are requested not to detain students after class or permit students to remain with them for part or all of a period to which they are not assigned without *prior approval by the teacher to whom the student is assigned.*

TELEPHONE (See Also: HANDBOOK; TARDINESS)

. . .Memo on Abuse of

(A) *district*

Re: Personal Telephone Calls

Please be advised that the use of the telephones in your building are primarily for official school business. It is understood that circumstances may require the placement of personal calls. However, the originator of all toll calls made for personal reasons must record these on the monthly telephone reporting form and make payment for such calls.

Monthly telephone reports are to be reviewed by your office. You will be notified of the actual N.J. Bell statements received for payment. At that time, you will be able to make your own reconciliation.

Recent New Jersey Bell telephone statements require that we advise all personnel that there must be an understanding of their individual responsibility.

Your cooperation is appreciated.

(B) *individual school*

After reviewing our recent phone bill may we please ask for your cooperation in terms of charging your personal phone calls to a telephone credit card, your home phone, or a third party. As you know, Mr. Miner is concerned about the district's escalating costs. We all should be!

On another matter, any and all calls to Sports Phone, Phone Games, and N.J. Lottery must be stopped immediately. We regret even writing the above and are embarrassed in doing so. There is really no reason whatsoever for making such calls!

Again the district will be closely monitoring our phone usage. Thank you for using our phone call form which should be at all phone locations. Needless to say we anticipate your full cooperation in this matter. All toll calls must be recorded.

. . .Sample Messages Concerning Use of

TELEPHONES

Public telephones are located on the first floor. The telephone in the office is to be used only in case of an emergency. No pupil or teacher will be called from a classroom to answer a telephone call.

*   *   *

There are two pay telephones for your use after school: one in the main hall and one near the door to the office. In the morning and before school and during the day, students who have urgent reasons for using the telephone are to have a written pass from their teachers and be excused from class in the regular manner.

Unless an emergency exists, students are requested to avoid asking permission to use the office phone.

*   *   *

There are five telephones in the building.

The phone in the hall is a call-out phone only. Students should be discouraged from using the telephone unless necessary. You should discuss this with the class so they get in the habit of checking with you ahead of time. It seems that the same students are often lined up using the phone day after day. Phone calls to go home with someone else to play, et cetera, are not really that necessary and should be discouraged so the lines are kept open for the child who really needs to call home. Children need to go directly home after school as parents expect them. Dial "7" first to get an outside line when using the hall phone.

There is also a phone in room #17. If you use this phone when classes are being held in either of those two rooms, please hold the volume down. There is a phone in the counselor's room and one in the fallout shelter.

Please do not use school time to make personal phone calls. Try to limit the time on calls so as not to tie up the phone for too long.

All long-distance phone calls should be cleared with the principal ahead of time. Long-distance calls are to be logged at the time the call is made on the record available from the secretary.

You can take calls that come into the office on the phones in the hall or in room #17. We try to take messages and encourage people to call back if calls come during classes—if we contact you in regard to a phone call, let us know if you are busy at that time. Try to avoid taking phone calls or making them during instructional sessions.

. . .Telephone Usage Form

ROCK TOWNSHIP HIGH SCHOOL
TELEPHONE USAGE REPORT

for the week from _____ to _____ , 19_____

DATE	TEACHER	# CALLED	REASON*	TIME & CHARGES**

*REASON—personal, school business, parent contact, etc.
**TIME & CHARGES—if a toll call.

The faculty is reminded that the expense of all toll calls for personal reasons must be borne by the individual.

TESTING (See Also: CHILD STUDY TEAM; EXAMINATIONS; SCHEDULES)

. . .General Information on

I. TEST   High School Proficiency Test—Grade 9

II. DATES AND   Tuesday, March 5, Periods 1–3 (8:15–10:38)
    TIMES   Wednesday, March 6, Periods 1–3 (8:15–10:38)
                 Thursday, March 7, Periods 1–3 (8:15–10:38)

III. GENERAL INFORMATION

    A. All ninth grade students will report to school Period 1. Mr. Kurz will inform aides and those students on a sixth period day to report for first period on the three days of testing.

    B. On Friday, March 1 and Monday, March 4, all Period 1 ninth grade teachers are to inform their students where to report

Period 1 on Tuesday, Wednesday, and Thursday (March 5–March 7). The students are to bring two #2 pencils and a magazine or book for quiet reading.

C. Students and teachers will report to their testing room as indicated on the attached schedule.

D. Seventh and eighth grade teachers whose rooms have been changed (see attached sheet) are also to inform their students of the room changes during testing.

E. The teacher assigned to pick up the tests can do so *each day* by 8:00 A.M. in the Guidance Office.

F. Attendance will be taken at regular times for all grades.

G. *Tardiness:* Students who arrive late to school will report to Mrs. Divis in the main office. They will then report to Mr. McCray in the library. They will be tested with the absentees at a later date.

H. During testing, bathroom passes are to be issued on an emergency basis only.

I. All other questions regarding testing are to be directed to Mrs. Douglass.

J. *Students Who Are Disruptive:* Send to Mr. McCray in the Library.

K. *Students Who Become Ill During Testing:* Send to Nurse.

. . .Letter to Parents Concerning

Dear Parents,

Next week, we will be giving the IOWA tests to all seventh grade students in our school. This is a lengthy process but one which is essential if we are to give the best possible education to every child.

The results of these tests are used by us to help determine a child's needs and find ways of meeting them. IOWA test results are an important (though not the only) factor in your child's placement next year. In short, the results of the IOWA test are very important.

We hope you will make every effort to impress this fact upon your son or daughter. So many students, particularly at this age, take a noncaring attitude about these tests. It is important that you, as parents, communicate to them the nature and import of these tests in their future academic career.

We will be sending you the individual results of the testing through the Guidance Office in the very near future.

Thank you for your continued cooperation and support.

. . .Message in Handbook

TESTS

IOWA tests are given in the spring of each year. Before the testing period, counselors meet with class groups to discuss the importance of the test and various test-taking and stress-reducing skills.

The test results, including a printed explanation, are distributed through guidance. Counselors are available for further help in interpreting the scores. Other tests may be given throughout the year. Counselors facilitate the process as well as explain the results.

TEXTBOOKS   (See Also: EQUIPMENT; SUPPLIES)

. . .Budget Form for Textbooks

NAME: _____ ROOM: _____

DIRECTIONS: Include all student books other than library books. An inventory of books on hand by *type*, not title, must be included.

TOTAL COST	Title or Program	Grade(s)	Quantity	Unit Cost	Total on Hand
	Total This Page				
	Total All Pages				

. . .Distribution Form

TEXTBOOK DISTRIBUTION

For the period from _____ to _____, 19_____

Department: _____ Chairperson: _____

TITLE OF TEXT	NO. OF COPIES	SENT TO	DATE SENT	RETURNED

Signature of Department Chairperson: _____

Date: _____

. . .Form for Suggesting New Textbooks

TEXTBOOK SUGGESTION FORM

NAME (of person making suggestion): _____

DEPARTMENT OR GRADE: _____

This form is to be used to suggest a new textbook for use in the school. This suggestion is then to be submitted to the Textbook Review Committee. You will be notified of the disposition of your request.

TITLE AND AUTHOR:

PUBLISHER:

SUBJECT AREA OF BOOK:

WHAT BOOK(S) WOULD THIS REPLACE:

COST PER UNIT:

BRIEFLY DESCRIBE CONTENT:

WHERE MAY A SAMPLE COPY BE OBTAINED:

BRIEFLY EXPLAIN WHY THIS NEW BOOK SHOULD
BE INTRODUCED INTO THE CURRICULUM:

. . .Messages Concerning

TEXTBOOKS

Textbooks are lent to you by the school districts so you can receive an education. These books are often used from year to year so the utmost care should be taken to preserve them. Your teacher will assess the condition of the books in September when they are given to you and in June when they are collected. If there is any damage done to the book during ownership, you will be asked to pay for the damage.

*   *   *

TEXTBOOKS AND LIBRARY BOOKS

All students are supplied with books at the opening of school. Deposits are not required, but students are responsible for keeping them covered at all times and seeing that they are returned in good condition. Textbooks are the property of the school district and lost or damaged books must be paid for by the student at the cost of replacement. Library books must also be replaced.

THANKS   (See Also: APPRECIATION; OPEN COMMUNICATIONS; PARENTS; P.T.A.; PUBLIC RELATIONS; RETIREMENT; SPORTS; STUDENT COUNCIL; VOLUNTEERS; AND ALL THOSE OCCASIONS WHERE THANKS WOULD BE APPROPRIATE)

. . .To an Administrator

Dear Dr. Carlson,

Please allow me to express my gratitude for your support of my candidacy for the position of assistant superintendent of schools. Naturally, I would be overjoyed to accept the position, but even if it is not offered to me, I shall always remember your kindness, your intercession on my behalf, and your most generous and gratifying letter of support.

You may rest assured that if I do obtain the position, I shall do everything in my power to justify your faith in me, as I shall continue to perform my present administrative duties to the best of my abilities and to your expectations should the Board select another candidate.

My heartfelt thanks for everything you have done.

Sincerely,

A. Kitteridge

. . .To Parents

Dear Mr. Herndon,

When our Drama Club ran into difficulty constructing the set for their production of *Oliver,* how could they know that their solution to the problem would involve a true friend of our school.

The help, guidance, and time you gave from your own busy schedule not only insured that the production went on, but the students themselves learned many valuable skills under your direction.

They also learned what it means to be a compassionate and caring human being who is always ready to help others, and that is a lesson which you taught by example.

On behalf of the Drama Club and on behalf of the school, I thank you for all you have done. And, may I add my personal thanks for your invaluable involvement.

Yours sincerely,

. . .To P.T.A.

Dear P.T.A.,

When we used to go to my grandmother's for Sunday dinner, and we would complain about this or that, the old lady would fold her arms across an ample bosom, gaze steadfastly at the ceiling, and say, "Lord, ain't it nice to be noticed!"

That was, of course, many years ago, but the sentiment still applies. Who could help but notice the beautiful changes that have taken place in the teacher's lounge? Who could fail to notice that concern, good taste, and obviously careful planning have manifested themselves in changes whose purpose is to make our time in school a bit more pleasant and comfortable? Who cannot see the positive reactions of the faculty to a P.T.A. who cares and whose warmth and affability is made manifest along with their concern for educational quality that we have always known?

On behalf of the faculty, may I express our thanks for your efforts in our behalf. Your notice of us has, indeed, been noticed by us, and "Lord, ain't it nice . . . !"

Yours sincerely,

. . .To Students

To: ALL STUDENTS
From: J. BENSON, PRINCIPAL
Re: THANK YOU

Only a few days remain of the present school year. At this time it is fitting that we think back on the time that has passed, that we recall those incidents which have made this a memorable year in our lives.

This is true for me no less than you, and when I remember the good times and the bad, the work and the play, the setbacks and the accomplishments, I keep coming back to you, the students of this school. In the final analysis, it is the student body that makes a school what it is, and you have made it an outstanding school, a place which is exciting to be in and of which we may all be justly proud. For your cooperation and your efforts, I am deeply grateful.

Have a wonderful summer, and thank you for making this such a wonderful year.

. . .To Teachers

To: ALL TEACHERS
From: J. BENSON, PRINCIPAL
Re: I'M THANKFUL

I'M THANKFUL—for the fine year which is about to end; for the high quality of education which has taken place; for a dedicated and professional faculty . . .

I'M THANKFUL—for having the chance to work with you; for your cooperation; for all the extra effort you have put into making this school such a wonderful place to be . . .

I'M THANKFUL—for knowing you; for the way you have made me feel at ease; for knowing that you are there and that I can always depend on you . . .

I'M THANKFUL—for YOU, the faculty, and I offer you my deepest gratitude . . .

HAVE A GREAT SUMMER!!!

TUTORS (See Also: ILLNESS; PERMANENT RECORDS; REFERRAL; SUSPENSION)

. . .Memo to Faculty

To: ALL MEMBERS OF THE PROFESSIONAL STAFF

I have just received an advisory from central administration that there is a pressing need for qualified tutors within our district. Indeed, we have a number of students (some from our own school) who are awaiting tutoring, only to be told that they must keep waiting until there is someone available.

Therefore, I really wish that each of you would seriously consider taking a tutoring assignment. Your qualifications are beyond question, the pay is good, and the rewards of teaching are very close to the surface in a one-on-one situation.

Certainly, it is worth your consideration. I assure you, it will be the homebound student who will benefit.

. . .Report to Parents

Dear _____,

I have tutored _____ for the period from _____

to _____, 19_____ in the subject(s) _____

_____.

In that time, we covered the following material:

Book(s) and Pages Covered: _____

_____

_____

I observed the following about your child's progress:

_____

_____

_____

_____

Sincerely,

_____

. . .Report to the Central Office on

MONTH: _____, 19_____

PUPIL: _____ SCHOOL: _____ GRADE: _____

ADDRESS: _____

INSTRUCTOR: _____ SUBJECT(S): _____

EACH AREA BELOW SHOULD BE COMPLETED IN DETAIL:

SUBJECT: (Reading, arithmetic, etc.—page numbers and skills being worked on, etc.)

TEACHER'S PROCEDURES: (Teacher-made materials, methods, and techniques used and which work best with student, tests given, and items of interest)

STUDENT'S PROGRESS: (Academic progress, attitude, and physical condition)

FURTHER RECOMMENDATIONS:

GRADE FOR MONTH:

TERMINATION: (Date of return to regular class, or moved, or date when instruction terminated, reason for, etc.)

SIGNATURE OF INSTRUCTOR: _____

DATE: _____

UNDERACHIEVERS (See Also: CHILD STUDY TEAM; EVALUATION; GRADES; OBSERVATION; REFERRAL)

. . .Form to Parents on

STUDENT _____ GRADE _____ DATE _____

SUBJECT _____ TEACHER _____

MARKING PERIOD ENDS _____

Dear Parents,

As your child's teacher, I am becoming concerned about a situation which is beginning to develop and which could have serious effects upon your child's school career if not handled soon. Therefore, I am sending you this in the hope that, acting as a team, we may help your child in his/her academic progress.

_____ appears to be working well UNDER the level at which he/she could be. He/she could be doing much better work than he/she is currently producing. I am certain that you are aware that should this trend continue, it could lead to poor grades, possible failure, and a lack of valuable skills on the part of your child.

I have checked below some of the things your son/daughter might do to help improve this situation. If you have any questions or if you believe that a conference would be helpful, please call the guidance department at _____.

Working together, I know we can help your child do the work he/she is capable of doing.

_____ be more attentive in class

_____ be more cooperative in class

_____ come prepared for class (bring books, pencils, etc.)

_____ listen to and follow directions carefully

_____ participate more actively in class

_____ learn to take notes in class

_____ learn to accept criticism and evaluation

_____ do the assigned work regularly (homework, classwork, etc.)

_____ find out about and make up assignments after absence

_____ try to improve the quality of assignments

_____ study more diligently for tests and quizzes

_____ respect the rights of others

_____ come for extra help when needed

_____ OTHER _____

_____

_____

_____

Please sign this report and return it to me via your child. If you have any comments, please use the back of this report. Thank you.

PARENT'S SIGNATURE: _____ DATE: _____

. . .Letter to Parents on

Dear Mr. & Mrs. Ontean,

As you know, I am Billy's math teacher this year. Indeed, we have spoken at Back-to-School Night and after the first marking period grades. I know that we are both concerned about Billy's progress in math this current academic year.

I really believe that Billy's grades in math do not reflect what Billy is capable of doing. It is obvious to me through observation alone that Billy has a much greater potential than he has manifested through his work in class or his homework. It is very disturbing to see a young man waste his abilities, and I know that we both agree on that.

I have spoken to Billy and told him about this letter. I have strongly urged him to apply himself to his math homework and class studies. I am certain that you will wish to inform Billy of this as well. Indeed, if the situation with Billy does not improve within two weeks, I feel that we should meet and develop stronger strategies for helping him.

I am certain that, working together, we can get Billy back on track as soon as possible.

Yours sincerely,

UNIT COORDINATION   (See Also: CHILD STUDY TEAM; GUIDANCE; MAINSTREAMING; OBJECTIVES; PSYCHOLOGICAL SERVICES; SPECIAL EDUCATION)

. . .Example of (for a Child Study Team)

The child study team of a local school district has the responsibility of examining, classifying, and recommending special education programs for pupils considered to be handicapped or needing special help. Guidelines are provided by the State Department of Education to determine what constitutes a local child study unit for the purposes of diagnosing learning handicaps and recommending educational programs. A basic child study unit in our state consists of a school psychologist, a school social worker, a learning disabilities specialist and appropriate medical personnel. The child study team may also include such professionals as medical specialists, the school nurse, the school administrator, reading and guidance personnel, speech correctionists, and classroom teachers.

How does a child needing help come to the attention of the Child Study Unit? Children who fail to make an adequate school adjustment emotionally, socially, or academically may come to the attention of the team in one of several different ways. Parents themselves may ask the superintendent of schools, the principal, or the director of special services to consider their child's special needs either before or after he or she enters school. Or the child may be brought to the attention of the team by the regular classroom teacher, the school principal, the guidance counselor, or the school nurse.

Once a referral is made, the Child Study Unit then obtains as much information as possible regarding the child through testing, observation, and conferences with the school staff and parents. Information from other sources may also be requested by the unit or submitted by the parents. In some instances the school district may obtain information from ophthalmologists, otologists, audiologists, neurologists, and other specialists.

After reviewing their findings on the child, the members of the unit then consider the educational alternatives which can be offered. These include the placement of the child in a special class in the home school district, or in another school district, or in a program operated by a state agency as a state college or state school. If none of these are available, the Board of Education may consider a suitable private nonsectarian program. Placement of children in such private facilities by school districts must be approved by the county supervisor of Child Study and the Department of Education.

If none of the above alternatives are available, arrangements may be made for the child to receive individual instruction at home or at school. Any handicapped child in a regular or special class who needs supplementary instruction, such as auditory training, speech correction, or instruction in Braille, may also receive it as part of his or her school program.

Upon completion of the case study, the child study team reports its recommendations to the local superintendent of schools who, in turn, makes the educational placement with full consideration given to the report of the examiners.

Another aspect of the child study unit is its role in educational planning and curriculum development. Often, when the child study team participates in educational planning, it can propose ways in which the curriculum can be developed to promote academic gain, proper mental health, and the prevention of emotional disturbances. The unit should also seek ways to provide opportunities for enrichment of superior students as well as to provide help for slower students. Often the team works closely with the Guidance Department to help those students who are having difficulty adjusting to high school.

In addition, preventive measures are often used by the unit in screening kindergarten and first grade children to determine the existence of possible educational difficulties and potential learning handicaps. It should be the overall aim of the Child Study Unit in educational planning to see that the school program is designed so that the individuality of each child will be given the fullest educational and social expression.

. . .Unit Report to Principal

To: J. BENSON, PRINCIPAL
From: CHILD STUDY UNIT
Re: REPORT ON ADAM BRADY (CONFIDENTIAL)

On February 17, 19XX, Adam Brady, a junior at your school, was referred to us by you for study and possible classification and placement.

Adam Brady was seen by the school psychologist and Dr. Harold Lacey of the Children's Center. Copies of both reports are enclosed for your information. A study was also made of Adam Brady's school records prior to his enrollment in the Rock Township school system and those since his enrollment. Interviews were also conducted with several of his teachers as well as his parents. Again, copies of the reports from these interviews are enclosed.

Our basic findings indicate that Adam Brady has had a history of violent incidents since the second grade. These outbreaks of violent behavior are becoming more frequent as well as more violent in nature. This is true at home as well as in school, and reports from outside agencies indicate a growing negative involvement with legal authorities.

On the basis of these interviews and the reports from the psychologists, we feel that Adam Brady may be classified as emotionally disturbed and placed in the E.D. class.

This is, however, our preliminary finding only. A full disposition will be made within two weeks. At that time we will inform you of all ramifications of the decision. In the meantime, we wanted to keep you abreast of the matter and thank you for bringing it to our attention.

V

VACATION (See Also: CLOSING OF SCHOOL; DISMISSAL PROCEDURES; YEAR-END MATTERS)

. . .Memo to Faculty on

To: ALL MEMBERS OF THE PROFESSIONAL STAFF

Well, here we are!

Where? Why at the end (almost) of another glorious year! In just a few days, the kids will be off and away, and there are times when I feel that I'm already "off and away" myself if only mentally.

It is my most sincere wish that your summer be filled with rest, relaxation, and just enough excitement to keep it from being dull! Enjoy it, because you have earned it. If anyone ever deserves a break, it is you, for you have done a difficult and marvelous job this year, and I am proud to be associated with you!

Have a great summer! See you in September!

. . .Teacher's Checklist Prior to

(TEACHER'S NAME)

With the exception of Item #1, which is to be checked out first in the Guidance Office, the following items are to be checked out in the Main Office on Friday, June 22, 19XX prior to leaving for summer vacation.

( ) 1. Marks recorded on office copies of student records (entire year).

( ) 2. Student Attendance Cards (Homeroom Teachers Only).

( ) 3. List of names of students who have failed the named subject with an explanation of the reason. If no students have failed, write "NONE."

( ) 4. Suggestions for Improvement sheet.

( ) 5. Events or Activities sheet.

( ) 6. Keys—ALL KEYS—tagged and identified in an envelope identified with your name and room number.

( ) 7. Name, summer address, and telephone number on two 3″ × 5″cards.

( ) 8. One self-addressed envelope provided by the office for every teacher returning in September. This envelope is to have your SUMMER address with zip code and will be used to send out your assignment sheet and information relative to opening school in September 19XX. You will receive them in late August. Teachers taking special contracts for next school year are to return TWO envelopes.

( ) 9. Unfinished business sheet.

( ) 10. Building report sheet.

( ) 11. This sheet.

_____

(CHECKED OUT BY)

DEPARTMENT CHAIRPERSONS ONLY

( ) 1. Percentage promotion sheet.

( ) 2. Textbook discard and storage sheet (in duplicate) for department.

( ) 3. Field trip requests by month.

( ) 4. Dates for student and parent events (for use in handbook).

. . .Welcome Back from

Dear Faculty and Staff,

Welcome back! While you may not be overjoyed with the prospect of another year of correcting papers and battling kids, it is nice to be back where you are appreciated, isn't it?

We hope you have had a marvelous summer, and it does our hearts good to be working with you once again. Please look over the forms and lists of meetings you received in this packet (our little "Welcome Back" surprise), and you will know that it is no dream; that you are truly back in the land of Oz (. . . or Kansas)!

Seriously, it is good to see you again, and I know that we are going to have another wonderful year and do it the way we always have— together!

Welcome back!

VANDALISM   (See Also: BEHAVIOR; CITIZENSHIP; DISCIPLINE; REFERRAL; SUSPENSION)

. . .Letter to Parents

Dear Parents,

I have shared with you many of our successes and achievements here at the school, and it is only right that I share with you one of our concerns as well.

There have been several incidents of vandalism recently. Some desks have been dismantled; windows have been broken; and, most serious of all, lavatory facilities have been rendered unusable. These are far from the "harmless pranks" of youth; these are criminal acts that deprive your child of the use of these facilities to which he or she is entitled.

A complete investigation is currently in progress, and I assure you that when they are caught it will *not* be a matter of an afternoon's detention. We have involved the police, and we fully intend to prosecute, whether or not the damages are reimbursed.

This is a serious matter; we intend to deal with it quite seriously; we would enlist your aid to impress upon your children the seriousness of this.

I know that I am assured of your cooperation in this most serious matter.

Sincerely,

. . .Principal's Message on

To: ALL STUDENTS
From: J. BENSON, PRINCIPAL
Re: VANDALISM

Lately, there have been a number of incidents of vandalism at our school. Windows have been broken, furniture and classroom fittings mutilated, and certain lavatory facilities seriously damaged.

I cannot help but think that whoever is responsible must have a very low opinion of you, the students of our school. After all, the broken windows mean an inconvenience for *you* in the classroom; the classroom fittings that have been wrecked mean that *you* cannot now use them; and certainly the lavatory facilities that have been damaged impose a hardship only on *you,* the students.

It disturbs me that some of our students would think so poorly of their fellow students that they would impose these hardships on them. It is my hope that if anyone knows someone who is guilty of these acts of cruelty against the student body, he or she will talk to these people and ask them to stop this assault on *your* safety, well-being, and comfort.

. . .Sample Statements Concerning

VANDALISM

If any student commits an act of vandalism on school property, the appropriate action will be taken by the school and parents will be held financially responsible for all damages.

*   *   *

VANDALISM

The Rock Township Board of Education has adopted stringent measures for dealing with school vandalism. The school administration is responsible for working with the Police Department in the investigation, apprehension, and prosecution of juveniles caught in the act of breaking, entering, or committing acts of vandalism on school property. After school punishment has taken place, parents of students who commit acts of vandalism will be held financially responsible for all damages.

VOLUNTEERS   (See Also: APPRECIATION; FIELD TRIPS; P.T.A.; PUBLIC RELATIONS; THANKS)

. . .Personal Letter to Specific Volunteer

Dear Phil,

I want you to know just how much I deeply appreciate the volunteer work that you have been doing for our students. It is obvious to me, to the faculty, and to anyone who cares to look that your time and your energy have helped to make this place a dynamic, functioning, and happy place to be. Without undue modesty, you must take your share of the credit for this.

I have received so many positive comments about your volunteer work with us, that I really do speak for the entire faculty, staff, and students when I thank you for all you have done and tell you how much we appreciate your efforts.

Thank you for being the giving, caring person that you are.

Yours sincerely,

. . .Soliciting Volunteers

Dear Parents,

We know how busy you are and what a premium time must be for you. Sometimes it seems that there are just not enough moments in the day for all we have to do.

And yet, if you can spare some of that valuable time, we can use your services.

Volunteers are needed now in all areas of our school. We need volunteers for our library, cafeteria, classrooms, after-school activities, dances, special events, and more. Be assured, if you volunteer, you will be used.

The pay is nonexistent, and the work is hard. Your reward is the knowledge that you are doing a service for our students and the school and, of course, our thanks and gratitude for your help.

Please call me at 234-5678 if you would like to give us a hand. I shall be happy to hear from you.

Sincerely,

J. Benson, Principal

. . .Thanking for Services

To: ALL VOLUNTEERS

The purpose of the volunteer program is to provide an opportunity for parents and other interested adults to assist school personnel in the operation of the schools. Over this past academic year, you have provided invaluable services in library work, the hot lunch program, aiding teachers in the classroom, and assisting in administrative offices. In all of these and more, your services have been beyond price.

You have every right to be proud of your accomplishments as we point with pride at you.

Please accept our deepest thanks for the gift you have given us this past year—the gift of your caring; the gift of yourself!

. . .Volunteer Solicitation Form (Sample)

P.T.A. VOLUNTEERS NEEDED

The Parent-Teacher Association of Rock Township High School needs the support of all parents. If you can help in any of the areas listed below, please indicate your interests. Please consider participating in some way. The P.T.A. needs your help.

1. Dance chaperones (parents to chaperone one or more school dances)
2. Library (one afternoon every other week)
3. Nurse's office (two hours per week typing and/or clerical)
4. Refreshments (baking for school functions)
5. Telephoning
6. Committees and fund raisers
7. Dinner Dance Committees (June)
8. P.T.A. Executive Board (positions still open to anyone wanting to get involved)

NAME _____

TELEPHONE _____

GRADE OF CHILD IN SCHOOL _____

COMMENTS _____

_____

WORK (See Also: EVALUATION; REPRIMAND; SCHEDULE; THANKS)

. . .Return-to-Work Form

RETURN-TO-WORK NOTICE

THE SCHOOL DISTRICT REQUIRES THE FOLLOWING INFORMATION FROM THE ATTENDING PHYSICIAN TO AN ON-THE-JOB INJURED EMPLOYEE BEFORE HE OR SHE MAY RESUME WORK:

INSURED EMPLOYEE _____

JOB DESCRIPTION _____

ACCIDENT DATE _____

RETURN-TO-WORK DATE _____

THIS EMPLOYEE HAS BEEN UNDER MY MEDICAL CARE FROM ___ TO ___ AND MAY RETURN TO WORK WITH NO RESTRICTIONS ☐, OR WITH THE FOLLOWING RESTRICTIONS:

_____

_____

_____

_____

PHYSICIAN'S SIGNATURE

_____

DATE

DISTRIBUTION:
1. Employee: give to your supervisor
2. Supervisor: forward to insurance office—original and copy
3. Retain one copy

. . .Statement on Worker's Compensation

The clarification of our policy concerning Worker's Compensation was made at the regular meeting of the School Board on September 8. It is the purpose and intent of the Board that our sick leave policy provide economic, physical, and psychological relief at a time when an employee must be absent due to illness. Full salary is paid for the period to which the employee is entitled. It is not the intent or purpose of our sick leave policy that our employee make a "profit" on an illness absence.

State law requires that the public school district carry Worker's Compensation liability insurance for all employees. This insurance provides certain payments for injuries that occur while on the job. For example, an employee may be absent for illness due to an injury. During the absence the employee may be on full pay from the school district, may be receiving hospital and surgical benefits from an insurance company, and in addition may receive payment from Worker's Compensation insurance. The clarification of the policy provides that

PAYMENTS MADE TO AN EMPLOYEE OF THE DISTRICT PROVIDED BY THE SICK LEAVE POLICY WILL BE REDUCED BY THE AMOUNT RECEIVED FROM WORKER'S COMPENSATION INSURANCE FOR THE SAME ABSENCE.

If the employee would prefer that no deduction be made, equal to the amount paid by Worker's Compensation, then the Worker's Compensation check shall be endorsed to the clerk of the school district.

Payment from Worker's Compensation is retained by the employer for those days an employee is absent over the number of sick leave days accrued.

. . .Work Order Request

Date Work ___/___/___ ___/___/___   Work Order No. __ __ | __ __ __ __
         Desired   *Required*   Account Code _____

Ordered by
School _____ No. _____   Budget Control No. _____

Teacher _____   Cost Limit _____
                                        (Cost limit must be stated for budgeted items)
Principal _____   Budget Control

Date _____   Approved by _____

Location in School _____

Description of Job: _____
_____
_____
_____
_____
_____
_____

Requisitions Necessary   To Be Completed by Maintenance:
to Complete Work Order:
                                Job Assigned to _____ Date _____
_____ _____
                                Job Completed by _____ Date _____
_____ _____   *(print name)*

_____ _____

WORKING PAPERS   (See Also: EVALUATION; MEDICAL; PERMANENT RECORDS; WORK)

. . .Confirmation of Employment Form

This is to certify that it is my intent to employ the following student:

STUDENT'S NAME: _____

TYPE OF BUSINESS: _____

NATURE OF STUDENT'S JOB: _____

DAYS AND HOURS PER DAY THAT STUDENT IS TO WORK: _____
_____

TOTAL WEEKLY HOURS: _____

WAGES PER HOUR: _____

TOTAL WEEKLY WAGES: _____

NAME OF EMPLOYER: _____

ADDRESS: _____ TELEPHONE: _____

_____ ZIP: _____

SIGNATURE OF EMPLOYER: _____

DATE OF THIS CERTIFICATION: _____

. . .Physician's Certificate for

DATE: _____

THIS IS TO CERTIFY THAT I HAVE EXAMINED THE FOLLOWING STUDENT:

NAME: _____

ADDRESS: _____ TELEPHONE: _____

_____ ZIP: _____

BASED ON THIS PHYSICAL EXAMINATION I FIND THAT THE STUDENT:

( ) IS PHYSICALLY FIT FOR EMPLOYMENT AS PERMITTED UNDER THE STATE CHILD LABOR LAW FOR MINORS UNDER 18.

( ) IS *NOT* PHYSICALLY FIT FOR SUCH EMPLOYMENT, BECAUSE: _____

_____

( ) IS FIT FOR EMPLOYMENT WITH THE FOLLOWING LIMITATIONS: ___

_____

PHYSICIAN'S SIGNATURE: _____

PHYSICIAN'S ADDRESS: _____ TELEPHONE: _____

_____ ZIP: _____

. . .Sample Handbook Statements on

WORKING PAPERS

Working papers are issued in the main office to students of Rock Township schools. Further information and forms can be obtained in the main office.

*   *   *

WORKING PAPERS

Students desiring working papers may obtain applications in the school guidance office. Students having questions concerning eligibility for work may check with their counselors.

*   *   *

WORKING PAPERS

Students between the ages of 14 and 18 must have working papers if they have jobs. As soon as there is a promise of a job, the student comes to the Guidance Office for a form that must be filled out by the prospective employer, a physician, the student and parent, and the principal. The completed form is returned with the student's birth certificate to the guidance office. They are then processed and sent to the Department of Labor. The working papers, themselves, are sent directly to the employer.

If a student wishes to work while the working papers are being processed, the counselor will send a letter to the employer stating that the working papers are being processed.

XEROX (See Also: BULLETIN; SECRETARY)

. . .Main Office Copier Notice

MAIN OFFICE COPIER

The Minolta copier is not to be used for mass copy production. Any work that is to be copied in large numbers must be accomplished by using mimeo machines and/or cutting stencils.

We can understand using this machine for *emergencies,* and believe up to 20 copies of any article, lesson, etc., does not present a problem. However, 20 copies of 20 pages of material (i.e., 400 pages) simply cannot ever happen!

. . .Xerox Copier Request

XEROX COPIER REQUEST

Instructional Media Center

Date/Time Received:
For IMC Use Only

_____ _____ _____
Name of Requester   School   Date Needed

_____ _____ _____
Title of Printing Request   Deliver to (name school)   Telephone

_____ Number of originals to be copied from.

_____ Number of copies to be made from each original.

YES   NO   Do you want to have your copies shot on both sides?
(circle one)

YES   NO   Do you want to have your copies reduced from the size of
(circle one)   the original?

If so, what percentage of reduction?

_____ 15% _____ 23% _____ 35% _____ 38½% _____ other

SPECIAL INSTRUCTIONS:

X-RAYS   (See Also: MEDICAL; PERMANENT RECORDS)

. . .Notice to Personnel of Possible X-ray Test

To: ALL SCHOOL PERSONNEL
From: ANSON KITTENGER, ASST. SUPERINTENDENT
Re: SCHOOL TUBERCULIN TESTING

Under the rules and regulations of the State Department of Education, you are required to have an intradermal test for evidence of tuberculosis infection. Board of Education policy requires that this be a Mantoux test, as it has been determined that this test is more reliable.

1. All employees who are positive reactors (10 or more m.m. of induration) or who have been exempted from the Mantoux test shall be required to have an annual chest X-ray unless documentation is provided that one year of chemotherapy has been completed.

2. All employees who are tuberculin negative shall be retested with an intradermal test every three years.

3. Any employee shall be exempt from intradermal testing upon presentation of documentation of a prior positive reaction (i.e., ten m.m. or more of induration) following a Mantoux test with five tuberculin units of stabilized PPD tuberculin or by presentation of a medical contraindication form signed by a physician which specifically states the reason(s) for the exemption.

All exempting documentation must be presented to the high school Health Office.

. . .X-ray Release Form

To Whom It May Concern:

I hereby freely grant permission for the release of the following X-rays to the Rock Township Board of Education and/or their assignees:

Type of X-ray: _____

Date Taken: _____

Place Taken: _____

Physician or Technician: _____

Signature: _____

Date of Release: _____

. . .X-ray Report Form

NAME Last, First, Middle Initial	SOCIAL SECURITY NUMBER (Student- Parent/Guardian)	BIRTH DATE	SEX	GRADE

RESIDENCE (Mailing Address)			
Number	Street	Municipality	Zip

EVALUATION
Retest Results

PPD	Mantoux	X-ray	PREVENTIVE THERAPY
DATE	SIZE MM	Positive	INH-Daily Dosage
Mo., Day, Year		Negative	Yes _____ MG
		Not Done	No

PHYSICIAN

YEARBOOK (See Also: APPRECIATION; CLUBS; EXTRACURRICULAR ACTIVITIES; PUBLIC RELATIONS)

. . .Dedication

Because she is always there when you need her; because she always has a smile and a kind word; because she listens and understands; because she can always be counted upon to do what is best; because she always stands ready to help; because she is more than a teacher and vice principal; because we are proud to call her our friend, this yearbook is gratefully dedicated to Mrs. Arlene Gibbons.

. . .Letter to Yearbook Advisor

Dear Harry,

It has just been my pleasure to review the copy of SIGNPOSTS which you were kind enough to present to me. It is an outstanding publication, and one which is highly reflective of the amount of work and dedication to excellence that went into its preparation. Not only does it serve as a record of the events of this past year, but it seems to capture the spirit, the very essence of our school. Years from now, it will continue to be a source of pleasant memory to faculty and students alike.

Your staff is to be congratulated on the fine job which they accomplished, and we are also mindful of the fact that a great deal of the excellence and professionalism they displayed is reflective of the leadership and guidance they received from you. I am certain you must find satisfaction and justifiable pride in your part in this undertaking.

Again, my heartiest congratulations on a most outstanding yearbook and my personal thanks for your concern and devotion.

Sincerely,

J. Benson, Principal

. . .Principal's Message in

(A) first form

A MESSAGE TO STUDENTS . . .

It is already tomorrow. Time, which never stops on its journey, will pass before your eyes, and in only a few moments you will be members of the community looking back on the years you spent at Rock Township High School. When you do, the photos, facts, and memories in this book will be your stepping stones to a happy reminiscence.

May your memories of Rock Township High School be pleasant ones, and may your futures be filled with happiness and success.

With every wish for a bright tomorrow,

(B) second form

A yearbook is more than printed pages, clever sayings, and photographs. It is, in a very real sense, a record of memories—your memories—the memories you hold both individually and in common as students of Rock Township High School. It is my sincere hope as well as the hope of the faculty and administration that those memories are pleasant ones; ones which you will cherish throughout your life. It is our hope that your days here at Rock Township High have been enjoyable as well as filled with learning and growth. You have received an education that will serve you well throughout your lives, and the memories within these pages will serve you in those quiet moments when you turn your thoughts back to your days spent with us.

On behalf of the faculty and administration, I wish you health, happiness, and success throughout your lives.

YEAR-END MATTERS   (See Also: CLOSING OF SCHOOL; EXAMINATIONS; GRADUATION; VACATION)

. . .End-of-Year Awards

To: DEPARTMENT COORDINATORS
From: ADMINISTRATION
Re: END-OF-YEAR AWARDS

In terms of end-of-year awards, please be advised of the following:

In terms of graduation:

1. Each department must identify one student who has the highest achievement within that department (top student).
2. The department awards are
   a. Mathematics
   b. Science
   c. Language Arts
   d. Social Studies
   e. Physical Education

The above awards will be given out at graduation by Kevin Graham.

   f. Foreign Language
   g. Industrial Arts
   h. Home Economics
   i. Art
   j. Choral Music
   k. Instrumental Music

These awards will be given out at graduation by Jill Humann.

3. The academic excellence award will be given to the student with the highest academic average of all subjects taken. This award will be given out by Pat Houston.
4. Don Kurz will give out the DAR Citizenship Award.

In terms of the awards assembly:

1. Each department member will identify one student per class taught for achievement and one per effort; that is, a teacher of five classes would identify five and five.
2. These awards will be given out by each department coordinator.

Please identify these students as soon as possible. Department coordinators turn in "graduation names" to Mark Kelly and "assembly names" to Lynn Williams.

. . .End-of-Year Review

To All Staff:

I just wish to take this opportunity to review the end of the year activities that we have planned. As you know, we are having our Tradewinds Beach Party for the eighth grade on Wednesday, June 7. Needless to say, there will be a blue sky and plenty of sunshine. Mrs. Williams will be asking some teachers to volunteer to ride the bus to and from Rock Township on that day. Obviously we need your help to assure student safety. There will be a stipend, and if you are interested please see Mrs. Williams.

As we did last year, we would like to invite any and all staff to stop in at the Tradewinds for any period of time. I am sure the eighth grade students would appreciate seeing you. Last year all faculty and staff had an enjoyable time.

On another matter, please know that we have formulated our plan for another graduation ceremony on Tuesday, June 20, 1989, at 6:30 P.M. at High School South. All staff are asked to be there at 5:45 P.M. Thank you for volunteering to help at the ceremony.

Mr. Pietkewicz, as he did last year, will be distributing the end-of-year procedures and deadlines. This greatly enhances the organization and efficiency needed at this particular time of year.

Since we are graduating early this year our eighth grade students will complete all exams before the ceremony. There is no change for the sixth and seventh grade schedules and there will be early dismissal on exam days. The eighth grade graduation practices will be as follows:

> Thursday, June 15 Periods 7 and 8
> Monday,   June 19 Second exam period
> Tuesday,   June 20 First exam and part of second (if necessary)

During exam days for staff only there will be coffee and _____ in the morning and sandwiches for lunch. All staff who may wish to go out for lunch should return at 1:30 P.M. We feel this is more than appropriate. Please know that there will be no cafeteria services on Thursday, June 22, which is the last day for teachers. (As you know Maureen, Ron, and I will be baking Wednesday evening from our own special and secret recipes for the staff continental breakfast on Thursday.) We are in the process of applying for a patent on this annual event.

Finally, please know that despite the problems the district has had this year, we have had, beyond any doubt, a very successful third year as a

Middle School. Without question our middle school philosophy has permeated the entire building, and we must continue to improve on this. It continues to be crucial that all of us realize we are teaching children and every care and consideration should be extended to our students in this child-centered atmosphere. We have truly earned the respect and admiration of the educational community . . . it now becomes imperative to keep the record we have earned intact.

In three years we have come a long way and we must continue to make this the exemplary school we all want it to become. Thanks for all your help, comments, and criticism.

. . .Inspirational Message to Students

To: ALL GRADUATES

Now that it's over, it is time to begin. Now it is time for *you* to take what you have learned and go out into the world to teach others as you have been taught, to lead others as you have been led, to love and help others as you would want them to love and help you, and to do all this in such a manner that when you have taught and led and helped and loved, you will be able to look at your students and say, "Now that it's over, it is time to begin . . . ."

. . .Notice Concerning

Dear Staff,

June is here and with it comes the need for all of us to "pull it together" for our own survival and our students' as well. Please be reminded of the following:

HALL DUTY TEACHERS

Challenge each and every student in the halls after the bell for the start of class has sounded. Students without a properly filled out pass, no matter what the reason, are to be returned to class immediately!

LUNCH DUTY TEACHERS

I know it's a tough duty, but tighten up. Get on the kids to clean up. Do not dismiss the students until the following times:

Lunch A   11:45 A.M.
Lunch B   12:28 P.M.
Lunch C   1:11 P.M.

CLASSROOM TEACHERS

Challenge students who come late to class. Passes should be issued only when you are convinced of the necessity. If you could monitor the halls by your classroom doorway during the passing between classes—what a help that would be!

ALL TEACHERS

Bring to the office immediately any student caught running or pushing anyone in the halls. Mrs. Powderly and Mrs. Staudt will assign Central Detention to these students. No discipline referral need be written if you escort the student to the main office.

Keep the faith, be on guard, and we'll certainly make it! Thanks.

. . .Year-End Thanks

Dear Parents,

One of the "neatest" statements I have heard in the past few weeks about middle-level education is certainly this one: "Between the sunset of childhood and the sunrise of the adolescence lies the twilight of transcendence." That is why the middle school may be fondly referred to as the "twilight zone." And so from the twilight zone of Rock Township Middle School, let me take the last opportunity I may have this year to say "thank you" to all our parents for your help and support during this school year.

THANK YOU, P.T.A. moms and dads, who certainly put forth tremendous effort to make Kaleidoscope, Star Lab, and the Chem Show a "go" for the benefit of our students.

THANK YOU, moms and dads, who supported our discipline effort this year, especially when the phone rang, we caught you off guard, perhaps, and had to relate to you some consequence of your child's misbehavior. Remember, we're not into punishment here at Rock Township, but "consequences." We know good kids make mistakes.

THANK YOU, moms and dads, for supporting our teachers, coming out to games, coming out to band and choral concerts, and to our Back-to-School and other information nights. I have said many times that when it comes to middle-level kids certainly we're all in this together, on the very same team. And what is the result of your efforts and support for all that we do at Rock Township? I believe that the result is a real middle school that is a place in your child's life where he or she can get a new image, a new talent, and a new set of skills and feel cared about by other human beings. Rock Township Middle School—not really a twilight zone.

Have a great summer!

ZONING (See Also: ADDRESS; PARENTS; PERMANENT RECORDS)

. . .Letter to Parents Regarding

Dear Parents,

The Board of Education has the responsibility to establish boundary lines for each elementary school, junior high school, and the senior high school. Because the township population shifts occasionally, the Board is called upon, periodically, to reexamine boundary lines and make appropriate adjustments to equalize student populations in all schools. The Board changes boundary lines only after careful study. Students must attend assigned schools as established.

The following diagram shows where the secondary schools receive their student populations:

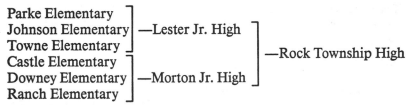

You may rest assured that the general public will be notified and a public meeting held prior to any zoning changes.

Sincerely,

Rock Township Board of Education

. . .Policy on Attendance Zones

A child attending the city schools must attend the school serving the attendance zone in which his or her parents or legal guardian reside.

If a child is residing with someone other than his or her parents or legal guardian and the place of residence is located in an attendance zone other than the zone in which the parents or legal guardian reside, proof must be submitted to the superintendent of schools that said place of residence is the permanent residence of the child.

Such proof must be submitted in the form of a statement, under oath, to the superintendent of schools to be presented to and acted upon by the city Board of Education. No transfer shall be made or become effective until approved by the city Board of Education. Said approval can be given only when verification by the superintendent of schools and Board attorney established that the proposed action is not violative of federal court order provisions which presently apply to the city school system.

Administrators of the city school system shall assure that students' admittance to respective schools is done through procedures that are in accord with policies adopted by this Board and with the federal court order exempt, "Attendance Outside System of Residence."

Adopted: September 11.

. . .Resolution on Attendance Zones

WHEREAS the City Board of Education is operating under an order from the United States Federal Court for the Middle District.

AND WHEREAS this order sets forth attendance zones for the said schools, which the City School Board is responsible for the enforcement thereof,

THEREFORE, NOW BE IT RESOLVED that if a student is attending a school other than the school he or she is assigned to by such zone lines, that student will not be allowed to continue in that school and will not be allowed to participate in extracurricular activities or represent the school to which he or she is zoned for the remainder of that school year.

BE IT FURTHER RESOLVED that this resolution become a part of the official City School Board Policy Manual and that it be included in each school's student handbook henceforth.

BE IT FURTHER RESOLVED that parents, teachers, and students assist in the enforcement of this policy so that no student will attend an overcrowded school and efficient use can be made of existing buildings and facilities. The enforcement of this policy will help ensure that no student will suffer because of another person's violation of this policy.

This will not conflict with the present policy which states: "Students whose parents move to another attendance zone will be permitted to remain in the school of original enrollment until the end of that school year, if they have been enrolled for 90 school days or more. Students who have not been enrolled for 90 school days or more must transfer to the school in which their parents or legal guardians reside."

Done this day, Monday, April 9, by vote.